THE CONSTITUTION AND THE CONDUCT OF AMERICAN FOREIGN POLICY

THE CONSTITUTION AND THE CONDUCT OF AMERICAN FOREIGN POLICY

EDITED BY DAVID GRAY ADLER AND LARRY N. GEORGE

FOREWORD BY ARTHUR SCHLESINGER, JR.

UNIVERSITY PRESS OF KANSAS

Published by the University Press of Kansas (Lawrence, Kansas 66049), which was organized by the Kansas Board of Regents and is operated and funded by Emporia State University, Fort Hays State University, Kansas State University, Pittsburg State University, the University of Kansas, and Wichita State University

Chapter 6 reprinted with permission of Yale University Press

Library of Congress Cataloging-in-Publication Data

The Constitution and the conduct of American foreign policy : essays
  in law and history / edited by David Gray Adler and Larry N. George.
      p. cm.
  Includes bibliographical references and index.
  ISBN 0-7006-0755-2 (cloth) — ISBN 0-7006-0756-0 (pbk.)
  1. United States—Foreign relations—Law and legislation.
2. Executive power—United States. 3. United States—Constitutional
history. I. Adler, David Gray, 1954– . II. George, Larry
Nelson.
  KF4651.C66   1966
  342.73′0412—dc20
  [347.302412]   96-5057

British Library Cataloguing in Publication Data is available.

Printed in the United States of America

10 9 8 7 6 5 4 3 2 1

The paper used in this publication meets the minimum requirements of the American National Standard for Permanence of Paper for Printed Library Materials Z39.48–1984.

To our parents
Robert and Marlene Adler,
Fran George, and
the late Howard George

CONTENTS

FOREWORD

Democracy faces no more momentous decisions than those of peace and war, and such decisions confront the conduct of foreign policy with its most crucial and sensitive challenges. If citizens are unwilling to study the processes by which foreign policy is made, they have only themselves to blame when they go marching off to war. The essays that follow splendidly analyze, illustrate, and document the leading issues in the relationship between foreign policy and the constitutional order.

Protection from attack is a prime obligation for any nation-state. In the United States, national security was a major motive in calling the Constitutional Convention of 1787. The Founding Fathers were acutely aware of the military vulnerability of the confederated ex-colonies. British in the Northwest, Spaniards in the South and Indians everywhere menaced the infant republic. The Articles of Confederation gave Congress no effective power to raise revenues, enforce treaties, create armies, or wage war. "We have," Alexander Hamilton wrote in *Federalist 15*, "neither troops, nor treasury, nor government." Nearly all of the first thirty *Federalist* papers dealt with national security and foreign relations.

The remedy was, in the Framers' view, a strong central government empowered to create a standing army and navy, to regulate commerce, and to make and enforce treaties. But the new Constitution was founded on the novel idea of the separation of powers. How then should foreign policy authority be distributed within the national government? Where especially should the power to go to war be located?

With the warmaking predilections of absolute monarchs in mind, the Framers assigned the vital powers in international affairs to Congress. Article I gave Congress not only the exclusive appropriations power—itself a potent instrument of control—but also the exclusive power to declare war, to raise and support armies, to provide and maintain a navy, to make rules for the regulation of the armed forces, and to grant letters of marque and reprisal, the eighteenth-century equivalent of retaliatory strikes. This last provision enabled Congress to authorize limited as well as general war.

Even Hamilton, the convention's most forceful proponent of executive energy, endorsed this allocation of powers. "The history of human conduct," he wrote in *Federalist 75,* "does not warrant that exalted opinion of human virtue which would make it wise to commit interests of so delicate and momentous a kind, as those which concern its intercourse with the rest of the world, to the sole disposal of . . . a President of the United States." As Abraham Lincoln remarked sixty years later about the warmaking power, the men in Philadelphia "resolved to so frame the Constitution that *no one man* should hold power of bringing this oppression upon us."

But the Framers also recognized that the structural characteristics of the presidency—unity, secrecy, decision, dispatch, superior knowledge of foreign politics—justified, in the words of *Federalist 75,* "the constitutional agency of the President in the conduct of foreign negotiations." The Constitution did not nullify presidential leadership. The executive was bound to be the seat of initiative in the tripartite system, but presidential leadership was to be exercised through discussion, persuasion, and consent, not through exclusion, secrecy, and command. The Framers envisaged the conduct of foreign affairs as a partnership between Congress and the president, with Congress, when it came to warmaking, as the senior partner. Hamilton's comment on the treatymaking power applies to the broader executive-legislative balance in foreign affairs: "The joint possession of the power . . . would afford a greater prospect of security than the separate possession by either of them."

From an early point, their structural advantages enabled presidents to undertake unilateral actions in foreign policy, including, on occasion, the commitment of military or naval force to combat. In the nineteenth century nearly all such instances were police actions against pirates, brigands, smugglers, mobs, and savages, not wars against organized governments and sovereign states and therefore not precedents for the presidential wars of the second half of the twentieth century. It is true that Abraham Lincoln in spring 1861 and Franklin D. Roosevelt in autumn 1941 did order major military initiatives without congressional authorization, but these were supreme emergencies when the life of the nation was at stake. Presidents on occasion transgressed their constitutional authority, but they did not claim inherent power to do so.

That claim was first made by President Truman when he went to war against North Korea in 1950 without congressional authorization. Most of his successors thereafter supposed that, contrary to the view of the Framers, the war-making power was the private property of presidents. The resulting transfer of the warmaking power from Congress, where the Constitution had carefully and deliberately lodged it, to the White House was, it should be added, as much a consequence of congressional abdication as of presidential rapacity for power.

Oddly, the loudest advocates in recent times of unilateral presidential authority in foreign affairs also proclaimed themselves champions of original intent as the criterion for constitutional interpretation. No one can doubt that the original intent of the Framers was to reject the heresy that foreign policy was an exclusive presidential preserve. The Reagan administration especially, while trumpeting "the Jurisprudence of Original Intention," repudiated and trampled upon original intention in the conduct of foreign policy.

In considering these matters, it would be a mistake to surrender to a romantic view of the superior wisdom of Congress. The legislative branch can be just as wrongheaded, impulsive, emotional, gullible, and dishonorable as the executive. It was Congress that turned down the League of Nations and the World Court and that during the rise of Hitler and Imperial Japan imprisoned the executive in rigid neutrality legislation forbidding any discrimination between aggressors and victims of aggression.

Sometimes presidents are wiser and better informed than Congress; sometimes they aren't. In the 1930s FDR was wiser and better informed than the isolationist senators William E. Borah, Burton K. Wheeler, and Gerald Nye. But in the 1960s the Senate Foreign Relations Committee made much more sense about Vietnam than the White House and the National Security Council. Yet, as I write, Congress is doing its best to undo the national commitment to collective security through the United Nations, leading the distinguished diplomat and former British ambassador to Washington Sir Nicholas Henderson to speak of "the rejection by the Republicans of the main plank of U.S. foreign policy for the last fifty years."

Neither branch of government is infallible. Neither has a divine right to prevail over the other. That is why the Constitution provides for "joint possession" and enjoins partnership. In this partnership, Congress must recognize that it cannot conduct day-to-day foreign relations. The president must understand that no foreign policy can last that is not founded on popular understanding and congressional consent. The search for ways to make the partnership real is the truest fidelity to the deeper intentions of the Framers.

Ultimately, the nature of the balance will be more a political than a legal question. "If the people ever let command of the war power fall into irresponsible and unscrupulous hands," Justice Robert H. Jackson wrote in *Korematsu* (323 US 416, 433), "the courts wield no power equal to its restraint. The chief restraint upon those who command the physical forces of the country, in the future as in the past, must be their responsibility to the political judgments of their contemporaries and to the moral judgments of history."

Arthur Schlesinger, Jr.

ACKNOWLEDGMENTS

It is a pleasure to acknowledge the encouragement and support that we have received from friends and scholars. The entire manuscript was read by Jules Lobel and Stephen Dycus, who offered numerous and very helpful suggestions. We have profited from their substantial contributions to the literature in this area.

Dean Alfange, Jr., Louis Fisher, and Donald Robinson have offered valuable insights, counsel, and advice on this project, which are appreciated almost as much as their friendship. We deeply appreciate the encouragement and friendship over the years from Tom Cronin, Ron Hatzenbuehler, Leonard Levy, Raoul Berger, Richard Falk, Fred Harris, Duane Lockard, Charles Noble, and the late Francis D. Wormuth. We express with deep gratitude our thanks to Arthur Schlesinger, Jr., whom we have viewed as a mentor from afar, for writing the foreword to this book. We are indebted as well to Cheryl Hardy, secretary of the Department of Political Science at Idaho State University, for her superb typing skill, enthusiasm, and good cheer. We are delighted to publish with the University Press of Kansas and to be counted among its outstanding list of works on the Constitution and the presidency. We owe a special thanks to Michael Briggs, our editor and the editor-in-chief of the press, for his support and encouragement of this project and, above all else, for his patience. Actually, he should be grateful for our demonstration of the boundless reach of his patience. Our brides, Mickie Fox Adler and Carmela Garcia-George, have been a constant source of inspiration and have shown more understanding, love, and support than either of us deserves. There, we said it; and, yes, we admit it. Finally, we are deeply pleased to dedicate this book to our parents, who have been with us every step of the way.

INTRODUCTION

Few areas of the Constitution are so little understood as those provisions that govern the conduct of U.S. foreign policy. As Americans contemplate their country's role in the post–Cold War world, they may be persuaded by the Iran-Contra affair and by recent military operations that have ranged from Grenada, Panama, and Haiti to Iraq, Somalia, and Bosnia to reexamine what is perhaps the most dangerous and pervasive of all constitutional myths—the myth that in foreign affairs, "the president is Zeus."[1] Like this greatest of Olympian gods, whose power was supreme and whose behavior was beyond control, the president, according to this myth, may do whatever he wishes in the conduct of American foreign policy. The myth, although constitutionally unfounded, corruptive of political democracy, and counterproductive to the nation's interests here and abroad, has nevertheless asserted itself with disturbing persistence over the past several decades, poisoning both practical foreign policymaking and rigorous constitutional interpretation.

The constitutional design for foreign affairs has been all but buried by an avalanche of newly contrived, self-serving executive branch missives that adduce an untenable theory of presidential monopoly of foreign relations powers. Over the past half-century, Democratic and Republican presidents from Harry S. Truman to William Jefferson Clinton have laid claim to sweeping executive powers in an unrelenting assault on the constitutional norms that govern American foreign policy.[2]

For most Americans who have matured politically since World War II, presidential dominance in foreign affairs has become a commonplace. This pervasive understanding rests on familiar, if flimsy, scaffolding. If one shines a lamp on the constitutional argument for unilateral presidential control, it goes something like this. The Framers of the Constitution gave the president a unique role in foreign affairs. His authority to define, manage, and conduct

1

the nation's foreign relations is unfettered. As the "sole organ" of American national policy, he alone is responsible for the nation's security. Thus congressional interference in this area is invidious. Indeed, any attempt by Congress to legislate in the realm of international relations violates the separation of powers doctrine. To fulfill this broad responsibility, the president is vested with certain "inherent powers" and all of the executive power of the nation. Accordingly, the president may, at his pleasure, unilaterally grant and withdraw recognition of foreign governments and countries, negotiate executive agreements without congressional approval, order covert activities of a peaceful or violent nature, withhold any or all information regarding foreign affairs from Congress and the American people, and raise and spend funds in defiance of congressional restraints. Moreover, he is commander-in-chief of the armed forces, a post which carries with it, executive proponents claim, the authority to do anything, anywhere, that can be done with military force, including the initiation of war. Apparently, he also possesses authority to violate the law.

These legal contentions and constitutional interpretations have sought sustenance in a variety of more practical policy arguments that seek to draw distinctions between the presumed decisiveness, efficiency, and unity of executive organizations and the alleged vacillation, languor, and fragmentation of parliamentary bodies. Proponents of presidential hegemony have frequently asserted that the difficulties inherent in the formulation and management of foreign affairs pose tremendous challenges to any constitutional democracy and leave little room for substantive legislative participation. The realm of foreign affairs, they insist, is intrinsically too secretive, mysterious, and technically complicated for ordinary citizens or legislators to understand at a level adequate to enable them to make sound policy judgments. The arcane maneuverings that epitomize international diplomacy are so sensitive and precarious that they preclude the kind of public discussion, deliberation, and confrontation typically associated with parliamentary processes. The tendency of legislatures to compromise, according to supporters of presidential dominance, can undermine the vigorous pursuit of the nation's interests. The need for quick and effective action in response to foreign emergencies, crises, or impending military conflicts is incompatible with the often cumbersome and time-consuming procedures characteristic of the legislative process, particularly when delays could jeopardize the lives or safety of American citizens. These proponents also claim that the many different values and interests of legislators, and the problem of factions in both the House and the Senate, can undermine the efficient pursuit of the national interest. Such divisiveness can also place the government at a disadvantage in its relations with foreign countries better able to speak and act with a single voice. The president, in contrast, possesses greater information, experience, and expertise than members of Congress and can speak for the entire nation with a single voice.[3]

This extravagance has served to obscure the architectural blueprint of the Framers, for whom the concept of presidential unilateralism in foreign affairs was intolerable. The Constitution assigns to Congress senior status in a partnership with the president for the purpose of conducting foreign policy. Article I vests in Congress broad, explicit, and exclusive powers to regulate foreign commerce, raise and maintain military forces, grant letters of marque and reprisal, provide for the common defense, and initiate all hostilities on behalf of the United States, including full-blown war. As Article II indicates, the president shares with the Senate the treatymaking power and the authority to appoint ambassadors. The Constitution exclusively assigns only two foreign affairs powers to the president. He is designated commander-in-chief of the nation's armed forces, although, as we will see, he acts in this capacity by and under the authority of Congress. The president also has the power to receive ambassadors, but the Framers viewed this as a routine, administrative function, devoid of discretionary authority. This list exhausts the textual grant of authority to the president with respect to foreign affairs jurisdiction. The president's constitutional powers pale in comparison to those of Congress.

The Framers' studied decision to vest the bulk of foreign policy powers in Congress marked a deliberate and dramatic departure from the practice in England which, like other nations, concentrated virtually untrammeled authority in the hands of the executive. In his *Second Treatise of Government* (1690), John Locke described three powers of government: legislative, executive, and "federative." The federative power, which we understand as the authority over foreign affairs, consisted of "the power of war and peace, leagues and alliances, and all the transactions with all persons and communities without the Commonwealth." The federative power was "almost always united" with the executive. Locke warned that the separation of executive and federative powers would invite "disorder and ruin."[4] Sir William Blackstone, the great eighteenth-century jurist, described in his distinguished work, *Commentaries on the Laws of England,* the vast foreign affairs powers that inhere in the king by virtue of the royal prerogative. Blackstone defined the king's prerogative as "those rights and capacities which the king enjoys alone."[5] The monarch's *direct* prerogatives, those which are "rooted in and spring from the king's political person," included the authority to send and receive ambassadors and the power to make war or peace. The Crown, moreover, could negotiate "a treaty with a foreign state, which shall irrevocably bind the nation," and he could issue letters of marque and reprisal, which authorized private citizens to perform military actions on behalf of the nation. The king, according to Blackstone, was "the generalissimo, or the first in military command," and he possessed "the sole power of raising and regulating fleets and armies." In the exercise of his lawful prerogative, the king "is, and ought to be absolute; that is, so far absolute, that there is no legal authority that can either delay or resist him."[6]

Placed in its historical context, then, the Constitutional Convention's decision to break from the prevailing foreign policymaking practices of other governments at the time was simply stunning. It is explicable, perhaps, only in terms of the Framers' intellectual orientation, their understanding of history, and their own practical experiences. The effective control and management of foreign policy and the use of armed force was, of course, a primary goal and an animating purpose of the convention. Indeed, given the widespread ramifications of foreign relations, "nothing," as Arthur Schlesinger, Jr., has written, "was more crucial for the new nation than the successful conduct of its external relations."[7] This concern was underscored by the convention's debate on the treaty power, during which delegates expressed a serious desire to halt the chronic infidelity that the nation had shown to its international obligations and treaty agreements under the Articles of Confederation. The inability of the United States to "maintain abroad its credit or position as a sovereign nation" had drawn contempt and derision from foreign countries and nearly destroyed its reputation overseas.[8] That debate reflected, in turn, the Framers' preoccupation with the tremendous impact of treaties on a wide range of economic, sectional, and security interests. As a consequence of these concerns they spent considerable time and energy on the issues surrounding the scope and structure of the "treaty-making power," a "fourth branch of government," which, in the words of Madison and Hamilton, would constitute the principal vehicle for the conduct of American foreign policy.[9]

The difficult search for an efficient foreign policy design was compounded by the Framers' heightened fear of the abuse of power. They were steeped in English history and they well knew that "the management of foreign relations," as Madison stated, "appears to be the most susceptible of abuse of all trusts committed to a Government." War, alone, could plunder the nation's treasury, ravage its society, and, of course, destroy its very lifeblood. The Framers contemplated the possibility and consequences of treasonous acts, realized that fortunes were to be made in the dark and secretive world of espionage, and feared "the loss of liberty at home" that could result from "danger, real or pretended, from abroad."[10] They were also greatly influenced by the constitutional crises and political convulsions of the seventeenth-century English Civil Wars. The absolutist claims of the Stuart kings and the abuse of authority by manipulative ministers had hardened their view toward the executive. The pervasive fear of unbridled power and the specter of an embryonic monarchy precluded presidential control of foreign policy. Even Hamilton— usually a staunch advocate of executive supremacy—shared these concerns as expressed in *Federalist 75:*

> The history of human conduct does not warrant that exalted opinion of human virtue which would make it wise in a nation to commit interests of so delicate and momentous a kind, as those which concern its intercourse with the rest of the world, to the sole disposal of a magistrate created and circumstanced as would be a President of the United States.[11]

All of these deep-seated trepidations regarding the abuse of power, which resonated from the colonial period and reflected the Framers' reading of history, made the quest for an effective foreign affairs system an arduous task. The pervasive fear of a powerful executive, particularly a president who might wield unilateral authority in an area so sensitive and critical as that of foreign relations, was reinforced by the republican ideology that permeated the convention. The Framers' attachment to collective judgment and their decision to create a structure of shared power in foreign affairs provided, in the words of James Wilson, "a security to the people," for it was a cardinal principle of republicanism that the conjoined wisdom of the many is superior to that of one.[12] The emphasis on collective decisionmaking came at the expense of unilateral presidential authority, of course, but that consequence was of little moment, given the overriding aversion to unrestrained executive power. The structure of shared powers in the conduct of international affairs proved satisfactory to the Framers since it would deter the abuse of power and provide a means of airing the various political, social, and economic values and interests that were bound up in the nation's external relations.

The conjunction of these historical, philosophical, and experiential influences compelled the convention to reject the model of executive control over foreign affairs prevailing in the rest of the world in favor of collective decisionmaking. The Framers' scheme brought Congress center stage in the foreign policy process and required institutional integrity, restraint, and forbearance on the part of both branches. In the past fifty years, however, this blueprint has been overshadowed by a mushrooming cloud of unilateral presidential actions in contravention of the Constitution, actions that exhibit appalling arrogance of power and an utter contempt for the rule of law in the conduct of foreign affairs.

This book is intended to afford several prominent writers an opportunity to air their most current thinking on issues central to the constitutional and democratic debates that surround the conduct of American foreign policy. More fundamentally, these chapters represent a direct response to the extravagant claims to executive power that have emanated from the White House in recent decades. The thesis of the book is simple: unilateral presidential control of U.S. foreign relations poses a grave threat to our democratic society and is without constitutional warrant.

Although there is, among our authors, some variation of opinion on issues surrounding the constitutional governance of foreign affairs, their respective angles of vision do not differ conspicuously. Indeed, they share several fundamental assumptions and understandings that define this collection of essays. These include above all a recognition that constitutional arrangements and democratic values should govern the conduct of foreign policy and a belief that the very marrow of constitutionalism consists of the subordination of the president to the rule of law. As a consequence, they are deeply critical of the postwar pattern of presidential usurpation of congressional powers. They embrace the Constitution's emphasis on collective decisionmaking in foreign affairs, which focuses the spotlight on Congress, while remaining keenly disappointed in the unwillingness of Congress to properly assert its constitutional powers and responsibilities. There remains, nevertheless, a deep and abiding belief in Congress as a national forum for discussion and debate. The contributors to this volume also agree that policy arguments cannot be permitted to supersede constitutional allocations of power. In all events, the Constitution, properly understood and interpreted, does not sanction presidential domination of America's international affairs.

In Part One, David Gray Adler and Larry George provide discussions of the constitutional and democratic principles that govern the conduct of American foreign policy. In Chapter 1, Adler examines the constitutional design for foreign affairs, a framework that reveals the Framers' preference for collective decisionmaking and establishes a preeminent role for Congress in the formulation of foreign policy. He discusses the policy preferences revealed during the convention and argues that those values are as relevant and compelling today as they were two centuries ago. Adler maintains that a wide gulf has developed in the past sixty years between constitutional principle and governmental practice in the conduct of foreign affairs and that this reflects a radical shift in power from Congress to the president. He shows how the Supreme Court has greatly facilitated the growth of presidential power in such areas as the war power, executive agreements, the right of citizens to travel abroad, and treaty termination by reliance on its own opinion in *United States v. Curtiss-Wright Export Corp.* (1936)—an opinion that Adler argues is misguided. In Chapter 2,

Larry George critically examines the arguments of political theorists and writers favoring presidential control over external relations. He notes that the American system of foreign policymaking is today more highly centralized and more thoroughly dominated by the executive than in virtually any other Western democracy and demonstrates that the traditional arguments made on behalf of centralized executive foreign policymaking fail to explain convincingly why U.S. foreign policy should be made outside normal democratic channels. He shows how this approach is inconsistent with the foundational principles and perennial concerns of representative democracy and calls for a democratization of the American foreign policy process.

Part Two focuses on executive-legislative relations in foreign policy. In Chapter 3, Robert J. Spitzer analyzes the interaction between the president and Congress on such important subjects as treaties, executive agreements, arms sales, foreign aid, intermestic issues, and intelligence activities. As Spitzer shows, despite the fact that Congress shares in these responsibilities and, in some instances, has begun to reassert itself, on the whole the idea of presidential authority over the realm of foreign policy has gained widespread acceptance. The dramatic rise in executive agreements, he argues, is symptomatic of presidential ascendancy in foreign affairs. Treaties on important subjects continue to appear on the Senate agenda, but they are no longer the primary or most important means of conducting business with other nations. Spitzer warns that unless Congress is prepared to surrender its foreign policy duties entirely, the separation of powers doctrine requires it to assert its powers and reclaim lost ground. He quotes, approvingly, Richard Pious's acute observation that in no other realm is it more clear that "the president claims the silences of the Constitution."[13] Spitzer is critical of what he regards as the Reagan administration's "Constitution-be-damned" attitude toward foreign affairs, and he sounds the trumpet for a foreign policy that strikes a prudent balance between democracy and efficiency while operating within the constitutional framework of shared powers.

The epitome of unrestrained presidential initiative is to be found in the assertion of the controversial doctrine of executive prerogative, which is the subject of Donald L. Robinson's analysis in Chapter 4. Robinson explains that the Constitutional Convention rejected Locke's notion that the rule of law could not apply to foreign affairs. The convention's conclusion on this point, reflected particularly in its decision to vest in Congress the sole power to authorize the use of military force—was protected and reinforced, in effect, by the absence of a standing army up through World War II. But, as Robinson points out, America's commitment to maintain large, permanent armed forces in the context of the Cold War, the Truman Doctrine, and a plethora of worldwide military and defense treaties provided scaffolding for presidential warmaking. In the past fifty years, presidents frequently have invoked the concept of emergency or prerogative powers to justify a wide range of military actions abroad. Robinson tracks and discusses the history of presidential invocation of prerogative powers and examines the Iran-Contra affair within the context of broadly construed executive powers. The essential question, he reminds us, is whether there are any limits at all on a president's prerogative power to act on behalf of the United States, in the absence of law or in the defiance of law.

In Chapter 5, David Adler examines the virtually ignored subject of the scope of the president's recognition power. Derived from the executive's authority to receive ambassadors, the recognition power has been transformed by twentieth-century presidents into an instrument of high prerogative to make and conduct the foreign policy of the United States. Presidents have used the reception clause as a source of broad discretionary authority to determine unilaterally both whether the United States will engage in relations with particular countries and what the tone and temper of those relations will be. Adler demonstrates that the Constitutional Convention, operating under the influence of the presuppositions of international law prevailing at the time, viewed the reception of ambassadors as a largely routine, administrative function. It was, in other words, understood to be essentially an act of diplomatic obligation, generally without meaningful political discretion, and it simply reflected an elementary principle of the law of nations: a sovereign state, with rare exceptions, has the duty to receive an ambassador sent by another sovereign. The Framers placed the duty in the executive rather than in Congress, primarily in the interest of convenience. Their intention was that the only issue before the president would be one of fact: is the ambassador or minister truly the representative of the competent organ of the nation in question? Interestingly, Madison, Hamilton, and Jefferson—who disagreed on so many other matters—concurred that the recognition power did not provide the president with discretionary authority to control American foreign policy.

The title of Harold Hongju Koh's chapter, "Why the President Almost Always Wins in Foreign Affairs: Executive Initiative and Congressional Acquiescence," suggests the pattern behind executive domination of American foreign policy. Koh argues that the executive branch is driven to take the initiative in foreign affairs for a number of reasons, including the structure of the Constitution itself and the effects of changes in international regimes. The president, it is argued, is ideally situated and well equipped to exercise power, in sharp contrast to Congress, which, with its dispersion of authority, is unable to move quickly or efficiently. This argument from structure does not, of course, explain why presidents choose to exercise this authority. Koh proposes that explanations of such decisions may be found in the shifting events in the international realm. But even when the president is inclined to initiate foreign policy moves, there remains the question of why Congress fails to restrain the executive. Koh grounds such legislative acquiescence in legislative myopia, inadequate drafting, ineffective legislative tools, and an institutional lack of political will and cites the 1973 War Powers Resolution as an illustration of the problem. Koh concludes on a grim but realistic note: the president, ordinarily, will be free to execute his intentions without congressional restraint, except in those rare cases where he is politically weak and where congressional will is unusually unified.

In Part Three, David Adler, Louis Fisher, and Edward Keynes analyze the exercise of the war powers under the Constitution and interrogate the constitutional and legal arguments that purport to locate a unilateral warmaking power in the presidency. In "The Constitution and Presidential Warmaking," Adler discusses the constitutional framework that governs the initiation of military hostilities, provides a historical analysis of the use of force, and examines the legal arguments that have been advanced on behalf of a putative executive power to commence war. He argues that the Framers vested in Congress the sole and exclusive power to initiate war and that the president was intentionally and explicitly given only the authority to repel invasions of the United States. According to Adler, no president claimed the constitutional power to commence war until 1950, when Harry Truman asserted the authority to plunge the United States into the Korean War. Since then, virtually every president has initiated hostilities somewhere in the world under the banner of unilateral presidential warmaking authority. Adler concludes that the legal claims invoked by presidents and their supporters are without merit.

In Chapter 8, Louis Fisher examines the congressional power of the purse as a means of controlling executive warmaking. He explains that the Constitutional Convention thought it necessary to separate the power to finance wars from the authority to prosecute them. As Madison noted, those "who are to *conduct a war* cannot in the nature of things, be proper or safe judges, whether *a war ought* to be *commenced, continued,* or *concluded.*"[14] Fisher surveys recent congressional efforts to use the spending power to limit foreign policy actions of the president, from Vietnam to Somalia. He also provides a penetrating critique of the startling constitutional claim, asserted during the 1987 Iran-Contra hearings, that Congress may not control foreign affairs by withholding appropriations. Fisher rejects on both policy and constitutional grounds the arguments made by some Reagan administration officials (including Lt. Col. Oliver North), that if Congress prohibits the use of appropriations for specific foreign affairs activities—as it did through the Boland amendment—the president may nevertheless pursue his agenda by soliciting funds from the private sector and from foreign countries. In addition to the damage that could be inflicted on our national reputation and the potentially corruptive influences associated with back-door solicitations, such initiatives could easily precipitate a constitutional crisis by merging the power of the sword with the power of the purse. Presidential defiance of congressional prohibitions placed on the solicitation of funds from foreign countries or private sources would, in Fisher's view, warrant impeachment of the president.

In "The War Powers Resolution and the Persian Gulf War," Edward Keynes reexamines the 1973 resolution within the context of the recent war in Kuwait. He argues that the resolution is constitutionally flawed because it represents an unconstitutional delegation of power to the president. Indeed, it confers upon the president authority to make war, a power that the Constitutional Convention denied to him. Moreover, the twenty-year history of the resolution reveals its relative ineffectiveness in curbing presidential initiation of hostilities. It is indeed counterproductive because it fails to direct attention in a timely manner to the critical military and foreign policy decisions underlying and preceding the outbreak of war and hostilities. It also fails, in various ways, to promote joint congressional-executive responsibility for the initiation of force. Keynes is thus critical of the congressional debate that preceded America's war against Saddam Hussein in 1991. He argues that Congress effectively granted open-ended authorization to the president to name the time and place in which the commencement of hostilities would occur, a grant of power similar to the Gulf of Tonkin Resolution that was inconsistent with properly understood constitutional restrictions. Before going to war, he contends, the American people deserve a genuine debate that gives consideration both to the issues that are precipitating hostilities and to the likely consequences and ramifications of the war.

The historical record of American foreign policy is important to the themes of this book for several reasons. First, the various foreign policy decisions made by national officials throughout the history of the republic have, for better or worse, effectively defined the issues at stake in current debates over foreign policymaking powers and have largely set the terms of those debates. Second, the historical record is important because the processes through which many pivotal and controversial foreign policy decisions were made have since acquired the status of historical precedents, informing and sometimes defining the parameters of subsequent controversies. Usually, such historical examples are simply brought forward analogically to illuminate or illustrate arguments in these later disputes, but sometimes accounts of past historical events are incorporated formally into arguments over matters of law. This procedure occurs regularly, for example, when judges ground their opinions in an evaluation of the practices of earlier foreign policymakers acting under historically similar conditions. It can also occur when a lawmaker enters an account of a historically comparable event into the official record as part of his or her arguments during deliberation over a piece of legislation relevant to the foreign affairs powers. In such instances, historical actions and decisions assume a greater status and, to some commentators, begin to approximate the status of actual legal precedents. This of course enhances the importance of accurately recounting and interpreting those events. Commentaries on such events, and responses to those commentaries, often accumulate until the stakes involved in the original events are far outweighed by the implications of the events as analogies in later debates. Many of the debates addressed in Part Four of this book concern precisely these sorts of interpretations of relevant historical precedents.

In Chapter 10, Gerhard Casper discusses the multifaceted diplomatic crisis known as the Algiers Episode. The event not only represented America's first encounter with hostage-taking but also occupied the eight years of George Washington's administration and posed one of the young republic's most intractable foreign affairs problems. Although the Algiers Episode was overshadowed by the Neutrality Proclamation and the Jay Treaty, it vividly illustrates the manner in which the executive and legislative branches could (and did) exercise their respective powers in a manner consistent with the constitutional framework. As Casper explains, the two branches demonstrated a prudent and cautious respect for secrecy, balanced with a healthy inclination toward disclosure of the pertinent information regarding the government's effort to resolve the crisis. Casper observes that Washington, in particular, exhibited considerable constitutional circumspection during the episode. He regularly consulted the House and sought advice from the Senate and, in all events, was concerned to achieve the highest possible degree of interbranch coordination of American policy toward Algiers. Casper also makes it clear that Washington never contemplated unilateral warmaking. The Algiers Episode provides an excellent illustration of a president working closely with Congress throughout a protracted crisis while displaying genuine concern for the integrity of the Constitution.

The United States' war with France in 1798, dubbed the Quasi-War, constituted the first instance of U.S. military action against a foreign nation. It has appeared on virtually every list of alleged examples of unilateral presidential warmaking. In 1966, for example, in an effort to justify American involvement in the Vietnam War, the office of the Legal Adviser to the Department of State described the Quasi-War as the first among some 125 instances in which the president has projected military force abroad without prior congressional authorization. But as Dean Alfange, Jr., demonstrates in Chapter 11, the remark was incautious in failing to recognize that Congress had in fact authorized military hostilities against France on the basis of no fewer than two dozen statutes and that at no time during the war did Pres. John Adams exceed his legitimate constitutional powers. The Quasi-War does not, then, belong on any list of instances in which the president has unilaterally ordered U.S. forces to initiate military hostilities. As Alfange notes, rather than serving as a precedent for executive warmaking, it provides strong evidence of the pervasive understanding among the individuals who drafted and ratified the Constitution that the president has no authority to initiate military hostilities unilaterally. Alfange shows further that such an understanding was endorsed not only by such leading Federalists as Adams and Hamilton but also by Jefferson, Madison, and other opponents of the war, as well as by the federal judiciary.

In Chapter 12, "Secrecy and Constitutional Controls in the Federalist Period," Daniel N. Hoffman examines the inherent tension between the principle of accountability and the occasional need to conceal information and actions by exploring several illustrative cases from the Federalist period. Although the Constitution says very little about secrecy, Hoffman explains that the Framers, aware of the conflict between publicity and secrecy, established a complex control system that consisted of three interwoven levels: explicit norms of official conduct, formal institutional checks, and procedures for public access and participation. Hoffman tracks a historical record of fits and starts, but one characterized by informal and relatively broad-based discussion. These early efforts to legislate standards for regulating secrecy in a polity governed by a Constitution that was largely silent on the issue were inhibited by the atmosphere of crisis that prevailed in the early republic and by the fact that secrecy issues were often bound up with many of the period's most intensely divisive issues surrounding foreign policy and democratization. In the Federalist period, as Hoffman explains, orthodox doctrine recognized the right of Congress to call for executive branch documents without restriction, but it also recognized a presidential power to censor the papers before supplying them—save perhaps where the Senate was acting in its executive capacity or where a question of impeachment or of declaring war was before Congress. In such cases, the right to know might be absolute. The only basis for presidential censorship that was unequivocally established in the Federalist period was the duty to protect the safety of individuals. Beyond this consensus there was debate about the exact legal status of secrecy, but in any event, Hoffman finds no basis for the claim of absolute executive secrecy that some observers have purported to find in the record.

The Barbary Wars of the early nineteenth century have often been adduced as precedent for unilateral presidential warmaking in foreign countries as far removed as Vietnam and Haiti. Various scholars and government officials have argued that as president, Thomas Jefferson dispatched forces to the Mediterranean against Tripolitan pirates on his own claim of power and without congressional authorization. But that claim, as Louis Fisher makes abundantly plain in Chapter 13, shatters upon analysis. Fisher shows how the historical record demonstrates that Jefferson's decision to carry out those military operations was in fact grounded in prior authorization from Congress in the form of some ten statutes. Comparing Jefferson's actions with President Clinton's recent statements authorizing American intervention in Haiti, Fisher underscores the central issue: "To the extent that Jefferson took initiatives before Congress acted, they were defensive in nature and not offensive (as contemplated for Haiti)."[15] Fisher explains that throughout his presidency, Jefferson, like his predecessors, honored the Constitution's assignment of the war power exclusively in Congress and, in fact, *refused* to initiate offensive measures without congressional authorization. Those who would hope to find precedential value for the concept of independent presidential warmaking in Jefferson's actions will search the records in vain.

In 1950 President Truman ordered the use of military force against North Korea without congressional authorization. The Truman administration purported to find legal sanction for his unilateral act of warmaking in resolutions that had been passed by the United Nations Security Council, but as Fisher demonstrates in Chapter 14, "Truman in Korea," this claim of derived authority was without merit. A proper understanding of the episode assumes increased importance in view of the fact that in 1991 Pres. George Bush invoked Truman's actions and his reliance on United Nations resolutions as "precedent" for the initiation of hostilities against Iraq. Fisher rejects Truman's contention that he needed authorization only from the Security Council and not from Congress. As Fisher explains, the Truman administration violated the plain language and the clear legislative history of the UN Charter and the UN Participation Act. Article 43 of the UN Charter provides that when member states supply armed forces in response to a request from the Security Council, they do so "in accordance with their respective constitutional processes." Fisher reminds us that Congress may not amend the Constitution by reading itself out of the warmaking power. Under the terms of the 1945 UN Participation Act, moreover, the president may not furnish troops without prior congressional authorization, which requires approval by both houses. Fisher also shows that despite the Truman administration's efforts to ground its actions in UN resolutions, the United States in fact committed its armed forces a day before the Security Council formally called for military action. In sum, the United Nations actually exercised no authority over the decision to go to war. It was ultimately a U.S. war fought on the basis of a presidential usurpation of power. Truman's arrogation of warmaking authority, like other presidential usurpations, recalls Great Britain's former Lord Chief Justice Denman's description of how such "precedents" are to be viewed: "The practice of a ruling power in the state is but feeble proof of its legality."[16]

Two appendixes round out this volume. The first consists of the principal essays in the *Federalist* papers that address the issue of the constitutional governance of American foreign policy. A firsthand examination of the Framers' reasoning will demonstrate their concern to sharply limit the role of the president in foreign affairs. The second gathers excerpts from the chief foreign affairs cases, judicial decisions that are central to an understanding of the contours of discussion in the academy, in the public realm, and in governmental departments. Instructors and readers alike will perhaps appreciate the convenience of this collection of key *Federalist* essays and judicial opinions within the covers of one book.

The conduct of the foreign policy of the United States vitally affects the lives and destinies of all Americans. An international course, once charted, too often leaves few escape routes. Foreign economic policies and international agreements have far-reaching and prolonged effects on the nation's security, prosperity, and political stability. The commitment of American armed forces abroad, whether for humanitarian purposes, to honor international obligations, or to advance U.S. interests may prove to be not only counterproductive, but it may lead as well to a tragic loss of life. Foreign policy stances and commitments may spark acts of terrorism or economic warfare directed against the nation or its citizens. And, most gravely, the decision to go to war in a world armed with modern conventional and nuclear weapons of mass destruction confers on fallible human beings powers that could eclipse humanity.

Yet despite its critical importance, far too many citizens, including government officials and members of the press, are underinformed or misinformed about the constitutional allocation of foreign policymaking powers. This book is intended to help fill that void and to provide appropriate corrections to these widespread misunderstandings. It has been written so as to be accessible to the reading public, a goal that reflects our belief that educated and active citizens can and do make a difference in our system of government. Finally, it is intended for the current generation of American students, tomorrow's leaders. Each chapter reflects the concerns and opinions of its author. To each of the contributors we owe our thanks for the high quality of their work, and for their patience during the book's long gestation period.

NOTES

1. We have borrowed this brilliant analogy from Gerhard Casper's influential article, "Constitutional Constraints on the Conduct of Foreign Policy: A Nonjudicial Model," *Chicago Law Review* 43 (1976): 477. See also Chapter 10 of this book.

2. Recently, for example, Clinton objected to various proposals that would have restricted presidential actions in Bosnia and Haiti. One measure, never enacted, would have prevented the deployment of additional U.S. forces in Bosnia and Herzegovina without prior authorization from Congress. Clinton objected that such measures would undercut his constitutional authority to make foreign policy and to deploy troops. He promised to "strenuously oppose such attempts to encroach on the President's foreign policy powers" (29 *Weekly Comp. Pres. Doc.* 2097 [1993]). Clinton also expressed "grave concern" about several proposals that would restrict the use of U.S. forces in Haiti, Bosnia, and UN peacekeeping operations. He was "fundamentally opposed" to measures that "improperly limit my ability to perform my constitutional duties as Commander-in-Chief, which may well have unconstitutional provisions." Amendments with respect to the "command and control" of U.S. forces "would insert Congress into the detailed execution of military contingency planning in an unprecedented manner" (ibid., p. 2104). Clinton was in error. Congress has full constitutional authority to place limits on the deployment of troops and to determine when the United States will initiate hostilities. See also Adler, Chapter 7.

3. For a thorough review of policy arguments that support presidential domination of foreign affairs, see Chapter 2.

4. John Locke, *Second Treatise of Government* (1690), secs. 146–48.

5. William Blackstone, *Commentaries on the Laws of England* (1803), 2:238.

6. Ibid., pp. 239–50.

7. Arthur Schlesinger, Jr., *The Imperial Presidency* (Boston: Houghton Mifflin, 1989), p. 2

8. Charles Warren, *The Making of the Constitution* (Cambridge: Harvard University Press, 1967), p. 5.

9. Hamilton, for example, told the New York Ratifying Convention that the Senate, "together with the President, are to manage all our concerns with foreign nations" (Jonathon Elliot, *Debates in the Several State Conventions on the Adoption of the Federal Constitution* [1861], 2:291).

10. Madison to Jefferson, May 13, 1798, quoted in Leonard D. White, *The Federalists* (New York: Macmillan, 1948), p. 65.

11. Hamilton, *Federalist 75*, in *The Federalist,* ed. Edward Mead Earle (New York: Modern Library, 1937), p. 487.

12. Elliot, *Debates,* 2:507. In the First Congress, Roger Sherman, who had been a delegate in Philadelphia, argued in defense of the shared-powers arrangement in foreign affairs and stated, "The more wisdom there is employed, the greater security there is that the public business will be well done" (*Annals of Congress* [1789], 1:1085).

13. Richard M. Pious, *The American Presidency* (New York: Basic Books, 1979), p. 333.

14. *The Writings of James Madison,* ed. Galliard Hunt, 9 vols. (New York: Putnam, 1900–1910), 6:148.

15. See first page of Chapter 13.

16. *Stockard v. Hansard,* 112 E.R. 1112, 1171 (Q.B. 1839).

PART ONE

CONSTITUTIONAL PRINCIPLES AND DEMOCRATIC NORMS

1
COURT, CONSTITUTION, AND FOREIGN AFFAIRS

DAVID GRAY ADLER

The unmistakable trend toward executive domination of U.S. foreign affairs in the past sixty years represents a dramatic departure from the basic scheme of the Constitution.[1] The constitutional blueprint assigns to Congress senior status in a partnership with the president for the purpose of conducting foreign policy. It also makes Congress the sole and exclusive repository of the ultimate foreign relations power—the authority to initiate war. The president is vested with only modest authority in this realm and is clearly only of secondary importance. In light of this constitutional design, commentators have wondered at the causes and sources of the radical shift in foreign affairs powers from Congress to the president.[2] Although a satisfactory explanation is perhaps elusive, it is nevertheless clear that the growth of presidential power in foreign relations has fed considerably on judicial decisions that are doubtful and fragile. It is, of course, beyond the scope of this chapter to attempt an exhaustive explanation, which has so far escaped the effort of others. The aim here is to examine the judiciary's contribution to executive hegemony in this area as manifested in its rulings regarding executive agreements, travel abroad, treaty termination, and the war power.

In this chapter, I provide a brief explanation of the policy preferences underlying the Constitutional Convention's allocation of foreign affairs powers and argue that those values are as relevant and compelling today as they were two centuries ago. I contend that a wide gulf has developed in the past fifty years between constitutional theory and governmental practice in the conduct of foreign policy. The courts have greatly facilitated the growth of presidential power in this area in three interconnected but somewhat different ways by adhering to the teaching of the sole-organ doctrine as propounded in the 1936 case of *United States v. Curtiss-Wright Export Corporation,* by invoking the politi-

19

cal-question doctrine and other nonjusticiable grounds, and by inferring congressional approval of presidential action by virtue of its inaction or silence.[3] I then offer an explanation of the Court's willingness to increase presidential foreign affairs powers well beyond constitutional boundaries. For a variety of reasons, the Court views its role in this area as a support function for policies already established. In this regard the judiciary has become an arm of the executive branch. Finally, I conclude with the argument that in order to maintain the integrity of the Constitution, the Court must police constitutional boundaries so as to ensure that fundamental alterations in our governmental system will occur only through the process of constitutional amendment. It is impermissible for the judicial branch to abdicate its function "to say what the law is."[4]

THE CONSTITUTION AND THE CONDUCT OF FOREIGN POLICY

The Preference for Collective Decisionmaking

The Constitution envisions the conduct of foreign policy as a partnership between the president and Congress. Perhaps surprisingly, Congress is assigned the role of senior partner. This assignment reflects, first, the overwhelming preference of both the Framers at the Constitutional Convention and the ratifiers in the various state conventions for collective decisionmaking in foreign as well as in domestic affairs and, second, their equally adamant opposition to unilateral executive control of U.S. foreign policy. This constitutional arrangement is evidenced by specific, unambiguous textual language, almost undisputed arguments by Framers and ratifiers, and by logical-structural inferences from the doctrine of separation of powers.[5] The design, moreover, is compelling and relevant for twentieth-century America for at least three reasons. First, separation of powers issues are perennial, for they require consideration of the proper repository of power. Contemporary questions about the allocation of power between the president and Congress in foreign affairs are largely the same as those addressed two centuries ago. Second, the logic of collective decisionmaking in the realm of foreign relations is as sound today as it was in the Founding period. Third, although it is true that the world and the role of the United States in international relations have changed considerably over the past 200 years it is nevertheless the case that most questions of foreign affairs involve routine policy formulation and do not place a premium on immediate responsive action. A slightly more detailed understanding of the constitutional landscape and the values that characterize it would prove beneficial both to the courts, which must forge policy in light of this background, and to liberal activists, who would find history friendly to their critiques of judicial decisions in the area of foreign affairs.

The preference for collective, rather than individual, decisionmaking runs throughout those provisions of the Constitution that govern the conduct of foreign policy. Congress derives broad and exclusive powers from Article I to regulate foreign commerce and to initiate all hostilities on behalf of the United States, including full-blown, total war. As Article II indicates, the president shares with the Senate the treatymaking power and the power to appoint ambassadors. Only two powers in foreign relations are assigned exclusively to the president. He is commander-in-chief, but he acts in this capacity by and under the authority of Congress. As Alexander Hamilton and James Iredell argued, the president, in this capacity, is merely first admiral, or general of the armed forces, after war has been authorized by Congress or in the event of a sudden attack against the United States.[6] And the president also has the power to receive ambassadors. Hamilton, James Madison, and Thomas Jefferson agreed that this clerklike function was purely ceremonial in character. Although the function has come to entail recognition of states at international law, which carries with it certain legal implications, this Founding trio contended that the duty of recognizing states was more conveniently placed in the hands of the executive than in the legislature.[7] This list exhausts the textual grant of authority with respect to foreign affairs jurisdiction. The president's constitutional authority pales in comparison to that of Congress. The preference for shared decisionmaking is stated strongly in the construction of the treaty power: "He shall have Power, by and with the Advice and consent of the Senate, to make Treaties, provided two-thirds of the Senators present concur." The compelling simplicity and clarity of the "plain words" of this clause hardly leave room for doubt as to its meaning.[8] Given the absence of any other clause that so much as intimates a presidential power to make agreements with foreign nations, it is to be supposed, as Hamilton argued, that the treaty power constitutes the principal vehicle for conducting U.S. foreign relations.[9] In fact, there was no hint at the Constitutional Convention of an exclusive presidential power to make foreign policy. To the contrary, all the arguments of the Framers and ratifiers were to the effect that the Senate and president, which Hamilton and Madison described as a "fourth branch of government" in their capacity as treatymaker,[10] "are to manage all our concerns with foreign nations."[11] Although a number of factors contributed to this decision,[12] the pervasive fear of unbridled executive power loomed largest.[13] Hamilton's statement in *Federalist 75* fairly represents these sentiments:

The history of human conduct does not warrant that exalted opinion of human nature which would make it wise in a nation to commit interests of so delicate and momentous a kind, as those which concern its intercourse with the rest of the world, to the sole disposal of a magistrate created and circumstanced as would be a President of the United States.[14]

The widespread fear of executive power that precluded presidential control of foreign policy also greatly influenced the convention's design of the war clause. Article I, section 8, paragraph 11 states: "The Congress shall have Power . . . to declare war." The plain meaning of the clause is buttressed by the fact of unanimous agreement among both Framers and ratifiers that Congress was granted the sole and exclusive authority to initiate war. The warmaking power, which was viewed as a legislative power by Madison and Wilson, among others, was specifically withheld from the president; he was given only the authority to repel sudden attacks.[15] James Wilson, second only to Madison as an architect of the Constitution, summed up the values and concerns underlying the war clause for the Pennsylvania Ratifying Convention:

This system will not hurry us into war; it is calculated to guard against it. It will not be in the power of a single body of men, to involve us in such distress; for the important power of declaring war is vested in the legislature at large. This declaration must be made with the concurrence of the House of Representatives; from this circumstance we may draw a certain conclusion that nothing but our national interest can draw us into war.[16]

No member of the Constitutional Convention and no member of any state ratifying convention ever attributed a different meaning to the war clause.[17]

Judicial Opinions and Policy Concerns

This undisputed interpretation draws further support from early judicial decisions, the views of eminent treatise writers, and from nineteenth-century practice. I have discussed these factors elsewhere; here the barest review must suffice.[18] The meaning of the war clause was put beyond doubt by several early judicial decisions. No court since has departed from this early view. In 1800, in *Bas v. Tingy*, the Supreme Court held that it is for Congress alone to declare either an "imperfect" (limited) war or a "perfect" (general) war. In 1801, in *Talbot v. Seeman*, Chief Justice John Marshall, a member of the Virginia Ratifying Convention, stated that the "whole powers of war [are] by the Constitution of the United States, vested in Congress." In *Little v. Barreme*, decided in 1804, Marshall held that Pres. John Adams's instructions to seize ships were in conflict with an act of Congress and were therefore illegal.[19] In 1806, in *United States v. Smith*, the question of whether the president may initiate hostilities was decided by Justice William Paterson, riding circuit, who wrote for himself and District Judge Tallmadge: "Does he [the president] possess the power of making war? That power is exclusively vested in Congress. . . . It is the exclusive province of Congress to change a state of peace into a state of war."[20] In the *Prize Cases* in 1863, the Court considered for the first time the power of the president to respond to sudden attacks. Justice Robert C. Grier delivered the opinion of the Court:

> By the Constitution, Congress alone has the power to declare a natural or foreign war. . . .
> If a war be made by invasion of a foreign nation, the President is not only authorized but bound to resist force, by force. He does not initiate the war, but is bound to accept the challenge without waiting for any special legislative authority. And whether the hostile party be a foreign invader, or States organized in rebellion, it is none the less a war, although the declaration of it be "unilateral."[21]

These judicial decisions established the constitutional fact that it is for Congress alone to initiate hostilities, whether in the form of general or limited war; the president, in his capacity as commander-in-chief, is granted only the power to repel sudden attacks against the United States.[22]

The convention's attachment to collective judgment and its decision to create a structure of shared power in foreign affairs provided, in the words of Wilson, "a security to the people," for it was a cardinal tenet of republican ideology that the conjoined wisdom of many is superior to that of one.[23] The emphasis on group decisionmaking came, of course, at the expense of unilateral executive authority. But this hardly posed a difficult choice, for among the Framers and ratifiers, there was a pervasive distrust of executive power, a deeply held suspicion that dated to colonial times.[24] As a result of this aversion to executive authority, the convention placed control of foreign policy beyond the unilateral capacity of the president. Furthermore, as Madison said, it "defined and confined" the authority of the president so that a power not granted could not be assumed.[25]

The structure of shared powers in foreign relations serves to deter the abuse of power, misguided policies, irrational action, and unaccountable behavior.[26] As a fundamental structural matter, the emphasis on joint policymaking permits the airing of sundry political, social, and economic values and concerns. In any event, the structure wisely ensures that the ultimate policies will not reflect merely the private preferences or the short-term political interests of the president.[27]

Of course this arrangement has come under fire in the postwar period on a number of policy grounds. Some critics have argued, for example, that fundamental political and technological changes in the character of international relations and the position of the United States in the world have rendered obsolete an eighteenth-century document designed for a peripheral, small state in the European system of diplomatic relations. Moreover, it has been asserted that quick action and a single, authoritative voice are necessary to deal with an increasingly complex, interdependent, and technologically linked world capable of massive destruction in a very short period of time. Extollers of presidential dominance also have contended that only the president has the qualitative information, the expertise, and the capacity to act with the necessary dispatch to conduct U.S. foreign policy.[28]

These policy arguments have been reviewed, and discredited, elsewhere; space limitations here permit only a brief commentary.[29] Above all else, the implications of U.S. power and action in the twentieth century have brought about an even greater need for institutional accountability and collective judgment than existed 200 years ago. The devastating, incomprehensible destruction of nuclear war and the possible extermination of the human race demonstrate the need for joint participation, as opposed to the opinion of one person, in the decision to initiate war. Moreover, most of the disputes at stake between the executive and legislative branches in foreign affairs, including the issues discussed in this chapter, have virtually nothing to do with the need for rapid response to crisis. Rather, they are concerned only with routine policy formulation and execution, a classic example of the authority exercised under the separation of powers doctrine. But these functions have been fused by the executive branch and have become increasingly unilateral, secretive, insulated from public debate, and hence unaccountable. In the wake of Vietnam, Watergate, and the Iran-Contra scandal, unilateral executive behavior has become ever more difficult to defend. Scholarly appraisals have exploded arguments about intrinsic executive expertise and wisdom on foreign affairs and the alleged superiority of information available to the president.[30] Moreover, the inattentiveness of presidents to important details and the effects of "group-think" that have dramatized and exacerbated the relative inexperience of various presidents in international relations have also devalued the extollers' arguments. Finally, foreign policies, like domestic policies, are a reflection of values. Against the strength of democratic principles, recent occupants of the

White House have failed to demonstrate the superiority of their values in comparison to those of the American people and their representatives in Congress.

The assumption of foreign relations powers by recent presidents represents a fundamental alteration of the Constitution that is both imprudent and dangerous. We turn now to an examination of the judiciary's contribution to executive hegemony in foreign affairs.

THE JUDICIARY AND FOREIGN AFFAIRS

The Influence of Curtiss-Wright

There can be little doubt that the opinion in *United States v. Curtiss-Wright Export Corp.* in 1936 has been the Court's principal contribution to the growth of executive power over foreign affairs. Its declaration that the president is the "sole organ of foreign affairs" is a powerful, albeit unfortunate, legacy of the case. Even when the sole-organ doctrine has not been invoked by name, its spirit, indeed its talismanic aura, has provided a common thread in a pattern of cases that has exalted presidential power above constitutional norms.

The domination of *Curtiss-Wright* is reflected in the fact that it is quite likely the most frequently cited case involving the allocation of foreign affairs powers.[31] It possesses uncommon significance even though it raised merely the narrow question of the constitutionality of a joint resolution that authorized the president to halt the sale of arms to Bolivia and Paraguay, then involved in armed conflict in the Chaco, in order to help stop the fighting. In an opinion by Justice George Sutherland, the Court upheld the delegation against the charge that it was unduly broad. If Justice Sutherland had confined his remarks to the delegation issue, *Curtiss-Wright* would have been overshadowed by *Panama Refining Co. v. Ryan* and would never have even surfaced in the tables of contents of undergraduate casebooks.[32] But Sutherland strayed from the issue and, in some ill-considered dicta, imparted an unhappy legacy—the chimerical idea that authority in foreign affairs was essentially an executive power, which he explained "as the very delicate, plenary, and exclusive power of the President as the sole organ of the federal government in the field of international relations—a power which does not require as a basis for its exercise an act of Congress."[33]

Let us consider the historical context from which Sutherland ripped the sole-organ doctrine. In short, the justice greatly expanded on Cong. John Marshall's speech in 1800 in which he noted that "the President is the sole organ of the nation in its external relations. . . . Of consequence, the demand of a foreign nation can only be made on him."[34] Marshall was defending the decision of Pres. John Adams to surrender to British officials a British deserter, Jonathan Robbins, in accordance with the Jay Treaty. The Robbins affair involved a demand upon the United States, according to Marshall, and it required a response from the president on behalf of the American people. At no point in his speech did Marshall argue that the president's exclusive authority to communicate with foreign nations included a power to formulate or develop policy. Edward S. Corwin has properly concluded: "Clearly, what Marshall had foremost in mind was simply the President's role as instrument of communication with other governments."[35] This point of procedure had been acknowledged in 1793 by then Secretary of State Thomas Jefferson.[36] And this view had not been challenged. Thus, it was Sutherland who infused a purely communicative role with a substantive policymaking function and thereby manufactured a great power out of the Marshallian sole-organ doctrine. To have done this, as Myres McDougal and Asher Lans observed, was to confuse the "organ" with the "organ grinder" and effectively to undermine the constitutional design for cooperation in the conduct of foreign relations.[37]

Curtiss-Wright, then, was a radical, path-breaking case. Despite the fact that it was a product of Justice Sutherland's imagination and that its rhetoric has been dismissed as "dictum," it has nevertheless enjoyed a long life—now more than fifty years—because the Court has trotted out the sole-organ doctrine whenever it has required a rationale to support a constitutionally doubtful presidential action in foreign affairs.[38] On such occasions, and they have been numerous, the ghost of *Curtiss-Wright* has been made to walk again. Even the most cursory review of the cases in which it has been invoked makes clear that the essence of this "spirit" is great "deference to executive judgment in this vast external realm" of foreign relations.[39]

The deference is perhaps attributable to the effects of "court-positivism." By this doctrine, the Court's decisions are treated "as a given, to be explained, manipulated, and systematized, but criticized only within narrow limits."[40] The doctrine culminates in the view that the Constitution means what the justices say it means; the tendency, therefore, is to treat as "oracles" the few cases that have dotted an otherwise barren constitutional landscape. Gerhard Casper has described it thus: "It has also the paradoxical effect of assigning a disproportionate importance to the few 'legal' precedents that do exist. Absent the continuous consideration and reconsideration of rules and principles, a few oracles have led to the emergence of a constitutional mythology that does not bear close analysis."[41] For all its shortcomings, *Curtiss-Wright* has assumed the status of an oracle. As we shall see, it has led the judiciary to defer to "executive judgment" in cases involving executive agreements, travel abroad, treaty termination, and the war power. Of course these judicial decisions have not totally relied on *Curtiss-Wright;* they have also drawn on the political-question doctrine, grounds of nonjusticiability, and the silence and inaction of Congress. But the spirit of *Curtiss-Wright* pervades these techniques.

Executive Agreements

Perhaps it is no exaggeration to observe that since *Curtiss-Wright,* presidents have used executive agreements as the primary means of dominating the conduct of foreign policy.[42] This practice, which has resulted in a flood of unilateral presidential agreements, obviously precludes a role for the Senate; therefore, it subverts the basic constitutional scheme established in Philadelphia. The structural design of the treaty clause, as we have seen, was to preclude the president from entering the field of foreign relations without the participation of the Senate, and fear of the abuse of power dissuaded the Framers from vesting the executive with such unilateral authority.[43]

There was apparently no doubt among the Framers and ratifiers that the treatymaking power was omnicompetent in foreign affairs; its authority covered the field. As explained by Hamilton:

> From the *best opportunity of knowing the fact,* I aver, that it was understood by *all* to be the intent of the provision to give that power the most ample latitude—to render it competent to all the stipulations which the exigencies of national affairs might require; competent to the making of treaties of alliance, treaties of commerce, treaties of peace, and *every other species of convention* usual among nations. . . . And it was emphatically for this reason that it was so carefully guarded; the cooperation of two-thirds of the Senate with the President, being required to make any treaty whatever.[44]

The text of the Constitution makes no mention of executive agreements. Moreover, there was no reference to them in the Constitutional Convention or in the state ratifying conventions. The *Federalist Papers* are silent on the subject as well. There is, then, no support in the architecture of the Constitution for the use of executive agreements. Yet their usage, since 1936, has flourished; presidents claim independent constitutional power to make them, and the judiciary has sustained such presidential claims of authority.[45] What is the source of the president's power to make executive agreements?

An examination of the leading cases involving executive agreements disclosed judicial reliance on two constitutional grounds: the sole-organ doctrine and the recognition power of the president. Neither claim is tenable. In *United States v. Belmont*, Justice Sutherland wrote the opinion for the Court upholding the validity of an executive agreement that Pres. Franklin D. Roosevelt negotiated with the Soviet Union in 1933 involving the assignment of assets in both countries. The Court took judicial notice of the fact that the Litvinov Assignment—an agreement on property claims between Roosevelt and Maxim Litvinov—was executed in conjunction with the 1933 recognition of the Soviet government and said that the pact derived its force from both the president's status as sole organ and his power to recognize foreign governments. Justice Sutherland stated that Senate consultation was not required.

We have already exposed the infirmities of Justice Sutherland's sole-organ doctrine. It fares no better in the *Belmont* setting. Moreover, his invocation of the president's "recognition power," which is derived from his duty under Article II, section 3, to "receive Ambassadors and other public ministers," is puzzling. It appears that there was not disagreement during the Founding period among Hamilton, Madison, and Jefferson, who shared the understanding that the recognition clause conferred upon the president merely a ceremonial function that does not include any "discretion" to reject foreign ministers.[46] Writing what Madison considered the "original gloss" on the meaning of the clause, Hamilton explained in *Federalist 69* that the authority

> to receive ambassadors and other public ministers . . . is more a matter of dignity than authority. It is a circumstance which will be without consequence in the administration of government; and it was far more convenient that it should be arranged in this manner, than there should be a necessity of convening the legislature, or one of its branches, upon every arrival of a foreign minister, though it were merely to take the place of a departed predecessor.[47]

By any measure, Hamilton was talking about the effectuation of a diplomatic function.

As Louis Henkin has observed, "receiving ambassadors" seems "a function rather that a 'power,' a ceremony which in many countries is performed by a figurehead." Indeed, the distinction between a power and a function cannot be stressed too strongly. Henkin has justly remarked that "while making treaties and appointing ambassadors are described as 'powers' of the president, receiving ambassadors is included in section 3, which does not speak in terms of power but lists things the President 'shall' or 'may do.' ''[48]

Given the apparent refusal of the convention to convert the recognition clause into a well of discretionary power and its refusal to clothe the president with the treatymaking power so that he alone might conduct foreign policy, *Belmont* certainly represents an ''extreme extension'' of presidential power in foreign relations.[49] The extension clearly contravenes not only the structure of the treaty power but also the policy reasons that predetermined that structure. Justice Sutherland did not discuss any of these points in *Belmont*.

The Court again considered the validity of the Litvinov Assignment in 1942 in *United States v. Pink*. Virtually echoing the opinion in *Belmont*, Justice William O. Douglas invoked the sole-organ doctrine as well as the recognition power as authorization for the executive agreement. Yet there was no need for Justice Douglas to attempt to sustain the assignment on purely presidential powers, for he had said that ''the executive policy had been 'tacitly' recognized by congressional appointment of commissioners to determine American claims against the Soviet fund.''[50] It would appear, however, that Chief Justice Harlan Stone's dissent, in which Justice Owen Roberts concurred, exposed the real question in the case: ''We are referred to no authority which would sustain such an exercise of power as is said to have been exerted here by mere assignment unratified by the Senate.''[51]

Clearly, *Belmont* and *Pink*, in drawing upon *Curtiss-Wright*, can be seen as facilitating the trend toward presidential control of U.S. foreign policy, at least with respect to the use of executive agreements. And beginning in 1937, a virtual torrent of such agreements was unleashed—at the expense of the Senate and its constitutional role in making treaties. The trend, which continues to this day, as seen in *Dames and Moore v. Regan*, constitutes a fundamental and extraordinary shift of power from Congress to the president.

In *Dames and Moore*, which clearly represented ''a political decision by a political court,'' the High Tribunal was at pains to sustain the constitutionality of Pres. Jimmy Carter's executive agreement with Iran that secured the release of American hostages.[52] In his opinion for the Court, then Justice (now Chief) William Rehnquist found *statutory authorization* for much of the agreement but none for a critical leg—the suspension of all claims pending against Iran in U.S. courts.[53] Undaunted, Justice Rehnquist held that Congress had ''tacitly'' approved the president's pact. Apparently, it had evinced its support in two ways. First, Rehnquist located two statutes, the ''general tenor'' of which, he said, had delegated broad discretionary power to the president. He conceded, however, that neither statute by itself provided sufficient authority for the agreement.[54] Second, he asserted that, by virtue of its silence, Congress had acquiesced in the agreement. The Court concluded that the absence of explicit delegation did not imply congressional disapproval but merely showed that Congress had not anticipated such a situation.[55]

To be sure, the doctrine of "tacit" delegation based on congressional acquiescence has its place in American jurisprudence. But it is an acquiescence of a particular kind; it is based on a settled congressional understanding of an administrative construction of a statute. In other words, suppose an administrative agency adopts an erroneous interpretation of a statute. If Congress reenacts the statute with knowledge of the administrative interpretation, it is said to incorporate that interpretation and to give statutory standing to what was previously unlawful.[56] In effect, it ratifies and adopts that construction. We find a signal decision in this tradition. In the nineteenth century, Congress passed a number of statutes that made available public lands for private occupation. However, on hundreds of occasions, without statutory authority, the president withdrew some land from the right of entry. In 1915, in *United States v. Midwest Oil Co.,* the Court upheld Pres. William Taft's withdrawal in 1909 of certain lands from the appropriation of oil rights offered to the public by an act passed in 1897. The Court, consistent with the doctrine of tacit delegation, might have held that the Act of 1897, passed as it was with the knowledge of earlier executive withdrawals, silently included the practice. But it stated that the "long-continued practice, known to and acquiesced in by Congress," had gained the "implied consent of Congress."[57] There is, of course, no merit to the argument that an executive abuse of power acquires legal status if Congress does not correct it. In a parallel case, the Supreme Court held that a well-established, well-known, and long-continued practice of granting suspended sentences did not justify the federal courts in following this practice when the statute did not authorize it.[58] Nevertheless, the case is one of statutory interpretation. It treated congressional acquiescence as statutory authorization, not as a gloss on the Constitution.

Justice Rehnquist invoked *Midwest Oil* as precedential authority for his theory that Congress may exhibit acquiescence regarding presidential practices through silence. Of course, *Midwest Oil* is inapposite to *Dames and Moore*. In *Midwest Oil,* the Court recognized that Congress had passed a number of statutes with full knowledge of prior presidential action. Those statutes provided the requisite ratification of an administrative action. There was no such ratification in *Dames and Moore*. Indeed, Rehnquist conceded that Congress had not passed a single statute to authorize the executive agreement in the Iranian hostage crisis. Finally, Congress did not even evince the "tacit" consent that it had in *Pink,* by virtue of its appointment of negotiators. There was no such congressional support in *Dames and Moore*.

What remained for Rehnquist at this point was to glean congressional support from congressional silence. This enterprise is problematic; indeed, the Court has stated that it is "treacherous to find in congressional silence the adoption of a controlling rule of law."[59] A failure to object does not necessarily mean that Congress approves of the action. There may be numerous reasons why Congress may not act even though a majority of the body may disagree with the president. Paul Gewirtz has written:

> When Congress is faced with an executive policy that is in place and functioning, Congress often acquiesces in the executive's action for reasons which have nothing to do with the majority's preferences on the policy issues involved. . . . In such a situation, Congress may not want to be viewed as disruptive; or Congresspersons may not want to embarrass the President; or Congress may want to score political points by attacking the executive's action rather than accepting political responsibility for some action itself; or Congresspersons may be busy running for reelection or tending to constituents' individual problems; or Congress may be lazy and prefer another recess.[60]

The implications of Justice Rehnquist's reasoning are staggering. Ineluctably, the "doctrine of silence" would sanction "an almost total transfer of legislative power to the executive, so long as Congress does not object."[61] Justice Rehnquist's argument is not a new one, of course, for it is but a page torn from Theodore Roosevelt's "stewardship theory" of the presidency:

> I decline to adopt this view that what was imperatively necessary for the nation could not be done by the President, unless he could find some specific authorization to do it. I did not usurp power but I did greatly broaden the use of executive power. In other words, I acted for the common well being of all our people whenever and in whatever measure was necessary, unless prevented by direct constitutional or legislative prohibition.[62]

Roosevelt's view, like Rehnquist's, "means that the President is free to undertake any folly, provided it is so gross that it has not occurred to Congress to forbid it."[63]

At bottom, perhaps *Dames and Moore v. Regan* should not be understood as having sustained a purely executive agreement; after all, Justice Rehnquist ruled that the president enjoyed congressional authorization through tacit delegation. But my contention is that he has misapplied that doctrine. As applied, it is a prescription for the exercise of arbitrary presidential power in foreign affairs.

Travel Cases

For the past thirty years, the Supreme Court has steadily increased the power of the president to restrict the right of U.S. citizens to travel abroad. Since the peak of the Court's respect for the wishes of citizens to visit foreign lands, as exhibited in its 1958 holding in *Kent v. Dulles* that the right to travel is guaranteed by the due process clause of the Fifth Amendment, the Court has managed to "find" exceptions to that right by bowing to painfully plastic invocations of national security needs.[64] Its vulnerability to the spirit of *Curtiss-Wright*—"deference to the judgment of the executive"—and its willingness to find, on the flimsiest of pretexts, congressional "approval" of State Department passport policies, has created an environment in which the administration is the sole judge of its policies. In just a handful of cases, the Court has transmuted what has been regarded as a congressional lawmaking function—to determine what, if any, restrictions are to be imposed in foreign travel—into a discretionary executive policymaking tool of great scope. In light of this fundamental shift of power, Justice Brennan has been moved to remark: "The reach of the Secretary's [of State] discretion is potentially staggering."[65]

The first national passport legislation passed in 1858 vested the exclusive authority to issue passports in the executive branch, and Congress codified its language in the Passport Act of 1926. The act did not grant specific authority to the secretary of state to refuse or revoke passports because at that time Congress did not require passports for international travel by U.S. citizens except during periods of war or national emergency. (The general passport requirement became law in 1952 with passage of the Immigration and Nationality Act.[66]) However, the Court held in *Kent v. Dulles* that in the 1926 Passport Act Congress had adopted earlier the prior administrative practice of the State Department. Apparently, the secretary of state had authority to resolve questions of the allegiance of a passport applicant, which meant verifying his or her citizenship as well as investigating the applicant's criminal activity. In the latter case the secretary could deny passports to people violating U.S. law or seeking to escape the law. As I have observed, the adoption of an administrative practice by statute constitutes a legalization of the practice.

The Court has ruled on only a few cases challenging the validity of State Department regulations developed under the Passport Act. In *Kent v. Dulles,* the first major case concerning this issue, the secretary of state denied the passport application of two Communists under a departmental regulation that prohibited the issuance of passports to Communist party members or to persons going abroad to engage in activities enhancing the Communist movement. The Court invalidated the regulation, per Justice Douglas, who ruled that the freedom to travel is a "liberty" protected by the Fifth Amendment and, moreover, that any regulation of the freedom to travel must be made pursuant to the congressional lawmaking function and must therefore be narrowly construed. Since the secretary lacked express authority to deny passports, only an administrative practice clearly adopted by Congress would imply a delegation of its lawmaking function. The Court found that neither the established administrative practice nor the specific delegation to the secretary were sufficient to deny a passport merely because of one's beliefs and associations.[67]

The bubble burst seven years later in *Zemel v. Rusk,* in which the Court, per Chief Justice Earl Warren, sustained the administration's total ban on travel to Cuba.[68] The Court applied the standard developed in *Kent* and claimed to have discovered a substantial and consistent State Department practice of restricting travel to named geographic areas, both in wartime and peacetime, sufficient to warrant a conclusion that Congress was aware of the secretary's policy and thus implicitly approved of such restrictions. The substance and "consistency" of such a practice is doubtful. Justice Arthur Goldberg, in a dissenting opinion, revealed that these "precedents" occurred during the proximity of war and were thus immaterial because they fell within the war power of the executive.[69]

The *Zemel* Court also dismissed the Fifth Amendment challenge, reasoning that if the government can restrict travel within the United States for safety and welfare purposes, then surely the State Department could similarly restrict travel to Cuba for the same reasons. Chief Justice Warren, invoking *Curtiss-Wright,* said that "the weightiest considerations of national security" permit these travel restraints without violating due process.[70]

Justice Hugo Black filed a strong dissenting opinion and took Warren to task for permitting the executive branch to make laws:

> Since Article I, however, vests "All legislative Powers" in the Congress, and no language in the Constitution purports to vest any such power in the President, it necessarily follows, if the Constitution is to control, that the President is completely devoid of power to make laws regulating passports or anything else. And he has no more power to make laws by labeling them regulations than to do so by calling them laws. Like my brother Goldberg, I cannot accept the Government's argument that

the President has "inherent" power to make regulations governing the issuance and use of passports.[71]

The *Kent-Zemel* standard, which required a consistent pattern of actual enforcement in order to establish the requisite congressional approval, was for all intents and purposes overruled in *Haig v. Agee*.[72] In this case, the Court recognized enforcement as one method of establishing congressional awareness and approval of the regulation. But it also stated, in terms echoing *Dames and Moore v. Regan*, that courts could likewise find approval from nothing more than congressional silence about a long-standing administrative practice. Chief Justice Warren Burger concluded that Congress had implicitly adopted the administrative construction because it had not made any changes in the executive's basic rulemaking power when it passed the Immigration and Nationality Act of 1952 or when it amended the Passport Act in 1978. He observed that Congress must have been aware of the "longstanding and officially promulgated view" of the State Department that the president could revoke passports for reasons of national security. There is, of course, no such official policy, and the cases advanced by Burger are not supportive.[73]

Haig v. Agee produced a new standard for establishing congressional approval: that Congress allows the State Department to construct its own regulations provides sufficient basis to assume implicit congressional approval of a passport regulation. The Court in *Kent* had rejected a similar assertion by the government, holding that only an established departmental practice can convince the Court that Congress is sufficiently aware of the claimed authority. But the Court in the *Haig* decision would not require frequent instances of enforcement in order to build a track record. Even if no enforcement occurred, the validity of the executive's authority would not be destroyed, nor would lack of enforcement preclude congressional awareness of the department's construction.

That the Court could assume this position is all the more incredible in view of the fact that in 1978 Congress amended the Passport Act so as to deprive the president of all discretion with respect to the issuance of passports except to those countries with which the United States is at war or where there is imminent danger to Americans.[74] Yet in the face of this statute the Court asserted the superiority of national security claims, stating that "it is obvious and unarguable that no government interest is more compelling than the security of the nation." Therefore, said the Court, the government may regulate foreign travel within the limits of due process. But the guarantees of due process demand nothing more than the offer of a prompt revocation administrative hearing and a statement of reasons for the action.[75]

Given the Court's view in *Haig* that the executive branch need merely assert a construction of its own regulation in order to satisfy the need for congressional awareness, it is little wonder that Justice Brennan would view the State Department's discretion as "potentially staggering." Perhaps his use of the word "potentially" was optimistic; the discretion already is "staggering."

The Political-Question Doctrine

The political-question doctrine, the "principle under which the courts defer the determination of an issue to the political branches of government," stems primarily from the Court's concern for the separation of powers and its own role within that scheme.[76] But there is a continuing debate about the scope of the doctrine, the essence of which involves two very different theories.

Chief Justice John Marshall espoused the "classical" view in *Cohens v. Virginia* (1821), stating that the courts "have no more right to decline the exercise of jurisdiction which is given, than to usurp that which is not given." Similarly, Herbert Wechsler has said that the existence of a political question in any particular issue is determined by "whether the Constitution has committed to another agency of government the autonomous determination of the issue."[77] Accordingly, a court must first decide the threshold separation of powers issue before it can invoke the political-question doctrine.[78] A second theory, the "prudential" view, holds that courts should weigh the consequences that a particular case might have on the judiciary before addressing the merits of the claim.[79]

The invocation of the political-question doctrine has been a major means by which the judiciary has strengthened the role of the president in the conduct of foreign affairs. This section examines the judicial application of the doctrine in the areas of treaty termination and warmaking. First we turn to *Goldwater v. Carter* (1979), in which Rehnquist, writing for a plurality, stretched the doctrine beyond its previous limits.

Treaty Termination

In *Goldwater v. Carter,* Sen. Barry Goldwater challenged President Carter's unilateral termination of the 1954 Mutual Defense Treaty with Taiwan.[80] In an opinion by Rehnquist (Burger, Stewart, and Stevens concurring), it was held that the issue of treaty termination represented a nonjusticiable political question precisely because it involved "the authority of the President in the conduct of foreign relations and the extent to which the senate or congress is authorized to negate the action of the President."[81]

The plurality's decision clearly is unfounded. In the words of Justice William Brennan's dissent, the quartet "profoundly" misapprehended "the political question doctrine as it applies to foreign relations." Indeed, in the opinion of Justice Lewis Powell, who concurred in the dismissal of the case, but on grounds of ripeness, the foursome's "reliance upon the political question doctrine" was "inconsistent with our precedents."[82]

In his notable opinion in *Baker v. Carr*, Justice Brennan drew order from the confusion surrounding the political-question doctrine. After a discussion of the previous cases, he set forth six alternative tests for identifying the political questions:

> Prominent on the surface of any case held to involve a political question is found a textually demonstrable constitutional commitment of the issue to a coordinate political department; or a lack of judicially discoverable and manageable standards for resolving it; or the impossibility of deciding without an initial policy determination of a kind clearly for non-judicial discretion; or the impossibility of a court's undertaking independent resolution without expressing lack of respect due coordinate branches of government; or an unusual need for unquestioning adherence to a political decision already made; or the potentiality of embarrassment from multifarious pronouncements by various departments on one question.[83]

The issue of treaty termination does not conform to any of these analytical components of the political-question doctrine. Justice Brennan's first test—a textual commitment—has been justly characterized by Wechsler as the governing principle of the doctrine. He stated that "all the doctrine can defensibly imply is that the courts are called upon to judge whether the constitution has committed to another agency of government the autonomous determination of the issue raised."[84] There is, of course, no textual commitment of the authority to terminate treaties, for the Constitution is silent on the point. Thus *Goldwater* certainly could not be labeled a political-question case on this ground. Nor is there "a lack of judicially discoverable and manageable standards" for resolving the issue. For example, the Court might have examined the logic of the treaty power's structure and drawn the inference that the authority to terminate treaties belongs to the treaty power. Support for this symmetrical construction was expressed by Justices Joseph Story and Benjamin Cardozo, two of our most eminent jurists. Or the Court might have studied the historical practice of treaty termination, which would have revealed three alternatives: termination by the president and Senate jointly, by congressional directive, or by independent presidential action. Any one of these inquiries would have disclosed "manageable standards."[85] Neither Brennan's third test, which prohibits a nonjudicial policy determination, nor his fourth, which precludes resolution of the issue if it would require the judiciary to exhibit insufficient respect toward a coordinate branch of government, is applicable here. Surely the courts may not undertake an initial policy determination to make or terminate a treaty, for this type of action is nonjudicial. But deciding whether the appropriate political branch has made that determination is clearly justiciable.[86] Moreover, the Court does not commit such a social solecism if it determines that the president has transgressed constitutional bounds. As Chief Justice John Marshall stated in *Marbury v. Madison,* "To what purpose are powers limited, and to what purpose is that limitation committed to writing, if these limits may, at any time, be passed by those intended to be restrained?" Whatever risk exists of insufficient respect toward the president, the overriding concern must attach to the integrity of the Constitution and its framework of limited government. "It is far more important," observed Justice Douglas, "to be respectful to the Constitution than to a coordinate branch of the government."[87] Brennan's fifth criterion is "an unusual need for unquestioned adherence to a political decision already made." Although it is not clear which cases might satisfy this criterion, outside of, perhaps, a declaration of war, it is hard to imagine that this test could encompass the termination of a treaty. The last reason cited by Brennan was "the potential embarrassment from multifarious pronouncements by various departments on one question." Probably Brennan had in mind *Luther v. Borden,* in which the Court was asked to decide which of two rival governments was the legitimate Republican government in Rhode Island.[88] That case represented the possibility of six pronouncements by six departments on one question. In *Goldwater,* however, we do not find "multifarious pronouncements"; indeed, only the president acted, and that action was challenged as unconstitutional. If the Court had ruled that Carter's termination of the Taiwan Treaty was invalid, the ruling no doubt would have been embarrassing to some people and annoying to Peking, but it would not have produced the chaos Justice Brennan had in mind.

For Justice Rehnquist the issue of treaty termination was a nonjusticiable political question merely because it raised the question of the allocation of power between the president and Congress in the realm of foreign affairs. Rehnquist thus ignored Justice Brennan's sagacious observation in *Baker v. Carr* that "it is error to suppose that every case or controversy which touches foreign relations lies beyond judicial cognizance."[89] Justice Rehnquist's obeisance to the president in the conduct of foreign policy recalls the folly of *Cur-*

tiss-Wright, the proposition that the president is sole organ in foreign affairs. Whatever authority the president has in the formulation of international policy, he is not the Pied Piper, and the other branches of government and the American public are not the children of Hamelin. Such a storybook view of presidential power cannot be reconciled with constitutional restrictions. To be sure, the allocation of power in the Constitution is not always clear. But when there is a question as to the repository of authority, determination of the matter is left to the courts. Justice Rehnquist's view that each of the branches "has resources available to protect its interests" would, as Raoul Berger has remarked, "return us to settlement of differences by Kentucky feud."[90] Rehnquist's adoration for this sort of legal Darwinism would not save us from a covetous or usufructuary executive, but a Court committed to the Constitution might.

In an astute study of the political-question doctrine, Fritz Scharpf has concluded that "the political question . . . had no place when the court was presented with conflicting claims of competence among the departments of the federal government."[91] That was the view of the Court in *Powell v. McCormack,* where it declared that its principal duty was to decide "whether the action of [another] branch exceeds whatever authority has been committed." In *Goldwater,* however, the Court abdicated that duty. Despite Justice Powell's reminder that in the past the Court had been willing to determine "whether one branch of our government has impinged upon the power of another,"[92] the Court declined to answer a straightforward question in *Goldwater:* In which department of government does the Constitution vest the authority to terminate treaties?

As a practical matter, the Court's action, or rather its inaction, left the termination of the Mutual Defense Treaty intact. Although the plurality opinion in *Goldwater* did not establish a legal precedent, it will nevertheless establish a foundation, however shaky, for future unilateral presidential treaty terminations.[93] This result will have the unfortunate effect of placing the exclusive authority to terminate defense, commercial, economic, and arms-control agreements, among others, in the hands of the president.

Political Questions and the War Power

Since 1950 the United States has been involved in a series of unilateral executive wars. Presidential usurpation of the war power has become a commonplace, a practice that obviously violates the policy objectives of the war clause. The delegates present at the Constitutional Convention, fearful that one man might rush the nation into war, vested in Congress the exclusive power to initiate hostilities. Apparently oblivious of the common sense underlying this allocation of power, the judiciary remains a coconspirator in this gross disjuncture between law and practice.

Indeed, its invocation of the political-question doctrine has been a major means by which the judiciary has strengthened the role of the president in the conduct of foreign policy. Throughout the Vietnam War, lower courts routinely invoked the doctrine in response to challenges to the constitutionality of that war, and many observers viewed the unwillingness to address the merits of the claims as a sign of judicial approval of administration policy.[94] This reticence certainly did not dissuade the president from continuing the war effort. Aside from the problematic inferences drawn from the silence of the courts, the Vietnam War—like the Korean War before it and the later wars in Grenada and Panama—did not receive congressional authorization, which the Constitution requires.[95] The fact that various presidents initiated war without congressional authorization created a constitutional crisis that might have been resolved by the judiciary. But it was not, and consequently, the United States has suffered a string of presidential wars from Korea to Panama. This actuality constitutes a fundamental shift of power from Congress to the president. In a few cases challenging Pres. Ronald Reagan's military adventures in Grenada, Nicaragua, and El Salvador, lower courts refused to rule on the merits. As might be expected, they have held that these cases constituted nonjusticiable, political questions. Judicial reluctance to enforce constitutional boundaries in the area of foreign policy has threatened, in Jefferson's phrase, to convert the "chains of the Constitution" into "ropes of sand." The effect has been to encourage the tendencies of the "imperial presidency." It is no surprise, therefore, that recent presidents have come to view the military of the United States as a private army at their beck and call to fulfill the goals of a foreign policy agenda. The shift threatens the foundation of our republican form of government as well as our tradition of constitutionalism.[96]

The nation's need for a judicial branch that will unflinchingly "say what the law is," therefore, is of greatest importance. The law, as we have seen, was articulated in a number of cases at the dawn of the republic: only Congress may constitutionally initiate war. Viewed in the light, the unwillingness of the judiciary to declare the Vietnam War unconstitutional clearly illustrates the fact that the judicial branch of government abdicated its institutional duties. There is no need here to review the judiciary's treatment of the cases challenging the legality of that war, for such reviews can be found elsewhere.[97] Suffice it to say that although no court affirmed the legality of the unilateral presidential war, only one court declared the war illegal. At the district and circuit court levels, judges routinely declared the issues nonjusticiable. The Supreme Court routinely denied certiorari.

In the tradition of the Vietnam War rulings, recent lower court decisions have dismissed challenges to presidential warmaking on various grounds of nonjusticiability. In *Crockett v. Reagan,* the D.C. Court of Appeals dismissed as a political question a suit filed by members of Congress that claimed Ronald Reagan had violated the War Powers Resolution when he failed to submit a report that American soldiers had been introduced into hostilities in El Salvador.[98] The court refused to engage in the fact-finding necessary to determine whether hostilities existed or were imminent and reasoned that "the question here belongs to the category characterized by a lack of judicially discoverable and manageable standards for resolution."[99] The court stated that it lacked "the resources and expertise" necessary "to resolve the disputed questions of fact concerning the military situation in El Salvador."[100] The difficulty involved in the fact-finding process did not justify the invocation of the political-question doctrine since the Supreme Court, in *Baker v. Carr,* had fenced off resolution of disputes characterized by uncertain legal standards and not those that entailed difficulties in settling questions of fact.

Members of Congress who claimed that Reagan's use of military force in the Persian Gulf in 1987 violated the procedures of the War Powers Resolution met a similar fate in *Lowry v. Reagan.*[101] In *Lowry,* 110 plaintiffs saw their suit dismissed on two grounds: political question and remedial discretion. Here, as in *Crockett,* the court misapplied the political-question doctrine. The court feared that a decision on the merits—whether a cease-fire in the Gulf meant that U.S. forces were in a situation in which hostilities were either present or imminent—would have required an evaluation of the stability of the cease-fire, a task "beyond judicial competence."[102] The existence of disputed questions of fact does not provide a basis for the application of the political-question doctrine; if that were so, judicial abstention would be the rule and not the exception. Disputed facts must be resolved through the traditional means of gathering evidence, not buried by resort to the doctrine of political question.

The district court in *Lowry* also dismissed the lawsuit on the basis of the doctrine of remedial discretion, a judicial tool that mandates dismissal of congressional claims where members have an effective in-house remedy for their injuries, such as the enactment, repeal, or amendment of a statute.[103] In 1985, in *Sanchez-Espinoza v. Reagan,* D.C. Circuit Judge (now Justice) Ruth Bader Ginsburg wrote a concurring opinion in which she dismissed as not ripe for review a suit brought by twelve members of Congress on issues arising from U.S. actions in Nicaragua.[104] Judge Ginsburg said of the war-clause claim: "The Judicial Branch should not decide issues affecting the allocation of power between the President and Congress until they reach a constitutional impasse." Moreover,

> Congress has formidable weapons at its disposal—the power of the purse and investigative resources far beyond those available in the Third Branch. But no gauntlet has been thrown down here by a majority of the Members of Congress. On the contrary, Congress expressly allowed the President to spend federal funds to support paramilitary operations in Nicaragua and "if the Congress chooses not to confront the President, it is not our task to do so."[105]

The message from the court was clear and familiar: if Congress fails to assert its powers, it cannot expect to be protected by the judiciary.

The *Lowry* court viewed the lawsuit as "a by-product of political disputes within Congress regarding the applicability of the War Powers Resolution to the Persian Gulf situation."[106] The court drew this conclusion from the numerous bills that had been introduced to "compel the President to invoke" the resolution, to strengthen it, and to repeal it. The tribunal embraced Justice Powell's concurring opinion in *Goldwater v. Carter* and stated that the "passage of legislation to enforce the Resolution . . . would pose a question ripe for review," but Congress had not passed a law and without it the court would be interfering in the legislative debate.[107] The court's major error in this line of reasoning was in its assumption that plaintiffs' dispute was with "fellow legislators" and not with the president. In fact, *Lowry* did not involve an intramural debate. Indeed, in the passage of the War Powers Resolution, Congress had required the president to submit a report when troops had been introduced into hostilities or hostilities were imminent.[108] Reagan had not complied with the law, and the plaintiffs simply sought enforcement of it.

In 1990, in the closely-watched case *Dellums v. Bush,* Federal District Judge Harold H. Greene dismissed as not ripe for review a congressional challenge to Pres. George Bush's claim of unilateral authority to wage war in Kuwait, but in his decision he forcefully rejected many of the sweeping claims made by the executive branch.[109] Judge Greene stated that if the president "had the sole power to determine that any particular offensive military operation, no matter how vast, does not constitute war-making but only an offensive military attack, the congressional power to make war will be at the mercy of a semantic decision by the Executive. Such an 'interpretation' would evade the plain language of the Constitution, and it cannot stand."[110] In response to the Department of Justice's contention that the issue was political and not judicial, Judge Green ruled:

The Department goes on to suggest that the issue in this case is still political rather than legal, because in order to resolve the dispute the court would have to interject itself into foreign affairs, a subject which the Constitution commits to the political branches. That argument, too, must fail.

While the Constitution grants to the political branches, and in particular to the Executive, responsibility for conducting the nation's foreign affairs, it does not follow that the judicial power is excluded from the resolution of cases merely because they may touch upon such affairs. . . . In fact, courts are routinely deciding cases that touch upon or even have a substantial impact on foreign and defense policy.[111]

Although Judge Greene rejected the Bush administration's sweeping assertions of independent presidential war powers, he nevertheless determined that the case was not ripe for judicial determination: "Unless the Congress as a whole, or by a majority, is heard from, the controversy here cannot be deemed ripe; it is only if the majority of the Congress seeks relief from an infringement on its constitutional war-declaration power that it may be entitled to receive it."[112]

Although there is merit to the judicial concerns underlying the doctrines of ripeness and remedial discretion, the judiciary's obligation to police constitutional boundaries remains a greater concern. As these matters stand, if a minority in either the House or the Senate is unable to move its chamber to repel a presidential usurpation of power, the minority cannot find relief in court. The problem is particularly acute in the case of warmaking since members of Congress will have been deprived of their constitutional authority to vote on the wisdom of initiating war. The application of these judicial barriers was defended in *Lowry* and *Dellums* by the resuscitation of Justice Powell's emphasis on the silence of Congress with respect to the issue of treaty termination in his concurring opinion in *Goldwater:*

Congress has taken no official action. In the present posture of this case, we do not know whether there ever will be an actual confrontation between the legislative and executive branches. . . . It cannot be said that either the Senate or the House has rejected the President's claim. If the Congress chooses not to confront the President, it is not our task to do so.[113]

The invocation of the doctrines of ripeness and remedial discretion in warmaking cases, on grounds that Congress has taken no action with respect to presidential warmaking, ignores the fact that the institutional indifference of members of Congress toward their constitutional responsibilities has no bearing whatever on the Court's duties, which are independent of those vested in Congress. Neither the judicial duty to "say what the law is" nor the scope of congressional power can be made to hinge on the interests, knowledge, or integrity of Congress.[114] History teaches, and the Constitution contemplates, the fact that public servants may not execute their duties faithfully, responsibly, or diligently.[115] How ironic it is that a majority of Congress, uninterested in exercising or defending its powers, as contemplated by the doctrines of separation of powers and checks and balances, would be rewarded for its irresponsibility, while a minority, committed to both constitutionalism and constitutionally allocated institutional values, can find no relief, support, or protection from the courts.[116]

It is true, of course, as the courts have held, that Congress has resources to draw upon in battle with the executive, among them the power of the purse, the power to abolish programs and departments, investigatory authority, and the ultimate weapon, impeachment of the president for encroachment on its powers or for subversion of the Constitution. However formidable the weapons may appear to be, they are difficult to effectuate.[117] Moreover, they require majorities and even a supermajority, in the event of impeachment, and thus will be unavailing to the ineffectual minority that seeks judicial protection. But is it the case that we really ought to prefer an interbranch conflict, with knives drawn and tempers frayed, to an impartial and dispassionate judicial resolution of competing constitutional claims?[118] Or, to put it in other terms, is the nation well served by a Court that sits idly by in the face of a manifest constitutional violation?[119]

The Constitution, it bears reminder, was written not for Congress but for the American people.[120] Presidential *usurpation* of power does not become more or less legal as a result of congressional acquiescence or challenge. The constitutionality of a presidential act is determined solely on the basis of whether it enjoys constitutional warrant. Thus, judicial settlement of a constitutional controversy between the president and members of Congress, as in *Dellums,* does not constitute an intrusion into the business of the House and Senate but a check on the president, not an unwarranted interference in the affairs of Congress but an exercise of the Court's duty to police constitutional boundaries.[121] As Chief Justice Edward White stated in 1892, in words that echo *Marbury v. Madison,* it is the "ever present duty" of the courts "to enforce and uphold the applicable provisions of the Constitution as to each and every exercise of governmental power."[122]

The duty of the Court to enforce the exclusive grant to Congress of the authority to initiate war is surely more vital and compelling than its solemn responsibility to safeguard the sole power of Congress to appropriate funds from the U.S. Treasury.[123] Who would excuse a judicial invocation of the doctrines of ripeness and remedial discretion in the face of a presidential usurpation of the appropriations power? The constitutional measure of the exercise of each power is whether Congress has acted affirmatively, that is by voting. Congressional silence is not the mechanism provided by the Constitution for the authorization of war or appropriations. Whether Congress has taken that affirmative action is a legal issue, subject to resolution by the courts.

If a quiescent Congress bows to a usurpatious president and the Court shirks its duty to "say what the law is," what is left in the way of governmental institutions to bring an errant executive to heel? Who, indeed, will act to maintain the integrity of the Constitution?

Judicial Deference to the Executive

As we have seen, the Court has been willing, even eager, to manipulate the Constitution and statutory law in order to justify executive action in the realm of foreign affairs. The Court's reflexive use of law to legitimate the international politics of the president and its concomitant paralytic refusal to invoke its paramount prerogative of invalidation have for all intents and purposes served to exalt the president's authority in these matters above constitutional norms.[124] In short, the Court has become an accomplice to the executive in foreign affairs.

The judiciary's subservience to the executive and its determination to clothe him with powers that are not tethered to the Constitution evokes questions about its motives. Why has the judicial branch been so loath to find usurpation of power? Why has it evinced no disposition to frustrate the tremendous growth of power in the executive, especially in the field of foreign relations? A complete explanation is beyond the reach of this chapter. The explanatory factors adequate to such a task are like pieces of a puzzle that cannot at this juncture be fitted properly. No more is hoped for here than to succeed in placing most of the pieces on the table.

It is quite likely that the Court views its function as supporting governmental policy once it has been established. Invariably, this perspective translates into support for presidential conduct of U.S. foreign relations. Certainly, any attempt to adduce an explanation would have to include the fact that the Court believes the president has plenary powers in the area of foreign policy that give him a broad discretionary authority to identify and define national interests and national security. Second, the Court seems to believe that it lacks competence, expertise, equipment, and guidelines for resolution of foreign affairs cases. Third, the Court fears the embarrassment, chaos, and confusion that may attend the exercise of judicial review against a presidential act. These factors have conduced to make the judiciary an arm of the executive in the conduct of foreign policy. As such we ought not to be surprised by the institutional loyalty it has shown toward the president.

There can be little doubt that *Curtiss-Wright* has overwhelmed the foreign relations law of the United States. The Court's penchant for precedent, even flimsy precedent, drives it almost inexorably back to *Curtiss-Wright,* the source of the view that the president exercises plenary authority over foreign affairs. The effect of court-positivism has given this case an oracular status that most likely will not be diminished.[125] Indeed, from *Belmont* and *Pink* to *Zemel* and *Haig,* the Court has regularly evinced its support of the president's dominant role. As an attribute of his authority, the president has virtually unlimited discretion to identify and define U.S. national security interests. And the Court has shown an exaggerated deference to the president's perception in this area, as manifested in *Zemel v. Rusk,* and again in *Haig v. Agee,* in which the Court withdrew all checks on the executive's power to regulate travel where national security interests are concerned. Of course, it is of no moment to the judiciary that the sole-organ doctrine has been savaged by constitutional scholars as utterly without foundation and support in Anglo-American legal history. Apparently, Thomas Reed Powell used to tell his students at Harvard Law School, "Just because Mr. Justice Sutherland writes clearly, you must not suppose that he thinks clearly."[126]

The Court's obeisance to the president cannot be explained solely in terms of its subscription to the sole-organ doctrine. Sixty years ago, Louis Jaffe was at pains to understand the Court's almost "unreasoning sense of incompetency" in foreign relations cases.[127] This sense of incompetency—which becomes, in the judges' minds, "no competency"—should be considered in the broader context of the Court's view that the president is superior in every aspect of policymaking. Thus, the president has superior information, expertise, foreign relations machinery, diplomatic skills, and a better understanding of the national interest. In short, the judges place more faith in the executive process of weighing values and measuring the gains and losses of policies than they do in the judicial process. Clearly, this mindset is evident in a number of the cases that we have reviewed, ranging from *Curtiss-Wright,* in which Justice Sutherland supported the president's lofty status with the claim of superior information, to its unwillingness to rule on the issue of unilateral presidential warmaking. It is also reflected in the political-question doctrine, as for instance in the test involving a lack of "judicially discoverable and manageable standards."

Given this backdrop—the judiciary's insecurity and lack of confidence—and the fact that the Court, usually, can check acts only *after* they have occurred, the idea of judicial deference becomes somewhat more comprehensible. There is, therefore, something of an urge to "go along" with the established policy. In reality, this trend provides a support function for the executive, as Congress rarely acts first. But this act of filial piety also can work tragedy, as it did in the internment of Japanese-Americans in World War II.

Finally, the Court has not been willing to ignore the political realities of the international realm. The contortions of Justice Rehnquist in *Dames and Moore*, the stretching and twisting to find congressional authorization for Jimmy Carter's agreement with Iran, reflected his understanding of realpolitik and the complexities of international negotiation. If the Court had ruled against the Iranian pact, chaos and confusion would have resulted and a carefully crafted diplomatic package would have been unraveled. A similar fate awaited Franklin Roosevelt in both *Belmont* and *Pink* if the Court had not contrived authority for the executive acts involved in those cases. Clearly, embarrassment is a weighty concern for the Court, as are its desires to promote order and tranquillity and to avoid confusion and stress.

For these reasons, and perhaps others, the Court is inclined to take a narrow view of its role in foreign affairs cases. The reasoning underlying this conception leads it to grant considerable respect, latitude, and discretion to other departments when it can, and in foreign affairs cases, as we have observed, it always follows this approach. In short, the Court believes it should not interfere with the policymaking organ, the president, but should give him virtually untrammeled authority. With this line of thought we have come full circle, for we have returned to the argument of *Curtiss-Wright*.

CONCLUSION: POLICING CONSTITUTIONAL BOUNDARIES

The growth of executive foreign affairs powers in the past sixty years has been tremendous. Although given only modest authority by the Constitution, the president's powers have become so great as to provide him with a virtual "monopoly" over foreign relations.[128] The judicial contribution to presidential hegemony is reprehensible. Beginning with *Curtiss-Wright,* the courts have steadily fed the springs of presidential power by showing great deference to the executive, sometimes by virtue of the political-question doctrine and other times by blanket disregard of congressional intentions. Whatever the method, the judiciary has played a pivotal role in the trend toward executive domination of foreign affairs. Its obeisance to the president betrays the wisdom of the deep-seated suspicion with which the Framers and ratifiers viewed executive discretion—an animus so powerful that it led them, virtually without dissent, to place the conduct of foreign policy beyond the presidency and in the more trusted hands of Congress. That decision, of course, also reflected their commitment to the republican principle of collective decisionmaking, a process they believed would produce foreign policy consistent with the national interests.

Acting as an arm of the executive branch, the Court has done much to undermine collective decisionmaking and shared powers in foreign affairs at the expense of its duty to police constitutional boundaries. As Justice Robert Jackson said, "Some arbiter is almost indispensable when power is . . . balanced between different branches, as the legislative and executive. . . . Each unit cannot be left to judge the limits of its own powers."[129] By policing constitutional boundaries, the Court not only would maintain the integrity of the Constitution, it also would protect the entire political community against usurpation. A political community like the United States expects that the allocation of governmental power by the Constitution will be maintained—barring, that is, fundamental changes through the amendatory process. Change through that method ensures the sovereign people a voice in the system by which they are governed. But a radical departure from the constitutional blueprint that the people ratified deprives them of such a voice. When the written Constitution is violated by usurpation of power, the people may wonder about the utility of limited powers "if these limits may, at anytime, be passed by those intended to be restrained." John Marshall, speaking as a member of the Virginia Ratifying Convention, had an answer: "To what quarter will you look for protection from an infringement on the Constitution, if you will not give the power to the judiciary? There is no other body that can afford such a protection."[130]

In recent years, the judiciary has failed to provide protection against executive usurpation of legislative power in foreign affairs; indeed, it has sanctioned it. As a result, the doctrine of shared powers has been virtually emasculated. If Marshall was right, then the Constitution and the republic are imperiled.

NOTES

1. For a discussion of this trend from a sharply critical perspective, see David Gray Adler, *The Constitution and the Termination of Treaties* (New York: Garland Publishing, 1986); Adler, "The Constitution and Presidential Warmaking: The Enduring De-

bate," *Political Science Quarterly* 103 (Spring 1988): 1; Raoul Berger, *Executive Privilege: A Constitutional Myth* (Cambridge: Harvard University Press, 1974); Arthur Schlesinger, Jr., *The Imperial Presidency* (Boston: Houghton Mifflin, 1973); Francis D. Wormuth and Edwin B. Firmage, *To Chain the Dog of War: The War Power of Congress in History and Law* (Dallas: Southern Methodist University Press, 1986); and Louis Fisher, *Presidential War Power* (Lawrence: University Press of Kansas, 1995).

2. For differing explanations, see Ira Katznelson and Kenneth Prewitt, "Constitutionalism, Class, and the Limits of Choice in U.S. Foreign Policy," in Richard Fagen, ed., *Capitalism and the State in U.S.-Latin American Relations* (Palo Alto, Calif.: Stanford University Press, 1979); Theodore Lowi, *The Personal President: Power Invested, Promise Unfulfilled* (Ithaca, N.Y.: Cornell University Press, 1985); Philip Kurland, *Watergate and the Constitution* (Chicago: University of Chicago Press, 1978); Leslie Gelb and Richard Betts, *The Irony of Vietnam: The System Worked* (Washington, D.C.: Brookings, 1979). See also the authors cited in note 1.

3. *United States v. Curtiss-Wright Export Corporation*, 299 U.S. 304 (1936).

4. *Marbury v. Madison*, 5 U.S. 137 (1803).

5. See Adler, *Constitution and Termination*, pp. 84–148.

6. For a discussion of the commander-in-chief clause see Adler, "Constitution and Presidential Warmaking," pp. 8–13, and Berger, *Executive Privilege*, pp. 60–64.

7. See Hamilton's explanation in *Federalist* 69 in *The Federalist*, ed. Edward M. Earle (New York: Modern Library, 1937), p. 451. Madison's remarks may be found in *The Letters of Pacificus and Helvidius*, ed. Richard Loss (Delmar, N.Y.: Scholar's Facsimile, 1976), pp. 76–77. See also Chapter 5 of this volume.

8. Such a straightforward, textualist approach provides a basis that, in the words of Prof. Philip Bobbitt, is "readily apprehendable by the people at large, namely, given common-language meaning to constitutional provisions" (Philip Bobbitt, *Constitutional Fate* [Oxford: Oxford University Press, 1982], p. 31). The significance of the plain meaning of the words should not be underestimated, for as Justice Joseph Story observed, "Constitutions . . . are instruments of a particular nature, founded on the common business of human life, adapted to common wants, designed for common use, and fitted for common understanding. The people make them; the people adopt them; the people must be supposed to read them . . . ; and cannot be presumed to admit in them any recondite meaning" (quoted in idem, *Constitutional Fate*, pp. 25–26).

9. Hamilton, *Federalist 75*.

10. Adler, *Constitutional Termination*, p. 93.

11. Hamilton made this point in the New York Ratifying Convention. Jonathan Elliot, *Debates in the Several State Conventions on the Adoption of the Federal Constitution*, 2d ed. (Washington, D.C.: J. Elliot, 1836), 2:305. For similar remarks, see pp. 291, 323. Senator Rufus King, a Framer, stated in Congress in 1818 that "to the validity of all . . . proceedings in the management of foreign affairs; the constitutional advice and consent of the Senate are indispensable" (*Annals of Congress* [1818], 31:106–7. See also Adler, *Constitution and Termination*, pp. 84–148.

12. For example, it was argued in the Constitutional Convention that the various political, economic, and security interests of the states could be protected *only* if each state had an equal voice in the treatymaking process. See Adler, *Constitution and Termination*, pp. 84–88.

13. In the North Carolina Ratifying Convention, William Davie, who had been a Framer, said "that jealousy of executive power which has shown itself so strongly in all the American governments, would not admit" of lodging the treaty powers in the president alone (Elliot, *Debates*, 4:120). In order to allay fears that the convention had created an embryonic monarchy, Hamilton launched into a minute analysis of presidential power in *Federalist* 69 and noted that nothing was "to be feared" from an executive "with the confined authorities of the President" (*Federalist* 69, p. 448). "Fear of a return of Executive authority like that exercised by the Royal Governors or by the King had been ever present in the States from the beginning of the Revolution" (Charles Warren, *The Making of the Constitution* [Cambridge: Harvard University Press, 1947], p. 173).

14. Hamilton, *Federalist* 75, p. 487.

15. When the Framers were discussing the repository of the war power, they considered a proposal to give the national executive the executive powers of the Continental Congress. But there was concern expressed that this power would include the power of war, which would make the executive a monarchy. James Wilson sought to reassure such concerns: "Making peace and war are generally determined by writers on the Laws of Nations to be legislative powers." He added that "the Prerogatives of the British Monarchy" are not "a proper guide in defining the executive powers. Some of the prerogatives were of a legislative nature. Among others that of war & peace" (Max Farrand, *The Records of the Federal Convention of 1787* [New Haven: Yale University Press, 1911], 1:73–74, 65–66. Madison agreed with Wilson (see p. 70). For discussion of the allocation of the war power and the president's authority to repel attacks against the United States, see Adler, "Constitution and Presidential Warmaking," pp. 3–13.

16. Elliot, *Debates*, 2:528.

17. For statements in the state ratifying conventions, see Adler, "Constitution and Presidential Warmaking," p. 5. For example, James Iredell stated in North Carolina: "The President has not the power of declaring war by his own authority. . . . Those powers are vested in other hands. The power of declaring war is expressly given to Congress." And Charles Pinckney, a delegate in Philadelphia, told the South Carolina Ratifying Convention that "the President's powers did not permit him to declare war" (Elliot, *Debates*, 4:107, 108, 287. Hamilton, moreover, had stated flatly that the "declaring of war . . . by the Constitution . . . would appertain to the legislature" (*Federalist* 69, p. 448).

18. See Adler, "Constitution and Presidential Warmaking," pp. 3–29.

19. *Little v. Barreme*, 4 Dall. 37, 40–42, 43, 45–46 (1800); 1 Cranch 1, 28 (1801); 2 Cranch 170, 177–78 (1804).

20. *United States v. Smith*, 27 F. Cas. 1192, 1230 (No. 16342) (C.C.D.N.Y. 1806).

21. *Prize Cases*, 67 U.S. 635, 668 (1863).

22. Some academics and various presidents—Truman, Johnson, Nixon, Ford, Carter, and Reagan—have invoked the commander-in-chief clause as a source of independent presidential warmaking authority. There is no merit to these claims. The Supreme Court never has held that this clause is a foundation of warmaking power for the president, and there is no foundation for the view in either the Constitutional Convention or the state ratifying conventions. See Adler, "Constitution and Presidential Warmaking," pp. 8–13, 28–29.

23. Elliot, *Debates*, 2:507. In the First Congress, Roger Sherman, who had been a

delegate in Philadelphia, argued in defense of the shared-powers arrangement in foreign affairs: "The more wisdom there is employed, the greater security there is that the public business will be done" (*Annals of Congress* [1789], 1:1085). This statement echoed the sentiment expressed by Benjamin Franklin at the close of the Constitutional Convention, when he urged the delegates to set aside their remaining differences in favor of the collective judgment (Farrand, *Records,* 2:641–43. For a discussion of republicanism, see, generally, Gordon S. Wood, *The Creation of the American Republic, 1776–1787* (New York: W. W. Norton, 1969), pp. 1–124.

24. Dread of executive power surfaced again and again in the various conventions; see Farrand, *Records,* 1:66, 83, 90, 101, 113, 119, 153, 425; and 2:35–36, 101, 278, 513, 632, 640; Elliot, *Debates,* 3:58, 60; and 4:311. This fear had been common among the colonists (Edward S. Corwin, *The President: Office and Powers,* 3d ed. [New York: New York University Press, 1948], p. 4).

25. Farrand, *Records,* 1:70. The convention believed the enumeration of presidential powers was essential. See Berger, *Executive Privilege,* pp. 49–59.

26. Gelb and Betts, *Irony of Vietnam,* p. 363; Mulford Q. Sibley, "Can Foreign Policy Be Democratic?" in Robert Goldwin and Harry Clor, eds., *Readings in American Foreign Policy,* 2d ed. (New York: Oxford University Press, 1971), pp. 20–28. See, generally, Robert Dahl, *Congress and Foreign Policy* (New York: Harcourt, Brace, 1950), and Adler, *Constitution and Termination,* pp. 344–55.

27. Dahl, *Congress,* p. 181, and Francis D. Wormuth, "The Presidency as an Ideal Type," in D. Nelson and R. Sklar, eds., *Essays in Law and Politics* (Port Washington, N.Y.: Kennikat Press, 1978), pp. 200–201.

28. See, e.g., Eugene Rostow, "Great Cases Make Bad Law: The War Powers Act," *Texas Law Review* 50 (May 1972): 833; William Rogers, "Congress, the President, and War Powers," *California Law Review* 59 (September 1971): 1194.

29. See, generally, Schlesinger, *Imperial Presidency;* Wormuth and Firmage, *Dog of War;* Berger, *Executive Privilege;* Adler, *Constitution and Termination,* pp. 344–62; Michael J. Glennon, *Constitutional Diplomacy* (Princeton, N.J.: Princeton University Press, 1990); John Hart Ely, *War and Responsibility* (Princeton, N.J.: Princeton University Press, 1993).

30. This view, as Schlesinger observed, "went down in flames in Vietnam" (*Imperial Presidency,* p. 282).

31. For some of the evidence, see Charles Lofgren, "*United States v. Curtiss-Wright Export Corporation:* An Historical Reassessment," *Yale Law Journal* 83 (1973): 1, 3–5.

32. *Panama Refining Co. v. Ryan,* 293 U.S. 388 (1935).

33. *United States v. Curtiss-Wright Export Corporation,* at 328.

34. *Annals of Congress* (1800), 10:613–14.

35. Corwin, *President,* p. 216.

36. *Writings of Thomas Jefferson,* ed. P. L. Ford (1895), 6:451.

37. Quoted in Raoul Berger, "The President's Unilateral Termination of the Taiwan Treaty," *Northwestern University Law Review* 75 (1980): 591.

38. In *Youngstown Sheet and Tube Co. v. Sawyer,* Justice Robert Jackson dismissed Sutherland's theory as "dictum" (343 U.S. 579, 635–36 n. 2 [1952]). The Court has repudiated the theory several times; see, e.g., *Reid v. Covert,* 324 U.S. 1 (1957). For discussion of the sole-organ doctrine, see Adler, "Constitution and Presidential War-

making," pp. 29–35; Lofgren, *"Curtiss-Wright"*; Berger, *Executive Privilege,* pp. 100–108.

39. See, e.g., *Regan v. Wald,* 468 U.S. 243 (1984); *Haig v. Agee,* 453 U.S. 280 (1981); *Dames and Moore v. Regan,* 453 U.S. 654 (1981); *Goldwater v. Carter,* 444 U.S. 996 (1979); *Zemel v. Rusk,* 381 U.S. 1 (1965); *United States v. Pink,* 315 U.S. 552 (1942); *United States v. Belmont,* 301 U.S. 324 (1937).

40. The term, I think, was coined by H. Jefferson Powell, "Book Review," *Northwestern Law Review* 80 (1986): 1128, 1136.

41. Gerhard Casper, "Constitutional Constraints on the Conduct of Foreign and Defense Policy: A Nonjudicial Model," *Chicago Law Review* 43 (1976): 463, 475. With respect to the conduct of foreign policy and its relationship to the Constitution, Casper observed that the "relative scarcity of case law in the field has made it easier for judges to engage in unchecked flights of fancy, which in turn have facilitated the creation of a constitutional mythology. In that mythology, the role of Zeus is usually assigned to the President" (p. 477).

42. "The Office of Legal Adviser of the State Department reports 368 treaties and 5,590 other international agreements concluded by the United States between January 1, 1946, and April 1, 1972" (Louis Henkin, *Foreign Affairs and the Constitution* [Mineola, N.Y.: Foundation Press, 1972], p. 420 n.1). See also Raoul Berger, "The Presidential Monopoly of Foreign Relations," *University of Michigan Law Review* 71 (1972): 1, and Spitzer, Chapter 3 of this volume.

43. William Davie, a Framer from North Carolina, stated that "jealousy of executive power" would not permit a grant of treaty power to the president alone; see Elliot, *Debates,* 4:120.

44. Hamilton, *Federalist 75,* pp. 486–87.

45. For a fine discussion of the constitutionality of executive agreements, see Berger, *Executive Privilege,* pp. 140–63.

46. See Chapter 5 of this volume.

47. Hamilton, *Federalist 69,* p. 451.

48. Henkin, *Foreign Affairs,* p. 41.

49. Hamilton stated that "the history of human conduct does not warrant" the commitment of "interests of so delicate and momentous a kind . . . to the sole disposal" of the president (*Federalist 75,* p. 487).

50. Berger, *Executive Privilege,* p. 160.

51. *United States v. Pink,* at 249.

52. Arthur S. Miller, *"Dames & Moore v. Regan:* A Political Decision by a Political Court," *UCLA Law Review* 29 (1982): 1104, 1107.

53. *Dames and Moore v. Reagan,* at 673–77.

54. Ibid., at 677–78.

55. Ibid., at 678–79. It has been held that unchallenged historical practice is no longer sufficient evidence of constitutionality (*United States v. Woodley,* 726 F. 2d 1328 [9th Cir. 1983], rehearing granted, 732 F. 2d 111 [9th Cir. 1984]).

56. See, e.g., *United States v. Arrendondo,* 6 Pet. 691, 713–14 (1832); *United States v. Alexander,* 12 Wall. 127, 180 (1871); *United States v. Safety Car Heating and Lighting Co.,* 297 U.S. 88, 95 (1936).

57. *United States v. Midwest Oil Co.,* 236 U.S. 459, 474, 478 (1915).

58. *Ex parte United States,* 242 U.S. 27 (1916).

59. *Girouard v. United States,* 328 U.S. 61, 69 (1946). See also *Scripps Howard Radio v. F.C.C.,* 316 U.S. 4, 11 (1942).

60. Paul Gewirtz, "The Courts, Congress and Executive Policy-Making: Notes on Three Doctrines," *Law and Contemporary Problems* 40 (1976): 46, 79.

61. Erwin Chemerinsky, "Controlling Inherent Presidential Power: Providing a Framework for Judicial Review," *Southern California Law Review* 56 (1983): 863, 889.

62. Theodore Roosevelt, quoted in William Howard Taft, *Our Chief Magistrate and His Powers* (New York: Columbia University Press, 1925), p. 144.

63. F. D. Wormuth, "The Nixon Theory of the War Power: A Critique," *California Law Review* 60 (1972): 623, 678.

64. *Kent v. Dulles,* 357 U.S. 116 (1958).

65. *Haig v. Agee,* at 319.

66. *Zemel v. Rusk,* at 31–32.

67. *Kent v. Dulles,* at 117–19, 124–25, 128, 130.

68. *Zemel v. Rusk,* at 15–16.

69. Ibid., at 17–18, 27–40.

70. Ibid., at 15–16.

71. Ibid., at 20.

72. *Haig v. Agee,* 101 S. Ct. 2766 (1981).

73. Ibid., at 2778–79. For example, although the Court relied on *Zemel,* the *Zemel* Court had asserted a consistent history of imposing area-travel restrictions both before the passage of the Passport Act of 1926 and afterward. That practice, or at least the claim of a practice, and not the State Department's construction of its own regulation, permitted the Court to sustain the travel ban to Cuba.

74. Passport Act, 92 Stat. 963, 22 U.S.C. sec. 211a (Supp. 111. 1979).

75. *Haig v. Agee,* at 2782–83.

76. Edwin B. Firmage, "The War Powers and the Political Question Doctrine," *Colorado Law Review* 49 (1977): 65, 66; *Powell v. McCormack,* 395 U.S. 486, 518–22 (1969); *Baker v. Carr,* 369 U.S. 210 (1962).

77. *Cohens v. Virginia,* 19 U.S. 264, 403 (1821); Herbert Wechsler, "Toward Neutral Principles of Constitutional Law," *Harvard law Review* 73 (1959): 1, 7–8.

78. *Powell v. McCormack,* 395 U.S., at 521; *Baker v. Carr,* 369 U.S., at 210–11.

79. See, e.g., Alexander Bickel, *The Least Dangerous Branch* (New Haven: Yale University Press, 1962); Philippa Strum, *The Supreme Court and Political Questions: A Study in Judicial Evasion* (Tuscaloosa: University of Alabama Press, 1974).

80. *Goldwater v. Carter,* 100 S. Ct. 533 (1979). Mutual Defense Treaty, December 2, 1954, United States–Republic of China, U.S.T. 6:433. Article 10 of the treaty provided that it "shall remain in force indefinitely. Either Party may terminate it one year after notice has been given to the other Party" (437). For details of the case and the history and law regarding treaty termination, see Adler, *Constitution and Termination,* pp. 149–307.

81. *Goldwater v. Carter,* at 536.

82. Ibid., at 534, 539.

83. *Baker v. Carr,* at 210.

84. Wechsler, "Neutral Principles," p. 7.

85. See Adler, *Constitution and Termination,* pp. 84–237, for a discussion of these points.

86. Justice Brennan said as much in his dissenting opinion: "The issue of decision-making authority must be resolved as a matter of constitutional law, not political
discretion; accordingly, it falls within the competence of the courts" (*Goldwater v.
Carter*, at 539). Moreover, Justice Powell stated: "We are asked to decide whether the
president may terminate a treaty under the constitution without congressional approval. Resolution of the question may not be easy, but it requires us to apply normal
principles of interpretation to the constitutional provisions at issue" (at 535).

87. *Marbury v. Madison*, 1 Cranch 137, 177 (1803); *Massachusetts v. Laird*, 400
U.S. 886, 894 (1970).

88. *Luther v. Borden*, 7 How. 1 (1849).

89. *Goldwater v. Carter*, at 536, and *Baker v. Carr*, at 211. In *Webster v. Doe*, 108
S.Ct. 2047 (1988), however, Chief Justice Rehnquist indicated he believed that judicial power extends to some cases affecting foreign affairs. In writing for an 8–1 majority, he held that the judiciary is not precluded from hearing a constitutional challenge
to the dismissal of a CIA employee, despite the fact that the executive branch had
claimed that sensitive material—security information—would be compromised. The
ruling was important, for as one editor observed: "To allow the executive to usurp the
judiciary's role as arbiter of conflicts between legitimate security interests and individual rights—the inevitable consequence of the government's . . . argument in Webster—would be to remove all external guarantees that the rule of law governs the national security apparatus of the United States" (see Note, *The Supreme Court—Leading
Cases, Harvard Law Review* 102 [1988]: 143, 337 n. 52, quoted in Glennon, *Constitutional Diplomacy*, p. 313). But this encouraging development was dwarfed by a cold reminder that the Court will reflexively invoke *Curtiss-Wright* to justify presidential
actions in foreign affairs. In *Sale v. Haitian Centers Council, Inc.*, 113 S.Ct. 2549, 2567
(1993), Justice Stevens spoke for an 8–1 majority, with Justice Blackmun dissenting,
which upheld an executive order issued by President Bush that directed the Coast
Guard to intercept vessels illegally transporting passengers from Haiti to the United
States and to return them to Haiti without first determining whether they qualify as
refugees. Although the legal focus was on whether the executive order violated a congressional statute and the United Nations Convention relating to the status of refugees, the Court grounded its ruling in *Curtiss-Wright*. The Court deferred to presidential decision in foreign affairs on the basis of the claim that such a "presumption has
special force when we are construing treaty and statutory provisions that may involve
foreign and military affairs for which the President has unique responsibilities."

90. Berger, "Taiwan Treaty," p. 625.

91. Fritz Scharpf, "Judicial Review and the Political Question: A Functional
Analysis," *Yale Law Journal* 75 (1966): 585.

92. *Powell v. McCormack*, at 521, 536, and *Goldwater v. Carter*, at 535.

93. In *United States v. Pink*, the Court observed that an equally divided vote on
the controlling "principle of law involved prevents [the case] from being an authoritative determination for other cases" (at 203, 216). In fact, the Goldwater case was vacated by the Court. Nevertheless, it already has been invoked as authority in *Beacon
Products v. Reagan*, 633 F. Supp. 1191 (D. Mass. 1986).

94. See, generally, Leonard Ratner and David Cole, "The Force of Law: Judicial
Enforcement of the War Powers Resolution," *Loyola of Los Angeles Law Review* 17
(1984): 715, and Casper, "Constitutional Constraints," p. 471 n. 30.

95. See notes 15–22, and Adler, "Constitution and Presidential Warmaking," pp. 1–29.

96. "The manner of the exercise of the war powers determines not only the nation's freedom from external danger, but also the respect which the national government has for law and for constitutional limitations on the exercise of power" (Wormuth and Firmage, *Dog of War,* p. 66).

97. See, e.g., Ratner and Cole, "Force of Law."

98. *Crockett v. Reagan,* 558 F. Supp. 893 (D.D.C. 1982), aff'd per curiam, 720 F. 2d 1355 (D.C. Cir. 1983). Pub. 1, no. 93–148, 87 Stat. 55 (codified at 50 U.S.C., sec. 1541–1548 [1976]).

99. Ibid., at 898.

100. Ibid. In a similar case, eleven members of Congress filed suit against President Reagan for his invasion of Grenada in 1983, contending that he had violated the power of Congress to declare war. The Court refused to exercise its jurisdiction because of the relief available to members through the regular legislative process. The message was a sobering one: if Congress wants to confront the president, it must assert its own powers; judicial relief is not available (*Conyers v. Reagan,* 578 F. Supp. 324 [D.D.C. 1984], dismissed as moot, and *Conyers v. Reagan,* 765 F.2d 1124 [D.C.Cir. 1985]).

101. *Lowry v. Reagan,* 676 F. Supp. 333 (D.D.C.1987).

102. Ibid.

103. Ibid.; *Riegle v. Fomc,* 656 F. 2d 873, 879 (D.C.Cir. 1981), cert. denied, 454 U.S. 1882 (1981).

104. *Sanchez-Espinoza v. Reagan,* 770 F. 2d 202 (D.C.Cir. 1985).

105. Ibid., at 204, 210.

106. 676 F. Supp., 338.

107. Ibid.; *Goldwater v. Carter,* 444 U.S. 996 (1979) (Powell, J., concurring).

108. War Powers Resolution, 87 stat. 555, 50 U.S.C. Sec. 1541–48 (1982) ed. Section 4(a)(1) of the resolution, in fact, does not give the president any discretion; if events occur that constitute "hostilities or . . . situations where imminent involvement in hostilities is clearly indicated by the circumstances," a report must be submitted.

109. *Dellums v. Bush,* 752 F.Supp. 1141, (D.D.C. 1990).

110. Ibid., at 1145.

111. Ibid., at 1146. Here, Judge Greene echoed the thoughts of an eminent international law scholar, John Bassett Moore: "There can hardly be room for doubt that the Framers of the Constitution, when they vested in Congress the power to declare war, they never imagined that they were leaving it to the executive to use the military and naval forces all over the world for the purpose of actually coercing other nations, occupying their territory, and killing their soldiers and citizens, all according to his own notion of the fitness of things, as long as he refrained from calling his action war or persisted in calling it peace" (J. B. Moore, *The Collected Papers of John Bassett Moore,* 7 vols. [New Haven: Yale University Press, 1944], 5:195–96).

112. 752 F. Supp., at 1146.

113. *Goldwater v. Carter,* 444 U.S. 979, 998.

114. Constitutional powers cannot be expanded or constricted by governmental departments but only through the amendatory process. In his explanation of the doctrine of separation of powers, Madison said that since "power is of an encroaching na-

ture . . . it ought to be effectively restrained from passing the limits assigned to it" (*Federalist 48*, p. 321). Moreover, it is a necessary consequence of the separation of powers, Edward S. Corwin rightly stated, that "none of the departments may abdicate its powers to either of the others" (Corwin, *President*, p. 9). See also *Panama Refining Co. v. Ryan*, 293 U.S. 388, 421 (1935).

115. The story of corruption in American politics is at least a thrice-told tale and requires no review here. The word Watergate says it all. The Constitution speaks to various government officials of the need for virtue in the exercise of their duties. Article II, section 3 states that the president "shall take care that the laws be faithfully executed." Article I, section 2 provides that "the House of Representatives . . . shall have the sole Power of Impeachment." Article I, section 3 vests the Senate with "the sole power to try all impeachments." Article II, section 4 sets forth impeachable offenses.

116. Too many members of Congress, like too many other Americans, "tend to be concerned with ends rather than means," wrote Phillip Kurland. He added, "Those who suggest a look at institutional values as a method of protection against tyranny are scorned as being concerned with a 'literary theory' rather than facts" (Kurland, "The Impotence of Reticence," *Duke Law Journal* [1968]: 619, 635).

117. Professor Michael Glennon finds "unpersuasive" the claim that "Congress has enough arrows in its legislative quiver to respond successfully to executive illegality" (Glennon, *Constitutional Diplomacy*, p. 319). He rightly notes the "practical problems that frequently render Congress's textbook tools too unwieldy" (p. 319). Chief among them is the ability of an administration to "delay" a congressional investigation (see his discussion, pp. 295–99). Dean Jesse Choper has said of the various tactics that Congress may employ against the executive that they "may reasonably be viewed as both unseemly and unreasonable" (Choper, *Judicial Review and the National Political Process* [Chicago: University of Chicago Press, 1980], p. 286).

118. When Congress collided with Pres. Andrew Johnson during the impeachment process, Chief Justice Salmon Chase took the view that conflicting claims would have been better resolved by the judiciary. See Raoul Berger, *Impeachment: The Constitutional Problems* (Cambridge: Harvard University Press, 1973), p. 300.

119. Professor Martin Redish justly stated: "The moral cost of such a result, both to society in general and to the Supreme Court in particular, far outweighs whatever benefits are thought to derive from the judicial abdication of judicial review" (Redish, "Judicial Review and the 'Political Question,' " *Northwestern University Law Review* 79 [1984–85]: 1031, 1060 (1984–85). Professor Glennon has rightly asked: "Why is judicial *inaction* in the face of controversy necessarily more prudent than judicial *action?*" (Glennon, *Constitutional Diplomacy*, p. 318). Raoul Berger has powerfully stated the case for judicial resolution: "The centrality of the separation of powers to our democratic system and to the protection of individual rights dictates that such injuries to a coordinate branch *must* be halted by the judiciary" (Berger, *Executive Privilege*, p. 334). The eminent judge and legal scholar, George Wythe, who also served as Thomas Jefferson's mentor, wrote that the protection of one branch of the legislative "against the usurpation of the others" protects "the whole community" (*Commonwealth v. Caton*, 4 Call 5, 8 [Va. 1782], quoted in Berger, *Executive Privilege*, p. 334 n. 144).

120. In *Powell v. McCormack*, 395 U.S. 486, 547–548 (1969), the Court emphasized the "basic principles of our democratic system," the right of the people to

"choose whom they please to govern them." For an excellent discussion of the
Founders' conception of a Constitution as a governing document that flows from the
sovereignty of the people, see, generally, Bernard Bailyn, *The Ideological Origins of the
American Revolution*, 2d ed. (Cambridge: Harvard University Press, 1992), and Wood,
Creation of the American Republic.

121. A manifest correlative of separation of powers was that no department of government was granted authority to act in excess of its constitutional power. The courts
were authorized to check transgressions (see Raoul Berger, *Congress v. the Supreme Court*
[Cambridge: Harvard University Press, 1969], pp. 8–16, 188–97). As Chief Justice
John Marshall stated in *Marbury v. Madison*, "To what purpose are powers limited,
and to what purpose is that limitation committed to writing, if these limits may, at any
time, be passed by those intended to be restrained?" (5 U.S. 137, 176 [1803]).

122. *Pacific States Tel. & Tel. Co. v. Oregon*, 223 U.S. 118, 150 (1912).

123. U.S. Constitution, Article 1, section 9 states: "No money shall be drawn
from the treasury, but in consequence of appropriations made by law."

124. See the development of this theme in Arthur S. Miller, "Reason of State and
the Emergent Constitution of Control," *Minnesota Law Review* 64 (1980): 585.
Harold Koh has concluded that "the Court's decisons on the merits of foreign affairs
claims have encouraged a steady flow of policy-making power from Congress to the executive" (Koh, *The National Security Constitution: Sharing Power After the Iran-Contra
Affair* [New Haven: Yale University Press, 1990], p. 146). In this regard, the courts
have become the "president's accomplices" (p. 146).

125. The Court cited *Curtiss-Wright* in *Sale v. Haitian Centers Council, Inc.*, 113 S.
CT. 2549, 2567 (1993), for the proposition that the president has "unique responsibilities" with respect to foreign and military affairs.

126. Quoted in Schlesinger, *Imperial Presidency*, p. 103.

127. Louis Jaffe, *Judicial Aspects of Foreign Relations* (New York: McGraw-Hill,
1933), p. 223.

128. Berger, *Executive Privilege*, p. 117.

129. Robert Jackson, *The Struggle for Judicial Supremacy* (New York: Knopf, 1949),
p. 9. Madison wrote that neither of the two departments "can pretend to an exclusive
or superior right of setting the boundaries between their respective powers" (*Federalist*
49, p. 328).

130. *Marbury v. Madison*, 5 U.S. 176 (1803), and Elliot, *Debates*, 3:554.

2

DEMOCRATIC THEORY AND THE CONDUCT OF AMERICAN FOREIGN POLICY

LARRY N. GEORGE

Throughout this century, and particularly since World War II, presidents have usurped authority over foreign affairs in ways that directly violate both the letter and the intent of the Constitution.[1] Despite sporadic congressional initiatives in recent decades, only two powers of the federal government today remain more insulated from democratic accountability: the Supreme Court's authority to interpret the Constitution and the Federal Reserve System's control over the national money supply. Widespread endorsement of the arguments commonly marshaled in support of the current American system of centralized executive foreign policymaking (hereafter CEFP) has encouraged the presidential arrogation of power. The appeal of such claims is nourished by broadly held misgivings regarding the innate capacity of legislatures or democratic governments to conduct their own foreign affairs—a skepticism that recalls Tocqueville's well-known comment in *Democracy in America:* "For my part, I have no hesitation in saying that in the control of society's foreign affairs democratic governments do appear decidedly inferior to others."[2]

Among American elites, this apprehensiveness spans the ideological spectrum. Liberals fear the unleashing of jingoistic sentiments among the general population and the attendant dangers of imperialism, militarism, and Caesarism. Throughout the Cold War, internationalists on both the Left and the Right harbored concerns that residual isolationism, fueled by the chronic public ignorance of foreign affairs, would undermine support for a vigorous American role in world politics. Conservatives despaired over flagging popular resolve in the face of the Communist menace. Presidents from both parties exploited the centralized executive foreign policymaking system for their own political ends and capitalized on popular doubts about more democratic alternatives to erect sturdy legal and institutional bulwarks against reform.

Although challenges to CEFP have emerged from time to time, they generally have taken on an overtly partisan or ideological character, which casts them in a rather tendentious light. During the Truman and Carter presidencies, for example, objections to presidential unilateralism came largely from House and Senate Republicans. Opposition to the Johnson, Reagan, and Bush administrations' military actions abroad stemmed primarily from liberal Democrats. Overall, during the post-Vietnam era it was primarily Republicans and conservative Democrats who defended CEFP while liberal Democrats were more likely to call for increasing the accountability of executive officials and broadening the process of foreign policymaking. And although the domestic and international political shake-ups that followed the collapse of communism have not diluted the allure of the case against democratic foreign policymaking, partisan and ideological realignments around the issue have begun to appear. Partisan conflicts and interbranch confrontations have erupted in recent years over, for example, the Persian Gulf War, U.S. policy toward Russia and the former Yugolsavia, NAFTA, the Clinton administration's interventions in Somalia and Haiti, and U.S.–Japan trade relations. The 1994 congressional election, which resulted in a Democratic president confronting a Republican-controlled Congress for the first time since the early 1950s, has produced splits within both parties, with some Republicans expressing a newfound enthusiasm for strict congressional oversight and some Democrats awakening to the virtues of presidential unilateralism. As these processes unfold, theoretical polemics over the issue of centralized executive foreign policymaking will continue to influence political developments in significant ways.

In this chapter I present and criticize the most prominent arguments typically mustered in support of CEFP and argue for a "democratization" of American foreign policymaking. Democratization is generally understood, by both proponents and opponents of CEFP, to entail reforms designed to decrease the unilateral powers of the president and other executive branch officials in foreign policymaking while increasing the openness of the process and the accountability of executive officials to Congress, public opinion, and the electorate. This shift is to be accomplished through a variety of reforms, including framework statute revisions, greater openness of debate, broader access to information, classification reforms, judicial clarification of congressional and presidential foreign policy powers, and more regular mechanisms and procedures for reviewing controversial executive foreign policy decisions. Such reforms would also be intended in part to force Congress to shoulder greater responsibility in foreign affairs as well as to educate and more actively involve the general citizenry. As other writers in this book demonstrate, recent constitutional scholarship on the issue has shown that a more democratically structured foreign policymaking system would not only be more consistent with well-established democratic principles of government but would also conform far more closely with the intentions of the Constitution's authors. In this light, the burden of proof falls on defenders of CEFP to demonstrate precisely why U.S. foreign policy should continue to be made largely outside normal democratic procedures. Their arguments must go beyond the trivial point that foreign affairs concern relations with foreigners while domestic affairs involve compatriots. They must show that this distinction is of such moral, practical, or political significance that although open democratic procedures may be appropriate for coping with domestic political issues, only CEFP arrangements are adequate to the demands of international relations. First I shall review the strongest of these arguments for CEFP, then criticize each of the arguments, and finally conclude with some brief comments.

THE CASE FOR CENTRALIZED EXECUTIVE FOREIGN POLICYMAKING

Three categories of arguments underlie most theoretical claims for CEFP. Although other, derivative, claims are sometimes asserted, the following general arguments provide the major premises for such secondary claims.[3]

National Representation Arguments

Defenders of CEFP often assert that in conducting its affairs with other nations, the United States must behave as a unitary political entity with indivisible and identifiable national interests. These interests effectively *define* the goals and purposes of foreign policy and are presumed to transcend and override competing parochial, ideological, partisan, or other divisive interests or concerns. "Politics," in the stock catchphrase, "stops at the water's edge."[4] In a pluralistic democracy, it is argued, the foreign policy positions adopted by senators, representatives, and ordinary citizens will unfortunately tend to be muddled and corrupted by partisan, regional, ideological, or other biases, and neither legislators nor the general population can be relied upon to hold the national interest above these parochial concerns.[5] Since the president is the only public official elected by all the country's citizens, and thus is the only official accountable to the entire nation, he is the proper and legitimate representative of the nation as a whole and the only official who can be entrusted to defend the country's national interests in the international arena.[6] As one authority put it not long ago, "In the areas of defense and foreign affairs, the Nation must speak with one voice, and only the president is capable of providing that voice."[7]

Expertise Arguments

Advocates of CEFP also claim that the executive branch is uniquely capable of developing the expertise necessary to the successful conduct of foreign policy. Foreign affairs, it is argued, are inherently more complex and abstruse than domestic issues. Although the background experiences of legislators or ordinary citizens may provide a solid basis for rendering commonsense judgments and decisions about local or national affairs, the arcane diplomatic, military, economic, and political problems that characterize the international arena lie well outside the experience or capacity of most citizens or members of Congress.[8] Again, the classical statement is Tocqueville's:

> Experience, mores and education almost always do give a democracy that sort of practical everyday wisdom and understanding of the petty business of life which we call common sense. Common sense is enough for a society's current needs, and in a nation whose education has been completed, democratic liberty applied to a state's internal affairs brings blessings greater than the ills resulting from a democratic government's mistakes. But, that is not always true of relations between nation and nation.[9]

In foreign affairs, the general ignorance of most citizens, their physical and psychological distance from most international events, and their isolation from the immediate impact and effects of foreign policy decisions create further problems.

> Few of the voters know more than the most elementary facts regarding the conditions and the policy of foreign countries, and to appreciate the significance of these facts, there is needed some acquaintance with the history of the countries and the character of the leading men. . . . One of the strongest arguments for democratic government is that the masses of people, whatever else they may not know, do know where the shoe pinches, and are best entitled to specify the reforms they need. In foreign affairs this argument does not apply, for they lie out of the normal citizen's range.[10]

Arguments like these gained particular momentum after World War II, when the perennial challenges of U.S. foreign policy were compounded by the labyrinthine responsibilities of orchestrating a global hegemonic order. Walter Lippmann underscored the difficulties in 1954, highlighting the increased demands on knowledge posed by postwar international society:

> If the task of governing the United States at home and conducting its foreign relations abroad, were as complicated as, and no more dangerous than, it was fifty years ago—then we could celebrate. . . . But we cannot measure the demands upon our people in the second half of the twentieth century—the demands in terms of trained intelligence, moral discipline, knowledge, and not least, the wisdom of great affairs—by what was demanded of them at the beginning of the first half of this century.[11]

Advocates of CEFP assert that only the president can adequately develop such expertise. As head of state, the president regularly travels abroad and confers with foreign leaders. At his or her disposal are the expertise of the cabinet, the public and secret information-gathering and interpreting resources of the various intelligence and investigative agencies, and the expertise and policy evaluation capabilities of the entire executive bureaucracy. The president has the power to appoint and the prestige to obtain the counsel of those persons most experienced in and informed about specific foreign policy matters.[12]

Members of Congress, by contrast, may not be expected to develop any international experience or foreign policymaking expertise whatsoever. The duties of legislative office, it is argued, do not typically leave enough time or give sufficient incentives for members of Congress to specialize in foreign policy issues.[13] Additionally, because of the open and adversarial nature of legislative deliberation, members of Congress cannot guarantee the sort of confidentiality and discretion enjoyed by the president and other executive officers and thus cannot safely be entrusted with the sort of secret information that enables the president to comprehend foreign policy issues in their full complexity.[14]

Structural Efficiency Arguments

Proponents of CEFP believe that executive institutions provide a more efficient organizational structure for the conduct of foreign policy than can legislative institutions or conventional mechanisms of popular citizen participation (such as voting, initiatives, referenda, town meetings, re-call elections, or public assemblies). Executive institutions, they argue, are empowered to function outside intrusive scrutiny or other interference and are designed to be efficient, decisive, and quick to respond in time of crisis. Executive branch hierarchies of authority are clear, and responsibility for decisions is easily assigned. By contrast, legislative and popular democratic institutions are by nature deliberative, cumbersome, and slow to respond to crises and are chronically plagued by volatility and inconsistency. Their procedural openness encourages the leaking of secret information. Legislative politicking also tends to lead to the contamination of foreign policy positions by side agreements and trade-offs that are often irrelevant to and not infrequently incompatible with the national interest.[15]

Defenders of CEFP argue that foreign policymaking is fundamentally different from the other activities of government and can be carried out effectively only by the executive branch. They argue that foreign policy must be conducted vigorously, expeditiously, and often covertly (qualities Hamilton and Jay described as "decision, activity, secrecy and dispatch").[16] Secret, quick, and decisive response is especially imperative during armed attacks or other sudden threats to Americans or their interests. Appropriate military responsiveness would be impossible if decisions had to await the deliberations of 535 members of Congress or a referendum process to test public support for such actions. Where secret intelligence or covert operations are involved, the risk of leaks increases with the number of decisionmakers.

It is also argued that the negotiation of treaties and international agreements, and the management of diplomatic affairs in general, must be conducted outside public or congressional scrutiny.[17] The practical difficulties of incorporating the public or Congress into the sensitive processes of formulating positions, tendering offers, accepting compromises, and formalizing agreements would be overwhelming and in most cases counterproductive.[18] A country that adopted more open and public negotiation procedures would find that its adversaries would exploit its openness to win more advantageous terms for themselves[19]—a particularly acute problem for democracies negotiating with authoritarian governments.[20] Secrecy is also frequently necessary to protect informants who might otherwise fear retaliation or to shield cooperative foreign leaders whose anonymity must be guaranteed because of their own citizens' hostility toward the United States.[21]

Furthermore, argue defenders of CEFP, the anarchic and frequently violent international environment often forces governments to take actions necessary to advance some national interest but that are technically illegal under international or domestic law or morally unacceptable according to conventional ethical standards. Open deliberation in Congress or the media over the propriety of such actions would raise inappropriate moral or legalistic concerns that could hamper the effective pursuit of national interests.[22] Conversely, public or legislative involvement in the violent anarchy of international relations could, over time, corrupt the nation's democratic values and institutions themselves.[23] Only the federal executive possesses both the centralized command structure necessary to conduct such activities and the internal discipline required to ensure "plausible deniability" so as to preserve the reputation of the national government from the taint of illegality or immorality and to protect the nation from the potential embarrassment or loss of international prestige that might result from public revelations of such actions.[24]

Finally, proponents of CEFP argue that a superpower's foreign affairs must be conducted in a steadfast and consistent manner so that its allies can anticipate its actions as they formulate their own foreign policy agendas. Only the president and the executive bureaucracy possess the stability and institutional integrity required to guarantee policy continuity over time. Although the Senate is the body endorsed by the authors of the *Federalist Papers* and entrusted by the Constitution to ensure policy stability,[25] the wide ideological and political fluctuations on foreign policy questions within that body during recent decades raise questions about its ability to guarantee long-term policy consistency.[26]

For these reasons, it is argued, American foreign policy should be formulated and implemented primarily by the president and the executive branch, with minimum interference from Congress or the general public.

THE CASE AGAINST CENTRALIZED EXECUTIVE FOREIGN POLICYMAKING

Each of these general arguments for CEFP is flawed, and their shortcomings reveal profound deficiencies underlying other arguments for such centralization.

National Representation Arguments

Arguments based on the executive's singular capacity to represent the nation and to pursue its interests in the international arena suffer from a number of flaws. First, the necessary priority of national interests—assuming these can be specified in any meaningful way at all—over individual, ethnic, local, religious, class, generational, human, environmental, or other conceptions of interest and rights can no longer simply be taken for granted. Although ties of nationalism may still bind, consensus on the national interests at stake in particular questions of foreign policy is rarely in evidence today. "Intermestic" political issues such as international trade, human rights, immigration, foreign investment, and environmental protection cut across national borders. The politics of such issues creates intersecting axes of international mutuality while driving wedges among compatriots with opposing positions on them. The ongoing construction of new international identities, exemplified by the political maturation of the European Community, the explosive reemergence of ethnic nationalisms worldwide, the growing appeal of transnational religious movements, the increasing relevance of gender issues in international affairs, and the technological reconstitution of the postmodern nation-state itself are challenging the priority of traditional national conceptions of identity and interest.[27]

Even conventional liberal democratic theory and practice has systematically pushed the bounds of obligations and rights beyond those traditionally accorded only to compatriots.[28] Extranational political, moral, and legal obligations as well as nearly universally recognized standards of justice incumbent on states and individuals are enshrined today in numerous international treaties, conventions, and binding judicial decisions. Humanitarian economic and political obligations are widely recognized in Western political theory and modern international law and are regularly expanded to include ever-broader areas of international activity.[29] The rise of intergovernmental organizations (IGOs) and of nongovernmental international organizations has created new kinds of parallel loyalties, political obligations, and moral commitments that frequently conflict with, and in some cases may override, national political duties or interests.[30]

What is important here is that all these interests, including presumptive national interests, are constituted politically. Foreign policies that advance some of these interests or subordinate others cannot reasonably therefore be considered impartial administrative or executive decisions. National representation arguments for closed executive treaty negotiations, for example, presume that unitary national interests in the issues to be addressed by the treaty already exist. Yet treaties, executive agreements, and other international compacts inevitably involve the suppression or subordination of some interests in favor of others. Indeed, such agreements effectively *define* the "national interest" with respect to the issues they cover. They *constitute* these interests retrospectively, through a process that is quintessentially legislative and political. Alexander Hamilton's oft-quoted claim that the president in the course of conducting foreign policy should have the power to "control and bind the legislative power of Congress" because the executive is, within its own sphere, "no less the organ of [the nation's] will than the Legislature" assumes wrongly that the nation has a single will reflecting unitary national interests in matters of foreign policy.[31]

A related problem is presented by the differential costs and benefits accruing to different individuals and groups as a result of foreign policy choices presumably made in the "national interest." Open international markets, for example, have always benefited exporters and import consumers more than import-competing sectors, even if the long-term benefits of free trade to the national economy are assumed. A presidential decision to postpone arms-control negotiations on national security grounds will economically benefit defense contractors and their employees at the expense of taxpayers employed in nondefense sectors. American immigration policy impacts different regions in diverse ways. Changes in U.S. policy toward Cuba, Israel, Mexico, or Northern Ireland will be of much greater relevance to some ethnic groups than to others. A decision to go to war will impose disproportionate costs on young persons of draft age and their families. Almost every foreign policy choice will benefit one of the dominant political parties and disadvantage the other. Indeed, it is difficult to imagine any foreign or domestic policy decision that would not entail such differential benefits and costs. And it is precisely to address such political problems that the complex mechanisms of bargaining, trade-offs, constituency mobilization, side compensation, and public deliberation that characterize both legislative policymaking and popular democratic politics have evolved in the first place. Arguments for isolating such decisions from the give-and-take of congressional politicking and executive-legislative compromise or from the petitions of those most likely to be helped or harmed by a particular policy cut directly against fundamental democratic principles of governmental legitimacy, accountability, and representation.

Clearly, politics no longer "stops at the water's edge." Viewed from the perspective of democratic theory, the bargaining environment of a legislative body like Congress provides a highly appropriate foreign policymaking forum. Because executive institutions are less conducive to the brokering of compensatory arrangements and compromises, they are as a consequence often forced to pursue suboptimal policies and are frequently tempted to adopt recklessly antidemocratic measures to disguise their actual foreign policy agendas—as occurred repeatedly during the early Cold War, the Vietnam conflict, the Iran-Contra events, and in Reagan-era Central America policy more generally.[32] The kaleidoscope of U.S. citizens' foreign policy concerns undermines those arguments for CEFP that derive from the purported representation by the president of consensual, unitary national interests in foreign policy.

Nor is it correct to assume, as did the Reagan administration, that national elections confer on the president any special popular mandate in foreign policymaking. As poll data indicate, even though some foreign policy concerns are at times highly salient for Americans and even though ordinary citizens actually have a stronger grasp of important foreign affairs issues than has traditionally been assumed, voters almost never elect presidents primarily on the basis of candidates' stances on particular foreign policy questions. Indeed, the popularity of individual presidents is often inversely related to public support for their foreign policies.[33]

In general, the history of twentieth-century American foreign policy controversies mocks the claim that such questions of "high politics" somehow transcend the robust partisanship and prevailing ideological discord of American political life. No more plausible is the notion that executive branch foreign policy decisionmaking is immune from parochial, partisan, or intergovernmental political considerations.[34] In the late twentieth century, U.S. foreign policymaking has become highly politicized, and postwar presidents bear the bulk of the responsibility for this development. As I. M. Destler, Leslie Gelb, and Anthony Lake, three respected students of American foreign policymaking, have noted:

> Before the breakdown [of the Cold War consensus], Presidents derived much of their power and authority over national security matters from the belief that they stood above politics, that they would sacrifice short-term political gains for long-term goals, and that they somehow embodied the enduring national interest. Too many times since 1964 have they used foreign policy to enhance their personal positions, thus personalizing, politicizing, and sometimes even trivializing the content and conduct of foreign affairs.
>
> In so doing they became almost like any other politician, and their words, facts, motives and actions became ever more subject to scrutiny and doubt. They thus squandered their own authority to construct steady majorities. By coming down into the political pits, they legitimized opposition on political grounds.[35]

As Destler, Gelb, and Lake remind us, Kennedy's endorsement of the Bay of Pigs invasion, Johnson's conduct of the Vietnam War, Nixon's overselling of détente and hurried negotiation of SALT I, Ford's stalling on SALT II, Carter's exploitation of human rights, nuclear nonproliferation, and the hostage crisis, and Reagan's trade-sanctions policies, policies toward the USSR and Lebanon, and exaggeration of America's military inferiority were motivated by political ambition or ideological myopia rather than by neutral assessments of national interests.

> Their . . . words and deeds made no sense on foreign policy grounds. Nor were they the acts of stupid people, acting carelessly and without information or without the benefit of other points of view. From all evidence they were calculated, driven by politics and ideology.[36]

This politicization of foreign policymaking by recent presidents has revived time-tested fears of executive abuse of the foreign affairs powers. Precisely because of his focal position at the intersection of domestic and international issues, the president is the public official most inclined to abuse the foreign policymaking power for domestic political purposes. Democratic theorists have long cautioned that executives will tend to create external enemies and exaggerate foreign threats in order to increase national unanimity, whether for purposes of tightening domestic political control, obstructing reform efforts, or simply to increase their own political capital. The evidence of postwar U.S. foreign policy can only confirm such fears. In addition, presidents, like other elected officials, are buffeted by political winds arising from foreign policy issues that provoke partisan or ideological controversies. Presidents thus are often forced to make politically difficult foreign policy decisions but must do so without Congress' capacity to arrange compensatory political bargains for those people disproportionately harmed by the decisions or to use open deliberation to evaluate competing policy recommendations and achieve compromise consensus. Although critical of recent congressional foreign policymaking initiatives, Destler, Gelb, and Lake conclude that

> democratic debate is more likely than doctrine to produce sensible foreign policy decisions. There neither can nor should be a return to the days of doctrinaire consensus. The question, rather, is how responsibly we use the foreign policy institutions that have become more open, more democratic. Will they be used to fashion mature policies of consistency and coherence, or will they be exploited for mere short-term political advantage?[37]

Expertise Arguments

Arguments for centralized executive foreign policymaking that rest on the presumed expertise of presidents and executive officials also entail serious factual distortions and logical inconsistencies. First, such arguments beg the question of political expertise itself and are predicated on the presumption that domestic political affairs are so fundamentally different from international relations that the openness, accountability, and pluralism democracies take for granted in domestic politics are wholly inappropriate to foreign policymaking. This assertion, however, seems far less compelling today than it once was. Although it may be true that most ordinary citizens and their representatives lack detailed knowledge about many important areas of foreign affairs, ignorance of factual details alone cannot vacate the right to influence policy. Juries and voters, after all, are not required to pass examinations before carrying out their civic responsibilities—since it is their commonsense judgment and collective wisdom, rather than any specialized knowledge, that justifies entrusting public decisions to them. Many contemporary political observers have come to doubt whether in the late twentieth century, the sorts of background understandings and values (as opposed to technical information) necessary to evaluate general policy alternatives in the international arena are in fact essentially different from those appropriate to domestic policymaking.

In comparison with the typically more immediate and pressing issues of local, state, and national politics, many foreign policy questions are, to be sure, intrinsically complex, demanding, and remote. But in the contemporary United States, the carving out of a distinct category of issues based on the degree of popular or congressional attention and knowledge is more misleading than illuminating, particularly as the end of the Cold War has brought about a widespread acknowledgment among political elites of the need both to educate and engage the public in the formulation of the nation's foreign relations.[38] Political decisions are simply not divisible by issue area into such distinct categories. At various times, certain foreign policy questions (e.g., tariff policy in the late nineteenth century, Vietnam in the 1960s) have exhibited much higher salience among both elites and ordinary citizens than have most contemporary domestic issues. Yet on most domestic as well as on foreign policy questions, the preferences and inclinations of voters, legislators, and, for that matter, executive officials may or may not rest on full prior possession of the relevant facts but on considered judgment, informed deliberation, and political calculation.

Expertise alone cannot delimit the democratic process. As Robert Dahl has shown with respect to decisions about nuclear weapons, for example, relevant technical knowledge is rarely if ever adequate for policymaking because the ends to which that knowledge is put cannot be determined technocratically.[39] This is true for foreign as well as for domestic affairs. A democracy cannot consistently demand levels of expertise that are prohibitive to citizen participation or congressional codetermination in one issue area but not in others. If technical expertise were a reasonable prerequisite for the right to exercise political rights, democratic government would stand on rather shaky footing across the entire breadth and range of political issues, internal as well as external, that face any modern nation. Indeed, proposals that Congress or the general population should be required to demonstrate some minimum level of expertise before participating in some area of legislation or policymaking tread dangerously close to more general arguments against democracy per se. It is hardly surprising that writers hostile to the democratization of foreign policymaking also tend to harbor deeper suspicions regarding legislative supremacy and popular democracy itself.

Moreover, the foreign policymaking expertise commonly attributed to presidents often has little to do with their personal background or experience and more with their administrative authority over bureaucratic organizations and executive departments. These agencies were originally placed under executive authority for practical reasons stemming from early experiences with committee foreign policymaking by the Continental Congress during the Articles of Confederation period.[40] Today, however, there seems little reason why Congress, or at least key members of foreign policy committees, once given similar staffing, access to vital information, and so forth, could not develop levels of expertise comparable or superior to those of presidents—as many have obviously done since the congressional "reassertionism" of the mid-1970s.[41]

The secrecy and diplomatic confidentiality integral to traditional international relations raise other, more difficult questions for proponents of a more democratized foreign policymaking system. The trade-off between accountability and executive secrecy is particularly acute within the American constitutional order, where the combination of a strong, independent executive and a weak party system precludes the sorts of parliamentary review and party accountability typical of most other modern democratic governments. In the United States today, presidents are essentially permitted to conduct foreign affairs as they see fit, openly or secretly, with occasional input from Congress. Their actions can only be partially and incompletely evaluated by voters, and final judgment is ultimately left up to future historians since most such decisions can be fully comprehended only after relevant documents have been declassified, which normally takes a generation. And because various executive agencies have now successfully established their own sources of funding—open and public as well as private and secret—even Congress' hallowed power of the purse has been disabled.

Yet it seems unwise to expect that the president of a nation that finds itself increasingly divided and often sharply polarized over foreign policy issues can automatically rely on the post hoc approval of the people or Congress to legiti-

mate his policies and that he should therefore be constrained only by anticipa-
tions of retrospective authorization in deciding whether to launch covert operations or other secret actions. Such a procedural framework might be
suitable in a more consensual polity or in countries where continuous threats
to national survival might require extraordinary executive powers to be institutionalized. But in a highly pluralistic United States, virtually any foreign policy
action sufficiently consequential to require being carried out in secret is quite
likely to have important implications for certain constituencies or fractions of
the public. Those groups and their representatives have the right to expect
that their desires and objections will be taken seriously in the policymaking
process, a right that quadrennial elections and other essentially plebiscitary
forms of ex post facto authorization cannot adequately guarantee.

Undeniably, governments must from time to time make decisions in secret
and limit access to certain types of information in order to prevent leaks that
could jeopardize operations, endanger agents or informants, or undermine
negotiations. But this is true in the domestic as well as in the international
arena. Equally evident are the hazards that such secrecy poses to democratic
institutions and processes. Democratically accountable governments should
be given the authority to conduct covert operations or to classify information
relevant to issues of public concern only under extraordinary circumstances.
The inevitable abuse of such secrecy to hide the incompetence, errors of judgment, and even criminal acts of public officials is simply too well documented
to believe otherwise.[42] Yet how is a democracy to grant those individuals entrusted with making its foreign policy the authority to determine which of
their own decisions should be made public and which classified? How can democracies permit secrecy where necessary while precluding actions designed to
evade legal restrictions or political accountability, such as those disclosed during the Watergate, Church Committee, or Iran-Contra hearings? On the other
hand, how can multiple access to vital secret information be broadened without increasing the danger of potentially calamitous leaks? Although these
questions remain extremely vexing (and are perhaps more difficult to resolve
under our constitutional framework than others), it seems clear that the balance between secrecy and accountability in the United States today has swung
dangerously far from sound principles of representative democratic government.[43]

The deeper threat of executive secrecy concerns the potential for political
exploitation of secret information by the president and other executive officials. The classification process can and has been used to deceive the public
and Congress, evade accountability, impede the exposure of government mis-
deeds, intimidate whistleblowers and investigative journalists, and generally to

manipulate the political process for ideological and partisan ends. The deception has been accomplished both by blocking the release of incriminating evidence and information detrimental to policies advocated by the president and by selectively leaking otherwise secret information favoring the president's position. Though it is the fear of congressional leaking of classified information for political purposes that lends plausibility to executive branch demands for secrecy restrictions, it has in fact been executive officials themselves who historically have committed the bulk of such politically motivated leaks.[44] One Orwellian consequence of institutionalized executive branch control over the power to leak secret information has been the growing evidence of fabricated or deceptive international "events" staged by executive branch functionaries and intended to manipulate public opinion in favor of controversial foreign policies. Recent examples here include (1) the unsuccessful plan to have Nicaraguan Contras assassinate the American ambassador to Costa Rica, Oliver Tambs, and blame it on the Sandinistas;[45] (2) the fictional "shipment" (revealed during the 1988 Noriega hearings) of Soviet-bloc armaments intended for illegal trans-shipment through Nicaragua to regional revolutionary groups, to be "intercepted" and "exposed" by Panamanian officials acting in collaboration with U.S. intelligence;[46] (3) several 1980s sting operations designed to implicate falsely the Sandinista government in drug trafficking; (4) various deceptive collaborations with the government of Iran, with Manuel Noriega, and even with Saddam Hussein—during the years before they became designated public enemies of the United States; and, of course, (5) the events of Iran-Contra.

Ostensibly such schemes were part of "disinformation" campaigns targeted primarily against foreign decisionmakers. But each of these fictional events was also contrived in such a way as to exploit the antidemocratic characteristics of centralized executive foreign policymaking in order to sabotage legitimate domestic political opposition to questionable administration policies. The real purpose of these bogus foreign "events" was to deceive the American press and public. Many of the actions were intentionally conducted so as to circumvent procedural restrictions and laws that had been explicitly established to prevent the U.S. intelligence agency's propaganda efforts from influencing political developments within the United States.[47] Such domestic fallout or "blowback" from the circulation within the United States of false information generated by disinformation campaigns directed against foreign governments can also undermine ongoing foreign policy efforts, threaten long-term international interests, and render public accountability impossible.

Such were the results, for example, of the spurious 1981 Reagan administration's accusations of Soviet sponsorship of most international terrorism,[48] the "rigging" by Reagan administration officials—apparently with the approval of then-Secretary of Defense Casper Weinberger—of a crucial SDI (Star Wars) test, and the falsification of other data "in a program of deception that misled Congress as well as the intended target, the Soviet Union."[49] Amicable relations with allies can be easily jeopardized by the covert manipulation of political events in their countries.[50] Executive classification restrictions—such as those covering presidential directives and agreements—can be used to conceal contingency policies and plans that, if disclosed, would force public discussion of important issues that an administration may prefer to suppress for partisan or ideological reasons. Revelations during the Iran-Contra hearings of contingency plans for annulling the Constitution during time of nuclear war or the Reagan administration's 298 National Security Decision Directives (NSDDs)—intended in part to circumvent public debate over controversial foreign policy questions—suggest disturbing patterns.[51]

Clearly some executive actions, especially those involving military operations, should normally be carried on without full and immediate public knowledge of their details. And some details of executive branch deliberations and decisions during unfolding crises may need to be kept secret from the public, at least for a time. The need to guarantee the anonymity and confidentiality of sources, to protect the safety of U.S. operatives, or to ensure the success of ongoing operations are plausible grounds for some degree of executive branch secrecy. None of these, however, provides a convincing argument against interbranch codetermination of both the overall trajectory of the nation's foreign policy and the management of crisis situations through the incorporation of representatives of the opposition party and Congress directly into the decisionmaking process. Indeed the very notion of a national interest requires codetermination, to prevent presidents from simply pursuing their own partisan political agendas while cloaking them in the rhetoric of national interests.

Such fears are not difficult to confirm. The sorts of foreign affairs issues in dispute during recent interbranch confrontations over secrecy have had, after all, little to do with protecting confidential sources or implementing policies derived from bipartisan conceptions of the national interest. Rather, they have involved profound interbranch, interparty, or ideological disagreements over the basic goals and direction of the nation's foreign policy. It has been the very refusal of recent presidents and other executive branch officials to stand by their administrations' publicly stated policy goals and to consult with Congress over the means to implement them that has created much of the chaos and counterproductiveness of recent American foreign policy. Indeed, many if not most of the conspicuous debacles of the last few decades are the direct result of executive branch secrecy, autonomy from congressional codetermination, and unaccountability. Recent disclosures about the conduct of the Vietnam War, for example, recall the numerous revelations uncovered during the Watergate and Church Committee hearings regarding systematic executive branch violations of both stated government policy and broadly endorsed conceptions of the national interest. By offering to trade arms for hostages as part of the Iran-Contra deals, Reagan administration officials effectively redefined the American negotiating position in a way that both contravened declared U.S. policy and made a mockery of aggressive administration pressures on our allies not to do the same thing. The illegal unilateral mining of Nicaraguan harbors led to a humiliating judgment against the United States by the International Court of Justice and severely undermined the credibility of the international legal system. The secret arming of the Contras effectively redefined a unilateral executive branch foreign policy that directly violated U.S. law and countermanded the official U.S. policy expressed in the Boland amendments and in ongoing diplomatic negotiations. Executive branch toleration and public denial of drug trafficking by the Corsican Mafia, Chinese KMT, Golden Triangle anticommunists, Lebanese Falangists, and Nicaraguan Contras, as well as by Manuel Noriega and other foreign "assets," obviously conflicted directly with U.S. and international law and with declared U.S. drug interdiction policies. Arms sales to Saddam Hussein during the 1980s helped set the stage for the Persian Gulf War. Terrorists recently convicted for the World Trade Center bombing were members of Afghan Mujahadeen groups funded by the CIA in the 1980s. Covert support for countless foreign dictators during the Cold War era created widespread distrust of and hostility toward the United States and significantly realigned American international commitments for the indefinite future, in many cases with grievous long-term implications for relations between Americans and their neighbors.

For decades, these and countless other secret executive branch activities effectively constituted a hidden American foreign policy, conducted almost entirely outside popular or congressional input and with often disastrous conseqences both domestically and internationally. Secrecy and expertise arguments gave presidents a cloak that enabled them to evade accountability for these policies and in so doing weakened American democratic institutions. Indeed, reflecting on the country's experience with CEFP during the post–World War II decades, the case for special executive branch expertise in foreign policy seems rather difficult to sustain. Ultimately, the whole question of executive versus congressional or popular expertise may well be simply a diversion from the more important questions of constitutionality and democratic accountability. The history of executive foreign policymaking in the United States is replete with fateful and often disastrous exhibitions of ignorance and mistakes in judgment by executive officials. The record suggests that the international arena is no more a technical domain accessible to expert management by administrative specialists than is the domestic political world. Nor is it readily comprehensible in ideological terms, as the myriad failures of Reagan administration policies demonstrated.[52]

Delegating foreign policymaking to purported experts in the executive branch has created a vicious circle of presidential hubris, congressional withdrawal, and increasing popular inattention to and ignorance about critical international problems. Conversely, involving Congress and the public more directly in foreign affairs would lead inevitably to an increasing awareness and understanding of foreign relations by both elected leaders and ordinary citizens. It would also contribute to a more robust democratic political culture and impel Americans to come to grips with an international system that influences more and more aspects of their lives each year. The simple point here is that in a representative democracy, expertise cannot be required as a precondition for the power to decide matters of policy, whether in domestic or foreign affairs.[53] Experts can be consulted and their advice solicited by elected leaders, but it is the rare policy choice, in either foreign or in domestic affairs, that is decided by resolving a factual dispute. Most issues of foreign policy are at their core *political* questions, and democracies do not wisely entrust these to centralized executive decisionmakers on grounds of technical expertise or the need for secrecy.

Structural Efficiency Arguments

The merits of structural and organizational efficiency arguments for centralized executive foreign policymaking are also generally exaggerated. Such arguments endorse one aspect of the *Federalist Papers*' case for separated powers—the practical efficiency of a separate administrative or executive branch—while ignoring or misconstruing Publius' other basic reason for separation: the need for a legislative check against the dangers of presidential concentration of power. Few people would deny that in an international crisis the "energy and dispatch" associated with executive power is desirable. But thus to infer that an elaborate, permanent system of unaccountable executive foreign policymaking is necessary makes no more sense than to suggest that the emergency powers granted to state or local executive officials during internal crises, such as riots or natural disasters, should provide a model for the conduct of ordinary domestic political affairs. Such arguments court the danger of Caesarism, which since ancient times has been the most common cause of the political degeneration of republics into tyranny.

Structural or practical arguments for centralized executive diplomacy and treaty negotiation and for the practical virtues of executive agreements run up against similar difficulties. Advocates of CEFP often argue that the Constitution's broad delegation of executive powers to the president was intended to include what Locke called "federative" or foreign policymaking powers.[54] In a mixed government, however, the theoretical difficulty with such arguments is straightforward: in those matters where diplomatic activity leads to treaties or other binding agreements or commitments, diplomacy functions by definition as a *legislative* power. This is, after all, the reason that the Senate is granted advice and consent power over treaties.

There are also sound pragmatic and political reasons for broadening the number of players in U.S. diplomatic negotiations beyond the executive branch. On practical grounds, earlier and more extensive congressional involvement could avoid the problem of lengthy and often arduous treaty negotiations being subsequently nullified by unanticipated Senate opposition to a final draft—as occurred with SALT II. Interbranch coordination can also prevent presidents from forcing a Hobson's choice on the Senate by presenting it with an all-or-nothing ultimatum, as occurred in the recent dispute over NAFTA, and as is quite likely to recur as more and more negotiating authority is delegated to the executive branch under similar fast-track rules. Concerns about the pernicious consequences of congressional "interference" in executive bargaining are highly exaggerated, as are fears of foreign manipulation of U.S. public opinion. After all, inasmuch as popular or congressional opposition to some aspect of a pending agreement is in evidence, the myth of national unity in foreign policy that underlies arguments for executive diplomacy in the first place is patently illusory. The ability of foreign leaders to appeal to domestic opponents of a particular negotiating position merely reflects the fact that the myriad ways in which Americans are active in the various realms of international affairs have given rise to innumerable conflicting and competing foreign policy interests and factions. Americans differ sharply over foreign policy issues along lines of cleavage that reflect party, ideology, region, ethnicity, occupation, business interests, religion, and a host of other factors. Moreover, in an internationally politicized world, the interests and positions of many domestic constituencies and interest groups are often more accurately represented by international organizations, nongovernmental organizations, or sometimes even foreign leaders than by their own president. The current trend toward executive agreements, fast-track negotiations, and executive branch monopoly over diplomatic activity works against the legitimate claims of such groups to representation in a pluralist democratic process. Conversely, more open deliberation and negotiation would help ensure that concluded agreements will genuinely reflect Americans' actual preferences.

Other pragmatic arguments for executive agreements and centralized executive diplomacy are no less dubious. The concern that foreign governments or leaders will often cooperate with the United States only if their cooperation can be concealed from their own citizens, for example, can be restated to imply that Americans' rights to democratic accountability should be subordinated to foreign leaders' political necessity to deceive their own people. Indeed the recent history of such practices points strongly to their impracticality and counterproductiveness over the long term. Anxieties over the difficulties created for foreign governments by the anticipated unpredictability and vacillation that purportedly accompany more open, democratic foreign policymaking grow out of several empirical and theoretical errors. First, the long-term foreign policy trajectories of democratic governments do not appear demonstrably more unstable or unpredictable, or more dangerous or counterproductive in general, than those of autocratic political systems, as opponents of democratization would expect.[55] Second, as already noted, because of the increasing politicization of foreign policy by recent presidents, the current American system of CEFP is far from predictable or invariable across or even within administrations. Finally, to the extent that U.S. foreign policymaking is democratized, policy positions can and should be expected to shift periodically as changes in the foreign or domestic political environment alter the composition of Americans' various international interests and concerns.

The realpolitik argument that popular sentiment may hinder the government from carrying out necessary but technically illegal or immoral actions is also questionable. Most obviously, the poor success rate of such practices, even strictly in terms of American interests, raises serious pragmatic doubts about them. The record is particularly damaging when the paucity of demonstrable triumphs is placed alongside the by now well-documented succession of often counterproductive and not infrequently disastrous covert operations, bribes, private arrangements, solicitations, coups, assassinations, assassination attempts, destabilizations, interventions, secret arms sales, subsidies to terrorists and drug traffickers, experiments on American citizens with drugs and nuclear materials, and any number of other questionable secret activities that have been conducted by executive branch officials and operatives in the name of national security since the last world war.[56] The damage done by such activities to Americans and their interests and the astronomical costs of executive branch conduct of foreign policy during the Cold War call into question even what it means to have "won" the Cold War through such means.[57] Moreover, many of the purported successes achieved through such legally or morally dubious operations might well have been accomplished through other, more legitimate means, although perhaps with different kinds of costs. In any case, the presumption that Americans are likely to be dangerously constrained by some endemic aversion to either violence or extralegal activities seems rather farfetched. Overall, little is gained politically, morally, or in terms of enduring national interests by denying the public and its elected representatives the responsibility to evaluate and approve such activities with full knowledge of their probable practical, legal, and moral consequences.

CONCLUSION

Examined individually, each of the traditional arguments for CEFP appears unconvincing. Yet such arguments underpin the current American system of unilateral presidential foreign policymaking. In a representative democracy, the burden of proof lies with those individuals who would except certain powers of government from direct public accountability and remove them from the authority of the elected representatives of the people affected by the exercise of those powers. Several such powers have in fact been largely isolated from normal political processes because sound arguments have persuaded the architects of the U.S. government that in some areas of governmental activity such exceptions are desirable. But the arguments for including foreign policymaking in this category are easily refuted, as I have sought to demonstrate.

Other contributors to this volume reveal how various aspects of the present system of CEFP are inconsistent with current interpretations of the Constitution or are unwarranted in light of relevant historical precedents. Taken as a whole, these discussions suggest that in a well-functioning democracy, the proper approach is not to isolate the foreign policymaking process within closed executive offices but to extend and broaden the decisionmaking process while simultaneously educating, informing, and organizing those ordinary Americans who may have stakes in international developments so that they may be better able to protect and advance those interests through their own democratic system.

NOTES

1. Louis Fisher, *Presidential War Power* (Lawrence: University Press of Kansas, 1995).

2. Alexis de Tocqueville, *Democracy in America* (New York: Anchor, 1959), p. 226.

3. The core arguments for CEFP are almost universally endorsed by proponents of presidential unilateralism. But because several of these claims are also accepted by even some opponents of CEFP—including some of the contributors to this volume—the standard caveat about the assertions in this chapter reflecting the opinions of its author alone should be underscored here. For solidly argued contemporary defenses of CEFP, see Robert Scigliano, "The War Powers Resolution and the War Powers," in Joseph M. Bassette and Jeffrey Tulis, eds., *The Presidency and the Constitutional Order* (Baton Rouge: Louisiana State University Press, 1981); John G. Tower, "Congress vs. the President: The Formulation and Implementation of American Foreign Policy," *Foreign Affairs* 60 (Winter 1981–82): 229–46; and the minority position report accompanying the report of the joint committees investigating the Iran-Contra events, published in Joel Brinkley and Stephen Engleberg, eds., *Report of the Congressional Committees Investigating the Iran-Contra Affair* (New York: Random House, 1988), pp. 397–406. More recent statements of such arguments can be found in the series of letters and critical essays issued by Bush administration attorneys Lawrence Block, Lee A. Casey, and David P. Rivkin, Jr.: Rivkin and Block, "The Constitution in Danger: An Exchange," *New York Review of Books,* May 17 and August 16, 1990; Rivkin and Casey, correspondence, *Foreign Affairs* (Summer 1991): 150–53; and Rivkin and Casey, " 'Presidential Wars': An Exchange," *New York Review of Books,* November 21, 1991, pp. 56–57.

4. In Dean Acheson's rather more unguarded version: "You can't run this damned country any other way . . . [than] to say politics stops at the seaboard—and anyone who denies that postulate is a son-of-a-bitch and a crook and not a true patriot. Now if people will swallow that then you're off to the races" (quoted in George Scialabba, "Citizen Karp," *Nation* 257, no. 6 [August 23/30, 1993]: 218).

5. J. Roland Pennock, *Democratic Political Theory* (Princeton, N.J.: Princeton University Press, 1979), pp. 404–5.

6. Tower, "Congress vs. the President," p. 232.

7. Ronald W. Reagan, "The Presidency: Roles and Responsibilities" *National Forum* 64 (Fall 1984): 24.

8. Louis J. Halle, "The American Experience" in *Foreign Policy and the Democratic Process,* ed. Halle and Kenneth W. Thompson (Washington, D.C.: University Press of America, 1978), p. 2.

9. Tocqueville, *Democracy in America,* p. 228.

10. James Bryce, *Modern Democracies* (New York: Macmillian, 1921), pp. 369–70.

11. Walter Lippmann, "The Shortage of Education," *Atlantic Monthly,* May 1954, p. 26.

12. Compare here *The Federalist Papers,* ed. Clinton Rossiter (New York: New American Library, 1961), *Federalist 3,* p. 43, with Tower, "Congress vs. the President," p. 232.

13. David R. Mayhew, *Congress: The Electoral Connection* (New Haven: Yale University Press, 1974), pp. 121–24.

14. Compare, for example, Jay's *Federalist 64,* pp. 390–96, Tower, "Congress vs. the President," pp. 241–42, and Bob Woodward, *Veil: The Secret Wars of the CIA* (New York: Pocket Books, 1988), pp. 168–69.

15. *Federalist 64,* pp. 390–96; and *75,* especially pp. 451–52; Tower, "Congress vs. the President," p. 233.

16. *Federalist 64,* p. 392, and *70,* p. 424.

17. *Federalist 64,* pp. 390–96; and *75,* p. 452.

18. Walter Lippmann, "When Diplomacy Is Too Open," *Today and Tomorrow,* December 22, 1932, p. 18.

19. Hans J. Morgenthau, *Politics Among Nations,* 6th ed. (New York: Knopf, 1985), p. 577.

20. Abba Eban, *The New Diplomacy* (New York: Random House, 1983), p. 355.

21. Compare Tower, "Congress vs. the President," p. 242, with *Federalist 64,* pp. 392–93.

22. George Kennan, *American Diplomacy: 1900–1950* (Chicago: University of Chicago Press, 1951), pp. 65–66, 84, 89–90, 93–96.

23. Compare *Federalist 22,* pp. 148–50; Marshall D. Shulman, "Problems in the Relationship Between Democratic Societies and Authoritarian Regimes," in Halle and Thompson, eds., *Foreign Policy and the Democratic Process,* pp. 222–30; Morton Halperin et al., *The Lawless State* (New York: Penguin, 1976), pp. 222–30; and George Kennan, "Morality and Foreign Policy," *Foreign Affairs* 64 (1985): 214.

24. See, for example, U.S. Congress, Church Committee, *Alleged Assassination Plots Involving Foreign Leaders* (New York: W. W. Norton, 1976), pp. 9–11.

25. *Federalist 63,* pp. 380–84.

26. On this idea, see Thomas E. Cronin, "President, Congress, and American Foreign Policy," in Charles Kegley and Eugene Wittkopf, eds., *Domestic Sources of American Foreign Policy,* 2d ed. (New York: St. Martin's Press, 1994), pp. 161–62; Michael Glennon, *Constitutional Diplomacy* (Princeton, N.J.: Princeton University Press, 1990); Louis Henkin, *Constitutionalism, Democracy, and Foreign Affairs* (New York: Columbia University Press, 1990).

27. A variety of statements along these lines can be found in Richard K. Ashley, "Living on Border Lines: Man, Poststructuralism, and War," and William E. Connolly, "Identity and Difference in Global Politics," both in James Der Derian and Michael J. Shapiro, eds., *International/Intertextual Relations* (Lexington, Mass.: Lexington, 1989); Charles R. Beitz, *Political Theory and International Relations* (Princeton, N.J.: Princeton University Press, 1979), pp. 3–66; David Campbell, *Writing Security* (Minneapolis: University of Minnesota Press, 1992); Miriam Cooke and Angela Woollacott, *Gendering War Talk* (Princeton, N.J.: Princeton University Press, 1993); James Der Derian, *Antidiplomacy: Spies, Terror, Speed, and War* (Cambridge, Mass.: Blackwell, 1992); Fred A. Sondermann, "National Interest," *Orbis* 21 (Spring 1977): 121–38; R. B. J. Walker, *Inside/Outside: International Relations as Political Theory* (Cambridge: Cambridge University Press, 1993).

28. Ferenc Feher, "Toward a Post-Machiavellian Politics," *Telos* 42 (Winter 1979–80): 56–64; Robert Amdur, "Rawls' Theory of Justice: Domestic and International Perspectives," *World Politics* 29 (April 1977): 438–61; Brian Barry, *The Liberal Theory of Justice* (Oxford: Clarendon Press, 1973), pp. 128–33; John Rawls, "The Law of Peoples," *Critical Inquiry* 20 (Autumn 1993): 36–38; and Fernando Teson, "The Kantian Theory of International Law," *Columbia Law Review* 92 (January 1992): 53–102.

29. See, for example, Michael Walzer, *Just and Unjust Wars* (New York: Basic Books, 1977); William Aiken and Hugo La Follette, *World Hunger and Moral Obliga-*

80   Larry N. George

tion (Englewood Cliffs, N.J.: Prentice-Hall, 1977); George Lopez and Drew Christiansen, eds., *Morals and Might* (Boulder, Colo.: Westview Press, 1993).

30. See Richard Falk, ed., *The Promise of World Order: Essays in Normative International Relations* (Philadelphia: Temple University Press, 1987), and Terry Nardin and David R. Mapel, eds., *Traditions of International Ethics* (Cambridge: Cambridge University Press, 1992).

31. From Hamilton's Letter to Camillus on the Jay Treaty, quoted in Clinton Rossiter, *Alexander Hamilton and the Constitution* (New York: Harcourt, Brace and World, 1964), p. 91.

32. See, for example, Theodore Draper, *A Very Thin Line* (New York: Hill and Wang, 1991); Jane Meyer and Doyle McManus, *Landslide: The Unmaking of the President 1984–1988* (Boston: Houghton Mifflin, 1988); David Wise, *The Politics of Lying: Government Deception, Secrecy, and Power* (New York: Random House, 1973); and Woodward, *Veil.*

33. See John H. Aldrich, John L. Sullivan, and Eugene Bordida, "Foreign Affairs and Issue Voting," *American Political Science Review* 83 (March 1989): 123–41; Robert Y. Shapiro and Benjamin I. Page, "Foreign Policy and the Rational Public," *Journal of Conflict Resolution* 32 (June 1998): 211–47; Eugene R. Wittkopf, *Faces of Internationalism: Public Opinion and American Foreign Policy* (Durham, N.C.: Duke University Press, 1990).

34. See James M. McCormick and Eugene R. Wittkopf, "Bipartisanship, Partisanship, and Ideology in Congressional-Executive Foreign Policy Relations, 1947–1990," *Journal of Politics* 52 (November 1990): 1077–1100; William B. Quandt, "The Electoral Cycle and the Conduct of American Foreign Policy," *Political Science Quarterly* 101 (1986): 825–37; and Gerald F. Seib, "Limits of Power," *Wall Street Journal,* September 11, 1989, p. A1.

35. I. M. Destler, Leslie H. Gelb, and Anthony Lake, *Our Own Worst Enemy: The Unmaking of American Foreign Policy* (New York: Simon and Schuster, 1984), p. 21.

36. Ibid., p. 26.

37. Ibid., p. 22.

38. Daniel Yankelovich and I. M. Destler, eds., *Beyond the Beltway: Engaging the Public in U.S. Foreign Policy* (New York: W. W. Norton and Company, 1994).

39. Robert A. Dahl, *Controlling Nuclear Weapons: Democracy vs. Guardianship* (Syracuse, N.Y.: Syracuse University Press, 1985), especially pp. 13–16, 42–47.

40. See Jennings B. Sanders, *Evolution of the Executive Departments of the Continental Congress* (Chapel Hill: University of North Carolina Press, 1935).

41. See Thomas M. Franck and Edward Weisband, *Foreign Policy By Congress* (New York: Oxford University Press, 1979), and the recommendations in Harold Hongju Koh, *The National Security Constitution: Sharing Power After the Iran-Contra Affair* (New Haven: Yale University Press, 1990), pp. 153–228.

42. Arthur M. Schlesinger, Jr., *The Cycles of American History* (Boston: Houghton Mifflin, 1986), pp. 299–300, and Victor Marchetti and John Marks, *The CIA and the Cult of Intelligence* (New York: Knopf, 1974).

43. See Itzhak Galnoor, ed., *Government Secrecy in Democracies* (New York: Harper and Row, 1977).

44. Allan E. Goodman, "Reforming U.S. Intelligence," *Foreign Policy* 67 (Summer 1987): 121–36.

45. Facts on File, December 19, 1986, p. 949.

46. *New York Times,* February 4, 1988, p. 1.

47. See Robert Perry and Peter Kornbluh, "Iran-Contra's Untold Story," *Foreign Policy* 72 (Fall 1988): 3–30.

48. Woodward, *Veil,* p. 426.

49. Tim Weiner, "Lies and Rigged 'Star Wars' Test Fooled the Kremlin, and Congress," *New York Times,* August 18, 1993, p. A1.

50. Woodward, *Veil,* p. 426.

51. Eve Pell, "White House Secret Powers," *Nation,* June 19, 1989, p. 833.

52. See Owen Harries, "Doctrine Overdose," *New Republic,* May 5, 1986, pp. 17–18, and Christopher Layne, "The Real Conservation Agenda," *Foreign Policy* 61 (Winter 1985–86): 73–93.

53. E. E. Schattschneider, *The Semi-Sovereign People* (New York: Holt, Rinehart, Winston, 1960), pp. 135–38.

54. Compare Hamilton's "Pacificus" letters in Harold Syrett et al., eds., *The Papers of Alexander Hamilton* (New York: Columbia University Press, 1961–79), vol. 15, with Scigliano's "War Powers Resolution and the War Powers."

55. On this point in general, see the essays by Michael Doyle, Nicholas Onuf, and Thomas Johnson and by Mark Zacher and Richard Matthew, in Charles Kegley, ed., *Controversies in International Relations Theory* (New York: St. Martin's Press, 1995); Lloyd Jensen, *Explaining Foreign Policy* (Englewood Cliffs N.J.: Prentice-Hall, 1982); Miroslav Nincic, *Democracy and Foreign Policy: The Fallacy of Political Realism* (New York: Columbia University Press, 1992); James Lee Ray, *Democracy and International Conflict* (Columbia: University of South Carolina Press, 1995); Bruce Russett, *Grasping the Democratic Peace* (Princeton, N.J.: Princeton University Press, 1993); and Kenneth Waltz, *Foreign Policy and Democratic Politics* (Boston: Little Brown, 1967).

56. Especially illuminating here are the records of the Church Committee hearings cited in note 24. See also Theodore Draper's *Very Thin Line* as well as his excellent series in the *New York Review of Books,* beginning with January 19, 1989, and continuing through September 26, 1991, November 21, 1991, and May 27, 1993; Carole Gallagher's disturbing *Secret Nuclear War* (Boston: MIT Press, 1993); Loch K. Johnson, *America's Secret Power* (New York: Oxford University Press, 1989); Jonathan Kwitny, *Endless Enemies* (New York: Congdon and Weed, 1984); Marchetti and Marks, *CIA and the Cult of Intelligence*; and Woodward's *Veil.*

57. Richard Ned Lebow and Janice Gross Stein, *We All Lost the Cold War* (Princeton, N.J.: Princeton University Press, 1994).

PART TWO

EXECUTIVE-LEGISLATIVE RELATIONS IN FOREIGN AFFAIRS

3
THE PRESIDENT, CONGRESS, AND THE FULCRUM OF FOREIGN POLICY

ROBERT J. SPITZER

It is impossible to understand the organic balance of power between the president and Congress without examining their interaction in the realm of foreign affairs. In this chapter I shall assess the important tools of foreign policy used by the two branches short of war.[1] They include treaties, executive agreements, arms sales, foreign aid, "intermestic" issues, and intelligence activities. In each area, modern presidents claim and often exert ascendancy, yet Congress in fact shares these responsibilities and has in some instances moved to reassert its involvement.

TREATIES AND EXECUTIVE AGREEMENTS

Treatymaking is treated succinctly in Article II, section 2 of the Constitution when it gives the president the power "by and with the advice and consent of the Senate, to make treaties, provided two-thirds of the senators present concur." The House of Representatives is excluded from the treaty process, yet it becomes involved out of necessity when enactment of appropriations or enabling legislation is required. The two-thirds vote requirement reflected the Founders' desire to avoid a treaty-approval process that was too easy. Many of them sought to avoid foreign entanglements or agreements entered into frivolously. As Gouverneur Morris noted, "The more difficulty in making treaties, the more value will be set upon them."[2]

Treatymaking power was discussed frequently at the Constitutional Convention. Initially, the Founders proposed that power over treaties remain solely in the hands of the legislature, as had been the case under the Articles of

Confederation. But late in the convention, the Founders yielded to the argument that the president should "make treaties" with the Senate. The exclusion of the House was defended by Alexander Hamilton and John Jay in the *Federalist Papers* when they argued that the Senate's smaller size and institutional continuity, attributable to senators' longer terms of office and staggered election cycle, would facilitate secrecy and dispatch in the treaty process.[3]

The Founders envisioned that the president actually would consult with the Senate while treaty formulation was under way and not simply present the Senate with a fait accompli. In fact, "the Senate was to be a kind of Presidential council affording him advice throughout the treaty-making process and on all aspects of it."[4] Writing in *Federalist 75*, Hamilton went even further by saying that power over treaties was more legislative than executive: "The particular nature of the power of making treaties . . . will be found to partake more of the legislative than of the executive character."[5]

President Washington attempted to implement joint presidential-Senate responsibility with an Indian treaty in 1789, seeking Senate advice by going to the chamber in person. In addition to informing the Senate about the most recent developments, he also sought the opinions of senators about how to proceed in future negotiations. Washington expected the Senate to provide its consent then and there, but senators felt that they were being rushed, needing time to analyze, discuss, and deliberate. When senators objected and proposed a delay, Washington became visibly angry, declaring *"This defeats every purpose of my coming here."*[6] Resolution of the issue was postponed until the following week; so ended the brief experiment with in-person consultation. Washington and his successors relied instead on consultation in written form. Yet some presidents have chosen to avoid Senate consultation, leading to a Senate role that has tended to emphasize the "consent" role more than the "advice" role.[7]

Despite this tendency, the Senate (and Congress as a whole) has been more active in peace-related matters than in war-related matters. According to one study, an inverse relationship exists between the active involvement of Congress and the presence of military hostilities in a situation. Stated another way, the greater the specter of armed conflict, the less likely Congress is to play a key role.[8]

Although the Senate as an institution typically enters the treatymaking process when treaties are presented to that body by the president, individual senators often have participated in negotiations with other countries. As early as 1814 President Madison appointed two members of Congress to negotiate a peace treaty with Britain. More recently, the United Nations Charter received key input from senators Arthur Vandenberg (R.-Mich.) and Thomas Connally

(D.-Tex.) in 1945. President Kennedy's negotiations with the Soviet Union over the Nuclear Test Ban Treaty of 1963 occurred with Senate members present. Many observers argue that the absence of senators during the Wilson administration's negotiations over the League of Nations agreement at the end of World War I contributed to the treaty's defeat by the Senate in 1919. After the Wilson experience, senators were often appointed to important international conferences, especially by presidents Warren Harding, Herbert Hoover, Franklin Roosevelt, Harry Truman, and Jimmy Carter.[9]

The relationship between the Senate and the president in the treaty process often is viewed as one of conflict, characterized by presidential defeat, especially in light of the two-thirds approval requirement. Examples such as the defeat of the League of Nations Treaty by the Senate, the withdrawal of the SALT II Treaty by President Carter in 1980 in the face of vocal Senate opposition, and Carter's protracted battle to win ratification of the Panama Canal Treaty in 1978 seem to support the proposition that the Senate is a graveyard for treaties. Yet from 1789 to 1988, only twenty treaties—about 1 percent— have been voted down on the floor of the Senate. About 15 percent have been accepted by the Senate after alteration.[10]

The very nature of treatymaking has provided the president with an immediate advantage in dealing with the Senate. Since the process of negotiating treaties falls clearly, although not necessarily exclusively, on the president, the executive and the staff are most closely associated with the construction of the treaty document. (The president may not only invite members of Congress to participate but may allow key legislators the opportunity to have a say in the selection of the negotiations team.) Thus, the administration is likely to have control over, if not a monopoly on, information about the content and political process leading up to an agreement. The proposed treaty is presented to the Senate as the president's document, carrying the weight and prestige of the chief executive. Since the president also is recognized as the nation's chief spokesperson to the rest of the world, the political initiative rests with the president in a way it does not with routine legislation.

The treatymaking process actually incorporates three stages. First, the president's representatives, usually including the secretary of state, engage in negotiations that culminate in a treaty with one or more other nations. Such negotiations sometimes span decades and several administrations, as was the case with the Panama Canal Treaty. Congress may offer advice and opinions about negotiations, but such opinions have no special legal weight. Second, the document is transmitted to the Senate, which has several options. It can approve the treaty, reject it, amend it (in which case it may have to go back to the foreign country for reapproval), or attach reservations and understandings designed to clarify treaty provisions and language. Third, at the conclusion of Senate deliberations, the treaty must be "proclaimed by"—that is, accepted by—the president.[11] As this sequence reveals, the president retains the political initiative throughout. At the same time, Senate involvement at every stage is by no means precluded. But if the Senate is to be involved at any stage other than ratification, it must be at the president's request.

Although the treaty process favors the president's political predilections, the chief executive cannot take Senate support for granted. Presidents must lay careful political groundwork to improve the likelihood of ratification, even when substantial support for proposed treaties already exists.

Ending Treaties

One question about which the Constitution is silent is that of treaty termination. Constitutional scholar Louis Fisher notes that Article VI of the Constitution vests federal statutes and treaties with the same status, yielding the conclusion that Congress possesses the power to end a treaty by the normal legislative process.[12] Other scholars have argued that since the Senate must ratify treaties, it follows that Senate consent is necessary to terminate a treaty, in legal parlance, a principle referred to as "symmetrical construction."[13] At the same time, several presidents have claimed for themselves the power to end treaties. For example, Pres. Franklin Roosevelt ended a commerce and friendship treaty with Japan two years before America's entry into World War II.

More recently, a political and legal challenge was raised against President Carter's termination of treaties with the Republic of China (Taiwan) as a prelude to full recognition of the People's Republic of China (mainland China). The key point of contention centered on the Mutual Defense Treaty of 1954, which allowed either party to end the treaty on a year's notice. Carter announced the termination of the treaty in December 1978, while Congress was out of session. Senator Barry Goldwater (R.-Ariz.) filed suit in federal court to block Carter's action. A federal district court sided with Goldwater, but the federal court of appeals ruled that the president possessed the power to terminate the treaty. In the case of *Goldwater v. Carter,* a divided Supreme Court dismissed Goldwater's complaint on grounds of nonjusticiability.[14] The ruling, however, had the practical effect of leaving the termination intact.

The ruling in *Goldwater* also clarified an important point about recognition of foreign governments. The termination of the treaty with Taiwan was a necessary step to the full recognition of the Beijing government, which was the goal of Carter's actions. Justice Brennan noted in his opinion that "our cases firmly establish that the Constitution commits to the President alone the power to recognize, and withdraw recognition from, foreign regimes.''[15] Brennan was not, however, speaking for a voting majority in the case.

If past actions are any judge, the power to end a treaty may indeed be shared. According to political scientist David Gray Adler's important study, treaty termination actually occurs rarely. But when it has occurred, from the period of 1789 to 1985, ten treaties were terminated by the president alone, seven by Congress, and two by the Senate.[16] In order to better appreciate the politics of the treaty process, I present two examples of recent treaty disputes. One ended in ratification, the other in withdrawal from the Senate. Both examples illustrate the fine presidential-Senate balance when each holds a vested interest in the outcome.

Treatymaking Success: The Panama Canal Treaties

Since the American-inspired Panamanian revolution in 1903, a ten-mile-wide strip of land running through the middle of Panama has been controlled by the United States. American control of the strip allowed the United States to construct the Panama Canal and to maintain complete control over its operation. The terms of the agreement granting American control ''in perpetuity'' were so favorable to the United States that, despite treaty renegotiations in 1936 and 1955, Panamanians grew increasingly resentful over continued American domination. In contrast, most American leaders felt little necessity to alter significantly the terms of the relationship, as it had been very advantageous to this country.

In the early 1960s riots broke out in Panama and the American-controlled Canal Zone. Although the immediate cause of the riots had to do with whether the Panamanian flag would be flown along with the American flag in the zone, the riots were symptomatic of growing resentment in Panama over continued American domination. In spring 1964 treaty renegotiations began. They did not conclude until 1977. During the long process, some members of Congress kept a watchful eye on negotiations development, especially the House Merchant Marine and Fisheries Committee and its subcommittee on the Panama Canal. Both committees were sources of opposition to changes that might arise from a new treaty, and in 1975 the House passed an amendment barring the use of funds to support relinquishing U.S. rights to the Canal Zone. The measure failed in the Senate but was reintroduced in the House in 1976 and 1977.

Treaty negotiations ended during summer 1977, and two treaties were transmitted to the Senate on September 16. One, the Panama Canal Treaty, superseded the 1903 treaty and abolished the Canal Zone. The United States maintained the right to manage, maintain, and operate the canal through a new administrative apparatus that would include Panamanians until the end of 1999, when complete control of the canal would pass to Panama. At that time, America would relinquish its control over administration of the canal and increase payments to Panama in order to continue to obtain favored treatment for the United States The other treaty, the Neutrality Treaty, asserted that the canal would operate under a permanent state of neutrality and that Panama alone would operate the canal after 1999. The only special concession for America stated that U.S. warships would be allowed expeditious canal transit.

From the start, treaty ratification was an open question. Polls showed a large number of undecided senators, and many people in the government and in the country simply assumed that the canal properly belonged to the United States. Indeed, public opinion surveys revealed overwhelming opposition to treaty ratification although citizens more well informed about the treaties were more likely to support them.[17] Part of the suspicion surrounding the treaty sprang from the concern that relinquishing legal control would mean that American security needs might be compromised.[18]

Thus, when President Carter tackled the task of winning treaty ratification in the Senate, he faced several political obstacles, and he began to lay the political groundwork in spring 1977 by meeting with key members of the Senate to apprise them of developments and to solicit their views. In addition to rallying public opinion, Carter needed to satisfy members of his own administration and a Congress that had maintained a long-term interest in the affairs of the Panama Canal. "Few foreign policy issues in the history of the United States have involved the Congress more than negotiations and relations regarding the Panama Canal."[19] Although such involvement is atypical of congressional involvement in foreign affairs, the Panama case reveals much about the interaction between the president and Congress pertaining to treaties.

Despite the fact that House ratification is unnecessary for treaties, the House had made its political weight felt in previous attempts to influence funding affecting the canal. During the ratification process, the House served as an important forum for generating both support for and opposition to the treaties. In particular, three House committees held hearings on the canal and the treaties: Merchant Marine and Fisheries, International Relations, and Armed Services. In the Senate, hearings were conducted by the Judiciary, Armed Services, and Foreign Relations committees; those of the latter were the most lengthy and extensive. In addition, no fewer than 42 of the Senate's 100 members traveled to Panama, as did many members of the House. Extensive activity was seen on the floor of the Senate as well as in committees. Floor debate continued for thirty-eight days and was the second longest treaty debate in the Senate's history; only the Treaty of Versailles debate was longer. No fewer than eighty-eight changes were proposed and voted on, and of these, over twenty reservations, understandings, and conditions were added.

Most of the senators who visited Panama did so to gather information, but some actually engaged in direct negotiations with the Panamanian leadership. The act of senators engaging in such negotiations after the conclusion of treaty terms between the executive heads of government was highly unusual and represented a degree of Senate involvement not seen since consideration of the Versailles Treaty. Carter found it necessary to respond to the specific concerns of undecided senators. In one key incident, a freshman senator—Dennis DeConcini (D.-Ariz.)—succeeded in attaching an amendment to the treaty (with Carter's consent) that allowed the United States to use military force to keep the canal open after the year 2000. The addition infuriated the Panamanians, and some emergency bargaining occurred to find compromise wording satisfactory to the Senate (including DeConcini) and to Panama. Carter's concession on the DeConcini amendment was obviously a move to win his support, yet it nearly collapsed the treaty process.

DeConcini's pivotal influence illustrated a larger point about ratification. Senators who remained undecided found themselves in the best political position to influence the terms of the treaty and also to extract concessions (often unrelated to the treaty issue) from the president in exchange for their support. Indeed, some senators who initially had committed themselves to the treaty backed off in an attempt to gain some leverage with the White House.[20] After months of intense investigation, bargaining, and debate the Senate approved the Neutrality Treaty on March 16, 1978, and the Canal Treaty the following April 18. Both passed by the same 68 to 32 margin—one vote more than the necessary two-thirds.

The unpopularity of the treaties, plus the keen interest of many members of Congress, made the ratification process exceptionally difficult for Carter. Yet he himself almost certainly made the process more difficult by underestimating Senate sensibilities. According to political scientist Richard Pious, Carter "bungled his dealings with the Senate. Some of the problems could have been avoided had the Senate been brought in at an early stage."[21]

Treatymaking Failure: The SALT II Treaty

Since 1968 the United States has engaged in systematic talks with the Soviet Union designed to control aspects of the nuclear arms race, known as Strategic Arms Limitation Talks (SALT) in the Nixon, Ford, and Carter administrations. The two most important treaties emerging from this process were SALT I, completed and ratified in 1972, and SALT II, completed in 1979 but withdrawn from the Senate shortly after completion. Although SALT II was not brought to a vote before the full Senate, it was withdrawn because of the clear sense that it could not achieve the necessary two-thirds affirmative vote.[22]

SALT II negotiations began in November 1972 and stretched over seven years, spanning three presidential administrations. The treaty dealt with a variety of complex issues, but in general it set limits on the numbers of "strategic delivery vehicles"—that is, the vehicles (including missiles and bombers) used to deliver nuclear warheads—that each side could have. It also included a three-year "protocol" addressing controversial issues dividing the two nations and a statement addressing President Carter's "deep cuts" proposal, which called for significant reductions in weapons numbers set out in prior agreements. The negotiations process dragged on during Carter's first two years in office because of disagreements over how to deal with particular weapons systems, such as the Cruise missile and the Soviet Backfire bomber.

As with the Panama Canal treaties, the president had to deal domestically not only with the Senate but also with the House, his own administration, and public opinion. In Congress, key members had been vocal about the negotiations process since the early 1970s. Certain House members had been influential in shaping the SALT debate in this country, and various attempts were made to influence the nature and direction of the treaty through control of funding (members of Congress had been excluded from actual negotiations up to this time).

In fact, Carter made good on his campaign promise of involving key legislators by including them within his inner circle of advisers, and some were actually involved in negotiations. Some Senate hardliners were also consulted by the Carter administration as a means of attempting to include their views ultimately to win their support. In all, a group of thirty senators and fourteen House members were appointed as advisers to, and participants in, the SALT negotiations. These efforts prompted Senate Minority Leader Howard Baker (R.-Tenn.) to praise Carter for his bipartisan approach. Moreover, prevailing congressional sentiment often was used as a bargaining chip with the Soviets, as the U.S. negotiators would sometimes argue for or against a certain proposed provision based on predictions about what the Senate would or would not accept.

Despite these careful steps, SALT II encountered a series of roadblocks. For example, many members of Congress sought to impose "linkage"—that is, they attempted to link the SALT agreement to other issues not related to the nuclear balance in an effort to alter Soviet policy in other areas. Other observers were concerned that some of Carter's negotiators, such as Arms Control and Disarmament Agency head Paul Warnke, would not be sufficiently tough negotiators. Some critics believed that the treaty gave away too much or that some provisions would be difficult to verify. These and related criticisms were presented forcefully at a time when Congress was moving to assert itself generally in policymaking and the presidency was still laboring under the consequences of Vietnam and Watergate.

The final provisions of the treaty were worked out in May 1979, and the agreement was signed on June 14. By the time the treaty was sent to the Senate, the public SALT debate had been going on for several years. Thus, the major issues were well known to the principals. The Senate Foreign Relations Committee held four months of both open and closed hearings on the treaty. Consideration of its military consequences were undertaken by the Senate Armed Services Committee.

After narrowly averting several attempts to kill the treaty, the Foreign Relations Committee reported it favorably by a lukewarm vote of 9 to 6. In addition, it attached twenty-three conditions to the ratification resolution. It thus became clear that the treaty would not be approved without changes; yet Carter had insisted that the treaty would not be renegotiated. The force of linkage also entered in, as congressional critics noted with alarm the presence of Cuban troops in Africa and the taking of American hostages in Iran in November. Shortly thereafter, a group of nineteen senators urged Carter to put off a vote on the treaty. Finally, Carter asked the Senate to postpone consideration of the treaty in the aftermath of the Soviet invasion of Afghanistan in December. The treaty was never brought back to the Senate although its terms were followed generally by both sides throughout the 1980s.

The withdrawal of SALT II was facilitated by external events but also by persistent divisions within the government over the goals and purposes of the SALT process. Some observers have suggested that the substantial involvement of Congress was instrumental to SALT's demise. Yet it was the exclusion of key congressmen from SALT I negotiations that did much to energize congressional opposition to the SALT process that followed.

Assessment: Treaties, the President, and Congress

The Panama Canal treaties and the SALT II Treaty were both high visibility treaty efforts involving a single presidency—that of Jimmy Carter. Nevertheless, they reveal much about the politics of treatymaking. First, the rise of congressional assertiveness in the 1970s has reinvigorated the role of Congress, such that presidents must now take greater care when laying the political

groundwork for approval of major or controversial treaties.[23] In any era, however, a president who ignores the Senate imperils any impending treaty.

Second, the president cannot ignore the House. Through the appropriations process, committee investigations, and the ability to gain public attention, the House (especially through key committees) can have a profound impact on the treaty process. Third, the door is clearly open for greater direct
involvement by members of Congress in the actual process of formulating
treaties, despite the possible pitfall of including too many hands in the negotiations process. Such involvement is consistent with the intent of the Constitution's Framers. Moreover, political circumstances make such efforts desirable, and nothing in the Constitution bars greater participation.

Fourth, political bargaining occurs over treaty support just as it does over
more mundane domestic political issues. Although one might question the
trading of a vote for an important treaty in exchange for funding an unrelated
pet project in a senator's home state, such processes are part of the currency of
presidential-congressional relations. Fifth, one of the central facts of the modern Congress is that it is organizationally more decentralized than in its past
history. Party and chamber leaders possess less control over the behavior of
members, and committees and committee chairs are extremely influential.
Thus, a president needing to win two-thirds support in the Senate must be
sensitive to the concerns of a variety of influential senators, including party
leaders, committee leaders, ideological leaders, and regional leaders.

Sixth, the two-thirds requirement means that thirty-four senators can veto any
treaty. The extraordinary majority requirement gives a relatively small number of
legislators disproportionately great influence. Most treaties are relatively uncon-
troversial and deal with minor matters, but those treaties that are likely to raise questions also invite senators to use the two-thirds threshold as a lever to extract concessions from the president, whether related or unrelated to the treaty issue at hand.

Seventh, treaties belong, in a political sense, primarily to the president. It is
the job of the chief executive to build coalition support by any available
means. The initiative belongs to the chief executive, but so too does the burden. Given the historical record, it is clear that presidents have carried the burden with considerable success. Yet in recent years presidents increasingly have
avoided the treaty route altogether in favor of a means of reaching international agreements that sidesteps the Senate.

Executive Agreements

Agreements with other countries may be achieved not only by treaties but
also by executive agreements, an understanding reached between heads of

state or their designees. It can be oral or written and may require either prior congressional authorization or later congressional approval. But key to an executive agreement is that it does not go to the Senate for approval. It does, however, have the force of law and also possesses "a similar dignity" as treaties.[24] Although executive agreement power is not stipulated in the Constitution, it is generally recognized as coming from four sources: the presidential responsibility of representing the country in foreign affairs, the authority to receive ambassadors, the role of commander-in-chief of the military, and the obligation to "take care that the laws be faithfully executed."[25]

Many executive agreements involve routine matters, from fishing rights to postal agreements. Yet some important international agreements have been concluded through this process, including the exchange of fifty American destroyers for some British military bases in 1940 between Pres. Franklin Roosevelt and British Prime Minister Winston Churchill and a series of agreements between U.S. presidents and South Vietnamese leaders promising military and other assistance in the 1950s and 1960s.

Executive agreements date back to the Founding of the country. In 1792 the postmaster general reached an agreement involving international postal arrangements, and executive agreements have been used frequently since then. Dating from World War II, however, the number of executive agreements has skyrocketed. In fact, about 95 percent of all international understandings since the war have taken the form of executive agreements.[26]

A Treaty or an Agreement? The rise in executive agreements is attributable partly to America's greater role in international military, political, and economic affairs since World War II. But it also represents presidential efforts to make foreign policy commitments without having to go through the laborious treaty process. This trend is founded partly on the president's relatively greater political influence, on congressional willingness to allow the president wide latitude in this area, and also in the fundamental legal ambiguity in deciding when an understanding ought to be viewed as a treaty and when it can be handled as an executive agreement. This ambiguity has been exploited for many years by presidents. Theodore Roosevelt, for example, found Congress unwilling to approve a proposed treaty with the Dominican Republic in 1905, and in response enacted the treaty as an executive agreement.[27]

The obscure difference between a treaty and an executive agreement has been nicely captured by constitutional scholar Bernard Schwartz, who relates an anecdote from 1954 pertaining to

a request addressed to the State Department by a Senator asking them how to distinguish a treaty, which must be approved by the Senate, from an executive agreement, which need not. The State Department unhelpfully defined a treaty as "something they had to send to the Senate in order to get approval by a two-thirds vote. An executive agreement was something they did not have to send to the Senate." This reply, said the Senator who had sent the request, "reminded me of the time when I was a boy on the farm, and asked the hired man how to tell the difference between a male and a female pigeon. He said, 'You put corn in front of the pigeon. If he picks it up, it is a he; if she picks it up, it is a she.' "[28]

In practical terms, the legal ambiguity has come to mean that an international understanding is likely to be handled as an executive agreement unless it deals with a politically important subject and Congress expresses sufficient objections to avoidance of treatymaking. Presidents often test the political waters by suggesting that an understanding might be treated as an executive agreement. President Carter followed exactly this path with both the Panama Canal treaties and the SALT II agreement. In both cases, however, congressional objections were sufficiently strenuous that he decided to deal with the negotiations as treaties.

The increased presidential reliance on executive agreements as a means to circumvent treaties has raised some objection, to the extent that it robs the Senate of advice and consent.[29] But absent a clear legal definition, political forces will probably continue to operate by forcing the president into treaty-making when Congress complains loudly.

The Case Act. Congressional dissatisfaction with the president's greater use of executive agreements, including some agreements arrived at secretly without the knowledge of Congress, culminated in the passage of the Case Act (also called the Case-Zablocki Act) of 1972. For example, Congress was not informed of important executive agreements reached between the president and Ethiopia in 1960, Laos in 1963, Thailand in 1964 and 1967, and Korea in 1966.[30] The Case Act provides that the secretary of state must transmit to Congress the text of all executive agreements within sixty days of their completion, including secret agreements (although access to information about secret agreements is restricted to key members of Congress).

Some observers have criticized the Case Act as being too weak. The act did not define executive agreements, and thus presidents have applied their own definitions, which have excluded understandings that many members of Congress believed were agreements. For example, President Nixon promised South Vietnamese President Thieu that the United States would "respond with full force" if North Vietnam violated the Paris Peace Agreement, but he did not inform Congress. The pledge proved to be an embarrassment, as Congress declined to provide assistance when South Vietnam was overrun in 1975. One congressman estimated in 1975 that from the time of the passage of the Case Act until then, presidents had entered into from 400 to 600 understandings with other governments that had not been reported to Congress.[31] The trend of noncompliance declined somewhat throughout the 1970s but still persists. Some agreements have been reported to Congress more than a year after completion; some are never reported.[32]

Despite the problems, Congress is probably in a better position because of the Case Act. Aside from refusing funding for agreements with which it disagrees, Congress can threaten public disclosure of controversial secret agreements. It can also act to amend or to counter them through legislation.[33] And although an executive agreement is by definition solely a presidential action, Congress can make a strong argument for at least being informed of agreements that bind the nation to obligations involving other nations.

ARMS SALES AND AMERICA'S CHANGING ROLE IN THE WORLD

For roughly the first twenty years after the end of World War II, American foreign policy was characterized by a relatively strong degree of bipartisanship. Republicans and Democrats in Congress and the White House shared deep antipathy for communism and the Soviet Union. During the Cold War era, arms sales, foreign aid programs, and direct military efforts usually focused on some aspect of anticommunism. The president provided the principal leadership, and Congress generally followed.

During the mid-1960s, however, dissent began to rise in Congress and throughout the country over conduct of the Vietnam War. Although conduct of the war was in many respects consistent with past policies, many Americans began to question the monolithic view of communism that had been the basis of U.S. policy up to that time. The questioning was evidenced in growing divisions between the executive and legislative branches of government. American involvement in the Vietnam War began with the approval and support of Congress, but it soon became identified with the two presidents most heavily committed to waging the war—Johnson and Nixon. As the institutional rift between the branches widened, so too did presidential-congressional differences over other aspects of foreign policy.

The immediate evidence of the rift was seen in repeated congressional efforts to end or otherwise limit American involvement in Vietnam. But it also was seen in other areas, such as in the handling of arms sales. In 1974, for example, an amendment passed by Congress required the president to report arms sales of over $5,000 to Congress (although multiple sales under that amount did not have to be reported), and it provided a mechanism whereby Congress could move to block some arms sales. The act helped prod Congress to challenge proposed presidential arms sales. In 1978 members of Congress fought unsuccessfully to block the sale of fighter jets to Egypt and Saudi Arabia. Congress succeeded, however, in stalling or forcing the withdrawal of proposed arms sales in the late 1970s to Turkey, Chile, Argentina, Libya, Iraq, and other nations.[34]

The Reagan administration revived efforts to exert greater presidential prerogative, but Reagan too encountered opposition to major arms sale proposals. For example, in 1985 he had planned to propose to sell a $1 billion arms package to Saudi Arabia, including F-15 jet fighters, M-1 tanks, helicopter gunships, and other equipment. The plan was scratched before it was formally proposed, however, because of informal but overwhelming Senate opposition that would have ensured defeat of the package. This sentiment grew partly from America's experience with Iran in 1979, when billions of dollars of recent vintage American military and other hardware that had been sold to the Shah of Iran fell into the hands of the unfriendly Khomeini regime during that country's revolution.[35]

In spring 1986, the Reagan administration proposed a scaled-down $354 million missile package for Saudi Arabia that included air-to-sea Harpoon missiles, air-to-air Sidewinder missiles, and ground-to-air, shoulder-held Stinger missiles. Congressional resistance even to this modified package was stiff because of Saudi support for Syria and the Palestine Liberation Organization (PLO), Saudi refusal to support Egypt and Jordan in the peace process, and the continued belligerence of Saudi Arabia toward Israel.

The arms sale would proceed unless Congress voted to block the sale within fifty days. Both the Republican-controlled Senate and the Democratic-controlled House voted to disapprove the sale, and Reagan then vetoed the disapproval on May 21. The relatively rapid and lopsided vote against the arms sale was partly a function of the administration's decision to prevent the negative vote by presidential veto rather than by working earlier to block the initial vote.

Congressional critics voiced concern over using arms sales as a primary means of diplomacy, and in particular over the inclusion of Stinger missiles in the package. Persistent objections were raised that, given the volatility of the Middle East, such weapons might find their way into the hands of terrorists (the Stinger was referred to as a "terrorist's delight" because of its small size, portability, and destructive capability). The White House argued that Saudi Arabia had remained a friend of the United States, was a key source of oil, and was a moderate voice in the Arab world. It also argued that the package was needed to counter Soviet and Iranian influence in the region. Then in a significant concession, the president eliminated the Stingers from the package. White House pressure to uphold the Reagan veto was facilitated by a recurring argument—namely, that the president's ability to conduct foreign policy could be impaired if his wishes were openly denied by Congress. At least one senator changed his vote in favor of the president in response to this argument. As a result of the last-minute pressure from the White House, the veto was upheld in the Senate by the exact margin required.[36]

FOREIGN AID

The pattern of presidential-congressional relations with respect to foreign aid has followed a similar path in recent years. In the 1970s Congress began to press the president to tie foreign aid assistance to progress on human rights. In 1973 Congress enacted the Foreign Assistance Act, in which it inserted two provisions expressing the opinion or "sense" of Congress that the president should deny foreign aid to any country that practiced incarceration of its citizens for political purposes. One provision stated such denial as a general principle; the other provision specifically addressed the government of Chile, which had recently undergone a coup (with the covert assistance of the American Central Intelligence Agency) that deposed its elected president, Salvador Allende, and replaced him with a harsh military regime. The human rights abuses of Chile's new Pinochet regime provoked Congress into tying American aid to human rights practices. Similar human rights–related restrictions were tied to aid packages for Argentina, Cambodia, El Salvador, Guatemala, Haiti, Mexico, Nicaragua, South Africa, South Korea, and Uganda.

Two members of Congress, Cong. Charles Vanik (D.-Ohio) and Sen. Henry Jackson (D.-Wash.), spearheaded an effort to link American trade relations with the Soviet Union to Soviet human rights practices, especially to prod more liberal emigration policies for Soviet dissidents, Jews, and others. Despite resistance from the White House, which felt that quiet diplomacy could accomplish more, the policy was enacted in 1974. Some critics have argued that the policy, often referred to as the Jackson-Vanik law, actually resulted in a constriction of emigration from the Soviet Union.[37]

Nevertheless, Congress strengthened the legal language tying aid to human rights practices in 1976, 1978, 1979, and 1980. The effort was facilitated during the Carter administration, as Carter elevated the concern for human rights as a coordinate policy goal, applying not just to foreign aid but to the overall conduct of foreign policy (including policy toward the Soviet Union). Congress worked progressively to apply rigorous standards concerning human rights in security assistance and multilateral aid programs but was less stringent in programs aimed toward development assistance and food aid since the latter programs were targeted at more fundamental human needs.

Interbranch struggle intensified during the Reagan administration, which sought a more conciliatory policy toward nations with records of human rights abuses like South Africa, El Salvador, Chile, and the Philippines under Ferdinand Marcos. The thinking of the Reagan administration was articulated by members of the administration such as United Nations representative Jeane Kirkpatrick, who argued that America should continue to aid its allies, even if human rights problems existed, because such nations supported America, did not violate human rights to the same degree as other nations, and would probably improve their human rights practices.[38] Other individuals in Congress and elsewhere argued that America was in the best position to influence the human rights practices of those nations.[39]

In the late 1980s Congress urged the president to support lifting some Jackson-Vanik restrictions. At the end of 1989, for example, thirty-three members of Congress signed a letter urging President Bush to waive Jackson-Vanik measures temporarily as a reward for the loosening of Soviet emigration restrictions before Bush met with Soviet president Mikhail Gorbachev. Such an action was seen as paving the way for improved Soviet–U.S. trade and for Soviet achievement of most-favored-nation (MFN) trading status.[40] Yet Bush resisted such efforts because of the Soviet Union's failure to meet the goal of an open emigration policy written into Soviet law.

Similar issues were raised with China. In this instance, Bush resisted pressure from Congress to eliminate China's MFN status in the aftermath of its ruthless suppression of the democratic movement during summer 1989. President Clinton faced a similar dilemma, wishing to retain China's MFN status but concerned that China was not moving fast enough to improve its human rights situation.

In general, the political pattern of presidential-congressional relations follows closely that noted for warmaking and other foreign policy areas. The president continues to be the dominant actor, even when Congress attempts to reassert its role in various foreign policy areas. Political initiative typically belongs to the president, but Congress can affect the course of policy meaningfully when it possesses the will.

INTERMESTIC ISSUES

Cheap and plentiful gas and oil supplies were taken for granted in America until 1973, when Arab nations imposed an oil embargo on nations that supported Israel during the Arab-Israeli War of that year. For the first time, Americans recognized the fact of interdependence and the relationship between gasoline prices in the United States and events around the globe. This situation is an example of an intermestic issue, an area in which political patterns between president and Congress resemble those of conventional domestic politics.

One long-standing intermestic policy has been the use of food. Since 1954 the Food for Peace program (also known as P.L. 480) has served the two-fold purpose of providing food for humanitarian, diplomatic, and political purposes abroad and also for providing a means for disposing of domestic agricultural surpluses. The program has expanded in high surplus years and contracted when surpluses were small; in the former instance, the program has provided American farmers with a major subsidy. The Food for Peace program has grown steadily over the years, largely because of domestic political pressure and support from the Foreign Agricultural Service of the Department of Agriculture, relevant agricultural commodity subcommittees, farmers' groups, and shipping interests. Although the program has served an important foreign policy objective, its political impetus lies in conventional interest group politics. In the 1970s an executive-legislative dispute arose over the increasing tendency to use the Food for Peace program abroad to reward political allies and to coax other nations toward greater cooperation with America. Many members of Congress opposed this trend, arguing that the program's purpose should be fundamentally humanitarian. Even though the debate persists, since strategic considerations continue to influence the distribution of food abroad, the program continued to thrive throughout the 1980s (despite budget cutbacks in other foreign aid programs), largely because of solid domestic support for the program.[41]

Domestic political forces also play an important role in trade and tariff policies. American steel and auto manufacturers, and the unions representing workers in these areas, take a keen interest in policies that affect the importation of foreign-made steel and autos. With American jobs apparently at stake, these groups lobby Congress and the president to ensure that they are not driven out of business by foreign competition. This fact was dramatically illustrated in 1993 when, after an intense political effort, President Clinton won passage of the North American Free Trade Agreement (NAFTA), which ends trade barriers between the United States and its North American neighbors.

Fears of American job losses and environmental degradation, among other concerns, prompted the furious opposition of unions, many environmentalists, some farm groups, and even the majority leader and majority whip of Clinton's own political party in the House. Thus in such intermestic issues, vital domestic concerns expressed through conventional domestic political means may shape foreign policy significantly.

Not all intermestic issues involve jobs and the economy. Jewish organizations take a strong interest in America's policy toward Israel. Greek-Americans and Turkish-Americans are represented by groups who work to influence American policy toward those traditionally antagonistic nations. Opponents of abortion have pressed Congress and the president to cut family planning aid to Third World nations that include abortion as a means of limiting population. Civil rights and other African-American groups pressed the U.S. government persistently and with considerable success to toughen America's stand toward the white supremecist apartheid regime ruling South Africa.[42] In all of these intermestic issues, domestic political forces substantially cast the political configuration of foreign policy as it is shaped by the president and Congress.

THE PRESIDENT, CONGRESS, AND INTELLIGENCE

Control over sensitive information pertaining to national security and intelligence matters represents a key source of presidential ascendancy. Virtually all of the intelligence-gathering that occurs is conducted through executive agencies. Executive Order 12333, issued by President Reagan in 1981, listed twelve agencies composing the intelligence community; five are affiliated with the Department of Defense and the rest with the Executive Office of the President or a cabinet agency. They are the Central Intelligence Agency; National Security Agency (NSA); Bureau of Intelligence and Research, Department of State; Defense Intelligence Agency (DIA); Navy Intelligence; Marine Intelligence; Air Force Intelligence; Federal Bureau of Investigation; Department of Energy Intelligence Office; Department of Treasury Intelligence Office; and Staff Elements of the director of Central Intelligence.[43]

In theory, the role of Congress in relation to intelligence is no different from that of other areas. It provides the legal basis for such agencies, approves their budgets, and oversees agency actions. In reality, however, Congress has had little impact on governmental intelligence until the 1970s.[44]

The need for intelligence has always existed, but the executive appetite for information and secrecy accelerated with America's expanded role in international affairs after World War II.[45] In 1947 Congress passed the National Security Act, which created the CIA (its forerunner was the Office of Strategic Services, formed to gather intelligence during the war). Yet Congress paid little attention to the agency or its activities, and other intelligence agencies like the DIA and the NSA were created by executive order. Because funds for these agencies were included in lump sum appropriations, members of Congress were unaware not only of the purposes but also of the actual amounts budgeted. Congressional interest in intelligence was aroused only when embarrassing problems arose, as when the Soviet Union shot down an American U-2 spy plane caught flying over Soviet territory in 1960 and in the aftermath of the disastrous Bay of Pigs invasion in 1961, when a CIA–sponsored invasion of Cuba by anti-Castro Cuban exiles failed. A handful of congressmen were informed of intelligence activities, but they rarely questioned executive priorities. As the chair of one watchdog committee, Sen. John Stennis (D.-Miss.) said, "You have to make up your mind that you are going to have an intelligence agency and protect it as such and shut your eyes and take what is coming."[46]

Congress was finally emboldened to engage itself more actively in intelligence-related matters when it was revealed that both the CIA and the FBI had been involved in illegal surveillance and investigation of Americans (mostly anti–Vietnam War protestors) in the late 1960s and early 1970s at the behest of the Nixon administration and that the CIA had played an active role in the violent overthrow of the popularly elected Allende regime in Chile in 1973. Several important congressional investigations helped bring these activities to light, especially the committee headed by Sen. Frank Church (D.-Idaho) in 1975 and 1976. Executive branch authorization of such activities at home and abroad raised fundamental questions about control over and misuse of the American intelligence establishment.[47]

In 1974, Congress passed the Hughes-Ryan amendment, which required that covert actions of the CIA—that is, operations designed to do more than gather information—be reported to appropriate congressional committees. The act did not have dramatic consequences since the executive was to report "in a timely fashion," and the CIA and the president interpreted this to mean after the conclusion of an operation.

In 1975 President Ford created a special commission to examine CIA activities. Based on the commission's findings, Ford directed the CIA to refrain from engaging in further assassination plots, an action that followed revelations that the CIA had plotted to assassinate Fidel Castro and other heads of government deemed unfriendly. As a result of these revelations, each house of Congress created a permanent Select Committee on Intelligence. Although the jurisdiction of each committee is slightly different, both are designed to provide some meaningful oversight. Each committee has a substantial staff and the power to compel testimony, demand information, and review reports. In addition, the committees exercise control over budgetary authorizations (that is, granting legal permission to spend appropriated money) for intelligence agencies. The concern for secrecy has meant that the committees cannot operate with the same openness as other congressional committees. Despite fears that Congress cannot keep secrets, both committees have favorable records of not disclosing national security information.[48]

To help ensure that the committees would engage in meaningful oversight and would not be co-opted by the intelligence agencies, as had happened in the past, a limit was put on the number of terms a member could serve on the committees, and the committee chair is rotated. In 1980 Congress passed the Accountability for Intelligence Activities Act, which stipulated that the two intelligence committees would be the sole funnels for information about covert activities. It required that the committees be fully informed of all intelligence activities, and it terminated the Hughes-Ryan amendment. Despite wording designed to strengthen and clarify the role of Congress, the act also granted the president wide discretion and freedom of action in covert operations.[49]

Although Congress assumed a more active role in intelligence activities, controversial covert operations continued. In 1981 the Reagan administration began engaging in a large-scale covert program to aid the Contra rebels fighting against the Sandinista regime in Nicaragua, and in December of that year the administration informed the intelligence committees of their support for the Contras. In 1982 Congress enacted for the first time an amendment aimed at curtailing Reagan's support for the Contras. Successively stronger amendments were enacted in 1983, 1984, and 1985 and were attached to authorization and appropriations bills. Twelve amendments appearing in six pairs of authorization and appropriations bills were known collectively as the Boland amendments, named after Cong. Edward Boland (D.-Mass.), their prime sponsor. The strongest wording was enacted in 1984 (attached to P.L. 98–473), and it barred all military and covert-related assistance to the Contras during fiscal year 1985 originating from the CIA, Defense Department, "or any other agency or entity of the United States involved in intelligence activities . . . for the purpose or which would have the effect of supporting, directly or indirectly, military or paramilitary operations in Nicaragua by any nation, group, organization, movement, or individual." Despite the inclusive nature of the wording, the Reagan administration argued during the Iran-Contra congressional hearings that it did not apply to the covert activities of the National Security Council (NSC), then under investigation.[50]

In 1985 and 1986 the administration succeeded in gaining from Congress permission to extend some support to the Contras. Yet in 1986 information also began to surface indicating that several of Reagan's National Security advisers and other members of the administration had been involved with an off-the-books operation to fund the Contras covertly by selling arms to Iran and using the profits to purchase weapons for them, despite the congressional ban. The revelations prompted Reagan to appoint a three-member board in November 1986 to investigate NSC operations. The three members, former senator and secretary of state Edmund Muskie, retired lieutenant-general Brent Scowcroft, and former senator John Tower (the group's head), were hamstrung by time and staff limitations and by a limited mandate. The Tower Commission Report was completed three months later.[51]

Throughout summer 1987, a joint House-Senate committee co-chaired by Sen. Daniel Inouye (D.-Hawaii) and Cong. Lee Hamilton (D.-Ind.), both former Intelligence Committee chairs, conducted its own hearings as part of a larger and more thorough investigation of the Iran-Contra affair. The committee majority report concluded that members of the NSC and other individuals (including private businesspeople) had consciously attempted to circumvent the law both through misuse of the NSC and private means. The political sting accompanying the revelations was sharpened because the scheme had included selling arms to Iran, an avowed enemy of the United States that was in the market for weapons to help in its protracted war with Iraq. Moreover, the activities represented an abuse of covert operations. In short, the findings against the Reagan administration included:

- violating the law—the Boland amendments—and America's stated foreign policy by funneling funds and other assistance to the Contras through other nations or private individuals;[52]
- disobeying legal reporting requirements to Congress about the covert activities. In particular, President Reagan issued a secret executive order in January 1986 authorizing the sale of American arms to Iran by the CIA. The purpose of the sale was to obtain the release of American hostages being held in Lebanon.[53] Reagan directed CIA director William Casey not to inform Congress of the order, which learned of the deal ten months later when a Lebanese newspaper broke the story.[54] According to the Intelligence Oversight Act of 1980, the president was required to report all such executive orders to Congress in a "timely fashion."[55] Reporting procedures within the executive branch were also circumvented;
- violation of antiterrorist laws and the administration's stated policy of

refusing to deal with terrorists for release of hostages. An administration report on terrorism released in 1986 had asserted that the United States "will make no concessions to terrorists. It will not pay ransoms, release prisoners, change its policies or agree to other acts that might encourage additional terrorism";[56]

- attempting to cover up the illegal activities by lying to Congress, shredding documents, and erasing computer memories.[57]

Congress' lengthy investigation did not, however, resolve all the pertinent questions. Subsequent charges leveled in the press claimed that the congressional investigation consciously avoided paths of inquiry that might have led to Reagan's impeachment. According to one participant in the committee inquiry, "We don't want to go after the President" because of Reagan's continued popularity, his advanced age, and the impending end of his term of office and because of a desire to avoid any inquiry that might disrupt negotiations with the Soviets.[58] The congressional effort was criticized for rushing to complete the inquiry, for failing to obtain Reagan's telephone logs, calendars, and computer-stored memos, and for failing to follow up on information suggesting that Reagan knew of the connection between the Iran arms deal and aid for the Contras.[59] In addition, it was severely criticized for granting immunity to Oliver North and John Poindexter during congressional hearings. The subsequent convictions of North and Poindexter were overturned on appeal because of the court's concern that the convictions might have been tainted by the immunity-covered testimony.[60]

One key fact about the Iran-Contra scandal is that it spanned the entire eight years of the Reagan presidency; without doubt, aiding the Contras was a priority goal of his administration. A second fact is that the endeavor was sweeping in its scope, involving a panoply of administration people and several foreign countries. A third is that it raises a central question about the entire venture: How much did Reagan know about the affair? We may never have a satisfactory answer to this question, but his desire to aid the Contras undoubtedly led to the violation of law and to the subversion of the separation of powers between president and Congress.[61] In his final report on the affair, special prosecutor Lawrence Walsh provided clear evidence—based in part on the diaries of former secretary of defense Caspar Weinberger and former secretary of state George Schultz—that impeachment grounds could have been marshaled against Reagan and that George Bush (contrary to his denials) was fully informed of the arms sales while serving as vice-president.[62]

At the same time, the Iran-Contra affair dramatized Congress' continuing difficulty in influencing the conduct of covert operations and in having a meaningful role in an intelligence process that is structured to serve the president. One potentially important agreement arising from Iran-Contra was reached between Congress and President Bush in 1989, when the latter agreed to define "timely notice" as within "a few days," except under unusual circumstances. The agreement, expressed in a letter, was the culmination of months of negotiations and was finally completed after Congress began moves to enact a definition legislatively.[63]

Despite its renewed efforts in the 1970s and 1980s, Congress continues to be handicapped because of its lack of involvement with, and influence over, the NSC, which has acquired principal control over the formulation and coordination of national security matters. Some observers have suggested that nominees for National Security adviser be subject to congressional ratification. Other suggestions have surfaced as well, but few significant reforms have been enacted.[64]

CONCLUSION

The distribution of powers between the executive and legislative branches outlined in the Constitution pertaining to foreign affairs verifies the sentiment that the president and Congress possess equivalent wisdom in directing the nation's course in international affairs. Yet the path of foreign policy from 1789 to the present is anything but a straight line since the realm of foreign policy has come to be accepted, with important exceptions, as primarily the domain of the president.

No piece of information more nicely summarizes this conclusion than the dramatic rise in executive agreements. Treaties on important subjects continue to appear on the Senate agenda, but they are no longer the primary means for conducting business, important or otherwise, with other countries. This evolution may be a necessary adaptation to America's modern role in a complex world—as may be the case with House involvement in the treaty process—but it also means a shift in the way president and Congress do business. Unless Congress is prepared to surrender its foreign affairs responsibilities entirely, the principle of separation of powers impels it to adapt appropriately, as it has attempted to do through such acts as the War Powers Resolution and the Case Act. In no other realm is it more clear that "the president claims the silences of the Constitution."[65] Congress will continue to hold a vested interest in policies and action pertaining to arms sales, foreign aid, intermestic issues, and intelligence activities. Its interest may consist merely of endorsing the president's proposals—an acceptable outcome but only if congressional acceptance is based on adequate information and time—or of reordering presidential priorities.

Though Congress continues to possess the capability to play a major role in foreign affairs, recent history demonstrates vividly what happens when one branch of the government abandons separation of powers and interbranch checks. The Iran-Contra affair may be taken as a classroom case of one-branch government in operation. Quite simply, the individuals in the executive branch who hatched and carried out the bizarre scheme—and it was bizarre, not only because it was illegal but also because it had so little chance of succeeding—formulated, enacted, and judged the plan within the confines of the National Security Council (including the CIA) in the basement of the White House.

Impatient with congressional and popular objections to Contra aid, individuals in the Reagan administration simply decided that their judgment was correct, Constitution-be-damned. According to a former staff director of the Senate Intelligence Committee, the CIA and other intelligence chiefs in the government of the 1970s differed from those of the Reagan administration in that the former were " 'so immersed in the constitutional questions that they could recite chapter and verse. Questions of law and balance occurred naturally to them.' By contrast, the Reagan leadership was dominated by 'advocates, people who were always trying to get around the roadblocks, who were looking for a way to get it done.' "[66] Commenting on Iran-Contra, Theodore Draper observed that "if ever the constitutional democracy of the United States is overthrown we now have a better idea how this is likely to be done."[67]

In short, an American foreign policy that is monopolized by the executive branch is liable to be more efficient but entirely at odds with the tenets of the American governing system. The concern for efficiency was, of course, one reason why the office of president was created and vested with authority in foreign affairs. Yet legislative involvement is no less vital a part. The sacrifice of some efficiency was readily accepted by the Founders in exchange for the necessary and important judgment of the legislative branch. It is, as has been often said, a cost of democracy. As James Madison presciently observed, "There can be no liberty where the legislative and executive powers are united in the same person."[68]

Many people have pondered this dilemma and the ways through which an appropriate balance between the branches might be struck. One thoughtful response was generated by Warren Christopher, President Clinton's secretary of state, who proposed "a new 'compact' between the Executive and Congress on foreign policy decision-making, based on mutually reinforcing commitments and mutually accepted restraints.''[69] Christopher's compact is predicated on the distinctive characteristics and capabilities of the two branches. It calls for (1) affirmation of the president's authority to articulate and manage foreign policy; (2) full executive cooperation with Congress in the latter's efforts to fulfill its foreign policy obligations, especially through the appropriations process and as a forum for generating and discussing ideas; (3) renewal of bipartisanship in foreign policy; (4) an acknowledgment by both Congress and the president that the government must provide sufficient resources for diplomatic and foreign aid efforts; and (5) acknowledgment that American foreign policy cannot operate as efficiently as that of undemocratic nations.[70]

The compact is important because it accepts, and works to operate within, the constitutional framework while also allowing for the more complex, dynamic, and executive-centered nature of contemporary American foreign policy. One cannot help but conclude that American foreign policy will operate best when it strikes a balance between democracy and efficiency. And that means working within the constitutional framework of shared powers, which is to say striking a balance between the executive and legislative branches.

NOTES

1. For more on the presidential-congressional balance in foreign and domestic affairs, see Robert J. Spitzer, *President and Congress: Executive Hegemony at the Crossroads of American Government* (New York: McGraw-Hill, 1993).

2. Max Farrand, *The Records of the Federal Convention of 1787* (New Haven: Yale University Press, 1966), 2:393; see also pp. 547–48.

3. See *Federalist 64, 69, and 75*, in *The Federalist*, ed. Edward Mead Earle (New York: Modern Library, 1937).

4. Louis Henkin, *Foreign Affairs and the Constitution* (New York: Norton, 1972), p. 131.

5. *Federalist*, p. 486. For an excellent discussion of the joint nature of the treaty power, see Louis Fisher, "Congressional Participation in the Treaty Process," *University of Pennsylvania Law Review* 137 (May 1989): 1511–22.

6. Quoted in Charlene Bangs Bickford and Kenneth R. Bowling, *Birth of the Nation: First Federal Congress 1789–1791* (New York: The First Federal Congress Project, 1989), p. 88.

7. See Larry Berman, *The New American Presidency* (Boston: Little, Brown, 1986), pp. 36–37.

8. See James A. Robinson, *Congress and Foreign Policy-Making* (Homewood, Ill: Dorsey Press, 1967), pp. 67–69.

9. Louis W. Koenig, *The Chief Executive* (New York: Harcourt Brace Jovanovich, 1986), pp. 205–6; Congressional Quarterly, *Guide to the Congress* (Washington, D.C.: Congressional Quarterly, 1971), p. 202; Fisher, "Congressional Participation in the Treaty Process," p. 1517.

10. See Spitzer, *President and Congress,* p. 197.

11. Cecil V. Crabb and Pat M. Holt, *Invitation to Struggle* (Washington, D.C.: CQ Press, 1989), pp. 13–14.

12. Louis Fisher, *Constitutional Conflicts Between Congress and the President* (Princeton, N.J.: Princeton University Press, 1985), p. 269.

13. This argument is made by David Gray Adler, *The Constitution and the Termination of Treaties* (New York: Garland, 1986), pp. 342–43.

14. *Goldwater v. Carter,* 444 U.S. 996 (1979).

15. Ibid, at 1007. For a discussion of the origins of the president's recognition power, see Adler, Chapter 5 of this volume.

16. According to Adler, the ten cases of presidential termination occurred in 1911, 1927, 1933, 1939, 1939, 1941, 1944, 1954, 1962, and 1985. The congressional cases occurred in 1865, 1874, 1883, 1915, 1936, 1951, and 1976. The two instances involving the Senate alone were 1856 and 1921. See *Constitution and Termination of Treaties,* pp. iv, 190, and 238. For more on treaty termination, see "Termination of Treaties: The Constitutional Allocation of Power," Committee on Foreign Relations, U.S. Senate, 95th Cong., 2d sess., December 1978 (Washington, D.C.: Government Printing Office, 1979).

17. Bernard Roshco, "The Polls: Polling on Panama—Si, Don't Know; Hell No!" *Public Opinion Quarterly* 42 (Winter, 1978): 551–62.

18. These and other basic facts are drawn from Crabb and Holt, *Invitation to Struggle,* chap. 3.

19. William L. Furlong, "Negotiations and Ratification of the Panama Canal Treaties," in *Congress, the Presidency and American Foreign Policy,* ed. by John Spanier and Joseph Nogee (New York: Pergamon Press, 1981), p. 78.

20. Crabb and Holt, *Invitation to Struggle,* p. 91.

21. Richard M. Pious, *The American Presidency* (New York: Basic Books, 1979), p. 338. A similar conclusion was reached by George D. Moffett III, who noted that despite the fact that Carter dealt "from a position of unusual strength," the victory "came at a debilitatingly high political price" (*The Limits of Victory: The Ratification of the Panama Canal Treaties* [Ithaca, N.Y.: Cornell University Press, 1985], pp. 9, 11). See also William L. Furlong and Margaret E. Scranton, *The Dynamics of Foreign Policymaking: The President, the Congress, and the Panama Canal Treaties* (Boulder, Colo.: Westview Press, 1984).

22. This account is drawn from Stephen J. Flanagan, "The Domestic Politics of SALT II: Implications for the Foreign Policy Process," in Spanier and Nogee, eds., *Congress, the Presidency and American Foreign Policy,* chap. 3. See also John Spanier and Eric M. Uslander, *American Foreign Policy Making and the Democratic Dilemmas* (New York: Holt, Rinehart and Winston, 1985), pp. 204–17.

23. See James Meernik, "Presidential Support in Congress: Conflict and Consensus on Foreign and Defense Policy," *Journal of Politics* 55 (August 1993): 569–87.

24. This was stated in *United States v. Pink,* 315 U.S. 203, at 230 (1942). For an analysis of *Pink,* see Adler, Chapter 1 of this volume.

25. See Fisher, *Constitutional Conflicts,* pp. 272–83.

26. See Spitzer, *President and Congress,* p. 208.

27. Bernard Schwartz, *A Commentary on the Constitution of the United States,* 2 vols. (New York: Macmillan, 1963), 2:150.

28. Quoted in ibid, 2:150–51. A useful scheme for understanding the distinctions between treaties and agreements can be found in Loch K. Johnson, *The Making of International Agreements* (New York: New York University Press, 1984), p. 7.

29. See Lawrence Margolis, *Executive Agreements and Presidential Power in Foreign Policy* (New York: Praeger, 1986).

30. See Benjamin I. Page and Mark P. Petracca, *The American Presidency* (New York: McGraw-Hill, 1983), pp. 269–70. The greater presidential reliance on executive agreements is discussed in Loch Johnson and James M. McCormick, "Foreign Policy by Executive Fiat," *Foreign Policy* 28 (Fall 1977): 117–38.

31. Robert E. DiClerico, *The American President* (Englewood Cliffs, N.J.: Prentice-Hall, 1990), p. 47. See also James W. Davis, *The American Presidency* (New York: Harper and Row, 1987), p. 216.

32. Johnson, *Making of International Agreements*, pp. 123–31.

33. See Harvey G. Zeidenstein, "The Reassertion of Congressional Power: New Curbs on the President," *Political Science Quarterly* 93 (Fall 1978): 397.

34. Spanier and Uslander, *American Foreign Policy Making*, pp. 12, 47, 88.

35. This account is taken from Robert J. Spitzer, *The Presidential Veto* (Albany, N.Y.: SUNY Press, 1988), pp. 94–96.

36. For more on the Saudi arms deal and other arms sales, see Bruce W. Jentleson, "American Diplomacy: Around the World and Along Pennsylvania Avenue," in *A Question of Balance*, ed. Thomas E. Mann (Washington, D.C.: Brookings Institution, 1990), pp. 161–66.

37. See Dan Caldwell, "The Jackson-Vanik Amendment," in Spanier and Nogee, eds., *Congress, the Presidency and American Foreign Policy*, chapter 1.

38. Jeane Kirkpatrick, "Human Rights and American Foreign Policy: A Symposium," *Commentary*, November 1981, pp. 42–45.

39. See, for example, Alan Tonelson, "Human Rights: The Bias We Need," *Foreign Policy* 49 (Winter 1982–83): 52–74.

40. Ronald D. Elving, "Hill Is Pressing Jackson-Vanik," *CQ Weekly Report*, December 2, 1989, p. 3311. Among other things, MFN status would reduce duties on Soviet goods.

41. Randall B. Ripley and Grace A. Franklin, *Congress, the Bureaucracy, and Public Policy* (Chicago: Dorsey Press, 1987), pp. 190–91.

42. See Jentleson, "American Diplomacy," pp. 156–61.

43. See 17 *Weekly Comp. Pres. Doc.* 1336–48 (December 7, 1981). For more on these organizations, see David Wise and Thomas B. Ross, *The Invisible Government* (New York: Random House, 1974); Jeffrey T. Richelson, *The U.S. Intelligence Community* (Cambridge, Mass.: Ballinger, 1985). See also Hoffman, Chapter 12 of this volume.

44. For more on this relationship, see Ripley and Franklin, *Congress, the Bureaucracy, and Public Policy*, chap. 7, and Christopher J. Deering, "National Security Policy and Congress," in *Congressional Politics*, ed. Deering (Chicago: Dorsey Press, 1989).

45. For more on the executive branch's obsession with secrecy and deception, see John M. Orman, *Presidential Secrecy and Deception* (Westport, Conn.: Greenwood Press, 1980). See also Gregory F. Treverton, *Covert Action: The Limits of Intervention in the Postwar World* (New York: Basic Books, 1987); Loch K. Johnson, *America's Secret Power* (New York: Oxford University Press, 1989).

46. Quoted in Frank Kessler, *The Dilemmas of Presidential Leadership* (Englewood Cliffs, N.J.: Prentice-Hall, 1982), p. 110.

47. See "Alleged Assassination Plots Involving Foreign Leaders," Interim Report of the Senate Select Committee to Study Government Operations with Respect to Intelligence Activities, no. 94–465, 94th Cong., 1st sess. (Washington, D.C.: Government Printing Office, 1975).

48. See Crabb and Holt, *Invitation to Struggle,* chapter 6, and Gregory F. Treverton, "Intelligence: Welcome to the American Government," in Mann, ed., *A Question of Balance,* pp. 78–80.

49. DiClerico, *American President,* pp. 48–52.

50. Joel Brinkley and Stephen Engelberg, eds., *Report of the Congressional Committees Investing the Iran-Contra Affair* (New York: Random House, 1988), p. 414.

51. *Arms for Hostages: The Official Report of the President's Special Review Board* (New York: Bantam Books, 1987).

52. Some individuals in the Reagan administration argued that Congress could not control foreign affairs by withholding appropriations and that if Congress did so, the president could continue to pursue his goals by soliciting private funding. These arguments are demolished in Louis Fisher, "How Tightly Can Congress Draw the Purse Strings?" *American Journal of International Law* 83 (1989): 758–66, and Fisher, Chapter 8 of this volume.

53. The background paper accompanying Reagan's directive, written by Oliver North, said that "this approach . . . may well be our *only* way to achieve the release of the Americans held in Beirut. . . . If all of the hostages are not released after the first shipment of 1,000 weapons, further transfers would cease" (quoted in Treverton, "Intelligence," p. 86).

54. The story appeared in a Lebanese weekly newspaper called *Al-Shiraa* on November 3, 1986.

55. Quoted in DiClerico, *American President,* p. 51. See also Johnson, *America's Secret Power,* pp. 224–25.

56. "Vice President's Task Force on Combatting Terrorism," *Public Report* (Washington, D.C.: Government Printing Office, 1986), p. 7.

57. Administration lies are summarized in David Hoffman, "The Political Sleights of the Contra Scandal," *Washington Post National Weekly Edition,* April 24–30, 1989.

58. Seymour M. Hersh, "The Iran-Contra Committees: Did They Protect Reagan?" *New York Times Magazine,* April 29, 1990, p. 64. See also Joel Brinkley, "The Cover-Up That Worked: A Look Back," *New York Times,* January 23, 1994.

59. Hersh, "Iran-Contra," pp. 47ff. See also Steven Waldman, "The Committee That Couldn't Shoot Straight," *Washington Monthly,* September 1988, pp. 43–50.

60. David E. Rosenbaum, "A Scandal That Fell Flat," *New York Times,* January 19, 1994.

61. This argument is carefully summarized in an episode of "Frontline," a television news and public affairs series broadcast on the Public Broadcasting System, entitled "High Crimes and Misdemeanors," hosted by Bill Moyers, broadcast November 11, 1990.

62. David Johnston, "Reagan Had Role in Arms Scandal, Prosecutor Says," *New York Times,* January 19, 1994; Peter Kornbluh and Malcolm Byrne, "Where the Bodies Are Buried," *New York Times,* January 19, 1994.

63. Stephen Engelberg, "Bush to Tell Congress of Covert Plans," *New York Times,* October 28, 1989. See also Johnson, *America's Secret Power.*

64. Harold Hongju Koh, "Why the President (Almost) Always Wins in Foreign Affairs: Lessons of the Iran-Contra Affair," *Yale Law Journal* 97 (June 1988): 1257–58. For more on Iran-Contra, see *The Iran-Contra Puzzle* (Washington, D.C.: Congressional Quarterly, 1987), and Frederick M. Kaiser, "Cause and Conditions of Inter-Branch Conflict: Lessons from the Iran-Contra Affair," paper delivered at the 1989 Annual Meeting of the American Political Science Association, Atlanta, Ga., August 31–September 3.

65. Pious, *American Presidency,* p. 333.

66. Quoted in Treverton, "Intelligence," p. 81. This attitude was reflected by Reagan who, according to former National Security Adviser Robert C. McFarlane, had "disdain" for Congress (reported in "High Crimes and Misdemeanors," PBS).

67. Quoted in Kornbluh and Byrne, "Where the Bodies Are Buried."

68. *Federalist 47,* p. 302.

69. Warren Christopher, "Ceasefire Between the Branches: A Compact in Foreign Affairs," *Foreign Affairs* 60 (Summer 1982): 998.

70. Ibid., pp. 999–1004.

4

PRESIDENTIAL PREROGATIVE AND THE SPIRIT OF AMERICAN CONSTITUTIONALISM

DONALD L. ROBINSON

In recent years, American constitutional theory has been agitated by debates about whether presidents do or do not have "prerogative."[1] The question is unlikely ever to be settled, for reasons I shall explain, but it cannot be ignored, for it raises an issue that goes to the heart of the American commitment to constitutional government and points to some crucial unfinished business on the agenda of American constitutionalism.[2]

The issue is this: What are the limits, if any, on a president's authority to act on behalf of the United States in the absence of law, or in defiance of it—that is, to exercise prerogative? And, if there are limits, what recourse other than impeachment does the nation have to prevent abuses or to punish those individuals who exercise prerogative without adequate justification?

The recent constitutional debate centers not so much on the claim that certain passages in the Constitution explicitly authorize a president to act without or against lawful authority but on the possibility that certain clauses were "intended" to leave that possibility. Thus, commentators do not debate, for example, the power of the president to pardon convicted persons but whether the vesting clause, or the presidential oath, or a president's duties as commander-in-chief might qualify his responsibility to "take Care that the Laws be faithfully executed," as Article II, section 3 of the Constitution directs.

It helps, in framing this debate, to recall the tradition underlying American constitutionalism. Its epitome is found in John Locke's *Second Treatise of Government,* in which Locke articulates a theory for constitutional monarchy. Locke is not a doctrinaire thinker. He is at pains to relate his ideas to political reality. Thus, alongside his insistence that the exercise of governmental power must be subject to the rule of law, he admits two bits of awkwardness: a power, distinct from "legislative" and "executive," called "federative," and mention of the need for "prerogative."

In defining the federative power (distinguished by Locke from the executive, though he notes that they were usually exercised by the same person), Locke contends that relations between nations take place in a zone close to anarchy. In these circumstances, he argues, it is unwise to bind the prince in every instance to "antecedent, standing, positive laws." In the conduct of relations with foreign nations, a nation must rely on the "prudence" of the prince and not try to bind him to law in the same way it does when he is exercising power within his own country.[3]

Locke's doctrine of prerogative goes even further. It is not confined to foreign affairs. He argues that, because it is impossible to foresee all accidents and because laws, if executed with inflexible rigor, may cause unintended and unnecessary harm, the executive must be permitted to do "many things . . . which the laws do not prescribe." Indeed, prerogative includes the power to act *against* law. It covers situations where laws do not yet exist (prelegal), where laws must be ignored (antilegal), and where there can be no law (alegal). Furthermore, Locke insists that prerogative is "undoubted," by which he apparently means that no common citizen and no sensible lawyer or theorist questions the authority of princes—indeed, their responsibility—to transcend the law, or to proceed in its absence, in order to serve the public good.[4]

How much influence did Locke's political ideas have in America? A slippery debate rages around that question,[5] but what seems beyond doubt is that his notions of constitutional engineering had less influence than his teaching about the foundations of civil government and the right to revolution (reflected, for example, in the Declaration of Independence). Specifically, there is no evidence that Locke's ideas about the federative power, or about prerogative, had any positive influence whatsoever at the Constitutional Convention of 1787. On the contrary, the "take-care" clause, with its uncharacteristically emphatic phrasing (the president shall *take care* that the law be *faithfully* executed), bears eloquent witness that the convention, dominated by lawyers, intended to brook no nonsense to the effect that the chief executive would have power to suspend, ignore, or transcend the rule of law. Monarchs claimed the power to act without lawful warrant, or even against it, whenever they discerned an emergency. The American chief executive was to obey the laws strictly and faithfully, carrying out their mandate energetically and without reservation.

To put the point another way, it seems that Locke's realism was not persuasive to most of the American Framers. On the other hand, it was not entirely lacking, either. Alexander Hamilton, for example, in *Federalist 23,* wryly notes that the world of nations will not tailor its demands to the capacities of a nation's preferred system of governance. Thus, republics (democracies, as we would call them) face the same opportunities and dangers as nations led by tyrants. We may prefer "open covenants, openly arrived at," but we must cope with cynical types who commit all sorts of skullduggery and do not wait for the polite exchange of diplomatic notes before starting hostilities. In context, Hamilton's argument is a plea to assign plenary powers to the federal government (rather than to the states), especially in foreign relations and national security, but its relevance to relations between the legislative and executive powers seems obvious. If so, Hamilton may have come close to the kind of expansiveness about governmental power that is willing to suffer prerogative. Yet even he, at least during this pre-Constitutional period, did not openly avow it.[6]

What is remarkable, however, is how quickly these men of the Founding generation, even the most Whiggish among them, found themselves taking actions not mandated by law in the realm of foreign relations. The first president, George Washington, was above all a scrupulous adherent to the rule of law.[7] As commander-in-chief of the American army during the War for Independence, for example, he had often put himself and his troops to great distress rather than assume power that Congress had been unable or unwilling to give him. As president, however, in conducting relations with the Indians, he had boldly used his command over military forces and his responsibility for negotiations with tribal leaders to mold American policy.[8] He apprised leading members of Congress of what he was doing, and he was certainly constrained by his sense of what his fellow-politicians in Congress would support. Nevertheless, he exercised considerable discretion. His conduct was not a matter of executing the laws. There was, in fact, hardly any relevant law on the matter (except tiny military appropriations) to execute.

In 1800 executive power passed to the leader of the opposition, Thomas Jefferson. He had campaigned for the presidency on a platform of "strict construction," a promise to restore the federal government to constitutional bounds, narrowly construed. Once in office, however, Jefferson discovered an opportunity to purchase from France, on irresistible terms, the port of New Orleans (the key to the Mississippi and Missouri river valleys) and the vast territory of Louisiana. The difficulty was that there was no constitutional authority to make such an acquisition. Jefferson hesitated and fretted for a while, deeply concerned about the precedent he was setting, but eventually he did what he had to do: he made the purchase. It is important to recognize that at no time in this episode did Jefferson assert his authority to act without the cooperation of Congress. On the contrary, Congress actively participated in the purchase by appropriating money for the negotiators and by passing a statute approving it. Meanwhile, several congressional leaders joined with the president in an anguished search for a way to repair what Henry Adams later called a "fatal wound to 'strict construction.'" In the end, Jefferson realized that even an ex post facto amendment to the Constitution would not make the purchase completely constitutional.[9]

A leading modern historian of these developments, Arthur M. Schlesinger, Jr., insists that they do not create a justifying precedent for modern presidents who invoke the doctrine of prerogative. Drawing on the diligent research of Judge Abraham Sofaer (who served during the Reagan administration as legal counsel to the State Department), Schlesinger points out that, although the first four presidents often employed military forces without explicit authorization in law, none of them claimed an inherent right to evade legislative accountability and the sanction of law. Paying the homage that pragmatism owes to principle, they performed their acts of warmaking in consultation with Congress.[10]

The distinction Schlesinger draws between the early and modern practice of prerogative is fair enough: whereas earlier presidents acted almost apologetically and kept in close informal contact with congressional leaders, modern presidents and their apologists perform their acts of prerogative boldly, often triumphantly, all the while insisting that they are following good constitutional doctrine.[11] He is wrong, however, I think, when he insists that the "pattern" of these early departures from strict constitutional orthodoxy has no bearing on modern practice. What early practice reveals—and modern experience routinely confirms—is that the Constitution has a blind spot. When modern apologists draw these earlier actions into precedent, they are showing that the performance of a president's responsibilities under the Constitution has never been possible without such behavior. Thus, modern presidents exercise the powers they deem necessary to their purposes, and they find precedents for their use. To be sure, doctrine and practice have evolved and grown more casual, but that is not unique to this area of governance.

One other antebellum precedent must be mentioned because it is so often cited in justification of modern presidents and because it anticipates modern practice so perfectly. In the winter of 1845–1846, following the annexation of Texas, President Polk moved American troops to southern Texas, into territory contested between the United States and Mexico. By April, skirmishes were leading to real fighting, and on April 25, eleven Americans were killed in battle. Declaring that "Mexico has shed American blood on American soil," Polk called on Congress to declare war. A few Whigs, including young Cong.

Abraham Lincoln, resisted. In a letter to a friend back home in Illinois, Lincoln insisted that the Framers intended that *"no one man* should hold the power" to take this nation to war (Lincoln's emphasis). Nevertheless, on May 13, the House declared war (the Senate had done so a day earlier). Vainly did Cong. Garrett Davis of Kentucky protest that it was "our own president who began this war." Yet even in this case, Polk did not doubt that he needed congressional action to legitimate his decision to apply military force.

We are dealing in this chapter primarily with prerogative in its bearing on foreign policy. It is worth noting that, more generally, prerogative is the power to deal with emergencies, and the greatest emergency in American history happens to have been a domestic struggle: the Civil War. Lincoln's performance as guarantor of the Constitution took him far beyond the bounds of constitutional orthodoxy. He suspended the writ of habeas corpus; he imposed a blockade on southern ports; he raised troops on his own authority; he directed his personal agents to spend public funds for military supplies. These were acts of "dictatorship," no less so for being undertaken in response to "a popular demand and a public necessity," as Lincoln put it in his special message to Congress. Lincoln's great example of course is drawn into precedent by apologists for modern presidents who act without lawful authority and in defiance of Congress, even though in Lincoln's case, as in Jefferson's, Congress gave ex post facto legitimation to the president's acts.[12]

During the twentieth century, the United States began to take its place as a world power. As Tocqueville had so astutely anticipated, this development precipitated a shift in the constitutional balance between Congress and the president. During World War I, Woodrow Wilson became Clinton Rossiter's second great exemplar (after Lincoln) of "constitutional dictatorship," for his exercise of emergency powers. Franklin Delano Roosevelt, steering the nation through the great international depression and then into and through World War II, was the third.[13]

Ever since the Citizen Genet affair, no one has questioned that the president and his agents must conduct the nation's foreign relations, whatever bounds Congress might set on the policy directing these relations. He appoints and dismisses ambassadors. His agents negotiate treaties of commerce and alliance. His speeches give authoritative articulation to the nation's foreign policy. As commander-in-chief, he directs the forces that give the ultimate response when the nation's vital interests are threatened.

Still, until the middle of the twentieth century, Congress had the means to resist presidential leadership when it was so inclined. Foremost was the legislature's exclusive constitutional authority to raise military forces and to appropriate funds for their support. Buttressing this power of the purse was the tradition against "entanglement" in foreign alliances. So long as the nation had no standing army to speak of and popular opinion was implacably opposed to involvement in European and Asian affairs (Central America was always a different matter), presidents had neither the means nor the political inclination to exercise their "almost royal prerogatives" in foreign affairs.[14]

All of this changed at mid-century, in the space of about five years. Roosevelt, steeped in these earlier traditions, assumed that the United States would very soon revert to its earlier isolationism when World War II ended. That is one reason he stubbornly resisted getting "roped into" Winston Churchill's plan to resist Stalin's ambitions for Eastern Europe. America's postwar planners did take the lead in building the United Nations, but it was conceived as a multilateral body, not an alliance centering on American military power.

When the ill-prepared Harry S. Truman suddenly acceded to the presidency, he inherited a terrible dilemma. His military commanders were inescapably responsible for the occupation of Japan and Germany, but the pressure for demobilization was immediate and intense. In addition, it soon became clear that Communists, spearheaded by the Soviet Union, were extending their influence into Europe and Asia. American military and diplomatic leaders, alarmed by this prospect and its implications for national security, began to concoct countermeasures, including alliance systems with provisions for mutual defense.

There ensued, in the late 1940s, a great national debate, the upshot being a decision to create a new system of worldwide alliances and to mount powerful military forces—a standing army—to back it up. Note that the alliances, beginning with the North Atlantic Treaty Organization in 1949, came first. The military forces were not immediately forthcoming.

The turning point came when Truman led the United Nations and the United States to war in Korea in June 1950. Certainly the decision to go to war sprang from a national consensus that was widely shared at the time. Its breadth is fairly indicated by the vote in favor of a resolution presented by Sen. Arthur Vandenburg (R. Mich.), a leading member of the Foreign Relations Committee and a major spokesman for isolationist opinion in the late 1930s. Vandenburg's resolution called for regional, collective-security arrangements to resist Communist aggression, and it passed on July 11, 1948, by vote of 64 to 4. Similar resolutions, aimed at Communist aggression in Europe and Asia, routinely and resoundingly passed through both houses of Congress in 1949 and 1950.

As this bipartisan foreign policy consensus solidified, it remained to be decided who now had the authority to determine when and where to take the nation to war. The Framers had made Congress full participants in that power, but Truman in 1950 took the position that the American responsibility to the United Nations was controlling and that it was his responsibility to give effect to that commitment. In point of fact, Article 43 of the UN Charter calls upon member nations to make troops available to the Security Council "on its call and in accordance with a special agreement or agreements." Article 43 further stipulates that special agreements must spell out the number and type of forces and be ratified "in accordance with [the contributing nations'] respective constitutional processes." The United Nations Participation Act, passed by Congress in 1945, authorizes the president to enter into special agreements, "subject to the approval of the Congress by appropriate act or joint resolution." Dean Acheson, testifying as undersecretary of state before the House Committee on Foreign Affairs, said, "It is entirely within the wisdom of Congress to approve or disapprove whatever special agreement the president negotiates." Until both houses of Congress accept a special agreement, said Acheson, "it has no force and effect."[15]

At the time of Truman's decision, in June 1950, to send an American army to Korea, it fell to Sen. Robert Taft (R.-Ohio) to argue that the president's action had no legal or constitutional justification. Prevailing opinion, backed by a chorus of learned argumentation from advocates of presidential prerogative, held that Taft's interpretation of the Constitution was old-fashioned, mean-spirited, and wrong.[16] And so we went to war—without a formal declaration and without adequate military forces. The latter deficiency was supplied in part by the resuscitation of a National Security Council blueprint called NSC-68. The design was for troop strength and weapons to wage the Cold War, not just in East Asia but in Europe and elsewhere around the world as well. Written in winter and early spring 1950, it was languishing on a White House shelf until the Korean emergency dramatized its argument: that the undertakings of our alliances and treaty commitments far exceeded our capacity to back them up.[17]

To repeat: that was the turning point. From 1950 onward, presidents claimed the authorization, in treaties and in a deeply convinced public opinion, to undertake the defense of "freedom-loving," Western-oriented peoples everywhere. They also had the means—standing military forces: no fewer than 2 million men and women in arms, equipped with nuclear weapons and rockets and airplanes that could deliver devastation anywhere on the globe on very short notice. Combined with the president's constitutional powers of military command and his responsibility for the conduct of foreign relations, these new commitments and capabilities changed the constitutional balances, creating new opportunities and demands for the exercise of presidential prerogative.

The question: Would the system's checks and balances, under these radically altered circumstances, still operate to keep the exercise of military power accountable, as American constitutionalism demands?

The courts, for their part, have given little encouragement to litigants who complained that the Constitution assigns no prerogative to presidents. On the contrary, the courts have sometimes gone out of their way to give judicial backing to presidential claims. The most spectacular example is *United States v. Curtiss-Wright Export Corporation* (1936) which involved a claim that President Roosevelt had exercised too much discretion in imposing a blockade against shipments of arms to the Chaco region in South America. The Court ruled that the congressional resolution authorizing the president's order did not delegate power unconstitutionally.

The case is remembered, not for its result, but for the Court's opinion, written by Justice George Sutherland. It went far beyond the need to defend the legislation upon which Roosevelt's action was based. Sutherland's dicta asserted that the conduct of foreign relations was inherent in sovereignty, that it was by nature executive, and that it existed prior to and independent of the Constitution.[18] In light of this understanding, constitutional provisions that qualified the executive's responsibility for foreign relations, such as the Senate's power to confirm ambassadorial appointments and to consent to treaties and the power of Congress to declare war, should be construed narrowly, as exceptions to the plenary power a president has by virtue of the executive powers vested in him.

Sutherland's opinion and the theory it presented have been ridiculed by historians and other commentators. They point out, among other criticisms, that nothing like it was ever broached by the Founders of the Constitution and that Sutherland's invocation of the authority of John Marshall is based on a misreading of a speech he gave in the House of Representatives.[19] One might add that, had Sutherland's interpretation of presidential powers been suspected during the ratification debates of 1787–1788, advocates of ratification would surely have had to disavow them or doom their project to defeat. (It is significant that Sutherland does not cite Hamilton's speeches at the convention or his essays in the *Federalist Papers*. If anyone among the founders had been sympathetic to such a doctrine, it would have been Hamilton.)

Even more remarkable than the bizarre content of Sutherland's opinion, however, is the fact that it has never been explicitly disavowed by the Supreme

Court. To be sure, it is rarely drawn into precedent by the courts. In fact, courts have sometimes allowed Congress to proceed on the opposite assumption: that powers in foreign relations that the Constitution assigns to Congress—such as the power to regulate international commerce, to define the rules for naturalization, and to punish piracy and offenses against the law of nations—should be construed generously and may be exercised aggressively, as part of the ongoing struggle for control over foreign policy that the Constitution is said to invite.[20]

There is also clear evidence that some justices view presidential powers very differently from Sutherland. Perhaps the most important statement of this more limited view is Justice Robert Jackson's concurring opinion in *Youngstown Sheet and Tube v. Sawyer* (1952), the steel seizure case decided during the agonized last spring of Harry Truman's presidency.[21] The owners' suit against Truman's taking of the mills, after Congress had refused the president's request for statutory authority to do so, brought before the Court the executive's claim that, in a national emergency, the president has "inherent" power and responsibility under the Constitution to do whatever is necessary to protect national security. The "opinion of the Court," written by Justice Hugo Black, gave no notice to this claim or to the alleged national emergency. It simply asserted that the order to seize the mills was "like legislation," but that, inasmuch as the Constitution gave Congress the power to legislate, the president had acted beyond his authority.

Jackson, in his concurrence, was more expansive. "Presidential powers," he wrote, "are not fixed but fluctuate, depending on their disjunction or conjunction with those of Congress." When a president acts pursuant to congressional authorization, express or implied (as in *Curtiss-Wright*), "his authority is at its maximum." When he acts in the absence of legislative authorization, he is in a "zone of twilight," where he and Congress may have concurrent authority or where the distribution of authority is uncertain. When he acts in defiance of the express or implied will of Congress (as here, according to the Court's majority), "his power is at its lowest ebb."[22] If the Court finds that the power in question is assigned by the Constitution to Congress, the president must show how the circumstances displace the Constitution. In concurring, Jackson concluded that Truman's solicitor general had not sustained that burden in this case, despite the fact that the nation was at war and the president insisted that the seizure of the mills was necessary to the prosecution of that war.[23]

Earlier, Justice Jackson had another occasion to comment on the danger of presidential "war powers" (a term he deeply distrusted, by the way).[24] Dissenting angrily from the Court's acquiescence in the internment of Japanese-Americans during World War II, he warned:

> If the people ever let command of the war power fall into irresponsible and unscrupulous hands, the courts wield no power equal to its restraint. The chief restraint upon those who command the physical forces of the country, in the future as in the past, must be their responsibility to the political judgments of their contemporaries and to the moral judgments of history.[25]

This is the modern, secular equivalent of Locke's "appeal to heaven."

American constitutional doctrine requires something more. It requires accountability for the exercise of power, and it depends on checks and balances to ensure that accountability. Thus, when presidents Eisenhower, Kennedy, Johnson, and Nixon gradually took this nation to war in Vietnam, without congressional authorization, and kept it there for several years, there was a strong popular reaction, though the courts consistently refused to provide any recourse. Suits were unavailing, whether brought by young men seeking to avoid service in an undeclared war or by members of Congress pleading that their constitutional powers were being usurped. The courts found sometimes that congressional appropriations were tantamount to a declaration of war; or they concluded that individual members of Congress, or small groups of members, could not act for the whole body in challenging the president's warmaking. Finally, they demurred from second-guessing Nixon's strategy for ending the conflict.[26] The effect of these demurrals, taken together, was to confirm Jackson's conclusion that the courts would not call the president to account for making war.[27]

Congress, during this period, was a good deal less supine. The institutional incentives to check the president were long delayed, but they did finally come into play. Legislative checks were terribly difficult to invoke, and they worked imperfectly, but Congress did try to extricate the nation from a war to which a succession of presidents, through their own dereliction, had committed us.

A few examples of the congressional effort will suffice to indicate its character and assess its effect. In 1973, over Nixon's veto, Congress passed the War Powers Resolution. The resolution is relevant here because it did not contradict—indeed, it confirmed—that the president had prerogative to take the nation to war without a congressional declaration. The product of intensive negotiations between lawyers representing the two branches, it presented itself as a clarification of constitutional provisions relating to warmaking, not as an attempt to restrict presidents. Indeed, in granting that the president had authority on his own to commit forces to hostilities, many critics thought it ceded authority where none had previously existed. In any case, the resolution declared that, if possible, the president should "consult Congress" before committing armed forces to situations that were potentially hostile. It required the president to report to Congress within forty-eight hours whenever he sent troops into such danger, and it said that, unless Congress affirmed the commitment of forces within sixty days, the president would have just thirty additional days to withdraw them.

In his veto message, Nixon not only called the resolution unwise but also warned that the attempt to alter the president's powers "by legislation alone is clearly without force."[28] The implication of Nixon's position—that a president might disregard such legislation, presumably unless and until the Supreme Court took the side of Congress as to its constitutionality—was restated by President Bush in a speech at Princeton May 10, 1991: "On many occasions during my presidency, I have stated that statutory provisions that violate the Constitution have no binding legal force."[29] According to this position, when the commander-in-chief moves troops abroad or when he orders them to fight back if attacked, he acts on powers vested in him by the Constitution; and he is not bound by the Constitution to consult with or report to anybody, nor is he under any time limit to remove troops. Presidents since Nixon have usually been less blunt, but each of them, from Ford and Carter to Reagan and Bush, has challenged the resolution's constitutionality and flouted its requirements (some more flagrantly than others).[30]

Congress has also been concerned about covert actions. Secret initiatives not only evade accountability to the law but also have sometimes proceeded without the president himself being fully informed. Accordingly, in 1974, Congress adopted the Hughes-Ryan amendment, requiring that, whenever a president deems that covert action is necessary to national security, he must prepare a "finding" to that effect and submit it in "timely" fashion to an appropriate congressional committee. In 1975, hearings by a Senate select committee chaired by Frank Church (D.-Idaho) revealed many activities by intelligence services that did not stand up to scrutiny, leading Congress to organize committees in each house for surveillance of intelligence activities. In 1980, Congress adopted a comprehensive Intelligence Oversight Act.[31]

The stage was finally set for better accountability. Or was it? If the abuses of the Johnson and Nixon years could be remedied by "framework" legislation there might have been progress toward the restoration of accountability under the Constitution.[32] But memories are short. New occupants of the White House are not much impressed by tales of earlier scandals. Framework legislation accepted by presidents only with severe reservations cannot prevail over a determination to pursue policies that cannot be publicized, for one reason or another, policies that presidents believe they are empowered by necessity and by the accumulated authority of their office to undertake.

Thus, President Reagan sent armed forces to El Salvador, Lebanon, Grenada, and Libya, ignoring reporting requirements of the War Powers Resolution. Each time, a few lonely voices questioned the constitutionality of the president's actions, trying vainly to be heard amid the chorus of national self-congratulation that the Vietnam syndrome was behind us. In Lebanon, in October 1983, the ghastly slaughter of 240 U.S. Marines serving in support of a doomed policy might have led to deeper questioning, but the wails of agony were quickly drowned out by the invasion of Grenada. Hardly anyone, it seemed, had any stomach to renew the unresolved debates of the 1970s. Time after time, comforting statements from the White House to the effect that a quick engagement would do the trick were enough to spike the guns of heavy constitutional disputation.

The climax of this lawlessness came with the Iran-Contra affair. While proclaiming that it would never make deals with terrorists, the Reagan administration secretly arranged the sale of arms to the Islamic regime in Iran, identified by the State Department as a prime instigator of terrorism, in the dizzy hope of winning the release of American hostages. Meanwhile, profits from this clandestine commerce were making their way to Nicaragua to support the Contra rebels, in circumvention of a series of amendments offered by Cong. Edward Boland (D.-Mass.) intended to block the supply of American assistance to the Contras. It later turned out that the administration was flouting the amendments, not only by redirecting the profits from arms sales to Iran but also by soliciting funds from private citizens and from other governments.

Foreign policy thus was being framed and implemented by covert actions—hidden, it turned out, even from the State and Defense departments and sometimes even from the president himself—and supported by means that bypassed the congressional power of the purse. It was prerogative run riot. It came to light only when an obscure Middle Eastern journal published a report of the sale of arms to Iran, and the attorney general acknowledged that some of the profits had been diverted to Nicaragua. A presidential commission, after a hasty inquiry, admitted that the Reagan administration's management methods were slipshod but recommended against any fundamental reform of institutions or new statutory authority. A special, bicameral congressional investigation tried to find out who was responsible for the fiasco but soon found itself on the defensive in its questioning of Oliver North, the National Security Council official who had directed the operation. The congressional committee constrained itself with an impossibly short schedule and showed little appetite for an inquiry that might reach the question of impeachment. Meanwhile, a special prosecutor was appointed to prepare indictments for any criminal behavior, but his investigation too was inhibited by grants of immunity to principals who had testified before the congressional committee and by litigation aimed at undermining its legitimacy.

In short, the system showed itself utterly incapable of coming to grips with an affront to constitutionality even so gross as the Iran-Contra affair. Nowhere was the issue joined over the contradictory assertions of constitutional authority advanced by the executive and legislative branches.[33] Is the president free to support rebels abroad if Congress enacts legislation to prevent that support? May the president seek funds elsewhere if Congress refuses to appropriate them?[34] The election of Vice-President Bush to the presidency suggested that the electorate had no strong political opinion that the actions of the Reagan-Bush administration were wrong. Indeed, the Republicans could well conclude that they at least politically were vindicated by the results of the 1988 election.

A graver and more lasting consequence of this aborted investigation is that Congress is left uncertain of its authority. Traditionally the power of the purse seemed to ensure that the legislative branch could terminate any activity that cost money to implement. It often seemed that a power so blunt and so cataclysmic could hardly be used, but its existence was never before questioned. The Iran-Contra affair leaves it very much in doubt.

The troubled state of constitutional accountability continued into the Bush administration. When Iraq attacked Kuwait in August 1990, the president decided very quickly, on his own authority, to meet the challenge with American military force. Almost no one raised any constitutional objection to the president's decision. Bush's responsibility to "respond to sudden attack" was not questioned. We have grown accustomed to the notion that our responsibilities as a world power extend the cover of that presidential power to areas of the world deemed vital to American and allied security. The president seemed well within his prerogative in August.

By October, however, we were crossing a decisive new line, and few people seemed to notice. The Bush administration decided that we needed to expand American forces in the Arabian peninsula in order to give us an "adequate offensive military option," in the president's phrase, to cope with Saddam Hussein's aggression.[35]

Why was this decision made on the president's authority alone? It placed the nation squarely on the road to war. Certainly there was sufficient time for a debate in Congress and a deliberate, joint decision. We were in the midst of midterm elections, however, and neither the president nor the congressional leadership seemed eager to force such a debate at that time.[36] So the debate was finessed, by tacit, mutual consent, and an announcement of troop buildup was delayed until after the elections.

During November and December the president assembled an international coalition in support of his policy and obtained resolutions of approval from the United Nations. He then set a deadline for the withdrawal of Iraqi troops from Kuwait and prepared for war.[37] At this point, in January 1991, Congress finally organized a debate on a resolution to support the use of military force if necessary to dislodge Iraq from Kuwait. The debate concluded with a narrow though decisive affirmation. War quickly ensued, and victory was shortly won by the anti-Iraq coalition, led by the American president.

Immense relief at the apparently satisfactory conclusion obscured the fact that the president had taken the nation to war by the exercise of his authority as commander-in-chief. It must be acknowledged, on the president's behalf, first, that he proceeded for the most part openly and candidly,[38] and, second, that Congress was at least a coconspirator in avoiding a full-scale debate before January 1991.[39] Furthermore, although the president later insisted that he had power to begin war in the Persian Gulf without an affirmative vote from Congress, it seems likely that he would have proceeded differently if the vote in January had gone against him.[40]

Even after one has granted these points on behalf of the argument that the president acted constitutionally, however, it is reasonably clear that the episode will contribute to the alleged precedents that seek to justify presidential prerogative, at the expense of constitutional mechanisms that reinforce accountability.[41] Certainly Bush seemed intent upon leaving this residue. During a campaign appearance in New Hampshire on the first anniversary of Desert Storm, he asserted, "When I moved those forces [to the Persian Gulf], I didn't have to ask Senator Kennedy or some liberal Democrat whether we were going to do it. We just did it."[42] Judging by accounts of the administration's decisionmaking that led to the war against Iraq, this was not an idle boast,[43] and its tone may reveal more about the prevailing understanding of the Constitution than all the carefully crafted briefs emanating from the White House.[44]

President Bush emerged from the war against Iraq with enormous prestige, and he was quick to use it to restate the case for presidential power. In a major address at Princeton University, just weeks after the surrender of Iraq, he spoke of the president's responsibility for "guiding and directing the nation's foreign policy." (He did disavow that presidents were at liberty "to keep Congress unnecessarily [*sic*] in the dark.") He complained that a hyperactive Congress often interfered with the discharge of the president's grave responsibility for foreign relations, and he charged that a recent piece of legislation, which he had vetoed, would have made the president "disclose a wide variety of sensitive diplomatic contacts and discussions" and resulted in a "dangerous timidity and disarray in the conduct of U.S. foreign policy."[45] He was presumably talking about a provision in the intelligence authorization bill for 1991 that would have required the president to disclose all "requests" from third parties, other countries, or private sources for assistance in mounting covert action. The provision in the legislation may have been stated too broadly, but the need to bring "indirect" covert action to the harness of the constitutional system is clear. Why was this elaborately negotiated piece of legislation (the president's veto was apparently unexpected) so carelessly worded? Its veto brought the post–Iran-Contra reform effort back to the starting gate, a full four years after the affair first came to light.

The argument of the chapter can be briefly summarized. The Framers and ratifiers of the Constitution of the United States intended that Congress alone make the decision to commit this nation to war. They did so despite a philosophical tradition, epitomized in Locke's *Second Treatise,* that insisted that the rule of law could not apply to foreign relations as it did to domestic affairs, that executives must have discretion to act without statutory authority, particularly in foreign relations. Events in America soon showed the wisdom of Locke's theory, but the defect of the Constitution (that its distribution of war powers erected mere "parchment barriers" against presidential prerogative, that it gave to the president, in de Tocqueville's phrase, "almost royal prerogatives") was obscured by the lack of a standing army, requiring presidents to obtain troops from Congress whenever they contemplated a significant military undertaking. When, in 1950, the nation committed itself to a massive standing army and to a worldwide network of mutual-defense treaties, the wraps on presidential warmaking came off. Congress presumably retained its power to control foreign relations by stopping or qualifying its authorizations and appropriations, but the president's command of troops, of the attention of the people through the media, and of means to raise funds from sources other than the public treasury gave him a tremendous advantage. The experience of Johnson and Nixon in Vietnam showed that presidents cannot sustain a costly and ill-defined war indefinitely; but Reagan (in Lebanon, El Salvador, Grenada, Nicaragua, the Persian Gulf, and Libya) and Bush (in Panama and the Persian Gulf) demonstrated that presidents, without any formal action by Congress, could take the nation to war without bringing the constitutional checks and balances into play.

Where does this leave us, as a nation committed to constitutional democracy? Arthur Schlesinger, Jr., pleads for a restoration of "comity" between the branches, and Harold Koh calls for new "framework" legislation and a watchdog agency, headed by independent lawyers.[46] Such proposals cannot bear fruit without a deep and abiding popular determination to rein in the presidency, but if that existed, new statutes and agencies would be unnecessary.

The problem is constitutional. It is inherited from the Founding period; it is a problem ducked, not solved, by the convention of 1787. Locke was right about the rule of law in its bearing on foreign relations. Laws may not adequately regulate foreign policymaking; it plays by different rules. If Congress is going to check and balance the president's warmaking, it must have greater *political* leverage. Statutory authority will not suffice.

The key to constitutional democracy is shared power. Thus we are left with this question: short of an "appeal to heaven," how can we force reluctant presidents to share their power, especially when they fear that Congress does not share their outlook on the national interest? The existing constitutional provisions are unavailing.

NOTES

1. An outstanding recent contribution is Thomas S. Langston and Michael Lind, "John Locke and the Limits of Presidential Prerogative," *Polity* 24 (Fall 1991): 49–68. Notes to this article cite the principal antecedent articles and books.

2. I acknowledge, with gratitude, the criticism of friends who read earlier drafts of this paper: David Gray Adler, Dean Alfange, Louis Fisher, and David Mervin.

3. John Locke, *Two Treatises of Government*, ed. Peter Laslett (Cambridge: Cambridge University Press, 1960), *Second Treatise*, sect. 147–48, pp. 365–66.

4. Ibid., chap. 14, pp. 374–80. For a recent analysis, see Langston and Lind, "John Locke," pp. 54–61. For an unusually sensible and comprehensive analysis of "crisis government in the modern democracies," see Clinton Rossiter, *Constitutional Dictatorship* (1948 rpt., New York: Harcourt, Brace and World, 1963).

5. A recent contribution is Oscar and Lilian Handlin, "Who Read Locke? Words and Acts in the American Revolution," *American Scholar* 58 (1989): 545–56. See also Donald L. Robinson, *"To the Best of My Ability": The Presidency and the Constitution* (New York, W. W. Norton, 1987), pp. 22–26, for a discussion of Locke's influence on the Framers of the presidency. See also pp. 28–31, on the thought of William Blackstone. There is substantial concurrence between Locke and Blackstone on the discretion of the executive, and Blackstone was considerably more influential, especially among the young lawyers who took a leading role in framing the Constitution.

6. Clinton Rossiter, *Alexander Hamilton and the Constitution* (New York: Harcourt, Brace and World, 1964).

7. In his eulogy for Washington, Jefferson remarked that Washington had enabled a nation, "new in its form and principles," to settle down into a "quiet and orderly

train," chiefly by "scrupulously obeying the laws through the whole of his career, civil and military" (quoted in Clinton Rossiter, *The American President* (New York: Harcourt, Brace, 1960), p. 93).

8. James Thomas Flexner, *Washington: The Indispensable Man* (New York: New American Library, 1974), pp. 250–55. For fuller accounts of Washington's relations with Indian tribes, see Reginald Horsman, *Expansion and American Indian Policy, 1783–1812* (East Lansing: Michigan State University Press, 1967), chaps. 5 and 6, and Francis Paul Prucha, *The Great Father: The United States Government and the American Indians* (Lincoln: University of Nebraska Press, 1984), especially pp. 52–57.

9. This story is told, with a delicious sense of irony, by the great-grandson of John Adams, the man Jefferson defeated in 1800. See Henry Adams, *History of the United States During the Administrations of Jefferson and Madison,* 2: chaps. 1–5; the relevant portions are conveniently available in an abridgment edited by George Dangerfield and Otey M. Scruggs (Englewood Cliffs, N.J.: Prentice-Hall, 1963), 1:57–77 (the reference to the "fatal wound" is on p. 75 of the Prentice-Hall edition).

10. Arthur M. Schlesinger, Jr., Introduction, in Abraham D. Sofaer, *War, Foreign Affairs and Constitutional Power: The Origins* (Cambridge, Mass.: Ballinger, 1976), p. xx.

11. George Bush boasted, during a campaign swing in New Hampshire, that he didn't have to have the permission of pygmies like Sen. Edward M. Kennedy (D.-Mass.) when he went to battle with Saddam Hussein.

12. Arthur M. Schlesinger, Jr., *The Imperial Presidency* (1973; rpt., Boston: Houghton-Mifflin, 1989), p. 64.

13. Rossiter, *Constitutional Dictatorship,* chaps. 16–28.

14. The quoted phrase is from Alexis de Tocqueville, *Democracy in America,* ed. and abr. Richard D. Heffner (New York: New American Library, 1956), p. 81.

15. See Chapter 14 of this volume. Fisher notes that amendments to the UN Participation Act adopted in 1949 permit the president on his own initiative to provide American military forces for "cooperative action" but only to serve as observers and guards, in a noncombatant capacity, and in numbers not to exceed 1,000 troops. These provisions obviously do not cover the action undertaken in Korea in 1950. Indeed, they would seem to be an attempt to reinforce the safeguards against it.

16. For a sample of this sentiment, see Arthur M. Schlesinger, Jr., "The Prerogatives of the Commander-in-Chief," in *The President: Roles and Powers,* ed. David Haight and Larry Johnson (Chicago: Rand McNally, 1965), p. 353. This valuable collection also includes a speech by Senator Taft, an essay by Henry Steele Commager taking Schlesinger's side, and an anguished rejoinder by Edward S. Corwin, calling the "high-flying prerogative men" to account. For Schlesinger's mea culpa, see *Imperial Presidency,* pp. 285–86.

17. Paul Y. Hammond, "NSC–68: Prologue to Rearmament," in *Strategy, Politics, and Defense Budgets,* ed. Warner Schilling, Paul Y. Hammond, and Glenn H. Snyder (New York: Columbia University Press, 1962), pp. 267–378.

18. *U.S. v. Curtiss-Wright,* 299 U.S. 299, at 315–29.

19. See Charles A. Lofgren, *Government from Reflection and Choice* (New York: Oxford University Press, 1986), pp. 167–205; see also, David Gray Adler, "The Constitution and Presidential Warmaking: The Enduring Debate," *Political Science Quarterly* 103 (1988): 1–36, especially pp. 30–34. A forthcoming book by Adler promises to be a definitive analysis of this important Supreme Court decision and its consequences.

20. Edward S. Corwin, *The President: Office and Powers,* 4th ed. (New York: New York University Press, 1957), p. 171. For a discussion of opportunities for Congress to legislate aggressively and effectively to curb presidential abuse of war powers, see Harold Koh, *The National Security Constitution* (New Haven: Yale University Press, 1990), pp. 123–33. Both Koh (especially chapter 5) and Louis Henkin, *Constitutionalism, Democracy, and Foreign Affairs* (New York: Columbia University Press, 1990), pp. 29–31, emphasize that the constitutional authority of Congress to legislate restrictions on foreign policy cannot be doubted.

21. Koh exaggerates when he says that Jackson "firmly rejected *Curtiss-Wright*" (*National Security Constitution,* p. 112), but his analysis of Jackson's "now-classic concurring opinion, . . . so familiar to first-year law students," is insightful (pp. 107–13).

22. *Youngstown Sheet and Tube v. Sawyer,* 343 U.S. 579, at 635–37.

23. Ibid., at pp. 647–49.

24. Koh, *National Security Constitution,* p. 110.

25. *Korematsu v. United States,* 323 U.S. 214 (1944), at 248.

26. Robinson, "To the Best of My Ability," pp. 244–45. See also Christopher H. Pyle and Richard M. Pious, *The President, Congress, and the Constitution* (New York: Free Press, 1984), pp. 350–51; cf. p. 361.

27. Professors Koh (Chapter 6 of this volume) and Henkin (*Constitutionalism,* pp. 81–91) severely chide the courts for their reluctance to pass judgment on claims that the president has exceeded his constitutional authority in foreign affairs. See Adler, Chapter 1 of this volume.

28. 9 *Weekly Comp. Pres. Doc.* 1286 (October 24, 1973). For a discussion of the War Powers Resolution see Keynes, Chapter 9 of this volume.

29. 27 *Weekly Comp. Pres. Doc.* 591b (May 13, 1991).

30. For further discussion, see Keynes, Chapter 9 of this volume.

31. Schlesinger, *Imperial Presidency,* pp. 451–52. See also Spitzer, Chapter 3 of this volume.

32. Professor Koh presents the case for "framework" legislation in *National Security Constitution,* pp. 166–81. See also, Koh, Chapter 6 of this volume.

33. This is the central point of Professor Koh's book, *National Security Constitution;* see especially chapter 1.

34. For an explanation of these issues, see Fisher, Chapter 8.

35. The decisionmaking process at the White House is described in Bob Woodward, *The Commanders* (New York: Simon and Schuster, 1991), pp. 318–20. The quoted phrase is from Bush's news conference of November 8, 1991, and is printed in Micah L. Sifry and Christopher Cerf, eds., *The Gulf War Reader* (New York: Random House, 1991), p. 229. For a detailed analysis of the legality of Bush's action, see Keynes, Chapter 9 of this volume.

36. The preparations for war did not go entirely unnoticed in the press. In late October 1990, the *New York Times* carried two stories reporting on efforts by congressional leaders to warn the administration not to take the nation to war without congressional authorization (October 25, p. A12, and October 31, p. A16); and the Op-Ed page carried two pieces devoted to the subject, one on October 22 by Anthony Lewis and another one October 30 by Gary Stern of the American Civil Liberties Union.

37. Again, there was speculation in the press about whether a congressional debate would be forthcoming (see, for example, Susan Rasky, "Congress and the Gulf," in

the *New York Times,* December 17, p. A1), but the president and the secretaries of state and defense insisted that the administration did not need congressional approval to go to war; congressional leaders, for political reasons, were not willing to force the issue at this point. For an explanation of Bush's invocation of UN authorization as a legal basis for his unilateral efforts, see Fisher, Chapter 14 of this volume.

38. Sifrey and Cerf, eds., *Gulf War Reader,* records a wide-ranging public debate throughout fall and winter 1990. The president's public announcements were not always timely, but Congress and the nation knew what he was doing. The fault was not so much that he was deceptive or that Congress had no opportunity to stop him but that he proceeded as if he felt it unnecessary to gain the formal support of Congress before proceeding; and Congress, by its failure to call him to account, seemed to acquiesce.

39. The *New York Times,* in mid-December, carried a story about congressional anxiety to avoid getting drawn into a "premature" debate over hypotheticals.

40. Speech at Princeton University, May 10, 1991, 27 *Weekly Comp. Pres. Doc.* 590b (May 13, 1991).

41. For a detailed analysis of the list of unilateral presidential acts of warmaking that purport to establish "precedential authority," see Francis D. Wormuth, "The Vietnam War: The President versus the Constitution," in *The Vietnam War and International Law,* ed. Richard Falk (Princeton, N.J.: Princeton University Press, 1969), 711–808.

42. *New York Times,* January 16, 1992, p. A16.

43. Woodward, *Commanders,* passim. See also Theodore Draper, "Presidential Wars," in the *New York Review of Books,* September 26, 1991, pp. 64–74, and "The True History of the Gulf War," in the *New York Review of Books,* January 30, 1992, pp. 38–45. For a critique of Draper, see the letter by David B. Rivkin, Jr., and Lee A. Casey, in the *New York Review of Books,* November 21, 1991, pp. 56–57; also, by the same authors, "xxx," *Foreign Affairs* (Summer 1991): xxx.

44. The war in the Persian Gulf produced a new outpouring of scholarly debate over the war powers. Notable were Michael J. Glennon, "War and the Constitution," *Foreign Affairs* (Spring 1991): 84–101 (see a reply by David B. Rivkin, Jr., and Lee A. Casey, *Foreign Affairs* (Summer 1991): 150–53); and two articles by Theodore Draper, "Presidential Wars," pp. 64–74, and "The True History of the Gulf War," *New York Review of Books,*, January 30, 1992, pp. 38–45 (see a reply to Draper by Rivkin and Casey in the November 21, 1991, issue, pp. 56–57).

45. 27 *Weekly Comp. Pres. Doc.* 591b (May 13, 1991).

46. Schlesinger, *Imperial Presidency,* p. 406, and Koh, *National Security Constitution,* pp. 157, 169–71, passim.

5
THE PRESIDENT'S RECOGNITION POWER

DAVID GRAY ADLER

The power of recognition has been exercised by presidents of the twentieth century as an instrument of high prerogative to make and conduct the foreign policy of the United States.[1] The exercise of this power rarely has engendered criticism or controversy. The practice scarcely has been questioned. Indeed, there is a prevalent assumption that the president may use the power "to receive Ambassadors" as a rudder with which to steer the Ship of State.[2]

At international law, the act of receiving an ambassador of a foreign government entails certain legal consequences. The reception of an ambassador constitutes a formal recognition of the sovereignty of the state or government represented. Without mutual recognition, generally speaking, governments are not free to engage in diplomatic intercourse. Lassa Oppenheim, an eminent international law commentator, has observed:

> As the basis of the Law of Nations is the common consent of civilized states, statehood alone does not imply membership in the Family of Nations. Those States which are members are either original members because of the Law of Nations which grew up gradually between them through custom and treaties, or they are members having been recognized·by the body of members already in existence when they are born. A State is, and becomes, an International person through recognition only and exclusively.[3]

Mindful of this, and other consequences of recognition under international law, presidents in this century, unlike those in the nineteenth, have seized the reception clause as a discretionary means by which they could direct the course of American foreign policy.[4] Though commentators and politicians have debated the relative merits of acts involving the use of the recognition power, there has not been, since the nineteenth century, serious challenge to an unrestricted presidential power to determine what is perhaps the most basic foreign policy question: whether and with which countries the United States will have diplomatic relations.[5] It has thus become an accepted prerogative of the president that, when bolstered by various opinions of Supreme Court justices,[6] has become, as Raoul Berger has observed, "a towering structure."[7]

This discretionary authority, when coupled with vast presidential claims to other foreign affairs powers—such as the war power and the power to conclude executive agreements—has given the executive a virtual monopoly over the conduct of foreign policy. Yet this state of affairs seems quite inconsistent with the Framers' distribution of the constitutional power regarding the conduct of American foreign relations. That distribution, according to Abraham D. Sofaer, former legal adviser to the State Department, provided "that Congress was to have the final say in foreign and military affairs."[8] Indeed, Alexander Hamilton, a favorite among extollers of a strong presidency, assured the ratifiers in the New York Ratification Convention that the Senate "together with the President, are to manage all our concerns with foreign nations."[9] The claims advancing a presidential prerogative over the conduct of foreign policy have been examined elsewhere and are beyond the competence of this study.[10] In this chapter the concern is only with the scope of the president's power of recognition. Specifically, does the reception clause confer upon the president a discretionary authority to determine whether and with which nations the United States shall have relations?

As demonstrated by the writings of Alexander Hamilton, James Madison, Thomas Jefferson, and others in the context of the debate surrounding Pres. George Washington's neutrality proclamation in 1793, the recognition clause was hardly viewed as a fountainhead of presidential power. On the contrary, the reception of ambassadors was understood as a routine, mechanical function, an almost dutiful act devoid of discretion on the part of the recognizing state or government. As I shall argue, the recognition clause was drafted against a background of international law presuppositions that clearly shaped the Framers' understanding of its nature. In no small way is this understanding attributable to the great influence on the Framers of the Swiss publicist Emmerich de Vattel, particularly, and, to a lesser degree, that of the Dutch jurist, Cornelius Van Bynkershoek. Moreover, given the Framers' fear of executive prerogative[11] and their consequent constitutional scheme to cabin and enumerate presidential powers,[12] as well as their decision to vest the principal authority to formulate and conduct American foreign policy in the treatymaking power, there was no reason to view the reception clause as a source of discretionary authority for the president. In fact, Article II, section 3 of the Constitution emphatically declares: "He *shall* [not "may"] receive Ambassadors and other public Ministers," an injunction that stands in sharp contrast with the discretionary constitutional powers that the president *may* choose to exercise, such as the decision to "convene both Houses" of Congress.[13]

RECOGNITION AT INTERNATIONAL LAW

On the eve of the Constitutional Convention, a settled understanding prevailed among international law commentators of the right, on the one hand, of a sovereign nation to send ambassadors, and a duty, on the other, to receive them. A brief examination of the evolution of this understanding indicates that its modern origins may have extended as far back as the sixteenth century and its roots, perhaps, to the Second Punic War.[14]

It appears that Pierino Belli, whose book, *A Treatise on Military Matters and Warfare*, was published in 1563, may have been the first publicist to consider the question.[15] Belli assumed a right of embassy but addressed it only indirectly. Examining the issue of the right of an ambassador to safe conduct, Belli noted that such a "right" is not written in the law "because, when something is allowed, we take for granted permission also for a preliminary that is essential to it, and without which the privilege would be nugatory; thus, where the drawing of water or the right of burial has been granted, we assume that the right to travel for either purpose is allowed also."[16] From Belli's perspective, then, the right of safe conduct is the "preliminary that is essential" to the right of embassy. Or, in other words, without the "privilege" of safe conduct, the right of embassy would be "nugatory."

Writing his seminal book in 1625, *The Law of War and Peace*, Hugo Grotius, justly known as the Father of International Law, stated: "Now there are two rights of ambassadors which we see are everywhere referred to the law of nations. The first is that they be admitted; the second that they be free from violence."[17] With respect to the admission of ambassadors, Grotius refers to Livy's report of how Hanno, a Carthaginian senator, sharply criticized Hannibal: "Our excellent commander has not admitted to his camp ambassadors coming from allies, and in behalf of allies. He has broken the law of nations." But Grotius observed that the "right" to send ambassadors is not absolute; ambassadors may be rejected on three grounds. First, there is no duty imposed on a government to receive an ambassador from a nation with which it is at war. Second, a government is not required to receive an ambassador whom it finds personally repugnant. Such a rejection does not terminate relations between the governments since another ambassador, perhaps less repugnant, can be sent in his stead. Finally, an ambassador whose underlying motive is to foment rebellion or otherwise "stir up the people" may be rejected as well.[18]

The most penetrating, detailed, and extended analysis to date of the right of legation came from the pen of the distinguished eighteenth-century Dutch jurist, Cornelius Van Bynkershoek. Perhaps the leading positivist of his day, Bynkershoek published *On Questions of Public Law* in 1737, which not only anticipated the views toward recognition held by his contemporaries—Christian Wolff and Emmerich de Vattel—but, seemingly, also provided the intellectual basis of the American doctrine of recognition as illustrated in the writings of Hamilton, Madison, and Jefferson.[19] As we shall see, Bynkershoek held that the right of a nation to send ambassadors is a function of its sovereignty. Its sovereign capacity, or its effective possession of territory and governmental functions alone, imposes a duty on other nations to receive its ambassadors. There is virtually no discretion in this regard for the receiving state; its recognition of the de facto power of the sending state, regardless of its relative legitimacy, closes the matter.

"Among writers on public law," observed Bynkershoek, "it is usually agreed that only a sovereign power has a right to send ambassadors." Thus, "if the prince who sends them is independent, they are accorded full rights of envoys; if the prince is not independent, the position of the envoys is left to the decision of the prince to whom they have been sent." The lack of "independence" or sovereign capacity implies a discretionary power with respect to the question of receiving ambassadors. But there is no such discretion if the ambassador is sent by a "sovereign power." There is only a duty to receive the ambassador.

Yet how is a state to determine whether a sending government is actually sovereign, as, for example, in a state torn by civil war? The question, as far as Bynkershoek is concerned, centers on "which faction retains the governmental functions; if one part has them wholly as they were, and this part does not need the consent of the other to perform the duties of government, this alone has the right of legation, and the representatives of this part are fully competent to act as envoys."[20] The test, then, is one of "effectiveness"; possession of the "governmental functions" carries with it the right of legation. This doctrine of de facto recognition precludes even the slightest consideration of whether the prince "holds his sovereignty by just title, or whether he has acquired it unjustly." Rather, "it is sufficient for those who receive the embassy that he is in possession of sovereignty."[21]

It was left to Wolff and Vattel, both Groatians, to supply—or at least to state directly what probably had been assumed all along—the basis for the right of legation: the necessity of nations to communicate with each other in an interdependent world.[22] Wolff, a German philosopher, wrote *The Law of Nations Treated According to a Scientific Method* in 1749, but it was not widely read.[23] Thus, Vattel, an admirer of Wolff's work, took it upon himself to "popularize" his work, which he did in his celebrated classic, *The Law of Nations,* published in 1758.[24]

"Nations," according to Wolff, "have a perfect right to send ambassadors to other nations."[25] This "perfect right," which is premised on the "self-evident" need of nations to treat with one another in order to consider "the many interests of state," cannot "be forbidden without wrong, nor can its request be harshly treated." The duty to receive ambassadors, moreover, is rooted in the law of nature. Wolff stated: "The necessity of dealings with each other carries with it a necessity for embassies without which dealings are impossible. Each, therefore, has a sufficient reason in the nature itself of nations, by which the law of nations is unalterably established. He who understands these points clearly, as they are understood if the points proved before should be carefully considered, can have no doubt of the right to send ambassadors."

Although legation is described as a "perfect right," Wolff nevertheless conceded two exceptions adduced by Grotius. First, an ambassador may be rejected "who is sent to disturb the peace." Second, an ambassador "who is guilty of treason" may be rejected. Apart from these exceptions, however, legation is not a matter of choice. Indeed, even an enemy should be received.[26]

During the Founding period and well beyond, Vattel was, in the United States, the unsurpassed publicist on international law.[27] Indeed, it has been observed that "when the law of nations is referred to, . . . its principles are to be understood in the sense in which Vattel defined them."[28] Writing in 1913, Charles Fenwick, a leading expert on the subject in his day, assessed the impact of Vattel's celebrated treatise, *The Law of Nations,* remarking:

> A century ago not even the name of Grotius himself was more potent in its influence upon questions relating to international law than that of Vattel. Vattel's treatise on the law of nations was quoted by judicial tribunals, in speeches before legislative assemblies, and in the decrees and correspondence of executive officials. It was the manual of the student, the reference work of the statesman, and the text from which the political philosopher drew inspiration. Publicists considered it sufficient to justify and give conclusiveness and force to statements as to the proper conduct of a state in its international relations.[29]

From the day Vattel's treatise arrived in America in 1775, it was invariably invoked as authoritative on matters of international law by the likes of Alexander Hamilton, James Madison, James Wilson, Edmund Randolph, Thomas Jefferson, John Marshall, Joseph Story, and James Kent, among others. Moreover, it was relied upon by the Second Continental Congress, the Constitutional Convention, and the U.S. Congress.[30]

In court, attorneys and judges alike invoked the authority of Vattel.[31] In 1814, in *Brown v. United States,* Chief Justice John Marshall and Associate Justice Joseph Story found themselves on opposite sides of the issue, but both appealed to Vattel. As one writer observed: "When a jurist is, as here, appealed to on both sides of the same case, it is incontestable proof of his authority."[32] Apparently, the weight of Vattel's work was so great that an attorney, Patrick Henry, before appearing before the U.S. Circuit Court in Richmond in 1790, persuaded his grandson to ride sixty miles on horseback to retrieve the work that would win his case.

The depth and longevity of Vattel's influence is in no small way attributable to the fact that by 1780 his treatise was already a classic and a text in the universities. At Jefferson's suggestion, *The Law of Nations* was first taught at William and Mary in 1779. Vattel's treatise was used at Yale from 1792 to 1795. In due course, Harvard, Columbia, Amherst, and Williams added courses on international law; each drew principally upon Vattel.[33]

Given Vattel's considerable stature in America, it is with particular interest that one examines his teaching with respect to the law of recognition. As we shall see, Oppenheim's observation that Vattel made no great contribution to the law of nations in general applies as well to his treatment of the law of embassy in particular. For Vattel's remarks on this subject owe a considerable intellectual debt to Grotius, Bynkershoek, and Wolff. Yet even if we were to treat Vattel's remarks as a mere echo of the voices before his, such a characterization still would be of great importance for this study because it was to his distillation, principally, that the Framers looked for authoritative application of international law.

Vattel's concept of recognition is premised on the equality and independence of every sovereign state. Nature, according to Vattel, "has established a perfect equality of rights between independent nations."[34] Because "it is necessary that nations should treat and hold intercourse together, in order to promote their interests," it follows that "every sovereign state then has a right to send and to receive public ministers; for they are necessary instruments in the management of those affairs which sovereigns have to transact with each other, and the channels of that correspondence which they have a right to carry on."[35]

Diplomatic intercourse is so vital from Vattel's perspective that a nation has no right to refuse an ambassador during peacetime. His doctrine is only slightly less rigid during a period of war. A nation's refusal to receive an ambassador is warranted if the minister arrives under "false appearances of peace," with the intention of overpowering his host by surprise. But a refusal to receive ministers during tranquil times is unwarranted. The *only* criterion that must be satisfied by a government seeking recognition, according to Vattel, is whether it is in "actual possession" of the nation's governmental functions. This principle of "effectiveness" renders irrelevant the question of the government's legitimacy. Thus a "usurper" will be recognized if it satisfies the test of possession. Of the doctrine of de facto recognition, Vattel states: "There cannot be a more certain rule, or one that is more agreeable to the law of nations and the independence of States." He adds, "as foreigners have no right to interfere in the domestic concerns of a nation, they are not obliged to canvass and scrutinize her conduct in the management of them, in order to determine how far it is either just or unjust." Such scrutiny or even an inquiry into the "justness" or form of government would constitute an injury to the nation's "sovereign dignity." And toward what end would such an inquiry aim? After all, every nation has, as a measure of its "sovereign dignity," the right to send and receive ambassadors.[36] It is this capacity—sovereign dignity—that entitles a state to recognition, not its military power or authority. As Vattel observed, "the dignity of independent nations is essentially the same; that a sovereign prince, however he may rank in the scale of power, is as completely sovereign and independent as the greatest monarch, in the same manner as a dwarf is a man equally with a giant."[37]

Given Vattel's emphasis on sovereign dignity and effective possession, the form of government is irrelevant to the right of embassy. Indeed, internal change is a prerogative of the body politic; it is of no concern to foreign powers. Vattel held that in this instance, other nations are to consider "what has been done as lawful."[38] In a certain sense, Vattel believed that all governmental changes ultimately would be "lawful" since they would reflect the will of the majority. This was so because even if the sovereign became a tyrant and failed to adhere to fundamental laws, the people would be justified in withdrawing their obedience and allegiance to his rule. In fact, Vattel went further and proclaimed a right of the people to oppose an evil sovereign with force. In less grievous circumstances, the people may change their form of government through constitutional procedures. Suppose that only a part of the people wants a change? In this instance, "the opinion of the majority must pass without question as that of the entire nation."[39] In theory, at least, the government would always represent the will of the nation.

EMERGENCE OF AN AMERICAN DOCTRINE OF RECOGNITION

The practice of receiving ambassadors was not born in the Constitutional Convention. As we have seen, the rules governing legation plumb the depths of legal history, perhaps as long ago as the Punic Wars. In any event, the influence of the presuppositions on the Framers was undoubtedly great. They had read, and obviously were familiar with, as evidenced by their frequent invocation, the works of the leading writers on the law of nations—Grotius, Bynkershoek, Wolff, and Vattel. If the Framers had decided to alter substantially the nature of the reception function from a duty to a high prerogative so as to infuse it with discretion and thus break from a long-settled practice under international law, they certainly gave no hint of such an intention. It is reasonable, therefore, to presume adherence to tradition. In fact, such a presumption would seem to be perfectly correct since statements by leading figures are consistently confirmatory in character.

The first post-convention commentary on the reception clause came from the pen of Alexander Hamilton, who, according to Forrest McDonald, was greatly influenced by Vattel.[40] In assaying the powers of the president, Hamilton was keenly aware of the "aversion of the people to monarchy," of their willingness to regard "the intended President . . . as the full-grown progeny of that detested parent," and he sought to allay fears by conducting a minute analysis of presidential powers.[41] Writing what Madison characterized as the "original gloss" on the meaning of the recognition clause, Hamilton wrote in *Federalist 69* that the authority

> to receive ambassadors and other public ministers . . . is more a matter of dignity than authority. It is a circumstance which will be without consequence in the administration of the government; and it was far more convenient that it should be arranged in this manner, than that there should be a necessity of convening the legislature, or one of its branches, upon every arrival of a foreign minister, though it were merely to take the place of a departed predecessor.[42]

By any measure, Hamilton was talking about the effectuation of a diplomatic function. As Louis Henkin has observed, "receiving ambassadors" seems "a function rather than a 'power,' a ceremony which in many countries is performed by a figurehead." Indeed the distinction between a power and a function cannot be stressed too strongly. The president is given the power, "by and with the Advice and Consent of the senate," to make treaties and appoint ambassadors, but the reception clause is placed in section three of the Constitution, which imposes duties or responsibilities on the president such as executing the laws and reporting on the state of the Union.[43]

The unpretentious nature of the president's duty to receive ambassadors is further affirmed by its comparison to the president's power to appoint ambassadors. In England, the king's prerogative included "the sole power of sending ambassadors to foreign states, and receiving ambassadors at home."[44] The Articles of Confederation retained the combination and vested it in Congress.[45] But the Constitutional Convention separated the appointment power from the reception function. The Framers recognized, as Prof. Arthur Bestor has explained, that "it was the sending of American ambassadors abroad that had implications for policy, not the reception of foreign ones, which they viewed as primarily a ceremonial function."[46]

Hamilton's understanding of the recognition power as merely ceremonial, a function devoid of consequence, which seems "more a matter of dignity than authority," reflects the teaching of Bynkershoek and Vattel. After all, the decision to receive an ambassador is of no moment in an environment in which nations have, as international law made clear, a "right" to send and receive ambassadors, the only issue being one of the de facto authority of the government in question. In the context of a virtual "duty" to receive ambassadors, the ceremonial nature of the reception would suggest emphasis on "convenience." Surely, it must be far more convenient for one person, the president, to shake hands with a foreign minister than it would be to trot out dozens of congressmen for purposes of an official greeting.

Clarification of the recognition power was wrought from the turbulence of the French Revolution, which afforded a backdrop from which emerged the American doctrine of de facto recognition. The seizure of power by the Jacobins in August 1792 and the consequent "suspension" of Louis XVI as King led Gouverneur Morris, then the U.S. minister to France, to inform Secretary of State Jefferson that another revolution had been carried out. In the midst of this turbulence, Morris awaited diplomatic instruction from Jefferson. On November 7, 1792, Jefferson advised Morris that in view of the circumstances, he would be justified in leaving Paris.

> With what kind of government you do business is another question. It accords with our principles to acknowledge any government to be rightful which is formed by the will of the nation substantially declared. The late government was of this kind and was accordingly acknowledged by all the branches of ours. So any alteration of it which shall be made by the will of the nation substantially declared will doubtless be acknowledged in like manner.[47]

Another matter complicated by the chaos in France was the debt the United States owed the French nation. Hamilton had persuaded Jefferson to instruct Morris to withhold payment until a stable regime had emerged, one that was clearly authorized by the nation to collect the debt.[48] Jefferson replied that the National Convention, then the presiding authority, would establish a definite form of government. Moreover,

> as we had recognized the former government, because established by the authority of the nation, so we must recognize any other which should be established by the authority of the nation. He [Hamilton] said we recognized the former because it contained an important member of the ancient, to wit: the King, and wore the appearance of his consent, but if in any future form, they should omit the King, he did not know that we could with safety recognize it or pay money to its order.[49]

Later that year, on December 30, Jefferson sent instructions to Charles Cotesworth Pinckney, the U.S. minister to London, regarding the policy that America intended to pursue toward France. Although conceding the impossibility of foreseeing future developments, he nevertheless believed that

> principles being understood, their application will be less embarrassing. We certainly cannot deny to other nations that principle whereon our own government is founded, that every nation has a right to govern itself internally under what forms it pleases and to change those forms at its own will; and externally to transact business with other nations through whatever organ it chooses whether that be a King, Convention, Assembly, Committee, President or whatever it be. The only thing essential is the will of the nation.[50]

Jefferson later observed that he had taken the opportunity to inform Pinckney of "the Catholic principle of republicanism, to wit, that every people may establish what form of government they please, and change it as they please."[51] He had done it as well in order to learn of Washington's opinion, which he wanted to make a matter of record. His letter was approved and a similar letter was sent to Morris. With Washington's consent, Jefferson thus recognized the National Convention as the de facto authority in France. He wrote:

> We learn that a Convention is assembled, invested with full powers by the nation to transact its affairs. Tho' we know that from the public pa-

pers only, instead of waiting for a formal annunciation of it, we hasten to act upon it, by authorizing you, if the fact be true, to consider the suspension of payment . . . now taken off . . . considering the Convention or the government they shall have established as the lawful representative of the Nation and authorized to act for them.[52]

Jefferson's act of recognition did not, of course, answer the question as to the nature of U.S. diplomatic relations with France. It is familiar that Washington's cabinet became involved in a heated controversy over whether Citizen Genet should be received as a minister from the French Republic. The controversy involved a cobweb of political and legal problems, but they shall be considered here only to the extent that they bear on the recognition power.

On April 8, 1793, President Washington submitted to his cabinet a series of questions which, among other queries, asked: "(1) Shall a minister from the Republic of France be received? (2) If received, shall such a reception be 'absolute' or qualified? (3) May the United States suspend the treaties of alliance and commerce concluded with the French Monarchy in 1778?"[53] By this time, France was involved in several wars, and thus there was concern as to the force and nature of the treaties: Did they obligate the United States to assist the French in their foreign adventures? This possibility clearly was Hamilton's greatest fear.[54] Therefore he directed his energies toward the goal of persuading the cabinet that the treaties should be considered void. He adduced two arguments. First, a nation has the right to renounce treaties if adherence to them would bring danger or harm to its interests.[55] We shall not consider this contention. His second argument, however, speaks volumes about his view on recognition. Hamilton contended that Genet should be received, but with the qualification that the reception would not in any way affect the operation of the treaties.[56] He thus severed the recognition question from the problem surrounding the treaties. "The acknowledgement of a government," wrote Hamilton, "by the reception of its ambassador and the acknowledgement of it as an ally, are things different and separate from each other."

Hamilton's statement nicely illustrates not only the essence of the doctrine of de facto recognition but also, more importantly for present purposes, the acute difference between viewing the recognition clause as a mere function and as a discretionary prerogative. When a president receives an ambassador he is merely acknowledging the de facto authority of the sending government or state. But "the acknowledgement of it as an ally," as Hamilton observed, is quite another matter. Such a consideration is a policymaking function, one left to the department charged with such authority; it is not one that is derived from the reception clause.

In a letter to Chief Justice John Jay, April 9, 1793, Hamilton indicated that both he and Jay, at least initially, had concluded that Genet should be received. Yet he voiced concern that perhaps Genet would not be representing the de facto government of France. In such a case, asked Hamilton, what would the United States do if another faction should announce itself as the de facto regime? In his reply of April 11, 1793, Jay stated: "I wd. not receive any Minister from a Regent untill [*sic*] he was Regent de facto." The chief justice further confirmed his adherence to the doctrine of de facto recognition in an enclosure for Washington. In language that invokes the spirit of Vattel, Jay wrote:

> Whereas every nation has a right to change and modify their constitution and government, in such manner as they may think most conducive to their welfare and happiness. And whereas they who actually administer the governmt. of any nation, are by foreign nations to be regarded as its *Lawful Rulers,* so long as they continue to be recognized and obeyed as such by the great body of their people.[57]

For his part, Jefferson thought the question of receiving Genet "the boldest and greatest that ever was hazarded."[58] From his perspective, there could be no doubt; after all, the United States already had extended recognition to the French Republic through Gouverneur Morris. He was pleased, of course, by Washington's official reception of Genet on May 20, but he was likewise most unhappy with the president's Proclamation of Neutrality.

The proclamation was defended by Hamilton in a series of newspaper articles that he wrote under the name Pacificus.[59] The celebrated articles prompted Jefferson to ask Madison to "select the most striking heresies and cut him to pieces in the face of the public" since "there is nobody else who can and will enter the lists against him."[60] Madison responded to Jefferson's pleas by publishing a series of letters under the name Helvidius.

In *Federalist 69,* Hamilton had engaged in a careful analysis of presidential power for purposes of allaying the public's concern that the Framers might have created an embryonic monarchy. As Pacificus, Hamilton clearly committed a volte face. Anyone is free to change his mind of course, but a reversal of one's opinion does not change the meaning of the Constitution. Hamilton's remarks on the recognition power in the first Pacificus essay, therefore, may be viewed as an elaborate, if unsound, effort to remake the reception clause. He not only broke with a centuries-old tradition of international law, in addition to contradicting what he had written in *Federalist 69,* but he also went beyond even what he had written in the spring as a means of attempting to persuade the cabinet of his viewpoint. Let us consider this confusion.

As Pacificus, Hamilton first described the reception of ambassadors as a presidential "duty."[61] He then said of the "right of the executive to receive ambassadors" that it "includes that of judging, in the case of a revolution of government in a foreign country, whether the new rulers are competent organs of the national will." So far this is consistent with the theme of *Federalist 69*, as it addresses recognition. But then he asserted that "where a treaty antecedently exists between the United States and such nation," the right of recognition "involves the power of continuing or suspending its operation." Moreover,

> this power of determining virtually upon the operation of national treaties, as a consequence of the power to receive public ministers, is an important instance of the right of the executive, to decide upon the obligations of the country with regard to foreign nations. To apply it to the case of France, if there had been a treaty of alliance, offensive and defensive, between the United States and that country, the unqualified acknowledgement of the new government would have put the United States in a condition to become an associate in the war with France, and would have laid the legislature under an obligation, if required, and there was otherwise no valid excuse of exercising its power of declaring war.[62]

Hamilton's reasoning is specious. First, the Constitution vests the legislative power in Congress. That includes the authority to suspend or repeal laws. Second, the Constitution also places the power to declare war in Congress. A treaty cannot commit the United States to war because the House is not part of the treatymaking power, and a declaration or authorization of war requires action by both chambers.[63] Finally, Hamilton's attempt to build on the basis of a mere ceremony an omnicompetent foreign affairs structure is nothing short of chimerical.

Given the poverty of his reasoning, Hamilton's position is explicable only as a partisan effort to disrupt the French-American alliance, something he might have accomplished if he had prevailed in his effort to prevent the reception of Genet. But it is altogether unlikely that even Hamilton believed that he could succeed in such an undertaking, for at least two reasons. First, Washington's cabinet had already decided to receive Genet. Second, it would have been very difficult to countermand Jefferson's instructions to Morris for the previous month. In all likelihood, as Prof. Lawrence Kaplan has justly concluded,

"What Hamilton may have sought was just to put the Secretary of State on the defensive and to make eventually an ostensible concession on a matter of recognition in order to extract an advantage in another area of Franco-American policy."[64] Viewed in the context of the ongoing Hamilton-Jefferson quarrel regarding the nature of U.S. ties to England and France, it is reasonable to assume that Hamilton saw in the recognition debate an opportunity to exert leverage against the secretary of state in the next round of their battle.

The Framers, wrote Madison in 1793, gave the president no prerogative whatever to reject foreign ministers. As the Father of the Constitution explained it,[65] "When a foreign minister presents himself, two questions immediately arise: Are his credentials from the existing and acting government of his country? Are they properly authenticated?"[66] He added that these questions are "of necessity" put to the executive because, as Hamilton explained in *Federalist 69*, it is more convenient for one person to ascertain the factual information than to burden the entire legislature with such a routine, ministerial function. Yet as Madison made pellucidly clear, these questions "involve no cognizance of the question, whether those exercising the government have the right along with the possession. This belongs to the nation, and the nation alone on whom the government operates."[67] To state it in its starkest terms, Madison wrote:

> The questions before the executive are merely questions of fact; and the executive would have precisely the same right, or rather be under the same necessity of deciding them, if its function was simply to receive *without any discretion to reject* public ministers.

Why is the president denied discretion to reject foreign ministers? Echoing the doctrine of Vattel, Jefferson, and the explanation provided by Hamilton in *Federalist 69*, Madison stated that

> little if any thing more was intended by the clause, than to provide for a particular mode of communication, almost grown into a right among modern nations; by pointing out the department of the government most proper for the ceremony of admitting public ministers, of examining their credentials, and of authenticating their title to privileges annexed to their character by the law of nations.

Moreover, "that being the apparent design of the Constitution, it would be highly improper to magnify the function into an important prerogative, even where no rights of other departments could be affected by it."[68]

The Madisonian-Jeffersonian-Hamiltonian doctrine that the recognition power is merely ceremonial, a clerklike administrative function devoid of discretion and consequence is quite clearly a product of the international law tradition, as explained by Grotius, Bynkershoek, Wolff, and Vattel. The reception of an ambassador would have been one of great consequence, one of considerable authority and not mere dignity, *if* the Framers had vested the president with the discretionary power to refuse ambassadors. But again and again, such a prerogative was denied. The only issue before the president is one of fact: Is the new ruler the competent organ of the nation?

Given the restrictive scope of the recognition clause, as comprehended by Hamilton, Madison, and Jefferson, it is virtually inconceivable that a unilateral presidential power to make and conduct foreign policy could be squeezed from such a narrow, clerklike administrative function. Moreover, there are at least two other policy factors that militate strongly against the expansive construction of the recognition power—the Framers' deep-seated fear of the executive prerogative and their decision to vest in the treatymaking authority the exclusive power to make and conduct U.S. foreign affairs. If the recognition clause truly were intended to confer upon the president a unilateral power to make foreign policy, such authority would have been contrary to both the constitutional design for collective decisionmaking in the formulation of foreign policy and the Framers' determination to place the primary responsibility for the conduct of foreign relations in the hands of the treatymaking power—the president and the Senate. Elsewhere I have detailed the story; here the barest summary must suffice.[69]

Until virtually the last moment of the Constitutional Convention, the treaty power was granted solely to the Senate.[70] The addition of the president was an afterthought; the aim was to provide a check on the Senate.[71] James Wilson, second only to Madison as an architect of the Constitution, thought this arrangement would "produce security to the people," since "neither the President nor the Senate solely, can complete a treaty; they are checks upon each other." This checking arrangement meant, as Patrick Henry observed, that "the President as distinguished from the Senate, is nothing" when it came to foreign affairs.[72]

Indeed, as we have seen, Hamilton believed that the president and the Senate, working in tandem, would conduct the foreign policy of the United States.[73] A fellow Framer, Rufus King, who, as a member of the Committee on Detail, had helped to draft the final provision for the presidential role in treatymaking, observed in 1819 that, except for receiving ambassadors, "the validity of all other definitive proceedings in the management of foreign affairs, the Constitutional advice and consent of the Senate are indispensable."[74]

The rationale underlying the Framers' decision to vest the authority to conduct foreign policy in the treatymaking power, as opposed to placing it in the hands of one person, was, as Wilson said, "to produce a security for the people." The decision was not a reflection of faith in mankind; to the contrary, it was a reflection of the fear of the abuse of power. In *Federalist 75*, Hamilton wrote:

> The vast importance of the trust, and the operation of treaties as law, plead strongly for the participation . . . of the legislative body in the office of making them. . . . The history of human conduct does not warrant [the commitment of] interests of so delicate and momentous a kind . . . to the sole disposal of [the President].

He added that "though it would be imprudent to confide in him solely so important a trust; yet it cannot be doubted that his participation would materially add to the safety of society."[75] William Davie, a delegate to the convention from North Carolina, explained to his state's ratifying convention that "jealousy of executive power which has shown itself so strongly in all the American governments, would not admit" of locating the power to make treaties in the president alone. His statement was echoed by Charles C. Pinckney, a Framer from South Carolina, who feared the president might "show an improper partiality."[76] Forty years later, Justice Joseph Story, perhaps the greatest scholar in the Supreme Court's history, wrote:

> Considering the delicacy and extent of the power, it is too much to expect that a free people would confide to a single magistrate the sole authority to act conclusively, as well as exclusively, upon the subject of treaties. . . . It would be inconsistent with that wholesome jealousy which all republics ought to cherish, of all depositories of power.[77]

The Framers' fear of expansive executive power, their attachment to collective decisionmaking in foreign affairs, and their conviction that a unilateral presidential power to conduct foreign policy threatened the security of the people conduced to preclude the placement of the treatymaking power in the president alone. These dangers would be no less real if the Framers had clothed the president with the discretionary power to make foreign policy by virtue of the recognition clause. Of course, they refused to grant such authority, as Hamilton and Madison made clear. As Hamilton said in *Federalist 75*, the historical record does not warrant such faith in one person; moreover, such a decision would be "imprudent."

CONCLUSION

Perhaps the classic statement of the first principle of American constitutionalism was uttered in 1819 by Chief Justice Marshall in *McCulloch v. Maryland:* "We admit, as all must admit, that the powers of the government are limited, and that its limits are not to be transcended."[78] The recognition "power" of the president was clearly delimited by the Framers to the capacity of a narrow, ministerial function. For Madison and Hamilton, the function was to be a matter without consequence; there was no discretion whatever involved in the exercise of the duty to recognize the de facto authority of a foreign nation. To be sure, the two Framers underestimated the potential power of the reception clause; perhaps they should have anticipated presidential transgression of its strictures. But perhaps the prescient Madison did anticipate the abuse of this and other clauses. Writing in 1793 in opposition to a novel construction of presidential power that, to him, seemed foreign to the Framers' conception of the office, Madison lamented:

> We are to regard it as morally certain, that in proportion as the doctrines make their way into the creed of the government, and the acquiescence of the public, every power that can be deduced from them, will be deduced, and exercised sooner or later by those who may have an interest in so doing. The character of human nature gives this salutary warning to every sober and reflecting mind. And the history of government in all its forms and in every period of time, ratifies, the danger. A people, therefore, who are so happy as to possess the inestimable blessing of a free and defined constitution, cannot be too watchful against the introduction, nor too critical in tracing the consequences, of new principles and new constructions, that may remove the landmarks of power.[79]

Born of unpretentious claim and design, the recognition clause has become a wellspring of presidential power to conduct foreign policy. Perhaps this interpretation was inevitable. After all, Madison did say that transgression is common to all governments. Thus the magnification of the clause serves to reaffirm the belief of the Framers that the great task confronting our political system is that of obliging the government to control itself. In this regard we place our hopes in constitutions and laws. In light of recent events, these hopes may yet prove to be false.

NOTES

I am indebted to Tom Cronin, Leonard Levy, Dean Alfange, Jr., Michael McCann, and Ron Hatzenbuehler for their careful readings of this chapter. A version of it was published as "The President's Recognition Power: Ministerial or Discretionary?" *Presidential Studies Quarterly* (Spring 1995): 267–87.

1. The Constitution of the United States does not expressly mention the power of recognition, nor does it confer that power in terms upon any one department of government. It provides, however, that the president "shall receive ambassadors and other public ministers" (Article II, section 3). The reception of an ambassador from a foreign nation entails various legal consequences under international law, the most basic of which is the recognition of the government or state represented. For a brief listing of these "consequences," see text accompanying notes 3–4.

2. For a history of the recognition policy of the United States through 1915, see Julius Goebel, Jr., *The Recognition Policy of the United States* (New York: Columbia University Press, 1915). For a continuation of the story, through the Ford administration, see L. Thomas Galloway, *Recognizing Foreign Governments: The Practice of the United States* (Washington, D.C.: American Enterprise Institution, 1978). Until President Carter granted recognition to the People's Republic of China on January 1, 1979, the use of the recognition power rarely had been given a second look. For a discussion of that recognition and its legal consequences for Peking and Washington, see David Gray Adler, "The Serbonian Bog: The Legal Relations of the United States and China," in *Essays in Honor of Francis Dunham Wormuth: Toward a Humanistic Science of Politics*, ed. D. H. Nelson and R. L. Sklar (Lanham, Md.: University Press of America, 1983), 345–59, reprinted in David Gray Adler, *The Constitution and the Termination of Treaties* (New York: Garland Publishing 1986), 362–88 (hereinafter referred to as Adler, *Termination*).

3. Lassa Oppenheim, *International Law: A Treatise*, ed. Hersch Lauterpacht, 2 vols., 8th ed. (London: Longmans, Green, 1955), 1:125.

4. A number of important consequences flow from the recognition of a state or government. As explained by Oppenheim: "(1) It thereby acquires the capacity to enter into diplomatic relations with other States and to make treaties with them; (2) within limitations which are far from being clear, former treaties (if any) concluded between the two States, assuming it to be an old State and not a newly-born one, are automatically revived and come into force; (3) it thereby acquires the right, which, at any rate according to English law, it did not previously possess, of suing in the courts of law of the recognizing State; (4) it hereby acquires for itself and its property immunity from the jurisdiction of the courts of law of the State recognizing it and ancillary rights which are discussed later—an immunity which, according to English law at any rate, it does not enjoy before recognition. (5) It also becomes entitled to demand and receive possession of property situated within the jurisdiction of a recognizing State which formerly belonged to the preceding government at the time of its supersession. (6) Recognition being retroactive and dating back to the moment at which the newly recognized government established itself in power, its effect is to preclude the courts of the recognizing State from questioning the legality or validity of such legislative and executive acts, past and future, or that government as are not contrary to International Law; it therefore validates, so far as concerns those courts of law, certain transfers of property and other transactions which before recognition the courts would have treated as invalid" (ibid., pp. 137–39).

Edward S. Corwin has justly stated that recognition has become "a most potent instrument of foreign policy, a remark that applies as well to its nonuse as its use. Presi-

dent Wilson encompassed the downfall of Huerta's regime in Mexico in 1915 by refusing to recognize it as even a government *de facto*, and the pivotal feature of our relations
with both Mexico and Russia for some years was the refusal of successive administrations at Washington to recognize as *de jure* the governments of those countries" (Corwin, *The President: Office and Powers, 1787–1957*, 4th ed. [New York: New York University Press, 1957], p. 190).

5. Henry Clay, among others, asserted in 1811, 1818, and 1836 a right of Congress to grant recognition. In 1836, in the midst of the debate on whether the United
States should grant recognition to Texas, Clay, then chairman of the Senate Committee on Foreign Relations, presented a report on June 18, 1836, in which he asserted
that, under the Constitution, there are four ways of recognizing a power as independent: (1) by treaty; (2) by the passage of a law regulating commercial intercourse; (3)
by sending a diplomatic agent; (4) by the executive receiving and accrediting a diplomatic representative. A Senate role was required by any one of the first three methods
while the president alone "is competent" to receive diplomatic representatives. See
Committee on Foreign Relations, Senate, S. Doc. 406, 24th Cong., 1st sess., June 18,
1836, quoted in J. B. Moore, *Digest of International Law* (Washington, D.C.: Government Printing Office, 1906) 5:97. On various other occasions, Congress has asserted a
right of recognition. See Taylor Cole, *The Recognition Policy of the United States Since
1901* (Baton Rouge: Louisiana State University Press, 1928), pp. 12–13, and Clarence
Berdahl, "The Power of Recognition," *American Journal of International Law* 14
(1920): 519.

6. In *Goldwater v. Carter,* 444 U.S. 996 (1979), for example, Justice Brennan, in a
dissenting opinion, wrote that President Carter's "abrogation of the defense treaty
with Taiwan was a necessary incident to Executive recognition of the Peking Government" and therefore was justified (at 1007). Brennan would thus clear the deck to permit a president to "remove obstacles to recognition of governments." One wonders
what limits apply to such presidential authority. The Court has acknowledged a limited power "to remove obstacles to recognition." See *United States v. Belmont,* 310
U.S. 324 (1937), and *United States v. Pink,* 315 U.S. 203 (1942). Is the termination of
a mutual defense treaty an "obstacle" that may be removed? For a discussion of this
question, see Adler, *Termination,* pp. 254–62.

7. This phrase has been borrowed from Raoul Berger, "The President's Unilateral
Termination of the Taiwan Treaty," *Northwestern University Law Review* 75 (1980): 580.

8. Abraham D. Sofaer, *War, Foreign Affairs and Constitutional Power: The Origins*
(Cambridge Mass.: Ballinger Publishing Company, 1976), p. 56.

9. Jonathan Elliot, *Debates in the Several Conventions on the Adoption of the Federal
Constitution,* 2d ed., 4 vols. (Washington, D.C.: J. Elliot, 1836), 2: 305.

10. See, for example, Raoul Berger, "The Presidential Monopoly of Foreign Affairs," *Michigan Law Review* 71 (1972): 1; Francis D. Wormuth and Edwin B. Firmage,
To Chain the Dog of War: The War of Congress in History and Law (Dallas: Southern
Methodist University Press, 1986); Adler, *Termination.* See also, Robinson, Chapter 4
of this volume.

11. The Framers severed all roots to the royal prerogative because, as Bernard Bailyn
has observed, they were frightened by the "endlessly propulsive tendency" of power
"to expand itself beyond legitimate boundaries" (Bailyn, *The Ideological Origins of the
American Revolution* [Cambridge: Harvard University Press, 1967], pp. 56–57). The

fear of unrestrained power was voiced frequently in the Virginia Ratifying Convention (Elliot, *Debates,* 3:32, 58, 60). See Adler, *Termination,* pp. 262–78.

12. The Framers were determined to limit the president's power sharply. Madison emphasized in the Constitutional Convention that it was essential "to fix the extent of the Executive authority . . . as certain powers were in their nature Executive; and must be given to that department" (Max Farrand, *The Records of the Federal Convention of 1787,* 4 vols. [New Haven: Yale University Press, 1911], 1: 66–67). He added that the executive power "should be confined and defined" (p. 70). Aware of the public's fear of a strong executive, Hamilton conducted a minute analysis of presidential power so as to allay those fears (see *The Federalist,* Modern Library Edition [New York: Random House, 1937], *Federalist 69,* pp. 445–54). Charles Pinckney told the South Carolina Ratifying Convention that "we have defined his powers, and bound them to such limits as will effectually prevent his usurping authority" (Elliot, *Debates,* 4:329). Pennsylvania's Chief Justice McKean told his state's ratifying convention that executive officers "have no manner of authority, any of them, beyond what is by positive grant . . . delegated to them" (Elliot, *Debates,* 2: 540). The eminent historian of the Supreme Court, Charles Warren, observed: "Fear of a return of Executive authority like that exercised by the Royal Governors or by the King had been ever present in the States from the beginning of the Revolution" (Warren, *Making of the Constitution* [Cambridge: Harvard University Press, 1947], p. 177). Further, Walter Bagehot noted that the Framers feared that sovereign power "would generate tyranny. George III had been a tyrant to them, and come what might, they would not make a George III" (Bagehot, *The English Constitution* [London: Paul Trench, Trubner and Company, 1964], p. 218).

13. As we have seen, Hamilton assured the New York Ratifying Convention that the Senate and the president "are to manage all our concerns with foreign nations" (Elliot, *Debates,* 2:305). For discussion, see text accompanying notes 66–73 and Adler, *Termination,* pp. 84–114. See Article II, section 3 of the Constitution (emphasis added). I thank Professor Randall Bland for this observation. The president "may" exercise other powers, e.g., "He may require the opinion, in writing, of the principal officer, in each of the executive Departments" (Article II, section 2). And, "He may, on extraordinary occasions, convene both Houses, or either of them, and in case of disagreement between them, with Respect to the Time of Adjournment, he may adjourn them to such time as he shall think proper" (Article II, section 3). See text accompanying note 43 below.

14. Hugo Grotius referred to a report that characterized Hannibal's refusal to receive an ambassador as a violation of international law since nations have a "right" to send ambassadors (Grotius, *On the Law of War and Peace,* ed. James Brown Scott (Oxford: Clarendon Press, 1925), p. 441. See text accompanying notes 35–39.

15. Pierino Belli, *A Treatise on Military Matters and Warfare,* ed. James Brown Scott (Oxford: Clarendon Press, 1936).

16. Ibid., p. 256.

17. Grotius, *Law of War.* Oppenheim has said that international law "owes its existence as a systematized body of rules largely to the Dutch jurist Hugo Grotius" (Oppenheim, *International Law,* 1:6).

18. Grotius, *Law of War,* pp. 440–41. For a response to these "exceptions" to the right of embassy, see the remarks of the eighteenth-century philosopher, Christian

Wolff, *The Law of Nations According to a Scientific Method,* ed. James Brown Scott (Oxford: Clarendon Press, 1934), p. 528; see also text accompanying notes 25–26.

19. Cornelius Van Bynkershoek, *On Questions of Public Law,* ed. James Brown Scott (Oxford: Clarendon Press, 1930). Oppenheim has described Bynkershoek's influence in the eighteenth century as "enormous" (*International Law,* p. 96). It is familiar that the Framers were guided by the works of Bynkershoek, among others. For example, Thomas Jefferson said that when it came to construing the law of nations as it applied to treaties, "Vattel has been most generally the grade. Bynkershoek often quoted, Wolf [*sic*] sometimes" (Jefferson to James Madison, August 5, 1793, in *The Papers of James Madison,* ed. Robert Rutland et. al. [Charlottesville: University Press of Virginia, 1985], 15: 50–51 [hereinafter cited as *Madison Papers*]). Alexander Hamilton made frequent reference to Bynkershoek on such matters of right of passage and neutrality. See, for example, *The Papers of Alexander Hamilton,* ed. Harold C. Syrett et. al. (New York: Columbia University Press, 1969), 15: 156, 187, 204, 225 (hereinafter cited as *Hamilton Papers*). Chancellor James Kent said, "Bynkershoek's treatise on the law of war has been received as of great authority in that particular branch of the science of the law of nations, and the subject is by him able and copiously discussed" (James Kent, *Commentaries on American Law,* ed. John M. Gould, 14th ed., 3 vols. [Boston: Little, Brown and Company, 1896] 1: 18). His writings on the international law of war during the eighteenth century still are recognized as authoritative. See Wormuth and Firmage, *To Chain the Dog of War,* p. 19.

20. Bynkershoek, *Public Law,* p. 157.

21. Ibid., p. 158. Bynkershoek quotes, approvingly, the statement of Carneades of Lactanius: "If all nations which had gained great empire, yea, even the Romans who have won possession of the whole world, should decide to become just, that is, to restore what did not belong to them, they would all have to return to dwelling in huts" (p. 158). In Bynkershoek's view, the attempt to draw a distinction between titles justly and unjustly acquired "would be impossible." He stated: "In political matters, at any rate, it is expedient that possession be nine points of the law. Otherwise, we would be compelled to examine into the origins of all states to find whether or not they were based upon justice, and then ultimately to decide whether or not they had the right of legation. This, however, would be utterly futile, and would provide an excellent excuse for disturbing the peace of nations" (p. 158).

22. The Grotians carved out a middle ground between the natural law theorists and the positivists. They maintained Grotius's distinction between the natural and the voluntary law of nations, but, in contrast to him, they viewed positive law and natural law as of equal importance.

23. Christian Wolff, *Law of Nations.*

24. Emmerich de Vattel, *The Law of Nations,* ed. James Brown Scott (Washington, D.C.: Carnegie Institution, 1916).

25. Wolff, *Law of Nations,* p. 526.

26. Wolff stated: "Since ambassadors are to be received and treated with respect, and since this obligation, being derived from the laws of nature, is natural and therefore unchangeable, consequently is not changed by the fact that the sender and the one to whom the ambassador is sent are enemies, ambassadors even when sent by an enemy are to be received and treated with respect" (ibid., p. 531).

27. James Kent, who wrote the first treatise on American law and was this nation's

first commentator on international law, described Vattel as the "most popular and most elegant writer on the law of nations" (Kent, *Commentaries*, 1:18). Kent's citations of Vattel on points of international law are too numerous to count (ibid., 1:1–191). In his introduction to a 1916 translation of Vattel's treatise, Albert de Lapradelle observed that in England, no writer on international law is "more copiously quoted than Vattel" (Emmerich de Vattel, *The Law of Nations*, trans. Charles G. Fenwick [1758; rpt., Washington, D.C.: Carnegie Institution, 1916], p. xxxiv). But he added: "In the United States the authority of Vattel is at least as great as in England." Vattel "was followed as the most competent, the wisest, and the safest guide, in all the discussions of Congress, in all the trials in court, and in diplomatic correspondence, especially that concerned with questions of legality" (p. xxxv). That view still has wide currency. Professors Wormuth and Firmage in *To Chain the Dog of War*, have described Vattel as "the most influential writer on the law of nations . . . at the time of the adoption of the Constitution" (p. 19). For similar encomia, see Stephen Peter Rosen, "Alexander Hamilton and the Domestic Uses of International Law," *Journal of Diplomatic History* 5 (1981): 183, 193; Theodore S. Woolsey, "International Law," in *Two Centuries' Growth of American Law*, ed. R. H. Helmholz and Bernard D. Reams, Jr. (rept., Buffalo, N.Y.: William Hein and Company, 1980), pp. 501, 516; David M. Levitan, "Executive Agreements: A Study of the Executive in the Control of the Foreign Relations of the United States, *Northwestern University Law Review* 35 (1940): 368; and Abraham Weinfeld, "What Did the Framers of the Federal Constitution Mean by 'Agreements or Compacts'?" *University of Chicago Law Review* 3 (1936): 453, 459.

28. James Brown Scott, *The United States of America: A Study in International Organization* (New York: Oxford University Press, 1920), p. 439.

29. Charles Fenwick, "The Authority of Vattel," *American Political Science Review* 7 (1913): 395.

30. Charles W. F. Dumas, a Swiss citizen living in Holland and an enthusiastic republican, apparently read Vattel with the United States in mind, published a new edition, and sent three copies of the book to Benjamin Franklin. Franklin observed that Vattel had arrived at the right moment: "It came to us in good season, when the circumstances of a rising State make it necessary frequently to consult the Law of Nations. Accordingly, that copy which I kept (after depositing one in our own public library here, and sending the other to the College of Massachusetts Bay, as you directed) has been continually in the hands of the members of our Congress now sitting, who are much pleased with your notes and preface, and have entertained a high and just esteem for their author" (letter from Franklin to Dumas, December 19, 1775, quoted in Scott, *United States*, pp. 439–40).

Kent, as we have seen, referred to Vattel as the most "popular and most elegant writer on the law of nations" (Kent, *Commentaries*, p. 18). A number of delegates to the Constitutional Convention invoked Vattel as authority on several issues. Edward Rutledge cited him in order to "prove" that individuals in a state of nature are equally free and independent and that the same may be said of states until they have relinquished their sovereignty (Farrand, *Records*, 1: 437–38). Luther Martin invoked the authority of Vattel for the proposition that the "first principle of government is founded on the natural rights of individuals, and in perfect equality" (Farrand, *Records*, 1: 440). Another Framer, Gen. Charles Cotesworth Pinckney, referred to "Vattel, one of the best writers on the law of nations," at the South Carolina Ratifying Convention and drew upon the weight of his reputation in urging the United States to remain faithful to the obligations of its treaties (Elliot, *Debates*, 4: 278). See Fenwick, "Authority of Vattel," p. 395, and Scott, *United States*, p. 440.

31. For example, in *Holmes v. Jennison*, Chief Justice Taney recognized a fundamental distinction between "agreements" and "treaties" and cited Vattel to support his opinion (39 U.S. 540 [1840]). Lapradelle has noted some of the many cases in which the judiciary has relied on Vattel; see his commentary in Vattel, *Law of Nations*, pp. xxxvi–xxxviii.

32. 8 Cranch 110 (1814).

33. Woolsey has compiled a list of schools that offered work in international law; see "International Law," pp. 518–20.

34. Vattel, *Law of Nations*, Book 2, sec. 36, p. 126.

35. Ibid., Book 4, sec. 55, p. 362.

36. Ibid., sec. 78, p. 369; see also pp. 362–66. Moreover, Vattel insisted that the form of government was irrelevant to the question of recognition (Book 2, sec. 38, p. 126; see also text accompanying notes 38–39).

37. Ibid., Book 4, sec. 78, p. 369.

38. Ibid., Book 2, sec. 39, p. 126; Book 4, sec. 68, p. 366.

39. Ibid., Book 2, sec. 33, pp. 18–19.

40. McDonald considers Vattel, Stewart, and Necker as the three greatest influences on Hamilton (Forrest McDonald, *Novus Ordo Seclorum: The Intellectual Origins of the Constitution* [Lawrence: University Press of Kansas, 1986], p. 188). Hamilton invariably invoked Vattel's treatise on matters of international law. For examples of Hamilton's invocations of Vattel on such questions as interpretation of treaties and neutrality, see *Hamilton Papers*, 14: 297, 328, 367, 372, and 15: 67, 192, 204, 225, 227, 258.

41. Hamilton, *Federalist 67*, p. 436.

42. Hamilton, *Federalist 69*, p. 451.

43. Louis Henkin, *Foreign Affairs and the Constitution* (Mineola, N.Y.: Foundation Press, 1972), p. 41. Article II, section 3 provides, for example, that "he shall take Care that the Laws be faithfully executed."

44. William Blackstone, *Commentaries on the Laws of England*, 4 vols. (1769), p. 253.

45. Articles of Confederation, Article 9, stated: "The United States, in Congress assembled, shall have the sole and enclusive right and power of sending and receiving ambassadors."

46. Arthur Bestor, "Respective Roles of Senate and President in the Making and Abrogation of Treaties—The Original Intent of the Framers of the Constitution Historically Examined," *Washington Law Review* 55, no. 1 (December 1979): 87. "Indeed, the Committee of Detail treated the power to 'receive Ambassadors' as a matter of providing a channel of communication, for they coupled it, in the same sentence of their draft constitution, with the President's power to 'correspond with the supreme Executives of the several states' " (p. 87).

47. Jefferson to Morris, November 7, 1792, in *The Writings of Thomas Jefferson*, ed. A. A. Lipscomb et al. (Washington, D.C.: Thomas Jefferson Memorial Association of the United States, 1904) 8: 436–38 (hereinafter cited as *Jefferson Writings*).

48. Ibid., Jefferson to Morris, October 15, 1972, pp. 419–21.
49. Quoted in Goebel, *Recognition Policy,* p. 103.
50. Quoted in ibid., pp. 103–4.
51. Ibid., p. 104.
52. *Jefferson Writings,* 9: 32–33.
53. Cited in J. A. Carroll and M. W. Ashworth, *George Washington: First in Peace* (New York: Scribner's, 1957) 7: 46.
54. See Goebel, *Recognition Policy,* pp. 107–12; Hamilton and Knox to Washington, April 18, 1793, in *Hamilton Papers,* 14: 367–96.
55. Hamilton invoked Vattel on this point (*Hamilton Papers,* 15: 67, 197). Jefferson and Madison argued that Hamilton misinterpreted Vattel (Jefferson to Madison, April 28, 1793, and Madison to Jefferson, May 8, 1793, *Madison Papers,* pp. 10–11, 12–13).
56. Hamilton and Knox to Washington, April 18, 1793, *Hamilton Papers,* 14: 367–68.
57. Ibid., Jay to Hamilton, April 11, 1793, p. 309.
58. Quoted in Carroll and Ashworth, *George Washington,* p. 49.
59. The Pacificus-Helvidius letters have been collected by Richard Loss, ed., *The Letters of Pacificus and Helvidius* (Delmar, N.Y.: Scholars' Facsimiles and Reprints, 1976).
60. Quoted in *Madison Papers,* 15: 65.
61. Loss, ed. *Letters,* p. 9.
62. Ibid., p. 13.
63. Prof. Michael Glennon has justly stated: "In mutual-security treaties to which the United States is a party, commitment is a myth" (Glennon, *Constitutional Diplomacy* [Princeton, N.J.: Princeton University Press, 1990], p. 193). See, generally, Wormuth and Firmage, *To Chain the Dog of War.*
64. Lawrence S. Kaplan, *Colonies into Nations: American Diplomacy 1763–1801* (New York: Macmillan, 1972), p. 221.
65. "It is Madison, not Hamilton," Henry Steele Commager justly observed, "who has a just claim to be considered not only the Father of the Constitution but its most authoritative interpreter." *Hearings on War Powers Legislation Before the Senate Committee on Foreign Relations,* 92d Cong., 1st sess., 1971, 19.
66. Quoted in Loss, ed., *Letters,* p. 77.
67. Ibid. This is straight out of Vattel's treatise; see Vattel, *Law of Nations,* Book 4, secs. 68 and 78, pp. 365–66, 369.
68. Loss, ed., *Letters,* p. 76.
69. Adler, *Termination,* pp. 84–148.
70. Westel W. Willoughby, *The Constitutional Law of the United States,* 2d ed., 3 vols. (New York: Baker, Voorhis, 1929), 1: 521.
71. Farrand, *Records,* 2: 540.
72. Elliot, *Debates,* 3: 353.
73. Ibid., 2: 305.
74. *Annals of Congress* (1818), 31: 106–7.
75. Hamilton, *Federalist 75,* pp. 486–87.

76. Elliot, *Debates,* 4: 120, 264–65.

77. Joseph Story, *Commentaries on the Constitution of the United States,* 5th ed., 2 vols. (1833; rpt., Boston: Little, Brown, 1905), 2: sec. 1512.

78. *McCulloch v. Maryland,* 4 Wheat. 316, 421 (1819).

79. Quoted in Loss, ed., *Letters,* p. 87.

6
WHY THE PRESIDENT ALMOST ALWAYS WINS IN FOREIGN AFFAIRS

HAROLD HONGJU KOH

Why does the president almost always seem to win in foreign affairs? The reasons may be grouped under three headings, which not coincidentally mirror general institutional characteristics of the executive, legislative, and judicial branches. First, and most obviously, the president has won because the executive branch has taken the initiative in foreign affairs and has done so by construing laws designed to constrain his actions as authorizations. Second, the president has won because, for all its institutional activity, Congress has usually complied with or acquiesced in what the president has done, through legislative myopia, inadequate drafting, ineffective legislative tools, or sheer lack of political will. Third, the president has won because the federal courts have usually tolerated his acts, either by refusing to hear challenges to those acts or by hearing the challenges and then affirming presidential authority on its merits.

The simple, three-part combination of executive initiative, congressional acquiescence, and judicial tolerance explains why the president almost invariably wins in foreign affairs. Indeed, this three-part reasoning enters directly into the calculus of an executive branch layer asked to draft a legal opinion justifying a proposed foreign affairs initiative. If asked, for example, whether the president can impose economic sanctions on Libya or can bomb Colonel Qaddafi's headquarters, the president's lawyer must answer three questions: Do we have the legal authority to act? Can Congress stop us? Can anyone challenge our action in court? Or, to use the framework outline above: Do the Constitution and laws of the United States authorize the president to take this executive initiative? If the executive branch takes the initiative, will Congress acquiesce? If Congress does not acquiesce and challenges the president's action (or if a private citizen sues), will the courts nevertheless tolerate the act, either by refusing to hear the challenge or by hearing it and ruling in the president's favor? The focus of this chapter is on the first two questions; the third is discussed elsewhere.[1]

EXECUTIVE INITIATIVE

What drives the executive branch to take the initiative in foreign affairs? Most critics of the Iran-Contra affair have offered no explanation, simply assuming that the president's men were overzealous, foolish, misguided, or evil. However true these explanations might be, two institutional explanations—based on domestic constitutional structure and international regime change—plausibly supplement them.

The simple yet sensible domestic explanation, offered by Charles Black, attributes executive seizure of the initiative in foreign affairs to the structure of the Constitution. Although Article I gives Congress almost all the enumerated powers over foreign affairs and Article II gives the president almost none of them, Congress is poorly structured for initiative and leadership because of "its dispersed territoriality of power-bases and . . . its bicamerality." The presidency, in contrast, is ideally structured for the receipt and exercise of power: "What very naturally has happened is simply that power textually assigned to and at any time resumable by the body structurally unsuited to its exercise, has flowed, through the inactions, acquiescences, and delegations of that body, toward an office ideally structured for the exercise of initiative and for vigor in administration. . . . The result has been a flow of power from Congress to the presidency."[2]

The notion that the presidency is institutionally best suited to initiate government action is hardly new. To the contrary, the notion dates back to Alexander Hamilton's statement that "energy in the executive is a leading character in the definition of good government."[3] Nor, in theory, is there anything wrong with the president initiating international action. As in the domestic context, a plebiscitary president is uniquely visible, and hence accountable, to the electorate. He is the only individual capable of centralizing and coordinating the foreign policy decisionmaking process. He can energize and direct policy in ways that could not be done by either Congress or his own bureaucracy.[4] His decisionmaking processes can take on degrees of speed, secrecy, flexibility, and efficiency that no other governmental institution can match. As Justice Sutherland declared in *Curtiss-Wright* (quoting from a Senate Report): "The President . . . manages our concerns with foreign nations and must necessarily be most competent to determine when, how, and upon what subjects negotiation may be urged with the greatest prospect of success. . . . The nature of transactions with foreign nations, moreover, requires caution and unity of design, and their success frequently depends on secrecy and dispatch.''[5] Over time, these structural considerations have largely explained why the president has assumed the preeminent role in foreign affairs, despite the clear textual preference of the Framers for Congress.

But the structural fact that the president may more easily exercise foreign affairs power than Congress does not explain why he *chooses* to wield it. The explanation may lie not simply in constitutional structure but in the complex relationship between domestic constitutional regimes and international regimes.[6] Theorists of international relations might explain the president's activist choices in terms of the rise and fall of American hegemony during the postwar era. It is familiar that Franklin Roosevelt's personalization and institutionalization of the presidency initiated an extrovert phase in American foreign policy, which marked America's emergence as the world's hegemonic power. During these years, which began before Pearl Harbor and ended with Vietnam, the president led America to erect the entire postwar multilateral political and economic order. An entire generation of Americans grew up and came to power believing in the wisdom of the muscular presidential leadership of foreign policy.[7]

The activist logic of this extrovert era made presidential initiatives virtually inevitable. Yet Vietnam caused an entire generation to rethink its attitude toward foreign policy. National elites became less willing to intervene to defend other nations and to bear the cost of world leadership.[8] Why, then, have presidential initiatives not only continued but appeared to accelerate during the post-Vietnam era?

In recent years, many distinguished scholars have made the claim that America is losing it hegemonic grip upon the world. Political economists David Calleo, Robert Gilpin, Robert Keohane, and Stephen Krasner, the historian Paul Kennedy, and economists Charles Kindleberger and Mancur Olson have recently examined the implications for world order of declining American hegemony. Although other distinguished scholars, including Samuel Huntington, Joseph Nye, Bruce Russett, and Susan Strange, have questioned the empirical basis underlying these claims of lost American hegemony, several policy analysts have steadfastly asserted the same claim.[9] The common strand that runs through this burgeoning literature is the suggestion that America is moving into a new historical era in its relationship with the rest of the world. This new phase, a posthegemonic era, is one in which the United States will act as an engaged global participant but will lack its former power to dominate singlehandedly the flow of international events.

Put simply, America's declining role as world hegemon has forced changes in the postwar structure of international institutions, which have in turn stimulated further presidential initiatives. In the place of formal multilateral political and economic institutions, which enact bodies of positive international law through treaties, have arisen new, informal regional and functional regimes. Those regimes, which the United States may not dominate but in which it must participate, now manage global economic and political events through bargaining and "soft," quasi-legal pronouncements. Examples on the political side include the international human rights regime, the international peacekeeping and nuclear nonproliferation regimes, and an evolving international dispute-resolution regime. On the economic side, the United States participates in the Group of Seven nations to manage exchange rates; in the Coordinating Committee on Multilateral Export Controls (CoCom) to manage strategic export trade; and in a debt regime that includes private bankers, multilateral organizations, and the informal Paris and London clubs for debt rescheduling, to give just a few examples.[10]

Within these regimes, the United States can no longer simply suppress conflicts of national interest; it must constantly manage relations even with close historic allies through repeated applications of economic carrots and political sticks. For example, recent developments in the world trading system have stimulated the United States to turn to an array of unilateral economic sanctions, bilateral free trade agreements and investment programs, and plurilateral monetary bargaining within the Group of Seven, in addition to (and often in lieu of) its traditional multilateral bargaining within the framework of the General Agreement of Tariffs and Trade (GATT). The rise of new and unanticipated problems not subject to the control of any nation-state, such as global terrorism and the debt crisis, has increasingly forced the United States into a reactive international posture.[11] Given the president's superior institutional capacity to initiate governmental action, the burden of generating reactive responses to external challenges has almost invariably fallen on him.

It is of course true that post-Vietnam congressional reforms also stimulated a resurgence of congressional interest and activism in foreign policy. Key foreign affairs committees have recently gained dramatically in both expertise and influence, and the number of informal congressional foreign policy caucuses has risen dramatically. Yet, ironically, those same reforms have left Congress too decentralized and democratized to generate its own coherent program of foreign policy initiatives.[12] Increasingly, Congress has exhibited its interest and activism in foreign affairs by exerting pressure on the president through means short of legislation. Particularly in fields such as international trade, which directly affect congressional constituencies, Congress has forced the president into a range of preemptive strikes to respond to or forestall even more drastic congressional activity. Recent well-publicized examples include the executive order imposing sanctions upon South Africa in order to preempt congressional enactment of comprehensive antiapartheid legislation; executive decisions in response to congressional pressures to close Palestinian Liberation Organization (PLO) offices in the United States and to deny PLO leader Yasir Arafat a visa; the expanded use of section 301 of the Trade Act of 1974 and so-called Super 301 of the 1988 Omnibus Trade and Competitiveness Act to open foreign markets; and the reluctance to fund the United Nations, a reflection in part of pressure imposed by Congress' enactment of the Kassebaum amendment.[13]

The same public opinion that has empowered the plebiscitary president has simultaneously subjected him to almost irresistible pressures to act quickly in times of real or imagined crisis. "Mass pressure on plebiscitary presidents requires results, or the appearance of results, regardless of the danger."[14] In many ways, the recent wave of treaty breaking and bending chronicled elsewhere reflects a reactive presidential role in leading both America's flight from international organizations and its movement toward alternative mechanisms of multilateral cooperation.[15] Similarly, President Reagan's use of short-term military strikes and emergency economic powers (to respond to terrorism), longer-term military commitments in Lebanon and the Persian Gulf (to respond to requests for peacekeeping), arms sales (to respond to military tensions in the Middle East), and covert actions (to effectuate neocontainment policies in Central America and Angola) reflect the modern American perception that crisis situations uniquely demand a presidential response.

Thus, the relative weakening of America in the world arena appears unexpectedly to have promoted an increase, rather than a decrease, in executive initiatives. In so suggesting, I do not deny the political scientists' insight that once such a crisis has been presented to the president, powerful domestic factors such as ideology, political philosophy, groupthink, or bureaucratic politics will combine to help drive his response.[16] My overriding claim, however, is that a pervasive national perception that the presidency must act swiftly and secretly to respond to fast-moving international events has almost inevitably forced the executive branch into a continuing pattern of evasion of congressional restraint.

This pattern has afflicted presidents of both political parties, without regard to whether they have generally been viewed as weak or strong, reckless or law-abiding. During the Iranian hostage crisis of 1979–1981, for example, President Carter reacted to both international and domestic pressures by conducting one of the most dramatic exercises of presidential power in foreign affairs in peacetime in U.S. history. During the 444 days that the U.S. hostages were held captive, he declared a national emergency under the International Emergency Economic Powers Act (IEEPA); imposed a trade embargo and an extra-territorial-assets freeze; cut off lines of communication and embargoed travel to Iran; sued Iran in the International Court of Justice; expelled Iranian diplomats; forced Iranian students to report to local immigration offices for visa checks; made a disastrous attempt to rescue the hostages by force; and concluded a wide-ranging executive agreement that suspended all private property claims against Iran while consigning American commercial claimants to arbitration before a newly established international tribunal. But when Carter left office, he was widely viewed not as an imperial president but as the weakest, most reactive president in recent memory. As one commentator observed, describing Carter's disastrous military attempt to rescue the hostages, "Public opinion had forced upon the president an act of the sheerest adventurism."[17]

Ultimately, an unholy synergy between the executive branch's ideological imperatives, international incentives, and domestic latitude to act drove it toward the Iran-Contra affair. A president dependent upon public opinion and sensitive to congressional pressure sought to respond to two perceived external threats—the taking of American hostages in Lebanon and the rise of a Communist regime in Nicaragua. In the same way as Oliver North saw the choice as one between "lies and lives," President Reagan saw the choice as between lives and law. As he reportedly told his secretary of state, "The American people will never forgive me if I fail to get these hostages out over this legal question."[18] As with earlier presidents, Reagan's commitment to action led him to condone an errant flow of decisionmaking power, not just from Congress to the executive branch but *within* the executive.[19] In his administration, power flowed away from the larger, more accountable but more cumbersome foreign affairs bureaucracies, such as the State and Defense departments, toward institutions such as the Central Intelligence Agency (CIA) and the National Security Council (NSC), which are closer to the Oval Office and more capable of swift, secret, and flexible action. To be sure, the resulting covert transfer of power to subexecutive entities facilitated swift and secret action. But at the same time, it inevitably sacrificed the technical expertise, institutional judgment, bureaucratic support, and bipartisan political approval that comes from consultative inter- and intrabranch decisionmaking in accordance with the National Security Constitution.

CONGRESSIONAL ACQUIESCENCE

In light of the president's strong institutional incentives to take initiatives, why in recent years has Congress so consistently failed to check or restrain him? The short answer is that, despite the initial flurry of post-Vietnam legislation, Congress has persistently acquiesced in executive efforts to evade that legislation's strictures. That acquiescence has institutional roots in legislative myopia, inadequate drafting, ineffective legislative tools, and an institutional lack of political will. The case in point is the War Powers Resolution of 1973, which has failed in its intended purpose for each of these four reasons.

Legislative Myopia

The first reason, already illustrated, is that Congress legislates to stop the last war. The War Powers Resolution was drafted principally to halt creeping wars like Vietnam, not short-term military strikes or covert wars of the kind that dominate modern warfare. Similarly, the covert action reform legislation that recently died in Congress would not have truly reformed the intelligence apparatus; it would have only finely tuned existing statutes to prevent the president from indefinitely delaying reports to Congress, which any future president mindful of the Iran-Contra affair would take care to avoid even without legislation. Why does Congress legislate this way? All explanations of congressional behavior, of course, must begin and end with politics. The institutional roots of congressional myopia lie in each phase of the legislative process.[20] As Morris Fiorina has observed, Congress legislates retrospectively largely because voters vote that way.[21] Like other legislation that attempts to be public regarding, proposed foreign affairs legislation is fully subject to undue influence or political veto by special interest groups. The trade field, of course, is the most extensively studied arena of private-interest-group influence upon Congress in foreign affairs. But in other areas, the defense and foreign aid lobbies have proved to be highly successful in promoting the maintenance of military spending and military aid. The Israeli lobby has exercised well-publicized influence over Middle East, Arab boycott, and arms sale policy. Even the intelligence committees are subject to lobbying by interest groups such as the Center for National Security Studies and the Association of Retired Intelligence Officers.[22]

Occasionally, these interest groups will press for, rather than against, legislative action. The international human rights lobbies, for example, successfully pressed for legislative action in obtaining the ratification of the Genocide Convention and the enactment of the South African sanctions bill. An influential ad hoc national interest group composed of students, parents of potential draftees, and alumni of the 1960s civil rights movement rose up to demand legislation to end the Vietnam War.[23] But more frequently, powerful interest groups will press to defeat or narrow pending legislation, thereby burying broader public policy reform objectives amid a welter of provincial or ethnic group concerns.

Even when interest groups successfully press individual members of Congress to act, rather than simply to refrain from action, there is no assurance that those members will take the broad view. The need of members to be seen as addressing this year's problem encourages them to address last year's problems by tinkering with existing statutes rather than by investing energy in introducing and passing large-scale reform programs. In 1973, for example, Sen. Thomas Eagleton (D.-Mo.) attempted to expand the War Powers Resolution to reach paramilitary forces under civilian command, but his efforts failed because his colleagues did not wish to legislate against speculative problems. As David Mayhew has noted, the desire of congressional members to choose legislative devices that can be easily explained to constituents leads to a "congressional penchant for the blunt, simple action," which may be insufficiently sensitive to the complexities of the underlying problem.[24] Congress' taste for the symbolic, easily comprehended legislative fix explains its decisions to enact a War Powers Resolution with an automatic sixty-day withdrawal provision; to consider carefully the Gephardt amendment to the 1988 trade bill (which, like the Gramm-Rudman-Hollings budget-balancing act, took an automatic phased numerical approach to reduction of the trade deficit); and to propose intelligence reform legislation after the Iran-Contra affair that declared a simple, mandatory forty-eight-hour-notice rule for all covert operations. The result of these institutional influences is that Congress lags behind public opinion in enacting major legislation and tends to wrap its policies in packages with largely symbolic value that offer particularized benefits to organized interest groups.[25]

Even when courageous congressional members overcome this institutional particularity and introduce sweeping legislative reforms, they must deal with committees. The competing objectives of the committees sharing jurisdiction over any omnibus bill or of members within particular committees may impede the coalition formation necessary to bring that bill to the floor. Committee chairs, who are still generally chosen based on seniority, may be less ready to challenge the president than more junior members, who may be subcommittee chairs at best. Thus, as in the case of the Boland amendments, several years of internal committee battles may ensue before the committee chair is willing to support, much less lend his or her name to, legislation that restricts presidential prerogative.[26]

The fate of the 1988 intelligence oversight reform legislation, the only Iran-Contra legislation to progress during the last Congress, provides a good illustration of these legislative problems. That bill was long delayed in coming to the floor, in part because it was referred for markup to both the House Intelligence and the House Foreign Affairs committees. Yet even after the committees finally reported the bill out late in the session, it was not brought to a floor vote; when it was reintroduced early in 1989, the leadership shelved it for extraneous political reasons. Even in the rare case where a floor vote occurs and floor majorities can be mustered in a bill's support, the Senate's rules require only forty-one votes to sustain a filibuster and defeat legislation.[27] Should the president veto the bill, as he threatens to do with most proposed legislation that would limit his freedom in matters of foreign affairs, the number of senators required to sustain the veto drops even further to thirty-four. For that reason, the supermajorities needed to overcome filibusters and vetoes usually coalesce around only those specific incremental changes that would correct known policy defects.

Bad Drafting

Even when enacted, legislation expressly designed to check executive adventurism has often failed because of faulty draftsmanship. The War Powers Resolution, the most ambitious piece of foreign affairs framework legislation enacted in the post–Vietnam era, offers three particularly glaring examples. First, the resolution's consultation requirements oblige the president to consult "in every possible instance" but then allow the president to decide what that term should mean. Thus, although prior consultation was clearly "possible," neither Carter nor Reagan consulted with Congress before sending troops to Iran and Grenada.[28] Second, the resolution requires the president to consult with Congress before he sends troops abroad but nowhere specifies how many members must be consulted or how far in advance. When Reagan sent warplanes to bomb Libya in April 1986, for example, he consulted with only fifteen congressional leaders and even then only after the planes were already in the air.[29] Third and most curious, depending upon the situation, the resolution permits the president to file three different types of reports to Congress upon committing armed forces abroad—whenever U.S. armed forces are introduced "into hostilities" or imminent hostilities; into foreign territory, airspace, or waters equipped for combat; or in numbers that substantially enlarge a preexisting combat unit. Yet the law's sixty-day clock for removing those troops runs automatically only from the date when a so-called hostilities report is submitted or "required to be submitted" and not when one of the other two types of report has been filed.[30] Simply by his choice of report, the president can thus satisfy the resolution's procedural reporting obligation while evading the resolution's substantive obligation to remove those troops within sixty days.

Some of these drafting errors were simply inadvertent. The legal counsel to the Senate Foreign Relations Committee during consideration of the War Powers Resolution recalls that the third drafting error just described was simply "unnoticed at the time the resolution was enacted."[31] Such inadvertence may also have institutional roots, however. Professor Mayhew has observed that once members decide to vote for a bill and exhaust its "credit-claiming" possibilities, they often "display only a modest interest in what goes into bills or what their passage accomplishes."[32] Other drafting errors—the perpetuation of the in-every-possible-instance language, for example—have resulted from the legislative tendency to draft new laws simply by transplanting boilerplate language from other post–Vietnam-era statutes.[33]

Perhaps what appears most frequently to outsiders to be poor drafting stems, in fact, from political deals or compromises struck among members of Congress, among staffers, members and staffers, congressional and executive staffers, members and executive officials, or among the drafting entities within the executive branch itself. Particularly when the president threatens a veto, a peculiar Capitol Hill ritual known as "being pecked to death by ducks" transpires, whereby more stringent procedural provisions are substantially watered down in conference in an often futile effort to avert the president's veto. This phenomenon accounts, for example, for the numerous loopholes in the 1986 South Africa sanctions bill, that passed into law over a presidential veto.[34] In much the same way, the 1980 Intelligence Oversight Act, which was originally drafted to require prior notice in all cases, was watered down to require only "timely" notice, language that lent itself to easy twisting during the Iran-Contra affair.[35]

Whatever the cause, the cumulative effect of these drafting failures has been to prevent the War Powers Resolution from being self-executing. Rather than put the pressure where it should be—on the president to start thinking about removing armed forces sixty days after he has committed them to a hostile situation—the War Powers Resolution now puts pressure on Congress to declare that U.S. forces are "in hostilities" in order to trigger the sixty-day clock for troop removal. If Congress as a whole is unwilling to make that declaration, aggrieved members must file suit in federal court seeking a judicial declaration that the resolution has been triggered, an option that thus far has yielded them no relief.[36] Even though Congress designed the War Powers Resolution to stop the last war—subtly escalating conflicts like Vietnam—in recent years, ironically, the resolution's drafting flaws have undercut its effectiveness in restraining just such creeping escalation in Lebanon, Central America, and the Persian Gulf.

Ineffective Tools

Why have its legislative solutions not worked even when Congress has both foreseen a problem and properly drafted provisions to address it? Post–Vietnam-era statutes applied an array of innovative procedural devices to bring executive action under control, including statutory sunset provisions, reporting and consultation requirements, committee oversight procedures, legislative vetoes, and appropriations limitations. Each of the statutes whose enactment has been described—the War Powers Resolution, the Case-Zablocki Act, IEEPA, the Arms Export Control Act, the Hughes-Ryan amendment, and the Intelligence Oversight Act—was designed not only to restrain executive discretion but also to increase congressional input into key foreign policy decisions. But if the Iran-Contra affair teaches anything, it is that most of these procedural devices simply have not worked, particularly when executive officials are intent upon evading them and courts are unwilling to enforce them.

Each of these devices has its defects. As Guido Calabresi has recognized, mechanical sunset laws force Congress to redo its work every few years, giving "a tremendous weapon to those who oppose regulation itself; the force of inertia shifts to their side." Not only does time not serve as an adequate measure of how obsolescent a statute may be, but complex legislative compromises will inevitably be difficult to replicate when a statute is sunsetted.[37] The War Powers Resolution experience shows that reporting and consultation requirements lack teeth and are all too easily evaded. Committee oversight invites committee capture and can usually be conducted only after the executive action has been completed.[38] The only supervisory methods that have proved their bite in foreign affairs—particularly in the areas of arms sales, transfer of nuclear materials, and covert action—have been the legislative veto and the appropriations cutoff.[39]

Legislative vetoes are simple or concurrent resolutions that have been approved by a majority of one or two houses, respectively, but that have not been presented to the president for signature or veto.[40] These provisions were the linchpins of the post–Vietnam-era framework legislation. Yet in 1983 the Supreme Court issued a sweeping decision, *INS v. Chadha*, which denied such vetoes legal effect.[41] Moreover, in the first years after *Chadha*, the Court embroidered it with a series of formalistic rulings whose broad language, read literally, would limit any congressional attempt to regulate executive exercises of delegated power by means other than legislation.[42] *Chadha*, which announced wide-ranging separation-of-powers language, could be read to restrict Congress' future authority to check presidential discretion in foreign affairs by using methods functionally similar to the legislative veto.

Moreover, as the saga of the Boland amendments has revealed, the alternative technique of appropriations cutoff does not necessarily ensure good executive behavior. When tacked to massive continuing appropriations measures, such limitations carry the political advantage of being nearly veto-proof.[43] At the same time, however, they possess the disadvantage of being subject to yearly reconsideration and modification. When, as in the case of the Boland amendments, the language of the restriction becomes more and less inclusive over time, executive officials can claim that the provision's vagueness impairs their ability to determine whether particular activities are proscribed.[44]

More explicitly drafted appropriations limits might not have more teeth, however. Two recent inconclusive Supreme Court rulings have left unclear how far Congress may go in exercising or enforcing its appropriations power to constrain the president's authorities in foreign affairs. More than forty years ago, in *United States v. Lovett,* the Court held that Congress could not use its appropriations power to effect a bill of attainder under Article I, section 9, clause 3 of the Constitution.[45] Although the Court has never extended *Lovett* beyond the bill of attainder context, presidential supporters have argued by analogy that the Boland amendments placed overly strict conditions upon presidential expenditure of authorized funds and thereby encroached unconstitutionally upon the executive's inherent authority to conduct foreign affairs.[46] Some commentators have argued that Congress may not constitutionally refuse to appropriate funds for the president to execute his exclusive, enumerated authorities in foreign affairs.[47] Until very recently, however, no federal court had ever invalidated an appropriations statute on the ground that it unconstitutionally impinged upon the president's ill-defined *unenumerated* foreign affairs authority, as described in *Curtiss-Wright.* In *Federal Employees v. United States,* however, a district court invoked the amorphous "role of the Executive in foreign relations" to invalidate a statute precluding the use of appropriated funds to implement or enforce government nondisclosure agreements. On appeal, the Supreme Court vacated and remanded that judgment for procedural reasons. Although the ruling removed district court precedent from the books, it also left both the underlying issue unresolved and the president free to challenge future appropriations limitations on executive branch actions as unconstitutional exercises of Congress' power of the purse.[48]

Indefinite judicial resolution has kept suspended constitutional objections not just to congressional creation of appropriations limits but also to the enforcement of such limits on the executive by the comptroller general. It appeared that the Supreme Court would clarify the constitutionally permissible scope of the comptroller general's authority when it recently consented to hear a case raising a constitutional challenge to his statutory authorities under the Competition in Contracting Act. Subsequently, however, the litigants agreed voluntarily to dismiss the case, leaving unresolved whether Congress may constitutionally direct the comptroller general to enforce executive compliance with spending limitations in foreign affairs.[49]

As the Iran-Contra affair revealed, the executive branch may also seek to escape Congress' power of the purse altogether by soliciting private entities to support U.S. foreign policy initiatives with wholly private monies. Although the Iran-Contra committees concluded that the Constitution prohibits such private solicitations "*where the United States exercises control over the receipt and expenditure* of the solicited funds," executive officials could foreseeably circumvent that conclusion by soliciting third parties directly to support foreign initiatives and by arguing that the solicited private monies never became part of the "public fisc" that is subject to Congress' appropriations power.[50] Oliver North made such a claim during the congressional Iran-Contra hearings when he acknowledged urging private citizens to support the Contras while maintaining that "we lived within the constraints of Boland, which limited the use of *appropriated funds*."[51]

Even when undeniably managing government monies, the president has developed over time a whole range of devices to exploit spending loopholes in the appropriations process. When Congress grants the president statutory "drawdown" authority, he may withdraw certain funds simply by determining that such withdrawals are vital to the security of the United States. Similar statutory provisions allow the president access to special or contingency funds based upon nebulous findings that the use of those funds is "important to the security of the United States" or "to the national interest." When given statutory "transfer" and "reprogramming" authority, the president may transfer to one appropriations account funds initially appropriated for another or may reprogram appropriated funds *within* a single appropriation account, often without specific statutory authority.[52] Even before the Iran-Contra affair broke, the Reagan administration had shown that these authorities could be used in combination to sustain the Central American conflict without seeking new appropriations. In the early 1980s the Reagan administration used drawdown authority over special funds to increase military aid to El Salvador by nearly five times the amount actually appropriated in a given year and routinely used the reprogramming authority to fund Central American projects that Congress had not approved.[53]

For all these defects, the appropriations limitation remains one of Congress' few effective legal tools to regulate presidential initiatives in foreign affairs. Even the most creative president cannot exploit spending loopholes indefinitely. Moreover, each of the open legal questions described above should, in my judgment, be resolved in favor of Congress' appropriations power if Congress' exclusive power over the purse is to have continuing meaning in the context of foreign affairs. But even if the courts rule for Congress on these matters, for purposes of Justice Jackson's category three, in his *Youngstown Sheet and Tube Co. v. Sawyer* (1952), Congress will retain only two meaningful ways to oppose a presidential initiative—by disapproving the president's action by joint resolution or by voting an unambiguous and complete denial of appropriated funds for the disfavored program. Yet in either case Congress would then need to override the president's inevitable veto by a two-thirds vote in each house. In the end, both solutions only trade one problem for another, for each requires Congress to exercise a measure of political will that it has rarely been able to muster.

Political Will

Congress could regularly block executive decisions by joint resolution or appropriations cutoff, so long as it could override a presidential veto by a two-thirds vote. Yet over the years, Congress has overridden only 7 percent of the presidential vetoes (excluding pocket vetoes) exercised between 1789 and 1989.[54] Why has Congress not overridden vetoes more often? In many cases, a critical mass of congressional members has simply been unwilling to take responsibility for setting foreign policy, preferring to leave the decision—and the blame—with the president. As Sen. William Fulbright (D.-Ark.) recalled, long before the mid-1970s "a majority [of Congress] may have wished to end the war [in Indochina], but less than a majority of the two Houses were willing to take the responsibility for ending it."[55]

The size of the critical mass necessary to kill legislation varies from bill to bill. In committee, sometimes even a single member can prevent a bill from reaching the floor; in the Senate, forty-one votes (less than a majority) can defeat cloture. Even in those cases in which a majority in both houses is willing to take a stand against the president, Congress often falls victim to simple numbers. For if Congress must muster a two-thirds vote in both houses to override a veto, only thirty-four senators can undercut its efforts. It is a crippled president indeed who cannot muster at least thirty-four votes for something he really wants, especially in foreign affairs. Even in the waning days of his administration, for example, Reagan secured forty-two votes for the confirmation of Robert Bork as a Supreme Court justice; early in his term, George

Bush won forty-seven votes for the ill-fated nomination of John Tower as secretary of defense. Reagan also succeeded in defeating Congress' effort to override his veto of the 1988 trade reform legislation, essentially by securing the
votes of two senators, even though the House had voted overwhelmingly for
an override.[56]

Charles Black has calculated that, assuming equal defections across party
lines, a House of Representatives would need 308 Democrats and 127 Republicans to be veto-proofed against a Republican president. At this writing, even
the large Democratic majority facing President Bush falls more than fifty votes
short of this number.[57] In theory, all members would have an incentive to enhance the power of Congress by enforcing an alternative solution—a binding
political agreement to override any presidential veto regardless of its substance.[58] Yet even in a repeat-player game, such an accord simply would not
hold up, for those members who favored the president's position on any particular bill would always have an incentive to defect and support the president,
even if their defection would weaken Congress' long-run strength vis-à-vis the
president. For precisely this reason, Congress has been unable to circumvent
the Supreme Court's decision in *Chadha* by entering a political compact to re-
enact all legislative vetoes by joint resolution regardless of their content.[59]

Collective-action problems aside, individual members face voting dilemmas
when the president violates congressionally imposed procedural constraints in
pursuit of substantive policies that they favor. When the Reagan administration sent troops to Grenada and bombers to Libya without complying with
the terms of the War Powers Resolution, for example, advocates of his policy
decision remained quiet rather than contest his procedural violation.[60] Similarly, parliamentary manipulation by the president's congressional allies may
force objecting legislators into untenable voting postures. In 1987 Sen. Lowell
Weicker (R.-Conn.), an opponent of the president's Persian Gulf policy, initially voted against a weak resolution protesting the president's acts on the
ground that it implied that the War Powers Resolution was not self-enforcing.
He ultimately decided to vote for it, simply to ensure that Congress would
register some objection to the president's noncompliance with the War
Powers Resolution in the Persian Gulf.[61] Nor is it unprecedented for a member
who led a drive to override the president's veto to vote to sustain the veto,
simply to preserve his right to call for the bill's reconsideration.[62]

Some legislative restraints are rarely applied simply because they leave members too vulnerable to political criticism. Appropriations cutoffs, for example,
expose legislators to charges of having stranded soldiers in the field. Even
though Congress had constitutional authority through its power of the purse
to terminate U.S. involvement in Vietnam long before 1973, "a large major-

ity of Congress felt it could not break with the President without jeopardizing the lives of American troops.''[63] Even when Congress has successfully forced the president to the bargaining table on a question of foreign affairs, as it did with regard to the 1982 commitment of forces to Lebanon, the president has usually been able to demand concessions or future support in exchange for agreeing to modify his conduct.[64] Thus, once again, the president remains largely free to execute his initiatives without congressional check, except in those rare cases where he is politically weak and where Congress' political will is unusually unified.

NOTES

This chapter was first published as Chapter 5 in Harold Hongju Koh, *The National Security Constitution* (New Haven: Yale University Press, 1990). It is reprinted with the permission of Yale University Press.

1. For a discussion of judicial tolerance of executive actions in foreign affairs, see Chapter 1 of this volume.

2. Charles Black, ''The Working Balance of the American Political Departments,'' *Hastings Constitutional Law Quarterly* 1 (1980): 13, 17, 20.

3. See *The Federalist,* ed. Edward Mead Earle (New York: Modern Library, 1937), A. Hamilton, *Federalist 70,* p. 454. For a more recent discussion of the same concept, see, generally, R. Neustadt, *Presidential Power: The Politics of Leadership from FDR to Carter,* rev. ed. (New York: John Wiley, 1980).

4. Cf. Cass Sunstein, ''Constitutionalism After the New Deal,'' *Harvard Law Review* 101 (1987): 421, 452–53, which articulates these three reasons as arguments favoring presidential control of the bureaucracy. See also, *Youngstown Sheet & Tube Co. v. Sawyer,* 343 U.S. 629, 629 (1952) (Douglas, J., concurring): ''All executive power—from the reign of ancient kings to the rule of modern dictators—has the outward appearance of efficiency. Legislative power, by contrast, is slower to exercise. . . . The ponderous machinery of committees, hearings, and debates is . . . cumbersome, time-consuming, and apparently inefficient.''

5. See *United States v. Curtiss-Wright Export Corp.,* 299 U.S. 304, 319 (1936), quoting U.S. Senate, Reports, Committee on Foreign Relations, vol. 8, at 24, Feb. 15, 1816. *Curtiss-Wright*'s language appears to derive from *Federalist 75,* in which Hamilton referred to the treaty process as one requiring ''decision, *secrecy* and despatch.'' But significantly, Hamilton used that reason to justify the House's exclusion from the treaty ratification process, not to justify the president's monopoly over it. See *Federalist 75,* p. 488 (emphasis in original).

6. For a political scientist's recent attempt to untangle the intricate relationship between domestic politics and international relations, see Robert B. Putnam, ''Diplomacy and Domestic Politics: The Logic of Two-Level Games,'' *International Organization* 42 (1988): 427. See also Spitzer, Chapter 3 of this volume.

7. See Michael Roskin, ''From Pearl Harbor to Vietnam: Shifting Generational Paradigms and Foreign Policy,'' *Political Science Quarterly* 89 (1974): 563–89.

8. Ole R. Holsti and James Rosenau, *American Leadership in World Affairs: Vietnam and the Breakdown of Consensus* (Boston: Allen and Unwin, 1984), pp. 29–78; Bruce Russett, "The Americans' Retreat from World Power," *Political Science Quarterly* 90 (1975): 1, 5; John A. Vasquez, "Domestic Contention on Critical Foreign-Policy Issues: The Case of the United States," *International Organization* 42 (1988): 643, 646; Vasquez, "A Learning Theory of the American Anti-Vietnam Movement," *Journal of Peace Resolution* 13 (1976): 299; Ernest May, *"Lessons" of the Past: The Use and Misuse of History in American Foreign Policy* (New York: Oxford University Press, 1973), pp. 143–71.

9. For claims of declining American hegemony, see David Calleo, *Beyond American Hegemony* (New York: Basic Books, 1987); Robert Gilpin, *The Political Economy of International Relations* (Princeton: Princeton University Press, 1987); Gilpin, *War and Change in World Politics* ((New York: Cambridge University Press, 1981); Gilpin, *U.S. Power and the Multinational Corporation* (New York: Basic Books, 1975); and Paul Kennedy, *The Rise and Fall of the Great Powers* (New York: Random House, 1987). For academic responses to those claims, see Samuel Huntington, "The U.S.—Decline or Renewal?" *Foreign Affairs* 68 (1988): 76; Joseph Nye, "Short-Term Folly, Not Long-Term Decline," *New Perspectives Quarterly* (Summer 1988): 33; Nye, "Understating U.S. Strength," *Foreign Policy* 72 (1988): 105; Nye, "Before the Fall," *New Republic,* February 13, 1989, 37–39; Bruce Russett, "The Mysterious Case of Vanishing Hegemony: Or, Is Mark Twain Really Dead?" *International Organization* 39 (1985): 207; and S. Strange, "The Persistent Myth of Lost Hegemony," *International Organization* 41 (1987): 551, all of which question the notion of America's lost hegemony. For policy analysis, see, e.g., B. Bosworth and R. Lawrence, "America's Global Role: From Dominance to Interdependence," in *Restructuring American Foreign Policy,* ed. J. Steinbruner (Washington, D.C.: Brookings Institution, 1989), p. 12, which makes policy recommendations based on the assumption of lost hegemony.

10. These regimes have been the subject of intensive political science analysis. For a description of particular political regimes, see, e.g., Robert Keohane and Joseph Nye, "Two Cheers for Multilateralism," *Foreign Policy* 60 (1986): 148, which describes debt, peacekeeping, and exchange rate regimes.

11. For discussion of developments in the trade area, see, e.g., Harold Koh, "Congressional Controls on Presidential Trade Policymaking After *INS v. Chadha,*" *New York University Journal of International Law & Politics* 18 (1986): 1191, 1227; Koh, "The Legal Markets of International Trade: A Perspective on the Proposed United States–Canada Free Trade Agreement," *Yale Journal of International Law* 13 (1987): 193, 240–48; and Gilpin, *Political Economy of International Relations,* pp. 171–230. For a description of the legal structure of the nascent antiterrorism regime, see, e.g., Harold Koh, "Civil Remedies for Uncivil Wrongs: Combatting Terrorism Through Transnational Public Law Litigation," *Texas International Law Journal* 22 (1987): 169, 170–73.

12. On the rise of congressional activism, see Harold Koh, "Congressional Controls," pp. 1211–21, which discusses the enhanced powers of the House Ways and Means and Senate Finance Committees under the 1984 Trade and Tariff Act; Richard Fenno, *Congressmen in Committees* (Boston: Little, Brown, 1973), 26–35, which discusses the power of foreign affairs committees; Paul Hammond, "Congress in Foreign Policy," in *The President, the Congress, and Foreign Policy,* ed. E. Muskie, K. Rush, and

K. Thompson (Lanham, Md.: University Press of America, 1986), p. 81, which lists informal congressional foreign policy caucuses. On the decentralization of the new congress, see Norman Ornstein, "The Constitution and the Sharing of Foreign Policy Responsibility," in Muskie et al., *President,* pp. 35, 57.

13. On the South African sanctions battle, see Exec. Order No. 12,532,50, Fed. Reg. 36,861, 1985 (South African sanctions order). On the PLO mission controversy, see Designation of Palestine Information Office as a Foreign Mission, 52 Fed. Reg. 37,035, Oct. 2, 1987 (executive decision to close Palestinian office to forestall enactment of the Anti-Terrorism Act of 1987, Pub. L. No. 100–204, Subsection 1001–1005, 101 Stat. 1331, 1406–7); U.S. Department of State, Statement on the Visa Application of Yasir Arafat, *American Journal of International Law* 83 (1989): 253. On recent presidential preemptive strikes in the trade field, see Koh, "Congressional Controls," pp. 1225–33; Note, "Defining Unreasonableness in International Trade: Section 301 of the Trade Act of 1974," *Yale Law Journal* 96 (1987): 1122, 1122–26, describing the Reagan administration's use of Section 301 of the Trade Act of 1974 to open foreign markets; "Statement on United States Action Against Foreign Trade Barriers," 25 *Weekly Comp. Pres. Doc.* 777 (1989), naming Brazil, India, and Japan as "priority" unfair trading countries under "Super 301" of the 1988 Trade Act. On the role of the Kassebaum amendment in the United Nations funding crisis, see Kassebaum Amendment, Pub. L. No. 99–93, Section 143, 99 Stat. 405, 424, 1985 (codified at 22 U.S.C. Section 287e note [Supp. 4 1985]), imposing preconditions upon U.S. payment of assessed contributions to the United Nations and specialized agencies; Nelson, "International Law and U.S. Withholding of Payments to International Organizations," *American Journal of International Law* 80 (1986): 973.

14. See Theodore Lowi, *The Personal President* (Ithaca, N.Y.: Cornell University Press, 1985), p. 173.

15. See generally, Koh, *National Security Constitution,* chap. 2.

16. The political science literature on each of these phenomena is massive. On ideology, see, e.g., Michael H. Hunt, *Ideology and U.S. Foreign Policy* (New Haven: Yale University Press, 1987). On the role of political philosophy in international affairs, see Michael Joseph Smith's probing discussion of the role of realism in Kissinger's thought in Smith, *Realist Thought from Weber to Kissinger* (Baton Rouge: Louisiana State University Press, 1986), pp. 192–217. On groupthink, see Irving Janis, *Victims of Groupthink: A Psychological Study of Foreign-Policy Decisions and Fiascoes* (Boston: Houghton Mifflin, 1972). On the role of bureaucratic politics and foreign policy, see Graham Allison, *Essence of Decision: Explaining the Cuban Missile Crisis* (New York: Harper Collins, 1971), and Morton Halperin, *Bureaucratic Politics and Foreign Policy* (Washington, D.C.: Brookings Institution, 1974).

17. See Lowi, *Personal President,* p. 173. For descriptions of Carter's actions during the Iranian hostage crisis, see Koh, "Congressional Controls," p. 1229 n. 112; Gaddis Smith, *Morality, Reason, and Power* (New York: Hill and Wang, 1986), pp. 180–207.

18. See *Newsweek,* Aug. 13, 1987, p. 16, statement of Secretary of State Shultz, quoting President Reagan; Oliver North, *Taking the Stand: The Testimony of Lieutenant Colonel Oliver L. North* (New York: Simon and Schuster, 1987), pp. 12, 256: "This is a nation at risk in a dangerous world. . . . [W]e all had to weigh . . . the difference between lies and lives."

19. Cf. Henry Kissinger, *White House Years* (Boston: Little, Brown, 1979), p. 806:

Because President "Nixon feared leaks . . . he thus encouraged procedures unlikely to be recommended in textbooks on public administration that, crablike, worked privily around existing structures." When Nixon ordered the Cambodian bombings, for example, he explicitly instructed the NSC that the "State [Department] is to be notified only after the point of no return" (p. 245). When Henry Kissinger returned from his secret mission to China, Nixon instructed him to give the secretary of state only a "sanitized" account of the trip (pp. 756–57).

20. The phenomenon is not restricted to the American legislature. See, e.g., Watson, "Legal Evolution and Legislation," *Brigham Young University Law Review* (1987): 353, 375–79, which provides a crosscultural explanation for why legislatures often reject revolutionary proposals.

21. See Morris Fiorina, *Retrospective Voting in American National Elections* (New Haven: Yale University Press, 1981).

22. For general discussions of the role of interest groups in the legislative process, see Jonathan R. Macey, "Promoting Public-Regarding Legislation Through Statutory Interpretation: An Interest Group Model," *Columbia Law Review* 86 (1986): 223; Cass Sunstein, "Interest Groups in American Public Law," *Stanford Law Review* 38 (1985): 29.

On interest-group politics in international trade, see, generally, Raymond Bauer, Ithiel de Solo Pool, and Lewis Dexter, *American Business and Public Policy: The Politics of Foreign Trade* (Chicago: Aldine, Atherton, 1963); Stephen Cohen, *The Making of United States International Economic Policy* ((Westport, Conn.: Praeger, 1988), pp. 121–39; I. M. Destler, *American Trade Politics: System Under Stress* (Washington, D.C.: Institute for International Economics, 1986); E. E. Schattschneider, *Politics, Pressure, and the Tariff* (New York: Prentice-Hall, 1935).

On the role of the defense lobby, see, e.g., Hedrick Smith, *The Power Game* (New York: Random House, 1988), pp. 173–215, which describes the "iron triangle" among the military services, defense contractors, and members of Congress.

On the influence of Israel's lobby, see Thomas Franck and Edward Weisband, *Foreign Policy by Congress* (New York: Oxford University Press, 1979), pp. 200–209, and H. Smith, *Power Game*, pp. 216–31, which discusses the role of the American Israel Public Affairs Committee [AIPAC] in opposing Arab arms sales.

On interest-group influence on the intelligence committees, see Loch K. Johnson, *America's Secret Power: The CIA in a Democratic Society* (New York: Oxford University Press, 1989), pp. 219–20.

23. On interest-group influence on U.S. human rights policy, see, generally, David Forsythe, *Human Rights and U.S. Foreign Policy* (Gainesville: University Press of Florida, 1988). On the Vietnam lobby, see Norman Ornstein, "Interest Groups, Congress and American Policy," in *American Foreign Policy in an Uncertain World*, ed. David Forsythe (Gainesville: University Press of Florida, 1984), pp. 49, 52–55.

24. David Mayhew, *Congress: The Electoral Connection* (New Haven: Yale University Press, 1974), p. 138. For Senator Eagleton's proposal, see 119 *Cong. Rec.* 25,079–86 (1973).

25. See, generally, Mayhew, *Congress*, pp. 126–40. For examples of legislative "fixes" easily comprehended by the public, see Balanced Budget and Emergency Deficit Control Act of 1985, Pub. L. No. 99–177, 99 Stat. 1037, 1985, codified as amended in scattered sections of 2, 31, and 42 U.S.C., Gramm-Rudman-Hollings

budget-balancing act, numerical approach to domestic deficit reduction; Trade and International Economic Policy Reform Act of 1987, H.R. 3, 100th Cong., 1st sess. sec. 126, 133 *Cong. Rec.* 2,755–57 (1987); the Gephardt amendment to the 1988 Trade Reform Act was subsequently dropped in conference. It required the president to retaliate against countries running excessive and unwarranted trade surpluses with the United States by forcing those countries to reduce their surpluses by 10 percent annually. Madison, "It's Congress's Move," *National Journal* 19 (1987): 2014, 2017–18, describes the "forty-eight-hour notice" intelligence reform bill.

26. I am grateful to Robert J. Kurz of the Brookings Institution (formerly a staff member of the House Subcommittee on Western Hemisphere Affairs during the period when the Boland amendments were enacted) for this observation.

27. See *Standing Rules of the Senate Revised to June 1, 1988,* S. Doc. no. 33, 100th Cong., 2d sess., Rule 22(2) at 15 (1988); see also, Molotsky, "A Senator Is Captured, but Not His Mind," *New York Times,* Feb. 25, 1988, p. A26 col. 4, which describes the Republicans' use of that rule, along with the quorum requirement, to defeat the Democrat-supported campaign reform bill.

28. Compare 50 U.S.C. Section 1542 (1982) with Jimmy Carter, *Keeping Faith* (New York: Bantam Books, 1982), p. 518, quoting from President Carter's diary: "I had planned on calling in a few members of the House and Senate . . . before the rescue team began its move into Tehran. . . . But I never got around to that" (emphasis omitted). As noted in chapter 4 of Koh, *National Security Constitution,* however, most presidents have complied in some form or another with the resolution's consultation requirement. See, generally, Note, "The War Powers Resolution: An Act Facing 'Imminent Hostilities' a Decade Later," *Vanderbilt Journal of Transnational Law* 16 (1983): 915 (citing examples).

29. Compare 50 U.S.C. Section 1542 (1982) with Robert Torricelli, "The War Powers Resolution After the Libya Crisis," *Pace University Law Review* 7 (1987): 661, 666.

30. See 50 U.S.C. Section 1543(a)(1)–(3), 1544(a) (1982). For further discussion of the resolution, see Keynes, Chapter 9 of this volume.

31. Michael Glennon, "The War Powers Resolution Ten Years Later: More Politics Than Law," *American Journal of International Law* 78 (1984): 571.

32. Mayhew, *Congress,* p. 122.

33. Compare the "in every possible instance" phrase in 50 U.S.C. Section 1542 (1982) with the identical phrase in IEEPA, 50 U.S.C. Section 1703(a), 1982.

34. See Comprehensive Anti-Apartheid Act of 1986, Pub. L. No. 99–440, 100 Stat. 1086 (1986); remarks of Richard Messick, former counsel to the Senate Foreign Relations Committee, Panel on Sustaining an International Human Rights Campaign in the United States; Passage of the Anti-Apartheid Act in Perspective, Symposium on Human Rights Advocacy and the U.S. Political Process, Yale Law School, April 9, 1988 (on file with author). For a description of the law's loopholes, see, generally, Paretzky, "The United States Arms Embargo Against South Africa: An Analysis of the Laws, Regulations, and Loopholes," *Yale Journal of International Law* 12 (1987): 133.

35. For further discussion, see Koh, *National Security Constitution,* chap. 2.

36. See, e.g., *Lowry v. Reagan,* 676 F. Supp. 333 (D.D.C. 1987), appeal dismissed, no. 87–5426 (D.C. Cir. Oct. 17, 1988), dismissing suit seeking to compel the president to comply with the reporting requirement of the War Powers Resolution with re-

gard to U.S. military activities in the Persian Gulf, and *Crockett v. Reagan,* 720 F.2d 1355 (D.C. Cir. 1983), cert. denied, 467 U.S. 1251 (1984), dismissing a similar suit with regard to U.S. military activities in El Salvador.

37. Guido Calabresi, *A Common Law for the Age of Statutes* (New Haven: Yale University Press, 1982), pp. 61, 62.

38. See Thomas Franck and Clifford Bob, "The Return of Humpty-Dumpty: Foreign Relations Law After the Chadha Case," *American Journal of International Law* 79 (1985): 912, 934.

39. For accounts of the use or threatened use of the legislative veto in the areas of arms control and transfer of nuclear materials, see Pomerance, "United States Foreign Relations Law After Chadha," *California Western International Law Journal* 15 (1985): 201, 262–80. For descriptions of Congress' efforts to use appropriations cutoffs in foreign affairs, see Louis Fisher, *Constitutional Conflicts Between Congress and the President* (Lawrence: University Press of Kansas, 1991), pp. 221–51, 318–23; Gregory F. Treverton, *Covert Action* (New York: Basic Books, 1987), pp. 156–60, which describes legislative cutoff of funds for covert activities in Angola under the Clark amendment; and Franck and Bob, "Return of Humpty-Dumpty," pp. 944–48.

40. For a fuller description, see Koh, "Congressional Controls," p. 1196 n. 16.

41. *INS v. Chadha,* 462 U.S. 919 (1983).

42. See *Bowsher v. Synar,* 478 U.S. 714 (1986); *Northern Pipeline Constr. Co. v. Marathon Pipe Line Co.,* 458 U.S. 50 (1982); *Buckley v. Valeo,* 424 U.S. 1 (1976). But see *Morrison v. Olson,* 108 S. Ct. 2597 (1988), and *Mistretta v. United States,* 109 S. Ct. 647 (1989).

43. See Clinton Rossiter, *The American Presidency* (New York: Harcourt, Brace, 1960), p. 157: "The President often feels compelled to sign bills that are full of dubious grants and subsidies rather than risk a breakdown in the work of whole departments."

44. See Engelberg, "Contra Aid: Loose Law?" *New York Times,* Jan. 15, 1987, p. A12 col. 1, which describes claimed loopholes in the Boland amendments.

45. *U.S. v. Lovett,* 328 U.S. 303 (1946). For an intriguing account of the decision, see Ely, "*United States v. Lovett:* Litigating the Separation of Powers," *Harvard Civil Rights Civil Liberties Law Review* 10 (1975): 1.

46. See, e.g., Gordon Crovitz, "Crime, the Constitution, and the Iran-Contra Affair," *Commentary,* October 1987, pp. 23, 28; Quade, "The President Is His Only Client," *Barrister* (Winter/Spring 1988): 5, 7, interview with A. B. Culvahouse, Jr., counsel to the president: "It was clear in our mind and remains clear that the Boland Amendment could not circumscribe the efforts of the President to speak with foreign leaders about supporting the Nicaraguan freedom fighters."

47. See, e.g., Louis Henkin, *Constitutionalism, Democracy, and Foreign Affairs* (New York: Columbia University Press, 1991), p. 47; Kate Stith, "Congress' Power of the Purse," *Yale Law Journal* 97 (1988): 1343, 1351, and n.32. For an excellent discussion of these issues, see Fisher, Chapter 8 of this volume.

48. See *Federal Employees v. United States,* 688 F. Supp. 671, 685 (D.D.C. 1988), vacated and remanded sub nom. *American Foreign Serv. Ass'n v. Garfinkel,* 109 S. Ct. 1693 (1989) (per curiam). Shortly before the district court's ruling in this case, another district judge declared that "we are aware of no case striking down federal legisla-

tion as an encroachment of the executive's authority to conduct foreign affairs." *Mendelsohn v. Meese*, 695 F. Supp. 1474, 1483 (S.D.N.Y. 1988) (Palmieri, J.).

49. See *Ameron, Inc. v. United States Army Corps of Eng'rs, Inc.*, 809 F.2d 979 (3d Cir. 1986), cert. dismissed, 109 S. Ct. 297 (1988); Stith, "Congress' Power," pp. 1390–92 and nn.232–47, which describes the constitutional difficulties of using the comptroller general to enforce appropriations requirements against the executive; Note, "The Role of the Comptroller General in Light of *Bowsher v. Synar,*" *Columbia Law Review* 87 (1987): 1529.

50. See House Select Committee to Investigate Covert Arms Transactions with Iran and Senate Select Committee on Secret Military Assistance to Iran and the Nicaraguan Opposition, *Report of the Congressional Comms. Investigating the Iran-Contra Affair,* 100th Cong., 1st sess., S. Rept. 216, H. Rept. 433, 1987, 16 (hereinafter *Iran-Contra Report*) (emphasis added); Stith, "Congress' Power," p. 1358 (only monies receivable by the U.S. government *and* subject to its control and expenditure are subject to Congress's appropriations power). Congress recently sought to redress this problem by passing an appropriations rider (which the president later vetoed) that would punish U.S. officials who solicit funds from foreign countries to carry out activities for which Congress has cut off aid. See S. Amend. 268, S. 1160, 101st Cong., 1st sess., 135 *Cong. Rec.* S8107–9 (daily ed. July 18, 1989), the Moynihan amendment to the FY 1990 State Department Authorization Act; H.R. 2939, 101st Cong., 1st sess. sec. 577, 135 *Cong. Rec.* H4071–72 (daily ed. July 21, 1989), a parallel provision in House foreign-aid bill.

51. North, *Taking the Stand*, p. 473 (emphasis added).

52. For descriptions of presidential devices to control spending, see Louis Fisher, *President and Congress: Power and Policy* (New York: Free Press, 1972), pp. 110–32; Fisher, *Presidential Spending Power* (Princeton: Princeton University Press, 1975); Meyer, "Congressional Control of Foreign Assistance," *Yale Journal of International Law* 13 (1988): 69, 74–75.

53. Sharpe, "The Real Cause of Irangate," *Foreign Policy* 68 (1987): 33–34.

54. See *Presidential Vetoes, 1977–1984* (Washington, D.C.: U.S. Government Printing Office, 1985), p. ix; *Congressional Quarterly Almanac* 43 (1987): 6 (103 of 1,417 have been overridden). See, generally, Robert Spitzer, *The Presidential Veto: Touchstone of the American Presidency* (Albany: State University of New York Press, 1988).

55. See William Fulbright, "Congress and Foreign Policy," in five Appendices to *U.S. Commission on the Organization of the Government for the Conduct of Foreign Policy* (1975), pp. 58, 59 (hereinafter Murphy Commission Report).

56. See 133 *Cong. Rec.* S15,011 (daily ed. Oct. 23, 1987), the Bork vote; Seib and Fialka, "Advise and Reject: Tower Fiasco Hurts Bush, but It Also Puts Congress on Defensive," *Wall Street Journal*, March 10, 1989, p. A1 col. 1, the Tower vote.

57. See Charles Black, "Some Thoughts on the Veto," *Law and Contemporary Problems* 40 (Spring 1976): 87, 93; *House of Representatives 1989–90, Cong. Index* (CCH) 24, 151 (Feb. 24, 1989): the House currently has only 257 Democrats versus 176 Republicans.

58. Cf. Bob Eckhardt and Charles Black, *The Tides of Power* (New Haven: Yale University Press, 1976), pp. 62–65; see statement of Professor Black, proposing that Congress simply follow the convention of overriding all presidential vetoes, regardless of substance.

59. See Spann, "Spinning the Legislative Veto," *University of Georgia Law Journal* 72 (1984): 813.

60. See Note, "War Powers Resolution," pp. 1008–14.

61. See, e.g., Feuerbringer, "Senate Defers Vote on Gulf Escort Policy," *New York Times*, October 22, 1987, p. A3 col. 4.

62. New Trade Legislation, p. 880, describes such an action by the Senate majority leader, who led the drive to override the president's veto of the trade bill. It would be highly unlikely, however, that a congressional leader would cast such a vote if it would be decisive in securing an override.

63. Louis Henkin, " 'A More Effective System' for Foreign Relations: The Constitutional Framework," in Appendices to Murphy Commission Report, pp. 9, 16. See also, Thomas Eagleton, *War and Presidential Power* (New York: Liveright, 1974), p. 146.

64. See Vance, "Striking the Balance: Congress and the President Under the War Powers Resolution," *University of Pennsylvania Law Review* 133 (1984): 79, 94–95, which describes the events leading to the enactment of the Multinational Force in Lebanon Resolution, Pub. L. no. 98–119, 97 Stat. 805 [1983]).

PART THREE

THE CONSTITUTION AND WARMAKING

7

THE CONSTITUTION AND PRESIDENTIAL WARMAKING

DAVID GRAY ADLER

A series of "presidential wars" over the past fifty years,[1] from Korea and Vietnam to Grenada and Panama, has triggered an intense and sometimes acerbic debate within both the scholarly community and the corridors of power on the question of whether Congress or the president is constitutionally empowered to commence war.[2] The issue of the constitutional repository of the power to decide for war is of surpassing importance for a nation faced with the specter of the nuclear holocaust, the overwhelming, perhaps incomprehensible destruction of an all-out atomic exchange.

Until 1950 it had long been established and well settled that the Constitution vests in Congress the sole and exclusive authority to initiate total as well as limited war. But since then, that firm understanding has been subjected to a continuing assault by revisionist contentions that purport to locate the power in the president.[3] In an effort to justify Pres. Harry Truman's unilateral decision to introduce U.S. troops into the Korean War in 1950, politicians and commentators, labeled "high-flying prerogative men" by Edward S. Corwin, asserted broad executive powers to commence war.[4] Emboldened by Truman's claim, subsequent presidents have likewise unilaterally initiated acts of war, often with the acquiescence of Congress. These executive assertions, which have by now established a consistent pattern of behavior, have been grounded on the alleged authority that the president derives from the executive power and commander-in-chief clauses of the Constitution his constitutional authority as the "sole organ" of American foreign policy and the inherent or prerogative power of the presidency.[5] Finally, it is contended that each presidential war constitutes a "precedent" that in turn legalizes the next such action. If taken at face value, the revisionists' arguments would eviscerate the constitutional grant of power to Congress to embark upon war.

Since the Korean episode, there has been considerable tension between the theory of the Constitution and the practice of recent presidents. A clear shift of the warmaking power from the legislative to the executive has given the president the dominant role. Of course, the substantive constitutional issues raised by the practice are numerous and momentous and not necessarily answerable by resort to the text of the Constitution: what right, if any, the executive has to commit troops into hostilities without congressional authorization; what control of the warmaking power remains to Congress once war has been declared; what authority the president might have in the face of invasion or the threat of imminent attack. The urgency of the circumstances has induced scholars to search the historical records for discussion of these questions in the Constitutional Convention and in the early years of the republic. Predictably perhaps, different interpretations of the sources have emerged and the questions have lingered in a state of confusion.

The critical nature of the issue and the challenge raised by revisionists compel reexamination of the Framers' understanding of the warmaking power. Accordingly, in the first part of this chapter I examine the debates and proceedings that accompanied the framing and ratification of the war clause, commander-in-chief clause, and the executive power clause. In the second part, I will briefly explore the late eighteenth- as well as the nineteenth-century understanding of the war power design as manifested in the contemporary statements of legislators and other political actors, in the practice itself, and in judicial decisions. In the final section I will consider recent arguments adduced by revisionists on behalf of unilateral presidential warmaking. It will be argued here that consistent with the understanding of the Framers and the Constitution, the authority to initiate hostilities, short of and including war, is vested solely and exclusively in Congress. The president has only the power to repel invasions.

THE CONSTITUTION AND WARMAKING

The War Clause

The war clause of the Constitution provides that "the Congress shall have power . . . to declare War (and) grant Letters of Marque and Reprisal."[6] The debate on the proper repository of the authority to make war occurred at the outset of the Constitutional Convention. On May 29, 1787, Gov. Edmund Randolph of Virginia proposed a constitution that included a provision "that a national Executive be instituted." The seventh paragraph stated that the executive "ought to enjoy the Executive rights vested in Congress of the Confederation."[7] The Randolph plan was taken up by the convention on June 1. In considering the proposal to give to the national executive the executive powers of the Continental Congress, Charles Pinckney objected that "the Executive powers of [the existing Congress] might extend to peace and war which would render the Executive a Monarchy, of the worst kind, to wit an elective one." Fellow South Carolinian John Rutledge said that "he was for vesting the Executive power in a single person, tho' he was not for giving him the power of war and peace."[8] James Wilson sought to reassure them: "Making peace and war are generally determined by writers on the Laws of Nations to be legislative powers." Wilson added that "the Prerogatives of the British Monarchy" are not "a proper guide in defining the executive powers. Some of the prerogatives were of a legislative nature. Among others that of war and peace."[9] James Madison agreed that the war power was legislative in character. Rufus King noted: "Mad: agrees with Wilson in his definition of executive powers—executive powers ex vi termini, do not include the Rights of war & peace and c. but the powers should be confined and defined—if large we shall have the Evils of elective Monarchies." Randolph did not defend his proposal but pressed for a plural executive: "A unity of the Executive he observed would savor too much of a monarchy. We had he said no motive to be governed by the British Governmt. as our prototype."[10] There was no vote on Randolph's resolution, but the discussion appears to reflect an understanding that the power of "war & peace"—the power to initiate war—did not belong to the executive but to the legislature.

On August 6 the Committee of Detail circulated a draft constitution providing that: "the legislature of the United States shall have the power . . . to make war."[11] This clause bore sharp resemblance to the Articles of Confederation, which vested the "sole and exclusive right and power of determining on peace and war" to the Continental Congress.[12] When the war clause was considered in debate on August 17 Charles Pinckney opposed placing the power in Congress. "Its proceedings were too slow. . . . The Senate would be the best depository, being more acquainted with foreign affairs, and most capable of proper resolutions."[13] Pierce Butler "was for vesting the power in the President, who will have all the requisite qualities, and will not make war but when the nation will support it." Butler's opinion shocked Elbridge Gerry, who said that he "never expected to hear in a republic a motion to empower the Executive alone to declare war." Butler stood alone in the Convention; there was no support for his opinion and no second to his motion.

The proposal of the Committee of Detail to vest the legislature with the power to make war proved unsatisfactory to Madison and Gerry. In a joint resolution, they moved to substitute "declare" for "make," "leaving to the Executive the power to repel sudden attacks."[14] The meaning of the motion is unmistakable. Congress was granted the power to make, that is, initiate war; the president, for obvious reasons, could act immediately to repel sudden attacks without authorization from Congress. There was no quarrel whatever with respect to the sudden-attack provision, but there was some question as to whether the substitution of "declare" for "make" would effectuate the intention of Madison and Gerry. Roger Sherman of Connecticut thought the joint motion "stood very well. The Executive shd. be able to repel and not to commence war. 'Make' better than 'declare' the latter narrowing the power [of the legislature] too much." Virginia's George Mason "was agst. giving the power of war to the Executive, because not [safely] to be trusted with it; or to the Senate, because not so constructed as to be entitled to it. He was for clogging rather than facilitating war; but for facilitating peace. He preferred 'declare' to 'make'." The Madison-Gerry proposal was adopted by a vote of seven to two. When Rufus King explained that the word "make" might be understood to authorize Congress to initiate as well as to conduct war, Connecticut changed its vote so that the word "declare" was approved, eight states to one.[15]

The debates and the vote on the war clause make it clear that Congress alone possesses the authority to initiate war. The warmaking power was specifically withheld from the president; he was given only the authority to repel sudden attacks. Confirmation of this understanding was provided by remarks of ratifiers in various state conventions, as well as by the early practice and contemporaneous statements of political actors.

James Wilson, perhaps only slightly less important than James Madison in the Constitutional Convention, told the Pennsylvania Ratifying Convention:

> This system will not hurry us into war; it is calculated to guard against it. It will not be in the power of a single man, or a single body of men, to involve us in such distress; for the important power of declaring war is vested in the legislature at large: this declaration must be made with the concurrence of the House of Representatives: from this circumstance we may draw a certain conclusion that nothing but our interest can draw us into war.[16]

Similar assurance was provided in other state ratifying conventions. In North Carolina James Iredell stated: "The President has not the power of declaring war by his own authority. . . . Those powers are vested in other hands. The power of declaring war is expressly given to Congress." And Charles

Pinckney, a delegate in Philadelphia, told the South Carolina Ratifying Convention that "the President's powers did not permit him to declare war." Likewise, in New York, Chancellor R. R. Livingston responded to objections that the Continental Congress did not have "the same powers" as the proposed Congress. He explained that the two bodies shared "the very same" power including the power "of making war and peace. . . . They may involve us in a war at their pleasure."[17]

In spite of the illuminating debate and vote on the war clause, the shift from "make" to "declare" has induced revisionists to find in the presidency a power to initiate war. Senator Barry Goldwater, for example, has observed that when the Convention deleted from the working draft of the Constitution the authorization of Congress to make war, "the Framers intended to leave the 'making of war' with the President."[18] Leonard Ratner explained that the declare clause recognized "the warmaking authority of the President, implied by his role as executive and commander-in-chief and by congressional power to declare, but not make, war."[19] John Norton Moore and others have suggested that acts of military force short of war might be committed by the president.[20]

We shall defer for the moment consideration of the executive power and commander-in-chief clauses, but these views ignore the fact that at the time of the Framing, the word "declare" enjoyed a settled understanding and an established usage. Simply stated, as early as 1552, the verb "declare" had become synonymous with the verb "commence"; they both meant the initiation of hostilities.[21] This was the established usage in international law as well as in England, where the terms to declare war and to make war were used interchangeably.[22] The usage was familiar to the Framers. As Chancellor James Kent of New York, one of the leading jurists of the Founding period, stated: "As war cannot lawfully be commenced on the part of the United States without an act of Congress, such an act is, of course, a formal official notice to all the world, and equivalent to the most solemn declaration." Though Kent interpreted "declare" to mean "commence," he did not assert that the Constitution requires a congressional declaration of war before hostilities could be lawfully commenced but merely that war is initiated by Congress. What "is essential," according to Kent, is "that some formal public act, proceeding directly from the competent source, should announce to the people at home their new relations and duties growing out of a state of war, and which should equally apprise neutral nations of the fact."[23]

Given the equivalence of commence and declare, it is clear that a congressional declaration of war would institute military hostilities. According to international law commentators, a declaration of war was desirable because it announced the institution of a state of war and the legal consequences that it entailed, to the adversary, to neutral nations, and to citizens of the sovereign initiating the war. Indeed, this is the essence of a declaration of war: notice by the proper authority of intent to convert a state of peace into a state of war.[24] But under American law only a joint resolution or an explicit congressional authorization of the use of military force against a named adversary is required. This can come in the form of a "declaration pure and simple" or in a "conditional declaration of war."[25] There are also two kinds of war, those which U.S. courts have termed "perfect" or general and those labeled "imperfect" or limited wars. In 1782, the Federal Court of Appeals, the prize court established by the Continental Congress, stated:

> The writers upon the law of nations, speaking of different kinds of war, distinguish them into perfect and imperfect: A perfect war is that which destroys the national peace and tranquillity, and lays the foundation of every possible act of hostility. The imperfect war is that which does not entirely destroy the public tranquillity, but interrupts it only in some particulars, as in the case of reprisals.[26]

It was decided at the dawn of the republic in three important Supreme Court cases that the power of determining perfect and imperfect war lay with Congress.[27] For example, the Court, per Chief Justice John Marshall, held in 1801 in *Talbot v. Seeman* that the power of Congress comprises the power to "declare a general war" and also to "wage a limited war."[28] The power of Congress to authorize limited war is, of course, a necessary concomitant of its power to declare general war. If, as John Bassett Moore has suggested, the president might authorize relatively minor acts of war or perhaps covert military operations in circumstances not demanding full-blown war, that power could be wielded in a way that would easily eviscerate the Constitution's placement of the war power in Congress. Moore, perhaps the most eminent American scholar of international law, justly rebuked that proposition:

> There can hardly be room for doubt that the framers of the Constitution, when they vested in Congress the power to declare war, they never imagined that they were leaving it to the executive to use the military and naval forces of the United States all over the world for the purpose of actually coercing other nations, occupying their territory, and killing their soldiers and citizens, all according to his own notion of the fitness of things, as long as he refrained from calling his action war or persisted in calling it peace.[29]

As a matter of fact, the Framers withheld from the president the power to work such mischief. As we have observed, he was granted only the authority to respond defensively to the initiation of war through sudden attack upon the United States. In 1806, in *United States v. Smith*, Justice William Paterson of the Supreme Court, who had been a delegate to the convention, explained the rationale for a presidential response:

> If, indeed, a foreign nation should invade the territories of the United States, it would I apprehend, be not only lawful for the president to resist such invasion, but also to carry hostilities into the enemy's own country; and for this plain reason, that a state of complete and absolute war exists between the two nations. In the case of invasive hostilities, there cannot be war on the one side and peace on the other. . . . There is a manifest distinction between our going to war with a nation at peace, and a war being made against us by an actual invasion, or a formal declaration. In the former case, it is the exclusive province of congress to change a state of peace into a state of war.[30]

As described by Paterson, the rationale for vesting the president with authority to repel sudden attacks rested on the fact that an invasion instituted a state of war, thus rendering a declaration of war by Congress superfluous. In such an event, the president was authorized to initiate offensive action against the attacking enemy. But the president's power of self-defense does not extend to foreign lands. The Framers did not give the president the right to intervene in foreign wars, or to choose between war and peace, or to identify and commence hostilities against an enemy of the American people. Nor did they empower him to initiate force abroad on the basis of his own assessments of U.S. security interests. These circumstances involve choices that belong to Congress under its exclusive province to change a state of peace into a state of war. The president's power is purely defensive and strictly limited to attacks against the United States.

All of the offensive powers of the nation, then, were located in Congress. Consistent with this constitutional theory, the convention gave to Congress the power to issue "letters of marque and reprisal."[31] Dating back to the Middle Ages when sovereigns employed private forces in retaliation for an injury caused by the sovereign of another state or his subjects, the practice of issuing reprisals gradually evolved into the use of public armies. By the time of the convention, the Framers considered the power to issue letters of marque and reprisal sufficient to authorize a broad spectrum of armed hostilities short of declared war. In other words, it was regarded as a species of imperfect war. For example, James Madison, Alexander Hamilton, and Thomas Jefferson, among others, agreed that the authorization of reprisals was an act of war and belonged to Congress.[32] As a direct riposte to the revisionists' claim of a presidential power to order acts of war, we may consider what Jefferson said in 1793 of the authority necessary to issue a reprisal: "Congress must be called upon to take it; the right of reprisal being expressly lodged with them by the Constitution, and not with the executive."[33]

In summation, when the Framers granted to Congress the power to declare war, they were vesting in that body the sole and exclusive prerogative to initiate military hostilities on behalf of the American people. The record reveals that no member of the Philadelphia Convention and no member of any state ratifying convention held a different understanding of the meaning of the war clause. Thus, if the revisionists are to find textual authority for a presidential power to make war, it must derive from another source.

The Commander-in-Chief Clause

Article II, section 2 of the Constitution provides: "The President shall be Commander in Chief of the Army and Navy of the United States, and of the Militia of the several States, when called into the actual Service of the United States." The commander-in-chief, in the words of Justice Robert H. Jackson, has been invoked for the "power to do anything, anywhere, that can be done with an army or navy."[34] Though stated in the context of reviewing President Truman's invocation of the clause to support his seizure of the steel mills, Jackson's observations certainly anticipated the claims of recent executives who have seized the provision as justification for their military adventures. Presidents Lyndon Johnson, Richard Nixon, Gerald Ford, Jimmy Carter, Ronald Reagan, George Bush, and Bill Clinton fall into this category.[35] The clause has also become the principal pillar for those commentators who would hope to vest in the president the constitutional power of war and peace.[36] As we shall see, however, the title of commander-in-chief conferred no warmaking power whatever; it vested in the president only the authority to repel sudden attacks on the United States and to direct war "when authorized or begun." In this capacity, he would direct those forces placed at his command by an act of Congress.

As Francis D. Wormuth observed, the "office of commander-in-chief has never carried the power of war and peace, nor was it invented by the framers of the Constitution."[37] In fact, the office was introduced by King Charles I in 1639, when he named the earl of Arundel commander-in-chief of an army to battle the Scots in the First Bishops War. In historical usage the title has been a generic term referring to the highest officer in a particular chain of command. With the eruption of the English Civil Wars both the king and Parliament appointed commanders-in-chief of armies in various theaters of action. In 1645 Sir Thomas Fairfax was appointed commander-in-chief of all of Parliament's forces, "subject to such orders and directions as he shall receive from both Houses or the committee of Both Kingdoms." The British government continued its practice of designating an officer commander-in-chief of each army and naval fleet with authority over subordinate commanders-in-chief. In the eighteenth century, with the development of the cabinet system, the various commanders-in-chief of armies were placed under the command of the secretary of war. So little discretion was granted that the duke of Wellington was moved to observe with some pain that "the commander-in-chief cannot move a Corporal's Guard from one station to another, without a Route countersigned by the Secretary of War. This is the fundamental principle of the Constitution of the British Army."[38] At all events, then, the ranking commander-in-chief, purely a military post, always was under the command of a political superior.

The government of England also transplanted the title to America in the eighteenth century by appointing a number of commanders-in-chief and by the practice of entitling governors of royal, proprietary, and chartered colonies as commander-in-chief, or occasionally as vice-admiral or captain-general. The appointment of Gen. Thomas Gage as commander-in-chief from 1763 to 1776 caused grave concerns for the colonists, for he interfered in civil affairs and acquired considerable influence over Indian relations, trade, and transportation. The bitter memories of his decision to quarter troops in the homes of civilians spawned the Third Amendment to the Constitution. These activities and others prompted the colonists to complain of King George III in the Declaration of Independence that he had "affected to render the Military independent of and superior to the Civil Power."

But colonists had no reason to fear the governors as commander-in-chief even though they controlled the provincial forces. After all, the assemblies claimed and asserted the right to vote funds for the militia as well as to call it into service. Ernest May has justly remarked that "under one or the other of these principles, they neutralized whatever pernicious power the executive might have had."[39] In fact, the grievances came from the governors; like the duke of Wellington, they complained of the relative impotence of their positions.

The colonial assemblies' (and later, the states') assertions of the power of the purse as a check on the commander-in-chief undoubtedly stemmed from the English practice, extending at least as far back as the middle of the seventeenth century. By 1665, as a means of maintaining political control of the military establishment, Parliament had inaugurated the policy of making annual military appropriations with a lifetime of but one year. This practice or strategy sharply emphasized the power of Parliament to determine the size of the army to be placed under the direction of the commander-in-chief. In 1678 Parliament provided such a meager fund that the king was forced to eliminate a portion of the army. A year later, Parliament provided for a special allocation to be used solely to disband the army. That act imposed a veto on the "King's prerogative as commander-in-chief." As a means of protecting its decisionmaking authority over military appropriations, Parliament passed in 1689 legislation that prohibited the diversion of funds from one service to another and provided for severe penalties for disobedience by administrative officials.[40]

The practice had a long influence, for under the Constitution Congress acquired the colonial and state assemblies' rights of voting funds for the armed forces under its powers to raise and support armies and to provide and maintain a navy. Moreover, we find another historical parallel in the clause that provides that "no appropriation of money to that use shall be for a longer term than two years." The requirement of legislative approval for the allocation of funds to raise troops, in England since the middle of the seventeenth century and through the framing of the U.S. Constitution, underscores the principle of political superiority over military command. It also constitutes a sharp reminder that a commander-in-chief is dependent upon the legislature for an army to command.

Most of the early state constitutions followed the colonial practice of making the governor commander-in-chief under the authority of state legislatures. For example, Article 7 of the Massachusetts Constitution of 1780 provided that the governor shall be "commander-in-chief of the army and navy." In carefully circumscribing his power, the governor was to "repel, resist [and] expel" attempts to invade the Commonwealth, and it vested him "with all these and other powers incident to the offices of captain general . . . to be exercised agreeably to the rules and regulations of the Constitution and the laws of the land, and not otherwise."[41]

The Continental Congress continued the usage of the title when on June 15, 1775, it unanimously decided to appoint George Washington as general. Dated June 17 his commission named him "General and Commander in Chief, of the Army of the United Colonies." The instructions of the Congress drafted by John Adams, Richard Henry Lee, and Edward Rutledge kept Washington on a short leash. He was ordered "punctually to observe and follow such orders and directions, from time to time, as you shall receive from this, or a future Congress of these United Colonies, or Committee of Congress." Congress did not hesitate to instruct the commander-in-chief on military and policy matters.[42]

The practice of entitling the office at the apex of the military hierarchy as commander-in-chief and of subordinating the office to a political superior, whether a king, parliament, or congress, was thus firmly established for a century and a half and thoroughly familiar to the Framers when they met in Philadelphia. Perhaps this settled understanding and the consequent lack of concern about the nature of the post account for the absence of any debate on the commander-in-chief clause at the convention.

In the plan he read to the convention on May 29, 1787, South Carolinian Charles Pinckney introduced the title of president and proposed, "He shall, by Virtue of his Office, be Commander in Chief of the Land Forces of U.S. and Admiral of their Navy."[43] Presumably, Pinckney had drawn on the traditional usage of the title employed in the South Carolina Constitution of 1776, which provided for a "president and commander-in-chief," and that of 1778, which included a provision for a "governor and commander-in-chief."[44] There was no such provision in the Randolph or Virginia plan, which was read to the convention on the same day. On June 15, William Paterson submitted the New Jersey plan, which called for a plural executive. It provided that "the Executives . . . ought . . . to direct all military operations; provided that none of the persons composing the federal executive shall at any time take command of any troops, so as personally to conduct any enterprise as General, or in other capacity."[45] The qualifying clause was meant to discourage a military takeover of the government.[46] When Alexander Hamilton submitted a plan to the convention on June 18 he probably did not propose the title commander-in-chief, but he undoubtedly had it in mind when he said the president was "to have the direction of war when authorized or begun."[47]

It was Hamilton's speech, then, that summarized the essence of the president's power as commander-in-chief: when war is "authorized or begun," the president is to command the military operations of American forces. There was no fear of the legal authority granted by the commander-in-chief clause, and in fact the clause seemed to excite little dispute. The lone concern was conveyed by the New Jersey plan in that a president who personally assumed command of army and naval forces might use them to institute a military coup. In the Virginia Ratifying Convention, George Mason, who had been a delegate to the Constitutional Convention, admitted

the propriety of his being commander-in-chief, so far as to give orders and have a general superintendency; but he thought it would be dangerous to let him command in person, without any restraint, as he might make a bad use of it. He was, then, clearly of opinion that the consent of a majority of both houses of Congress should be required before he could take command in person.[48]

James Monroe was concerned that a president could escape punishment because he commanded the military forces. And Patrick Henry, in his typically colorful speech, opined that "the President, in the field, at the head of his Army, can prescribe the terms on which he shall reign master, so far that it will puzzle any American ever to get his neck from under the falling yoke."[49] In a report to the Maryland legislature on the Constitutional Convention, Luther Martin expressed similar sentiments: "Objections were made to that part of this article by which the President is appointed commander-in-chief of the army and navy of the United States, and of the militia of the several states; and it was wished to be so far restrained, that he should not command in person; but this could not be obtained."[50]

Their concerns were allayed in the North Carolina Ratifying Convention, however. Richard Spaight, who had been a delegate to the Constitutional Convention, said that the commander-in-chief could be controlled by Congress, which had the exclusive authority to raise and support armies.[51] Similar assurance was offered by James Iredell, later an associate justice of the Supreme Court, who laid bare the authority of the commander-in-chief and drew a sharp distinction between the powers of that office and those of the king of England.

I believe most of the governors of the different states have powers similar to those of the President. In almost every country, the executive has command of the military forces. From the nature of the thing, the command of armies ought to be delegated to one person only. The secrecy, dispatch, and decision, which are necessary in military operations, can only be expected from one person. The President, therefore, is to command the military forces of the United States, and this power I think a proper one; at the same time it will be found to be sufficiently guarded. A very material difference may be observed between this power, and the authority of the king of Great Britain under similar circumstances. The king of Great Britain is not only the commander-in-chief of the land and naval forces, but has power in time of war, to raise fleets and armies. He also has the power to declare war. The President has not the power of declaring war by his own authority, nor that of raising fleets and armies. The powers are vested in other hands. The power of declaring war is expressly given to Congress, that is, to the two branches of the legislature. . . . They have also expressly delegated to them the powers of raising and supporting armies, and of providing and maintaining a navy.[52]

Iredell's speech echoed *Federalist 69* in which Hamilton sought to calm fears surrounding the commander-in-chief clause:

> The President is to be commander-in-chief of the army and navy of the United States. In this respect his authority would be nominally the same with that of the King of Britain, but in substance much inferior to it. It would amount to nothing more than the supreme command and direction of the military and naval forces, as first General and Admiral of the Confederacy; while that of the British kings extends to the *declaring* of war and to the *raising* and *regulating* of fleets and armies,—all which, by the Constitution under consideration, would appertain to the Legislature.[53]

In sum, the president as commander-in-chief was to be "first General and Admiral" in "the direction of war when authorized or begun." But all political authority remained in Congress, as it had under the Articles of Confederation. As Louis Henkin has observed, "Generals and admirals, even when they are 'first,' do not determine the political purposes for which troops are to be used; they command them in the execution of policy made by others.' "[54] The commander-in-chief in the tradition of a century and a half was made subordinate to a political superior. The office carried with it no power to declare war; as Hamilton and Iredell explained, that power is the exclusive prerogative of Congress.

The Executive Power Clause

Article II, section 1 of the Constitution provides: "The executive power shall be vested in the President of the United States of America." In recent years various presidents and commentators have sought to squeeze from the executive power clause a presidential authority to make war. In 1966, for example, the State Department cited the president's role as chief executive to adduce constitutional support for Lyndon Johnson's entry into the Vietnam War.[55] Richard Nixon's legal advisers similarly invoked the clause to justify his adventures in Southeast Asia.[56] In 1975 Gerald Ford found constitutional warrant in the "President's Constitutional executive power" for the military activities he ordered in Cambodia. On April 26, 1980, Jimmy Carter authorized an attempted rescue of American citizens held hostage by Iran. He justified the attempt as being "pursuant to the President's powers under the Constitution as Chief Executive and as Commander in Chief."[57]

The claim asserted by Johnson, Nixon, Ford, and Carter—that the grant of executive power includes authority to initiate hostilities—was considered and rejected in the Constitutional Convention; indeed, it caused the delegates much alarm. As we have seen, the Randolph plan provided for a "national executive," which would have "authority to execute the national laws . . . and enjoy the executive rights vested in Congress by the confederation." Charles Pinckney said he was "for a vigorous executive but was afraid the executive powers of the existing Congress might extend to peace and war which would render the executive a monarchy, of the worst kind, to wit an elective one." John Rutledge shared his concern, saying "he was for vesting the Executive power in a single person, tho' he was not for giving him the power of war and peace." James Wilson sought to ease their fears; he "did not consider the Prerogatives of the British Monarch as a proper guide to defining the Executive powers. Some of these prerogatives were of a legislative nature. Among others that of war and peace. The only powers he conceived strictly Executive were those of executing the laws, and appointing officers not [appertaining to and] appointed by the legislature." He added: "Making peace and war are generally determined by the writers on the Law of Nations to be legislative powers—executive powers ex vi termini, do not include the Rights of war and peace."[58]

No delegate to the convention ever suggested or even intimated that executive power is a fountainhead of power to make war. For the Framers, the phrase "executive power" was limited, as Wilson said, to "executing the laws, and appointing officers." Roger Sherman "considered the Executive magistracy as nothing more than an institution for carrying the will of the Legislature into effect." Madison agreed with Wilson's definition of executive power. He thought it necessary "to fix the extent of Executive authority . . . as certain powers were in their nature Executive, and must be given to that department" and added that "a definition of their extent would assist the judgment in determining how far they might be safely entrusted to a single officer." The definition of the executive's powers should be precise, thought Madison; the executive power "shd. be confined and defined."[59] And so it was. In a draft reported by James Wilson, the statement "The Executive Power of the United States shall be vested in a single person" first appeared. His draft included an enumeration of the president's powers to grant reprieves and pardons and to serve as commander-in-chief; it included as well the charge that "it shall be his duty to provide for the due and faithful execution of the Laws." The report of the Committee of Detail altered the "faithful execution" phrase to "he shall take care that the laws of the United States be duly and faithfully executed." This form was referred to the Committee on Style, which drafted the version that appears in the Constitution: "The executive power shall be vested in a president of the United States of America. . . . He shall take care that the laws be faithfully executed."[60]

The debate, to the extent there was one, centered almost entirely on whether there should be a single or plural presidency. The first sentence of Article II, section 2, "The Executive Power shall be vested in a President," depicts the conclusion reached.[61] Aside from this, there was no argument. There was no challenge to the definition of executive power held by Wilson and Madison, nor was there even an alternative understanding advanced. And there was no argument about the scope of executive power; indeed, any latent fears were quickly arrested by assurances from Madison and Wilson that the power of peace and war was not an executive but a legislative function. Given the Framers' conception of the chief executive as little more than an institution to effectuate the "will of the legislature," that is, to execute the laws and to appoint officers, there was little about the office to fear. As Raoul Berger has observed, "the 'executive power' was hardly a cornucopia from which could pour undreamed of powers."[62]

Of course, the widespread "aversion of the people to monarchy," the "unhappy memories of the royal prerogative; fear of tyranny, and distrust of any one man, kept the Framers from giving the President too much head."[63] That the Framers did not vest the president with too much authority is evidenced by the relative calm with which the state ratifying conventions discussed the presidency. No doubt this is attributable to the careful and specific enumeration of the president's full powers. In South Carolina, Charles Pinckney reported that "we have defined his powers, and bound him to such limits, as will effectually prevent his usurping authority."[64] Similarly, Chief Justice Thomas McKean told the Pennsylvania Ratifying Convention that executive officers "have no . . . authority . . . beyond what is by positive grant . . . delegated to them." In Virginia, Governor Randolph asked, "What are his powers? To see the laws executed. Every executive in America has that power." That view was echoed by James Iredell in North Carolina and James Bowdoin in Massachusetts, who said the president's powers were "precisely those of the governors."[65]

And the powers of the governors were strictly limited. The Virginia Constitution of 1776, for example, stated that the governors shall "exercise the executive powers of government, according to the laws of the Commonwealth; and shall not, under any pretense, exercise any power or prerogative, by virtue of any law, statute, or custom of England."[66] Thomas Jefferson's "Draft of a Fundamental Constitution for Virginia," written in 1783 and inspired in part by the excesses of the Virginia legislature, explained that "by Executive powers, we mean no reference to those powers exercised under our former government by the Crown as of its prerogatives. . . . We give them these powers only, which are necessary to execute the laws (and administer the government)."[67] In short, as James Madison said, state executives across the land were "little more than Cyphers."[68]

It is not at all surprising that the Founding generation would so sharply limit the power of its executives. In colonial America, the belief was prevalent, wrote Corwin, that "the 'executive magistracy' was the natural enemy, the legislative assembly the natural friend of liberty."[69] There was a deep fear of the potential for abuse of power in the hands of both hereditary and elected rulers. The colonial experience had laid bare the source of despotism. "The executive power," wrote a Delaware Whig, "is ever restless, ambitious, and ever grasping at increase of power."[70] Thus James Madison wrote in *The Federalist:* "The founders of our republics . . . seem never for a moment to have turned their eyes from the over-grown and all-grasping prerogative of an hereditary magistrate."[71]

It was in this context that the Framers designed the office of the presidency. Far from establishing an executive resembling a monarchy, the Framers, in fact, severed all roots to the royal prerogative. Executive powers amounted to little more than the execution of laws and the appointment of various officers. There is no intimation whatever in the records of the Constitutional Convention or in any state ratifying conventions that executive power includes the right to make war or even to initiate hostilities.

A critical review of the proceedings and debates in the Constitutional Convention and in the various state ratifying conventions inescapably leads to the conclusion that the warmaking power, including the authority to initiate both limited and general war, was vested exclusively in Congress. The record establishes that neither the commander-in-chief clause nor the executive power clause affords any support for the claim of presidential power to commence hostilities. Indeed, such authority was specifically withheld from the president. That this was the settled understanding of the war power is evidenced by statements of the Founding generation, views of eminent treatise writers, early judicial decisions, and by nineteenth-century practice.

THE EARLY UNDERSTANDING

Practice and Commentary

In early 1793 war broke out between Great Britain and France. President George Washington declared that the treaty of alliance of 1778 did not obligate the United States to defend French territory in America, and he issued a proclamation of neutrality. Whether this power belonged to the president or Congress was debated by Alexander Hamilton and James Madison.[72] Hamilton sought to defend the proclamation:

> If the legislature have the right to make war on the one hand—it is on the other the duty of the Executive to preserve Peace till war is declared; and in fulfilling that duty, it must necessarily possess a right of judging what is the nature of the obligations which the treaties of the Country impose on the Government; and when in pursuance of that right it has concluded that there is nothing in them inconsistent with a state of neutrality, it becomes both its province and its duty to enforce the laws incident to that state of the Nation.[73]

In response Madison contended that if the proclamation was valid it meant that the president had usurped congressional power to decide between a state of peace or a state of war. Despite this difference, both men agreed that the power to commence war is vested in Congress. Madison wrote:

> Every just view that can be taken of this subject admonishes the public of the necessity of a rigid adherence to the simple, the received, and the fundamental doctrine of the constitution, that the power to declare war, including the power of judging of the causes of war, is *fully* and *exclusively* vested in the legislature; that the executive has no right, in any case, to decide the question, whether there is or is not cause for declaring war; that the right of convening and informing Congress, whenever such a question seems to call for a decision, is all the right which the constitution has deemed requisite or proper; and that for such, more than for any other contingency, this right was specially given to the executive.[74]

It is to be emphasized that throughout their lives both Hamilton and Madison maintained the doctrine that it is for Congress alone to initiate hostilities. The president has only the power to repel invasions.[75]

In 1798 France repeatedly raided and seized American vessels. On April 27, 1798, Congress passed a law that increased the size of the navy.[76] Secretary of War James McHenry, who seemed to want war, asked Hamilton if the legislation authorized the president to initiate hostilities. Hamilton responded on May 17:

> Not having seen the law which provides the *naval armament,* I cannot tell whether it gives any new power to the President; that is, any power

whatever with regard to the employment of the ships. If not, and he is left at the foot of the Constitution, as I understand to be the case, I am not ready to say that he has any other power than merely to employ the ships as convoys, with authority to *repel* force by *force* (but not to capture) and to repress hostilities within our waters, including a marine league from our coasts. Anything beyond this must fall under the idea of *reprisals,* and requires the sanctions of that department which is to declare *or make war.*[77]

During his first administration Thomas Jefferson was confronted with attacks on American shipping in the Mediterranean by the pasha of Tripoli, who also demanded annual tribute from the United States. Jefferson wrote the pasha on May 21, 1801, to inform him that he was ordering a "squadron of observation" to the Mediterranean to protect U.S. commerce. Though the ships were forbidden to take offensive action, one U.S. vessel, the *Enterprise,* was attacked. Lieutenant Andrew Sterrett of the *Enterprise* rendered the attacking ship dead in the water and released it. On the occasion of his first annual message to Congress on December 8, 1801, Jefferson adopted the Hamiltonian position and explained:

> Unauthorized by the Constitution, without the sanction of Congress, to go beyond the line of defense, the [Tripolitan] vessel, being disabled from committing further hostilities, was liberated with its crew. The Legislature will doubtless consider whether, by authorizing measures of offense also, they will place our force on an equal footing with that of its adversaries. I communicate all material information on this subject, that in the exercise of this important function confided by the Constitution to the Legislature exclusively their judgment may form itself on a knowledge and consideration of every circumstance of weight.[78]

But Jefferson's legal argument was met with harsh criticism from Alexander Hamilton, who thought the release of the Tripolitan vessel contemptible but nonetheless maintained:

> "The Congress shall have power to declare war"; the plain meaning of which is, that it is the peculiar and exclusive province of Congress, *when the nation is at peace,* to change that state of war; whether from calculations of policy, or from provocations or injuries received; in other words, it belongs to Congress only *to go to war.* But when a foreign nation declares or openly and avowedly makes war upon the United

States, they are then by the very fact *already at war,* and any declaration on the part of Congress is nugatory; it is at least unnecessary. . . .

Till the Congress should assemble and declare war, which would require time, our ships might, according to the hypothesis of the message, be sent by the President to fight those of the enemy as often as they should be attacked, but not to capture and detain them; if beaten, both vessels and crews would be lost to the United States; if successful, they could only disarm those they had overcome, and might suffer them to return to the place of common rendezvous, there to equip anew, for the purpose of resuming their depredations on our towns and on our trade.[79]

Hamilton probably attacked Jefferson for partisan reasons. The Tripolitan vessel had been rendered impotent; and Hamilton's hyperbole notwithstanding, there was no further threat to "our trade," let alone "our towns." Thus it was proper for Jefferson to refer the matter to Congress as the body that has the authority to change a state of peace into a state of war. At any rate, on February 6, 1802, Congress passed an act that met the concerns of Jefferson and Hamilton. The act empowered the president "fully to equip, officer, man, and employ such of the armed vessels of the United States as may be judged requisite by the President of the United States, for protecting effectually the commerce and seamen thereof on the Atlantic Ocean, the Mediterranean and adjoining seas"; to direct the ships' commanders to "subdue, seize, and make prize of all vessels, goods and effects, belonging to the Bey of Tripoli, or to his subjects . . . and also to cause to be done all such other acts of precaution or hostility as the state of war will justify, and may, in his opinion, require."[80]

Jefferson's understanding of the war clause underwent no revision. On December 6, 1805, he informed Congress of the dispute with Spain over the boundaries of Louisiana and Florida. Jefferson said that Spain evidenced an

intention to advance on our possessions until they shall be repressed by an opposing force. Considering that Congress alone is constitutionally invested with the power of changing our condition from peace to war, I have thought it my duty to await their authority for using force. . . . But the course to be pursued will require the command of means which it belongs to Congress exclusively to yield or to deny. To them I communicate every fact material for their information and the documents necessary to enable them to judge for themselves. To their wisdom, then, I look for the course I am to pursue, and will pursue with sincere zeal that which they shall approve.[81]

Like Jefferson, Pres. James Madison was aggrieved by the punishment and harassment inflicted on U.S. vessels. On June 1, 1812, he expressed to Congress his extreme resentment of the British practice of seizing American ships and seamen and of inducing Indian tribes to attack the United States. Madison complained:

> We behold, in fine, on the side of Great Britain a state of war against the United States, and on the side of the United States a state of peace toward Great Britain.
>
> Whether the United States shall remain passive under these progressive usurpations and these accumulating wrongs, or, opposing force, to force in defense of their national rights, shall commit a just cause into the hands of the Almighty Disposer of Events, avoiding all connections which might entangle it in the contest or views of other powers, and preserving a constant readiness to concur in an honorable reestablishment of peace and friendship, is a solemn question which the Constitution wisely confides to the legislative department of the Government. In recommending it to their early deliberations I am happy in the assurance that the decision will be worthy the enlightened and patriotic councils of a virtuous, a free, and a powerful nation.[82]

This exercise in presidential restraint speaks volumes for the intentions of the Framers with respect to the initiation of hostilities. As the leading architect of the Constitution and as a principal actor in the debate on the war clause, Madison certainly knew that when the question arises of whether the United States should oppose force with force it is a "solemn question which the Constitution wisely confides to the legislature department of the Government." This view exactly coincides with his earlier position. In 1793 Madison had written that "the power to declare war, including the power of judging the causes of war, is *fully* and *exclusively* vested in the legislature; that the executive has no right, in any case, to decide the question, whether there is or is not cause for declaring war." And in 1793 he stated, "Those who are to *conduct a war* cannot in the nature of things, be proper or safe judges, whether *a war ought* to be *commenced, continued, or concluded*. They are barred from the latter functions by a great principle in free government, analogous to that which separates the sword from the purse, or the power of executing from the power of enacting laws."[83]

Following his announcement of what has become known as the Monroe Doctrine, on December 2, 1823, Monroe was confronted with international circumstances that seemed to invite the use of force, but he repeatedly disclaimed any constitutional power to initiate hostilities.[84] In 1824 Colombia feared an attack by France. Citing the Monroe Doctrine, the Colombian government inquired of Secretary of State John Quincy Adams "in what manner the Government of the United States intends to resist on its part any interference of the holy Alliance for the purpose of subjugating the new Republics or interfering in their political forms." The question was considered in a cabinet meeting, which Adams summarized in his diary: "The Colombia republic to maintain its own independence. Hope that France and the Holy Allies will not resort to force against it. If they should, the power to determine our resistance is in Congress. The movements of the Executive will be as heretofore expressed. I am to draft an answer." While the matter was on the table, Monroe wrote James Madison to explain the problem: "The subject will of course be weighed thoroughly in giving the answer. The Executive has no right to compromise the nation in any question of war." And John Quincy Adams informed Colombia: "You understand that by the Constitution of the United States, the ultimate decision of this question belongs to the Legislative Department of the Government."[85] The threat dissolved, and no force was used.

On December 7, 1824, President Monroe reported that American shipping off the coast of Florida was being plundered by pirates. Various measures might be employed to stop the pirates, but Monroe referred the matter to Congress: "Whether those robbers should be pursued on the land . . . or any other measure be resorted to suppress them, is submitted to the consideration of Congress." When the Senate asked for more information, Monroe responded with three proposals and asked that "a power commensurate with either resource be granted to the Executive."[86]

Although Pres. Andrew Jackson probably resented some congressional decisions regarding international affairs during his administration, he nonetheless agreed that Congress controlled the warmaking power. On December 6, 1831, Jackson delivered his third annual address, in which he said that an American ship had been seized "by a land acting, as they pretend, under the authority of the Government of Buenos Ayres [*sic*]." He augmented the naval squadron in the area but asked Congress to "clothe the Executive with such authority and means as they may deem necessary for providing a force adequate to the complete protection of our fellow citizens fishing and trading in those areas."[87] Congress did not act on his proposal.

In his annual message on December 1, 1834, Jackson informed Congress that France had not honored an 1831 treaty by which the French government agreed to meet claims for damages to American shipping between 1800 and 1817. He asked for legislation "authorizing reprisals upon French property, in case provision shall not be made for the payment of the debt at the approaching session of the French Chambers.''[88] Jackson's request met opposition later that day when Cong. Nathaniel Claiborne warned: "If this power be conferred upon him, it will be virtually conferring upon the President unconstitutional power—a power to declare war. . . . Gentlemen have read history to little effect, if they are ready to clothe a single individual with the power of making war.''[89] It was also opposed by Albert Gallatin, who on January 5, 1835, wrote to Edward Everett: "The proposed transfer by Congress of its Constitutional powers to the Executive, in a case which necessarily embraces the question of war or no war, appears to me a most extraordinary proposal, and entirely inconsistent with the letter and spirit of our Constitution, which vests in Congress the power to declare war and grant letters of marque and reprisal." The Senate denied Jackson's request, basing its refusal on a report issued by the Senate Foreign Relations Committee, read by Henry Clay on January 6, 1835:

> In the first place the authority to grant letters of marque and reprisal being specially delegated to Congress, Congress ought to retain to itself the right of judging of the expediency of granting them under all the circumstances existing at the time when they are proposed to be actually issued. The committee are not satisfied that Congress can, constitutionally, delegate this right. It is true that the President proposes to limit the exercise of it to one specified contingency. But if the law be passed as recommended, the President might, and probably would, feel himself bound to execute it in the event, no matter from what cause, of provision not being made for the fulfillment of the treaty by the French Chambers, now understood to be in session. . . . Congress ought to reserve to itself the Constitutional right, which it possesses, of judging of all the circumstances by which such refusal might be attended; of hearing France, and of deciding whether, in the actual posture of things as they may then exist, and looking to the condition of the United States, of France, and of Europe, the issuing of letters of marque and reprisal ought to be authorized, or any measure adopted.[90]

As secretary of state, Daniel Webster echoed the views of his predecessors on the meaning of the war clause. In 1851 he denied a request for the United States to aid Hawaii in its dispute with France.

> In the first place, I have to say that the war-making power in this Government rests entirely with Congress, and that the President can authorize belligerent operations only in the cases expressly provided for by the

Constitution and the laws. By these no power is given to the Executive to oppose an attack by one independent nation or the possessions of another. We are bound to regard both France and Hawaii as independent states, and equally independent, and though the general policy of the Government might lead it to take part with either in a controversy with the other, still, if this interference be an act of hostile force, it is not within the Constitutional power of the President; and still less is it within the power of any subordinate agent of government, civil or military.[91]

James Buchanan was insistent on the constitutional repository of the war power. As secretary of state in 1848 he responded to a request from Hawaii for the United States to lend military aid to collect claims by stating that "the President could not employ the naval force of the United States to enforce its payment without the authority of an act of Congress. The war-making power alone can authorize such a measure." In 1860 Buchanan directed Secretary of State Lewis Cass to explain to an American company in Nicaragua that asked the administration to use force to collect claims that such a measure would constitute "an act of war," which "is a measure which Congress alone possesses the constitutional power to adopt."[92]

There was no departure from this understanding of the war clause throughout the nineteenth century; indeed, a search of historical records for a claim to presidential power to initiate hostilities is made in vain.[93] In fact, it was left to twentieth-century officeholders and commentators to adduce constitutional power for the president to make war.

The Mexican War, which lasted from 1846 to 1848, deserves attention in this context. Following the annexation of Texas, a dispute arose over the title to territory between the Nueces River and the Rio Grande. President James Polk ordered an army into the area, and it defeated the Mexican forces. In a message to Congress, Polk offered the rationale that "Mexico has passed the boundary of the United States, has invaded our territory and shed American blood on American soil." It was on the basis of this report that Congress declared, "by the act of the Republic of Mexico, a state of war exists between that Government and the United States."[94]

If Polk's rationale was correct, then his action could not be challenged on constitutional grounds, for it was well established that the president had the authority to repel sudden attacks. If, however, he had been disingenuous, if he had in fact initiated hostilities, then he had clearly usurped the warmaking power of Congress. It is worth noticing that he made no claim to constitutional power to make war.

The Whigs greatly resented Polk's actions, and in 1847 the two houses of Congress commenced an inquiry into the circumstances surrounding the outbreak of the war. On January 3, 1848, the House concluded, by a vote of 85 to 81, that the war had been "unnecessarily and unconstitutionally begun by the President of the United States."[95] Congressman Abraham Lincoln of Illinois voted with the majority. Lincoln's law partner, William H. Herndon, had written a letter in which he assumed Polk had initiated the hostilities but nevertheless defended the action as a legitimate means of preventing an invasion by Mexico. Lincoln answered his friend in words that have become famous:

> Let me first state what I understand to be your position. It is that if it shall become necessary to repel invasion, the President may, without violation of the Constitution, cross the line and invade the territory of another country, and that whether such necessity exists in any given case the President is the sole judge. . . .
>
> Allow the President to invade a neighboring nation whenever he shall deem it necessary to repel an invasion, and you allow him to do so whenever he may choose to say he deems it necessary for such a purpose, and you allow him to make war at his pleasure. Study to see if you can fix any limit to his power in this respect, after having given him so much power as you propose. . . .
>
> The provision of the Constitution giving the war-making power to Congress was dictated, as I understand it, by the following reasons: Kings have always been involving and impoverishing their people in wars, pretending generally, if not always, that the good of the people was the object. This our convention understood to be the most oppressive of all kingly oppressions, and they resolved to frame the Constitution that no one man should hold the power of bringing oppression upon us. But your view destroys the whole matter, and places our President where kings have always stood.[96]

As president, Abraham Lincoln did not alter his view of the war power. This conclusion may be drawn from his first annual message on December 3, 1861, when he referred to prior congressional authorization for American ships to "defend themselves against and to capture pirates." It was his opinion that congressional authorization was necessary "to recapture any prizes which pirates may make of United States vessels and their cargoes," which was exactly the understanding of the war clause held by Madison, Hamilton, and Jefferson.[97] It bears reminder, moreover, that none of Lincoln's actions in the

Civil War constitutes a precedent for presidential initiation of war. The attack on Fort Sumter represented a "sudden attack" that Lincoln had the constitutional power to repel.[98]

The treatise writers of the nineteenth century were uniformly in agreement on the meaning of the war clause: war cannot lawfully be initiated by the president but only by Congress. Chancellor James Kent, one of the republic's most eminent jurists, wrote in his *Commentaries* in 1829:

> But, though a solemn declaration, or previous notice to the enemy, be now laid aside, it is essential that some formal public act, proceeding directly from the competent source, should announce to the people at home their new relations and duties growing out of a state of war, and which should equally apprise neutral nations of the fact. . . . As war cannot lawfully be commenced on the part of the United States without an Act of Congress, such an act is, of course, a formal official notice to all the world, and equivalent to the most solemn declaration.[99]

In his celebrated *Commentaries* of 1833, Joseph Story, then an associate justice of the Supreme Court, likened the congressional power to declare war to the "similar exclusive power under the Articles [of Confederation]" and assessed Charles Pinckney's motion in the Constitutional Convention that the Senate be vested with the war power for the sake of dispatch, secrecy, and vigor:

> On the other hand, it may be urged in reply that the power of declaring war is not only the highest sovereign prerogative, but that it is in its own nature and effects, so critical and calamitous, that it requires the utmost deliberation, and the successive revise of all the councils of the nation. . . . The representatives of the people are to lay the taxes to support a war, and therefore have a right to be consulted as to its time, and the ways and means of making if effective. The co-operation of all branches of the legislative power ought, upon principle, to be required in this highest act of legislation as it is in all others.[100]

In 1864, William Whiting wrote:

> Congress has the sole power, under the constitution, to sanction or authorize the commencement of *offensive* war. . . . But this is quite a different case from a defensive or civil war. The constitution establishes the mode in which this government shall *commence* wars, and what author-

ity shall ordain, and what declarations shall precede, any act of hostility; but it has no power to prescribe the manner in which others should begin war against us. Hence it follows, that when war is commenced against this country, by aliens or by citizens, no declaration of war by the government is necessary. The fact that war is levied against the United States, makes it the duty of the President to call out the army or navy to subdue the enemy, whether foreign or domestic. . . . The Constitution, made as it was by men of sense, never leaves the nation powerless for self-defence. That instrument, which gives the legislative authority to declare war, whenever war is *initiated* by the United States, also makes it the duty of the President, as commander-in-chief, to engage promptly and effectually in war; or, in other words, to make the United States a belligerent nation, whenever he is legally called upon to suppress rebellion, repel invasion, or to execute the laws against armed and forcible resistance thereto. . . . It must not be forgotten that by law of nations and by modern usage, no formal *declaration* of war *to the enemy* is necessary. All that is now requisite is for each nation to make suitable declarations or proclamations to their own citizens, to enable them to govern themselves accordingly.[101]

In his treatise on the Constitution in 1868, John Norton Pomeroy wrote: "It is sufficient to know that the people considered the act and state of war a matter of such transcendent importance and magnitude, involving such untold personal and material interests, hazarding the prosperity, and perhaps the very existence of the body politic, that they committed its formal inception to that department of the government which more immediately represents them,—the Congress."[102]

Thomas Cooley, one of the most learned legal scholars of the nineteenth century and chief justice of the Michigan Supreme Court, said in 1880 of the president as commander-in-chief: "The power to declare war being confided to the legislature, he has no power to originate it, but he may in advance of its declaration employ the army and navy to suppress insurrection or repel invasion."[103]

In 1887 Hermann von Holst wrote:

The right "to declare war" belongs to Congress alone. . . . Of course, the United States may get into a war without Congress' having declared war. War is, in the first place, a state of fact, the appearance of which cannot be made wholly dependent, by any constitutional provisions whatever, upon the pleasure of one of the nations concerned. As far as that is possible, however, Congress has the exclusive right of the initiative. If a foreign power brings war against the United States, then it is not only the right, but the duty, of the president to oppose the enemy with all means placed at his disposal by the constitution and the laws.[104]

In his learned treatise on the Constitution, Westel W. Willoughby reflected the teaching and understanding of the nineteenth century when he stated that "the right of making war belongs exclusively to the supreme or sovereign power of the State. This power in all civilized nations is regulated by the fundamental laws or municipal constitution of the country. By our own Constitution, the power is lodged in Congress."[105]

Judicial Precedents

The meaning of the war clause was put beyond doubt by several early judicial decisions. No court since has departed from this early view. In 1800 in *Bas v. Tingy*, the Supreme Court considered for the first time whether Congress might declare an imperfect or limited war, as well as a perfect or general war.[106] The case was decided in the context of a limited war between the United States and France from 1798 to 1801. Of immediate concern to the court was the legal status of the hostilities. Justice Bushrod Washington held:

It may, I believe, be safely laid down, that every contention by force between two nations, in external matters, under the authority of their respective governing, is not only war, but public war. If it be declared in form, it is called solemn, and is of the perfect kind; because one whole nation is at war with another whole nation; and all the members of the nation declaring war, are authorized to commit hostilities against all the members of the other, in every place, and under every circumstance. In such a war all the members act under a general authority, and all the rights and consequences of war attach to their condition.

But hostilities may subsist between two nations, more confined in its nature and extent, being limited as to places, persons, and things; and this is more properly termed imperfect war; because not solemn, and because those who are authorized to commit hostilities, act under special authority, and can go no further than to the extent of their commission. Still, however, it is a public war, because it is an external contention by force between some members of the two nations, authorized by the legitimate powers. It is a war between two nations, though all the members are not authorized to commit hostilities such as in a solemn war, where the government restrains the general power.

Now, if this be the true definition of war, let us see what was the situation of the United States in relation to France. In March, 1799, Congress had raised an army, stopped all intercourse with France; dissolved our treaty, built and equipped ships of war; and commissioned private armed ships; enjoining the former, and authorizing the latter, to defend themselves against the armed ships of France, to attack them on the high seas, to subdue and take them as prize, and to recapture armed vessels found in their possession. Here, then, let me ask, what were the technical characters of an American and French armed vessel, combating on the high seas, with a view the one to subdue the other, and to make prize of his property? They certainly were not friends, because there was a contention by force; nor were they private enemies, because the contention was external, and was authorized by the legitimate authority of the two governments. If they were not our enemies, I know not what constitutes an enemy. . . .

What then is the evidence of legislative will? In fact and law we are at war: an American vessel fighting with a French vessel, to subdue and make her prize, is fighting with an enemy, accurately and technically speaking: and if this be no sufficient evidence of the legislative mind, it is explained in the same law.[107]

Thus Congress, the "legitimate authority," had passed legislation that had taken the United States into a state of imperfect war, a limited war. Justice Samuel Chase was of the same opinion:

Congress is empowered to declare a general war, or Congress may wage a limited war; limited in place, in object, in time. If a general war is declared, its extent and operations are only restricted and regulated by the *jus belli,* forming a part of the law of nations; but if a partial war is waged, its extent and operation depend on our municipal laws.

What then is the nature of the contest subsisting between America and France? In my judgment it is a limited, partial war. Congress has not declared war in general terms; but Congress has authorized hostilities on the high seas by certain persons in certain cases.[108]

Justice William Paterson, who had been a leading delegate to the Constitutional Convention, shared the view of his brethren:

The United States and the French republic are in a qualified state of hostility. An imperfect war, or war, as to certain objects, and to a certain extent, exists between the two nations; and this modified warfare is authorized by the constitutional authority of our country. It is a war *quoad hoc*. As far as Congress tolerated and authorized the war on our part, so far may we proceed in hostile operations. It is a maritime war, a war at sea for certain purposes. . . . It is therefore a public war between the two nations qualified, on our part, in the manner prescribed by the constitutional organ of our country.[109]

In 1801, in *Talbot v. Seeman,* the Court upheld the right of a U.S. vessel to take a prize. Chief Justice John Marshall, who was a member of the Virginia Ratifying Convention, delivered the opinion:

The whole powers of war being, by the Constitution of the United States, vested in Congress, the acts of that body can alone be resorted to as our guides in this inquiry. It is not denied, nor in the course of the argument has it been denied, that Congress may authorize general hostilities, in which case the general laws of war apply to our situation; or partial war, in which case the laws of war, so far as they actually apply to our situation, must be noticed.[110]

In *Little v. Barreme,* decided in 1804, Marshall held that John Adams's instructions to seize ships were in conflict with an act of Congress and were therefore illegal.[111]

In 1806, in *United States v. Smith,* the question of whether the president may initiate hostilities was decided by Justice Paterson, riding circuit, who wrote for himself and district judge Matthias Tallmadge: "Does he [the president] possess the power of making war? That power is exclusively vested in Congress." He continued: "There is a manifest distinction between our going to war with a nation at peace, and a war made against us by an actual invasion, or a formal declaration. In the former case, it is the exclusive province of Congress to change a state of peace into a state of war."[112]

In the *Prize Cases* in 1863 the Supreme Court considered for the first time the power of the president to respond to sudden attacks. Justice Robert Grier delivered the opinion of the court:

By the Constitution, Congress alone has the power to declare a national or foreign war. . . . If a war be made by invasion of a foreign nation, the President is not only authorized but bound to resist force, by force. He does not initiate the war, but is bound to accept the challenge without waiting for any special legislative authority. And whether the hostile party be a foreign invader, or States organized in rebellion, it is none the less a war, although the declaration of it be "unilateral."[113]

These judicial decisions established the constitutional fact that it is for Congress alone to initiate hostilities, whether in the form of general or limited war; the president is granted only the power to repel sudden attacks. Moreover, the Supreme Court has never held that the commander-in-chief clause confers power to initiate war. In 1895 in *United States v. Sweeny*, Justice Henry Brown wrote for the Court that the object of the clause was to give the president "such supreme and undivided command as would be necessary to the prosecution of a successful war."[114] In 1919 Sen. George Sutherland, who became an associate justice of the Supreme Court, wrote: "Generally speaking, the war powers of the President under the Constitution are simply those that belong to any commander-in-chief of the military forces of a nation at war. The Constitution confers no war powers upon the President as such."[115] In 1942, in *Ex parte Quirin*, Chief Justice Harlan Stone said of the commander-in-chief's power:

> The Constitution thus invests the President with power to wage war which Congress has declared, and to carry into effect all laws passed by Congress for the conduct of war and for the government and regulation of the Armed Forces, and all laws defining and punishing offenses against the law of nations, including those which pertain to the conduct of war.[116]

It is thus against the intentions of the Framers, against the debate and vote on the war clause, and against a wealth of executive, legislative, and judicial precedents of the nineteenth century that recent executives have invoked a presidential power to initiate military hostilities. The evidence against their case is overwhelming. Their claims ignore the text of the Constitution, and they find no authority in our legal history.

THE CONTINUING CONTROVERSY

Until 1950, it has been justly observed, "No judge, no President, no legislator, no commentator ever suggested that the President had legal authority to initiate war."[117] Since then, however, a steady pattern of presidential warmaking has developed, and its legality has been defended on a number of grounds. We have reviewed those claims that are based on constitutional grants of authority and have found them to be without merit; in fact, there is not the slightest hint of evidence to support such claims. Defenders thus have contrived additional arguments that, for the sake of completeness, require consideration. First, it has been contended that the president may initiate hostilities by virtue of an ''inherent power'' that is derived from extraconstitutional sources. Second, it has been asserted that the president derives a warmaking authority from his status as the ''sole organ'' of American foreign policy. Third, it has been argued that executive warmaking acquires legal validity through repetition.

Advocates of inherent executive power typically ground their argument in the dictum of Justice George Sutherland in the 1936 case, *United States v. Curtiss-Wright Export Corporation*.[118] It is quite likely that *Curtiss-Wright* is the most frequently cited case involving the allocation of foreign affairs powers.[119] It carries uncommon significance even though it raised merely the narrow question of the constitutionality of a joint resolution that authorized the president to halt the sale of arms to Bolivia and Paraguay, then involved in armed conflict in the Chaco, if it would ''contribute to the re-establishment of peace between those countries.''[120] The Court, per Justice George Sutherland, ultimately upheld the delegation against the charge that it was unduly broad. If in his opinion for the Court Justice Sutherland had stuck to the delegation issue, *Curtiss-Wright* would have been overshadowed by *Panama Refining Co. v. Ryan* and never even would have surfaced in the table of contents of undergraduate casebooks.[121] But Sutherland strayed from the delegation question and in some ill-considered dicta imparted an unhappy legacy, the idea that the external sovereignty of the nation is vested in the presidency and is neither derived from nor restrained by the Constitution.

Sutherland's theory of inherent presidential power stems from his reading of Anglo-American legal history. According to him, domestic and foreign affairs are different, ''both in respect of their origin and nature.'' The ''domestic or internal affairs'' are confined by the reach of the Constitution. But authority over foreign affairs is not dependent upon a grant from the Constitution since the powers of external sovereignty ''passed from the Crown not to the colonies severally, but to the colonies in their collective and corporate capacity of the United States of America.''[122] Sutherland's historical excursion is without factual foundation. Scholars have demolished his thesis by demonstrating that in 1776 states were sovereign entities.[123] Proof is found in the Articles of Confederation, approved by the Continental Congress in November 1777 and ratified in March 1781. Article II of that governing document stated, "Each State retains its Sovereignty, freedom and independence, and every power . . . which is not . . . expressly delegated to the United States, in Congress assembled." Further, in Article III, it was provided, "The said states hereby severally enter into a firm league of friendship with each other, for their common defense . . ." Finally, Article IX stated: "The United States in Congress assembled, shall have the sole and exclusive right and power of determining on peace and war . . . [and of] entering into treaties and alliances."[124] From this it should be understood that the states entered into a "league of friendship"; they did not attempt to create a "sovereign" or "corporate" body. Indeed, the thirteen sovereignties, "which emerged from the principles of the Revolution," only grudgingly *delegated* powers to the Continental Congress.[125] This was, in Randolph's words at the Constitutional Convention, because of the "jealousy of the states with regard to their sovereignty."[126] Thus the "states, in their highest sovereign capacity," delegated powers to the Continental Congress; among these powers was an express grant, per Article IX, of the war and treaty powers.[127] As Raoul Berger has observed, this grant "alone undermines Sutherland's central premise that these powers were derived from 'some other source' than the several states."[128]

Even if we were to assume that the power of external sovereignty had been by some method transferred directly from the Crown to the Union, it remains to be explained why that power would be vested in the president. As Justice Felix Frankfurter stated, "The fact that power exists in the Government does not vest it in the President."[129] Indeed, the Supreme Court has ruled on several occasions that the sovereign power in foreign affairs is held by Congress.[130] At any rate, there is nothing in Sutherland's theory that would explain the location of this power in the presidency.[131]

Finally, Sutherland was plainly in error in his contention that the conduct of foreign policy is not restricted by the Constitution. James Madison put the question beyond doubt when he wrote in *Federalist 45* that "the powers delegated by the proposed Constitution are *few and defined*. . . . [They] will be exercised principally on external objects, as war, peace, negotiation, and foreign commerce," to demonstrate that foreign relations powers were derived from the Constitution.[132] Clearly there is no evidence from the Constitutional Convention to suggest even the slightest flirtation with the concept of an undefined reservoir of presidential power.

Moreover, since *Curtiss-Wright* the Court consistently has taken the position that powers are tethered to the Constitution. In the *Steel Seizure* case, Justice Hugo L. Black, speaking for the Court, delivered a weighty rebuke to the claim of extraconstitutional "executive power."[133] In the same case Justice Robert Jackson sharply dismissed Sutherland's discussion of inherent presidential power as mere "dictum."[134] In *Reid v. Covert,* the Court rejected the contention that foreign affairs powers are beyond the reach of the Constitution's due process clauses. Writing for the Court, Black stated: "The United States is entirely a creature of the Constitution. Its powers and authority have no other source. It can only act in accordance with all the limitations imposed by the Constitution."[135] The assertion of an inherent presidential power to initiate war is unlikely to find aid and comfort in the *Curtiss-Wright* decision. Arthur Schlesinger, Jr., has justly remarked:

> The case itself involved the power to act under congressional authorization, not the power to act independently of Congress. Moreover, it involved the power over foreign commerce, not the power over war. Its actual holding was restricted. Its expansive contentions were in the nature of *obiter dicta.* And, as Thomas Reed Powell used to tell his students at the Harvard Law School, "Just because Mr. Justice Sutherland writes clearly, you must not suppose that he thinks clearly."[136]

Further, the text of the Constitution and the debates in the Constitutional Convention and the state ratifying conventions as well as early judicial decisions—in short, all the evidence—incontrovertibly establish that Congress alone has the constitutional power to commence war. And, as John Quincy Adams said, "The war power is strictly constitutional."[137]

Extollers of a unilateral executive warmaking authority also have invoked the Lockean prerogative as a source of inherent presidential power. Drawing on John Locke's defense of the right of an executive to act for the common good, even if it requires breaking the law *(salus populi supreme lex)*, defenders have adduced a similar claim for the president.[138] There is not a scintilla of evidence whatever that the Framers intended to incorporate the Lockean Prerogative in the Constitution. And lacking a textual statement or grant of power to that effect, such an intent is indispensable to the claim of a constitutional power. In fact, the evidence runs in the other direction. Fears of executive power led the Framers to enumerate the president's power to "define and confine" the scope of his authority. And clearly, an undefined reservoir of discretionary power in the form of Locke's prerogative would have unraveled the carefully crafted design of Article II and repudiated the Framers' stated aim of corralling executive power.

The absence of such authority means that by definition any presidential assertion of a prerogative power to violate the law is an extraconstitutional claim; an action based on such an assertion is definitionally unconstitutional. This claim then does not afford a president any constitutional or legal authority to initiate war. The issue is merely whether a president would commence war in violation of the supreme law of the land and then attempt to justify it on the grounds of necessity. Of course, he cannot be the judge of his own actions. He must seek immunity and exoneration from Congress in the way of retroactive authorization, a practice that is deeply imbedded in American tradition.[139] Whether or not congressional approval of the claimed prerogative is granted, the review itself is an admission of presidential usurpation of power.

Revisionists have also asserted a presidential warmaking authority on the basis of his role as the "sole organ" of American foreign policy.[140] This sentiment recently found expression in somewhat different language when Ronald Reagan drew upon his "prime responsibility for the conduct of foreign relations" to defend his invasion of Grenada.[141] The argument has acquired a certain following and therefore deserves close scrutiny.

In *Curtiss-Wright* Justice Sutherland stated that the authority in foreign affairs was essentially an executive power, which he explained "as the very delicate, plenary and exclusive power of the President as the sole organ of the federal government in the field of international relations—a power which does not require as a basis for its exercise, an act of Congress."[142] Let us consider the historical context from which Sutherland ripped the sole-organ doctrine. In short, Sutherland greatly expanded on Cong. John Marshall's speech in 1800 in which he noted that "the President is the sole organ of the nation in its external relations. . . . Of consequence, the demand of a foreign nation can only be made on him."[143] Marshall was defending the decision of Pres. John Adams to surrender to British officials a British deserter, Jonathan Robbins, in accordance with the Jay Treaty. The Robbins affair involved a demand upon the United States, according to Marshall, and it required a response from the president on behalf of the American people. At no point in his speech did Marshall argue that the president's exclusive authority to communicate with a foreign nation included a power to formulate or develop policy. Corwin properly concluded: "Clearly, what Marshall had foremost in mind was simply the President's role as an instrument of communication with other governments."[144] This point of procedure had been acknowledged in 1793 by Thomas Jefferson, who remarked that the president,

> being the only channel of communication between this country and foreign nations, it is from him alone that foreign nations or their agents are to learn what is or had been the will of the nation; and whatever he communicates as such, they have a right, and are bound to consider as the expression of the nation, and no foreign agent can be allowed to question it.[145]

And this view has not been challenged. Thus, it was Sutherland who infused a purely communicative role with a substantive policymaking function and thereby manufactured a great power out of the Marshallian sole-organ doctrine. To have done this, as Myres McDougal and Asher Lans observed, was to confuse the "organ" with the "organ grinder," and to undermine the Framers' design for cooperation in the conduct of foreign affairs.[146]

The persistence of the claim that the president is constitutionally empowered with the prime responsibility for the conduct of American foreign policy, that he is the sole organ, is really quite puzzling, because the claim cannot survive close scrutiny. As Article II of the Constitution indicates, the president shares the treatymaking power and the power to appoint ambassadors with the Senate. In fact, the Framers assumed that the treaty power would constitute the primary mechanism by which American foreign relations would be conducted. Hamilton echoed the sentiment of the convention when he assured the New York State Ratifying Convention that the Senate, "together with the President are to manage all our concerns with foreign nations."[147] Moreover, Congress has complete power over foreign commerce and, of course, it alone is the repository of the power to declare war. Only two powers in foreign relations are assigned exclusively to the president. He is commander-in-chief, but he acts in this capacity by and under the authority of Congress. And he has the power to receive ambassadors. Hamilton, Madison, and Jefferson agreed that this clerklike function was purely ceremonial in character. Although it has come to entail recognition of states at international law, which carries with it certain legal implications, the Framers declined to make it a discretionary policymaking instrument. As Hamilton explained it, the duty of recognizing states was more conveniently placed in the hands of the executive than with the legislature.[148] This examination exhausts the textual grant of authority to the president with respect to foreign affairs jurisdiction. The Framers clearly granted the bulk of foreign relations powers to Congress. The president's constitutional authority pales by comparison. It appears that the sole-organ doctrine is simply so much fanciful rhetoric.

Finally, the extollers of executive power have fashioned the argument that executive warmaking, if repeated often enough, acquires legal validity. This is the contention as expounded by Henry P. Monaghan that "history has legitimated the practice of presidential war-making."[149] The argument rests on the premise that the president frequently has exercised the war power without congressional authorization. The actual number of these episodes varies among the several compilations, but defenders usually list between 100 and 200 unilateral acts, each of which constitutes a legitimizing precedent for future executive wars.[150]

In detail and in conception the argument is flawed. In the first place, the revisionists' lists are inaccurately compiled. Francis D. Wormuth has thoroughly deflated their claims with what Raoul Berger has rightly characterized as a "painstaking analysis."[151] Space does not permit a critical analysis of each alleged assertion of executive precedents. Consider, however, an error common to the lists: the claim that unilateral warmaking was initiated by the "undeclared" war with France in 1798. That claim, as Wormuth justly observed, "is altogether false. The fact is that President John Adams took absolutely no independent action. Congress passed a series of acts that amounted, so the Supreme Court said, to a declaration of imperfect war; and Adams complied with these statutes."[152] Moreover, many of the episodes involved initiation of hostilities by a military commander, not by authorization from the president. If practice establishes law, then the inescapable conclusion is that every commander of every military unit has the power to initiate war. What is perhaps most revealing about presidential understanding of the constitutional locus of the war power is that in the one or two dozen instances in which presidents have personally made the decision unconstitutionally to initiate acts of war, they have *not* purported to rely on their authority as commander-in-chief or chief executive. In "all of these cases the Presidents have made false claims of authorization, either by statute or by treaty or by international law."[153]

Moreover, it cannot be maintained that constitutional power, in this case the war power, can be acquired through practice. In *Powell v. McCormack*, Chief Justice Earl Warren wrote, "That an unconstitutional action has been taken before surely does not render that action any less unconstitutional at a later date." Earlier, Justice Felix Frankfurter, writing for a unanimous Court, echoed a centuries-old principle of Anglo-American jurisprudence: "Illegality cannot attain legitimacy through practice."[154] The Court has repeatedly denied claims that the president can acquire power by a series of usurpations. If it were otherwise, the president might aggrandize all governmental power. Neither Congress nor the judiciary could lawfully restrain the exercise of the president's accumulated constitutional powers. Clearly, this practice would scuttle our entire constitutional jurisprudence. Thus, the most recent act of usurpation stands no better than the first.

Finally, it is unwarranted to conclude that presidential usurpation, indulged by congressional acquiescence or passivity, attains a legal status. Congress cannot divest itself of those powers conferred upon it by the Constitution, a necessary predicate of the separation of powers doctrine.[155] Neither congressional abdication nor acquiescence can accomplish a transfer of power to the executive. As the Court has held, harking back to an old axiom of English law, once powers are "granted, they are not lost by being allowed to lie dormant, any more than non-existent powers can be prescripted by an unchallenged exercise."[156]

Of course, in recent years the congressional power to decide for war and peace has at times been usurped by the executive. In this regard there is a fundamental conflict between the theory of the Constitution and the practice of the government. It is sometimes observed that the intentions of the Framers are outdated and irrelevant. But before we too readily acquiesce in this verdict we might do well to consider the policy reasons underlying the decision to vest the war power in Congress and not in the president. Painfully aware of the horror and destructive consequences of warfare, the Founders decided that before the very fate of the nation was put to risk there ought to be some discussion, some deliberation by Congress, the people's representatives. The Founders did not, as James Wilson explained, want "one man to hurry us into war."[157] As things stand in the United States today, however, the president has been exercising that power. Perhaps in this case the intentions of the Framers are not irrelevant. Perhaps their policy concerns are even more compelling today than they were two centuries ago.

NOTES

A version of this chapter was published as "The Constitution and Presidential Warmaking: The Enduring Debate," *Political Science Quarterly* 103 (Spring 1988): 1–36.

1. The phrase is borrowed from Francis D. Wormuth, "Presidential Wars: The Convenience of 'Precedent'," *Nation*, October 9, 1972, p. 301.

2. A considerable body of literature has examined this question. See Louis Fisher, *Presidential War Power* (Lawrence: University Press of Kansas, 1995); Francis D. Wormuth, "The Nixon Theory of the War Power: A Critique," *California Law Review* 60 (May 1972): 623; his earlier monograph, *The Vietnam War: The President versus the Constitution* (Santa Barbara, Calif: Center for Study of Democratic Institutions, 1968), reprinted in Richard Falk, ed., *The Vietnam War and International Law*, 4 vols. (Princeton, N.J.: Princeton University Press, 1969), 1:711; and F. D. Wormuth and Edwin Firmage, *To Chain the Dog of War: The War Power of Congress in History and Law* (Dallas: Southern Methodist University Press, 1986). See also John Hart Ely, *War and Responsibility* (Princeton, N.J.: Princeton University Press, 1994); Leonard Ratner, "The Coordinated Warmaking Power—Legislative, Executive and Judicial Roles," *Southern California Law Review* 44 (Winter 1971): 19; Eugene Rostow, "Great Cases Make Bad Law: The War Powers Act," *Texas Law Review* 50 (May 1972): 833; J. Terry Emerson, "The War Powers Resolution Tested: The President's Independent Defense Power," *Notre Dame Lawyer* 51 (1975): 187; Raoul Berger, "War-Making by the President," *Pennsylvania Law Review* 121 (November 1972): 29; William Rogers, "Congress, the President, and War Powers," *California Law Review* 59 (September 1971): 1194; Charles Lofgren, "War-Making Under the Constitution: The Original Understanding," *Yale Law Journal* 81 (March 1972): 672.

3. See Ratner, "Co-ordinated Warmaking Power," Rostow, "Great Cases," and Emerson, "War Powers."

4. Corwin denounced Arthur Schlesinger, Jr., and Henry Steele Commager for their support of Truman's action. Edward S. Corwin, *The President: Office and Powers, 1787–1957,* 4th rev. ed. (New York: New York University Press, 1957), p. 14. By the late 1960s both Schlesinger and Commager had altered their views and favored a more powerful congressional role in the conduct of foreign policy (cited in Louis Fisher, *Constitutional Conflicts Between Congress and the President* [Princeton, N.J.: Princeton University Press, 1985], p. 291. The list of revisionists continues to grow (see text accompanying note 35 of this chapter).

5. Sutherland enunciated the sole-organ doctrine in *United States v. Curtiss-Wright Export Corporation,* 299 U.S. 304 (1936).

6. U.S. Constitution, Article I, section 8, paragraph 11.

7. Max Farrand, *The Records of the Federal Convention of 1787,* 4 vols. (New Haven: Yale University Press, 1911), 1:21.

8. Ibid., p. 65.

9. Ibid., pp. 73–74, 65–66.

10. Ibid., pp. 70, 66.

11. Ibid., 2:182.

12. Henry Steele Commager, *Documents of American History,* 7th ed. (New York: Appleton, 1963), p. 133. Charles Warren observed that this power, as well as others, came "bodily from the old Articles of Confederation" (Warren, *The Makings of the Constitution* [Cambridge: Harvard University Press, 1947], p. 389).

13. Farrand, *Records of the Federal Convention,* 2:318.

14. Ibid.

15. Ibid., 2:318, 319.

16. Jonathan Elliot, *Debates in the Several State Conventions on the Adoption of the Federal Constitution,* 2d ed., 4 vols. (Washington, D.C.: J. Elliot, 1836). Robert McCloskey wrote that Wilson was the "most learned and profound legal scholar of his generation" (*Works of James Wilson,* ed. R. G. McCloskey, 2 vols. [Cambridge: Harvard University Press, 1967], 1:2).

17. Elliot, *Debates,* 4:107, 108, 287, and 2:278.

18. 119 *Cong. Rec.* S14141 (daily ed. 19 July 1973).

19. Ratner, "Co-ordinated Warmaking Power," p. 467.

20. John Norton Moore, "The National Executive and the Use of Armed Forces Abroad," in Falk, ed., *Vietnam,* 2:814. Senator Paul Douglas defended President Truman's unauthorized venture in Korea on this ground (96 *Cong. Rec.* 9648 [1950]).

21. Huloet's dictionary provided this definition: "Declare warres. Arma Canere, Bellum indicere." We have here two meanings: to summon to arms; to announce war (quoted in Wormuth and Firmage, *To Chain the Dog of War,* p. 20).

22. In 1744 *Comyn's Digest,* an authoritative treatise on English law, stated: "To the king alone it belongs to make peace and war," as well as "the king has the sole authority to declare war and peace" (quoted in Wormuth and Firmage, *To Chain the Dog of War*). For a discussion of the understanding of international law, see Lofgren, "War-Making," pp. 685–95.

23. James Kent, *Commentaries on American Law,* 2d. ed., 4 vols. (Boston: Little, Brown, 1896), 1:55.

24. Lofgren, "War-Making," pp. 685–95.

25. According to Emmerich de Vattel, the leading international law publicist, a conditional declaration of war, an ultimatum demanding satisfaction of grievances, ought properly to precede a declaration of general war (Vattel, *The Law of Nations,* trans. C. Fenwick [Washington, D.C.: Carnegie Institution, 1916], pp. 254–57).

26. *Miller v. The Ship Resolution,* 2 U.S. (2 Dall.) 12, 21 (1782).

27. See notes 109–14 of this chapter.

28. *Talbot v. Seeman,* 5 U.S. (1 Cranch) 1, 28 (1801).

29. J. B. Moore, *The Collected Papers of John Bassett Moore,* 7 vols. (New Haven: Yale University Press, 1944), 5:195–96.

30. *United States v. Smith,* 27 F. Cas. 1192, 1230 (C.C.D.N.Y.) 1806).

31. For an excellent discussion of the origins and development of the use of letters of marque and reprisal, with an application to contemporary covert war, see Jules Lobel, "Covert War and Congressional Authority: Hidden War and Forgotten Power," *Pennsylvania Law Review* 134 (June 1986): 1035.

32. Ibid., 1045–47.

33. Quoted in J. B. Moore, *A Digest of International Law,* 8 vols. (Washington, D.C.: U.S. Government Printing Office, 1906), 7:123.

34. *Youngstown Sheet and Tube Co. v. Sawyer,* 343 U.S. 579, 643 (1952) (concurring opinion).

35. For example, the State Department justified Johnson's involvement in Vietnam on the basis of his power as commander-in-chief (*Department of State Bulletin* 54 [1966]: 474, 484). For the same justification by Reagan with respect to his actions in Lebanon and Grenada respectively, see 18 *Weekly Comp. Pres. Doc.* 1232 (September 29, 1982), and 19, 1494 (October 25, 1983). President Clinton has followed the same path when he adduced the commander-in-chief clause as authority for his decision to order air strikes against Iraq on June 26, 1993, in response to an alleged assassination plot against George Bush (29 *Weekly Comp. of Pres. Doc.* 1181, 1183 [1993]). For a good, brief discussion and review of presidential invocation of the commander-in-chief argument, see Fisher, *Presidential War Power,* pp. 134–61.

36. Senator Barry Goldwater, for example, has asserted that the commander-in-chief clause gives the president "the power of war and peace" (117 *Cong. Rec.* S5640 [daily ed. April 26, 1971]).

37. Wormuth, "Nixon Theory," p. 630.

38. Quoted in ibid. See also Ernest May, ed., *The Ultimate Decision: The President as Commander in Chief* (New York: George Braziller, 1960), pp. 3–19.

39. Quoted in May, ed., *Ultimate Decision,* pp. 9–10.

40. Abraham D. Sofaer, *War, Foreign Affairs and Constitutional Power: The Origins* (New York: J. B. Lippincott, 1976), pp. 9, 382, 383.

41. Ben P. Poore, *Federal and State Constitutions, Colonial Charters,* 2 vols. (Washington, D.C.: U.S. Government Printing Office, 1877), 1:965–66; for the New Hampshire Constitution, which was identical to Massachusetts', see 2:1288; for Delaware, Art. 9, 1:275; for South Carolina, Art. 26, 2:1619.

42. For example, the Continental Congress ordered Washington to Massachusetts to take command of the United Colonies. See *Journals of the Continental Congress,* 34 vols. (1904–1937), 2:101. Washington was directed to intercept two British vessels on October 5, 1775 (3:276).

43. Farrand, *Records of the Federal Convention*, 3:606.

44. F. Thorpe, ed., *The Federal and State Constitutions, Colonial Charters, and Other Organic Laws*, 7 vols. (Washington, D.C.: U.S. Government Printing Office, 1909), 3:3243, 3249.

45. Farrand, *Records of the Federal Convention*, 1:20, 244.

46. See text accompanying notes 50–53 of this chapter.

47. Farrand, *Records of the Federal Convention*, 1:292.

48. Elliot, *Debates*, 3:496.

49. Ibid., pp. 220, 59.

50. Ibid., 1:378.

51. Ibid., 4:114.

52. Ibid., 4:107–8. As a member of the Supreme Court, Justice Paterson held that it was for Congress alone to declare war. *United States v. Smith*, 27 F. Cas. 1192, 1196–97 (No. 16342) (C.C.D.N.Y., 1806).

53. *Federalist 69*, in *The Federalist*, ed. Edward Mead Earle (New York: Modern Library, 1937), p. 448 (emphasis in original).

54. Louis Henkin, *Foreign Affairs and the Constitution* (Mineola, N.Y.: Foundation Press, 1972), pp. 50–51.

55. Leonard Meeker, "The Legality of the United States Participation in the Defense of Vietnam," *Department of State Bulletin* 54 (1966): 474.

56. William P. Rogers, "War Powers," pp. 1207–12.

57. Carter justified his attempted rescue of the hostages on April 24, 1980, on his powers as chief executive and commander-in-chief (126 *Cong. Rec.* H2991 [daily ed. April 28, 1980]).

58. Farrand, *Records of the Federal Convention*, 1:62–70.

59. Ibid., pp. 65–70.

60. Ibid., 2:171, 185, 572, 574, 597, 600.

61. Edward Corwin fairly remarked, "The Records of the Constitutional Convention make it clear that the purposes of this clause were simply to settle the question whether the executive branch should be plural or single and to give the executive a title" (Corwin, "The Steel Seizure Case: A Judicial Brick Without Straw," *Columbia Law Review* 53 [January 1953]: 53).

62. Raoul Berger, *Executive Privilege: A Constitutional Myth* (Cambridge: Harvard University Press, 1974), p. 52.

63. Hamilton, in *Federalist 67*, p. 436; Henkin, *Foreign Affairs*, p. 33. Henkin has observed that the "powers explicity vested in [the president] are few and seem modest, far fewer and more modest than those bestowed upon Congress" (p. 37).

64. Elliot, *Debates*, 4:329.

65. Ibid., 2:540; 3:201; 4:107; 2:128.

66. Poore, *Federal and State Constitutions*, 2:1910–11.

67. Quoted in Warren, *Makings of the Constitution*, p. 177.

68. Farrand, *Records of the Federal Convention*, 2:35.

69. Corwin, *President*, pp. 5–6.

70. Quoted in Gordon Wood, *The Creation of the American Republic 1776–1787* (Chapel Hill: University of North Carolina Press, 1969), p. 135. The colonists were virtually obsessed with power, "its endlessly propulsive tendency to expand itself be-

yond legitimate boundaries'' (Bernard Bailyn, *The Ideological Origins of the American Revolution* [Cambridge: Harvard University Press, 1967], pp. 56–57).

71. *Federalist 48*, p. 322.

72. Hamilton wrote under the pseudonym ''Pacificus''; Madison used the pen name ''Helvidius.'' The debate is reprinted in Richard Loss, ed., *The Letters of Pacificus and Helvidius* (Delmar, N.Y.: Scholars Facsimiles, 1976).

73. ''Pacificus, No. 1,'' in *The Papers of Alexander Hamilton*, ed. Harold C. Syrett, 27 vols. (New York: Columbia University Press, 1961–1987), 15:40. Hamilton noted specifically ''the right of the Legislature to declare war and grant letters of marque and reprisal'' (15:39).

74. ''Helvidius, No. 1,'' in *Writings of James Madison*, ed. G. Hunt, 9 vols. (New York: Putnam, 1900–1910), 6:174 (emphasis in original).

75. See notes 79–86 of this chapter.

76. 1 U.S. Statutes at Large (Stat.) 552, 5th Cong. 2d sess., chap. 31 (April 27, 1798). For a discussion of the war with France see Chapter 11 of this volume.

77. *The Works of Alexander Hamilton*, ed. H. C. Lodge, 2d. ed., 12 vols. (New York: Putnam, 1904), 10:281–82 (emphasis in original).

78. Quoted in James D. Richardson, *Compilation of the Messages and Papers of the Presidents, 1787–1897*, 10 vols. (Washington, D.C.: U.S. Government Printing Office, 1897), 1:326–27.

79. ''Letters of Lucius Crassus, No. 1,'' quoted in *Hamilton Works*, 8:249–50 (emphasis in original).

80. 2 Stat. 129, 7th Cong. 1st sess., chap. 4 (February 6, 1802).

81. Richardson, *Messages and Papers of Presidents*, 1:389–90.

82. Ibid., 2:489–90.

83. *Madison Writings*, 6:174, 148 (emphasis in original).

84. Richardson, *Messages and Papers of Presidents*, 2:218.

85. Moore, *International Law*, 6:446. See also, W. S. Robertson, ''South America and the Monroe Doctrine, 1824–1828,'' *Political Science Quarterly* 30 (March 1915): 89.

86. Richardson, *Messages and Papers of Presidents*, 3:258, 279.

87. Ibid., 1:1116.

88. Ibid., 2:1325.

89. Quoted in Wormuth, *Vietnam*, p. 44.

90. Moore, *International Law*, 7:126–28.

91. Ibid., p. 163.

92. Ibid., pp. 165–66.

93. Albert Putney, ''Executive Assumptions of the War-Making Power,'' *National University Law Review* 7 (May 1927): 1.

94. 9 Stat. 9 29th Cong., 1st sess., chap. 16 (May 13, 1846). Richardson, *Messages and Papers of Presidents*, 3:2292.

95. *Congressional Globe*, 30th Cong., 1st sess., 95.

96. Quoted in Wormuth, *Vietnam*, p. 11.

97. Richardson, *Messages and Papers of Presidents*, 6:47.

98. Arthur Schlesinger, Jr., has written: ''There is no suggestion that Lincoln supposed he would use this power in foreign wars without congressional consent'' (Schle-

singer, "Congress and the Making of American Foreign Policy," *Foreign Affairs* 51 [1972]: 78, 89).

99. Kent, *Commentaries*, p. 55.

100. Joseph Story, *Commentaries on the Constitution of the United States*, 4th ed., 2 vols. (Boston: Little Brown, 1873), 2:87.

101. William Whiting, *War Powers Under the Constitution of the United States*, 10th ed. (Boston: Little Brown, 1864), pp. 38–40 (emphasis in original).

102. John Norton Pomeroy, *Introduction to the Constitutional Law of the United States*, 10th ed. (Boston: Houghton, Mifflin, 1888), p. 373.

103. Thomas Cooley, *The General Principles of Constitutional Law in the United States of America*, 3d. ed. (Boston: Little Brown, 1898), p. 316.

104. Hermann von Holst, *The Constitutional Law of the United States of America*, 8 vols. (Chicago: Callaghan and Company, 1887), pp. 164–65.

105. Westel W. Willoughby, *The Constitutional Law of the United States*, 3 vols. (New York: Baker, Voorhis and Company, 1929), p. 1560

106. *4 Bas v. Tingy*, Dall. 37 (1800). The Federal Court of Appeals, the prize court established by the Continental Congress, had distinguished perfect from imperfect war in *Miller v. the Ship Resolution*, 2 Dall. 19, 21 (1782). See text accompanying notes 26–34 of this chapter.

107. 4 Dall. 40–42.

108. 4 U.S. (Dall.) 43.

109. Ibid., 45–46.

110. *Talbot v. Seeman*, 5 U.S. (1 Cranch) 1, 28 (1801).

111. *Little v. Barreme*, 6 U.S. (2 Cranch) 170, 177–78.

112. *U.S. v. Smith*, 27 F. Cas. 1192, 1230 (No. 16342) (C.C.D.N.Y. 1806).

113. *Prize Cases*, 67 U.S. (2 Black) 635, 668 (1863).

114. *U.S. v. Sweeny*, 157 U.S. 281, 284 (1895).

115. George Sutherland, *The Constitution and World Affairs* (New York: Columbia University Press, 1919), p. 73.

116. *Ex parte Quirin*, 317 U.S. 1, 26 (1942).

117. Wormuth and Firmage, *To Chain the Dog of War*, p. 28.

118. *U.S. v. Curtiss-Wright*, 229 U.S. 304 (1936).

119. For some of the evidence, see Charles Lofgren, "*United States v. Curtiss-Wright Export Corporation:* An Historical Reassessment," *Yale Law Journal* 83 (November 1973): 1, 3–5; Gerhard Casper, "Constitutional Constraints on the Conduct of Foreign and Defense Policy: A Nonjudicial Model," *University of Chicago Law Review* 43 (Spring 1976): 463, 475.

120. 299 U.S. 304, 312.

121. *Panama Refining Co. v. Ryan*, 293 U.S. 388 (1935).

122. 299 U.S. 304, 315–16.

123. See Lofgren, "*Curtiss-Wright*," p. 1; David M. Levitan, "The Foreign Relations Power: An Analysis of Mr. Justice Sutherland's Theory," *Yale Law Journal* 55 (April 1946): 467.

124. Commager, *Documents*, pp. 111–14.

125. *Chisholm v. Georgia*, 2 U.S. (2 Dall.) 419, 470 (1793) (Jay, C.J.).

126. Farrand, *Records of the Federal Conventions*, 1:19.

127. In *Rhode Island v. Massachusetts*, 37 U.S. (12 Pet.) 657, 720 (1838), the Court

held that by virtue of the revolution, the power of the Crown and Parliament devolved on the "states in their highest sovereign capacity."

128. Raoul Berger, "The President's Unilateral Termination of the Taiwan Treaty," *Northwestern Law Review* 75 (November 1980): 591–94.

129. *Youngstown Sheet and Tube Co. v. Sawyer,* 343 U.S. 579, 604 (1952).

130. See *Chae Chan Ping v. United States* (Chinese Exclusion Case), 130 U.S. 581, 603–4 (1889); *Perez v. Brownell,* 356 U.S. 44, 57 (1958).

131. Henkin, *Foreign Affairs,* p. 27.

132. *Federalist 45,* p. 303 (emphasis added).

133. 343 U.S. 587 (1952).

134. Ibid., at 634.

135. *Reid v. Covert,* 354 U.S. 1, 16–17 (1957).

136. Arthur M. Schlesinger, Jr., *The Imperial Presidency* (Boston: Houghton, Mifflin, 1973), p. 103.

137. 12 *Cong. Debates* 4037–4038 (1836).

138. See Kenneth M. Holland, "The War Powers Resolution: An Infringement on the President's Constitutional and Prerogative Powers," in *The Presidency and National Security Policy,* ed. R. Gordon Hoxie (Montpelier, Vt.: Capital City Press), p. 378. For a discussion of prerogative, see Donald L. Robinson, "Presidential Prerogative and the Spirit of American Constitutionalism," chapter 7.

139. For discussion of this point, see Wormuth and Firmage, *To Chain the Dogs of War,* pp. 12–15; Fisher, *Conflicts,* pp. 287–92.

140. See *United States v. Curtiss-Wright Export Corp.,* 299 U.S. 304 (1936).

141. 19 *Weekly Comp. of Pres. Doc.* 1494 (October 25, 1983).

142. 299 U.S., at 320.

143. 10 *Annals of Cong.,* pp. 613–14 (1800).

144. Corwin, *President: Office and Powers,* p. 178.

145. Thomas Jefferson, *The Writings of Thomas Jefferson,* ed. P. L. Ford, 10 vols. (New York: Putnam, 1892–1899), 6:451.

146. Quoted in Berger, "Taiwan Treaty," p. 591.

147. Elliot, *Debates,* 2:305.

148. Hamilton, *Federalist 69,* p. 451.

149. Henry P. Monaghan, "Presidential War-Making," *Boston University Law Review* 50 (Spring 1970): 19.

150. For example, in 1967 the State Department published a study that listed 137 cases of unilateral presidential action (Department of State, Historical Studies Division, *Armed Actions Taken by the United States Without A Declaration of War, 1789–1967* [Washington, D.C.: U.S. Government Printing Office, 1967]). J. Terry Emerson, legal assistant to Sen. Barry Goldwater, published a list in 1973 in which he alleged 199 incidents of presidential acts of war without congressional authorization (119 *Cong. Rec.* S14174 [daily ed. July 20, 1973]).

151. Berger, *Executive Privilege,* p. 76. See Wormuth, "Nixon Theory," pp. 652–64, and Wormuth and Firmage, *To Chain the Dog of War,* pp. 133–49.

152. Wormuth, *Vietnam,* p. 718.

153. Wormuth and Firmage, *To Chain the Dog of War,* p. 149.

154. *Powell v. McCormack,* 395 U.S. 486, 546 (1969); *Inland Waterways Corp. v. Young,* 309 U.S. 518, 524 (1940).

155. Corwin observed that "none of the departments may abdicate its powers to either of the others" (Corwin, *President,* p. 9). See also *Panama Refining Co. v. Ryan,* 293 U.S. 388, 421 (1935).

156. *United States v. Morton Salt Co.,* 338 U.S. 632, 647 (1950).

157. Elliot, *Debates,* 2:528.

8
THE SPENDING POWER

LOUIS FISHER

The power of the purse represents a powerful tool used by Congress to control presidential warmaking. The Framers were familiar with efforts by English kings to rely on extraparliamentary sources of revenue for their military expeditions and other activities. Kings, denied money by Parliament, turned to foreign governments and private citizens. Because of these transgressions, England lurched into a civil war and Charles I lost both his office and his head.[1] The rise of democratic government is rooted in this legislative control over expenditures.

Although Parliament gained the power of the purse, the power to go to war remained a monarchial prerogative. William Blackstone, the great eighteenth-century jurist and author of *Commentaries*, assigned to the king absolute power over foreign affairs and war: the right to send and receive ambassadors, make treaties and alliances, make war or peace, issue letters of marque and reprisal, command the military, raise and regulate fleets and armies, and represent the nation in its intercourse with foreign nations.[2]

U.S. CONSTITUTIONAL PRINCIPLES

The U.S. Constitution attempted to avoid the British history of civil war and bloodshed by vesting the power of the purse squarely in Congress. Under Article I, section 9, "No Money shall be drawn from the Treasury, but in Consequence of Appropriations made by Law." In *Federalist 48,* James Madison explained that "the legislative department alone has access to the pockets of the people." In Article I, section 8, Congress is empowered to lay and collect taxes, duties, imposes, and excises; to borrow money on the credit of the United States; and to coin money and regulate its value. This power of the purse, said Madison in *Federalist 58,* represents the "most complete and effectual weapon with which any constitution can arm the immediate representatives of the people, for obtaining a redress of every grievance, and for carrying into effect just and salutary measures.''

The delegates to the Constitutional Convention in Philadelphia decided to vest in Congress many of Blackstone's royal prerogatives. They repeatedly expressed their determination to give the power of peace and war to Congress, not to the president.[3] As James Wilson noted, it was incorrect to consider ''the Prerogatives of the British monarch as a proper guide in defining the Executive powers. Some of these prerogatives were of a Legislative nature. Among others that of war & peace, &c.''[4] Although the president was made commander-in-chief, it was left to Congress to raise and regulate fleets and armies.

Madison and other delegates wanted to keep the power of commander-in-chief separate from the power to finance a war. To protect constitutional liberties, that liberty had to be reserved to Congress:

> Those who are to *conduct a war* cannot in the nature of things, be proper or safe judges, whether *a war ought* to be *commenced, continued, or concluded*. They are barred from the latter by a great principle in free government, analogous to that which separate the sword from the purse, or the power of executing from the power of enacting laws.[5]

This understanding of the war power was widely accepted. Thomas Jefferson praised the transfer of the war power ''from the executive to the Legislative body, from those who are to spend to those who are to pay.''[6] At the Philadelphia Convention, George Mason urged that the ''purse & the sword ought never to get into the same hands whether Legislative or Executive.''[7]

The congressional power of the purse is not unlimited. Congress cannot use appropriations bills to enact bills of attainder, to restrict the president's pardon power, or to establish a national religion.[8] The Constitution prohibits Congress from diminishing the salaries of the president or federal judges.[9] Congress would overstep its boundaries if it ''refused to appropriate funds for the President to receive foreign ambassadors or to make treaties.''[10] It is often said that Congress, in adding conditions and provisos to appropriations bills, may not achieve unconstitutional results. But this merely restates the issue. What types of conditions are unconstitutional? It is false to assume that conditions on appropriations bills are proper for domestic legislation but impermissible for legislation governing foreign affairs and the war power. In foreign affairs as in domestic affairs, presidents acknowledge that Congress can use conditions to tailor its spending power.[11]

The issue does not change simply because legislation affects the president's role as commander-in-chief. The president is empowered "to direct the movements of the naval and military forces placed by law at his command, and to employ them in the manner he may deem most effectual to harass and conquer and subdue the enemy."[12] The discretion accorded to the president is substantial, but it is the power *placed by law* at his command. Congress used its power of the purse to halt military operations in Southeast Asia in 1973.[13] Three years later, with the Clark amendment, Congress prohibited all assistance for conducting military or paramilitary operations in Angola.[14] More recently, in 1986, Congress used language in an appropriations bill to prohibit U.S. forces from operating within twenty miles of the Nicaraguan border while providing assistance to the Contras. And in 1993 Congress established a deadline for troops to leave Somalia. No funds could be used for military action after March 31, 1994, unless the president requested an extension from Congress and received legislative authority.[15]

The CIA uses a contingency fund to initiate covert operations before notifying Congress. If administrations abuse this authority and claim a constitutional right not to notify Congress, even within forty-eight hours or some minimal period, Congress can abolish the contingency fund and force the president to seek congressional approval in advance for each covert action.

With regard to war powers in general, Congress may pass a concurrent resolution (not subject to the president's veto) stating that it shall not be in order in either House to consider any bill, joint resolution, or amendment that provides funding to carry out any military actions inconsistent with an enabling statute, such as the War Powers Resolution. Under the ruling of *INS v. Chadha,* concurrent resolutions may not direct the president or the executive branch, but they can control the internal procedures of Congress.[16]

THE VIETNAM WAR

During the Vietnam War the question arose in the federal courts whether Congress, by appropriating money for the Defense Department, had sanctioned the president's war policy. A State Department memorandum in 1966 argued that Congress had shown its support for the war policy of the Johnson administration by enacting the necessary appropriations. Defense appropriation constituted "a clear congressional endorsement and approval of the actions taken by the President."[17]

In 1968 a federal district judge rejected the notion that Congress had been forced against its better judgment to appropriate money for military operations in Vietnam. Congress had the power—both political and constitutional—to terminate military action. The court could not "infer that courage is lacking among the members of Congress, should the majority of the elected representatives of the people conclude to take such action."[18] Nor could a federal judge in 1970 believe that defense appropriations had been "extorted by the exigencies created by presidential seizures of combat initiatives."[19]

Expert witnesses advised the courts that House and Senate rules prohibited major declarations of policy in appropriations bills. The parliamentary process limited substantive legislation to authorization bills. They also pointed out that some members had voted for military appropriations not because they endorsed the war policy but because they felt an obligation to support American soldiers already committed to battle. Initially the courts were unimpressed by this line of argument. As a district judge noted in 1970: "That some members of Congress talked like doves before voting with the hawks is an inadequate basis for a charge that the President was violating the Constitution in doing what Congress by its words had told him he might do. . . . The entire course of legislation shows that Congress knew what it was doing, and that it intended to have American troops fight in Vietnam."[20]

Members of the judiciary began to backtrack from the proposition that Congress could indirectly endorse a war simply by appropriating funds. Federal appellate judge Arlin Adams, in 1972, said that such a determination would require the interrogation of legislators regarding the intent behind their votes, followed by a synthesis of the various replies. He concluded that it would be impossible to gather and evaluate such information.[21] Federal appellate judges Charles Wyzanski and David Bazelon, who had earlier accepted appropriations acts as identical with congressional consent, reversed their positions by 1973. They could no longer be

> unmindful of what every schoolboy knows: that in voting to appropriate money or to draft men a Congressman is not necessarily approving the continuation of a war no matter how specifically the appropriation or draft act refers to that war. A Congressman wholly opposed to the war's commencement and continuation might vote for the military appropriations and for the draft measures because he was unwilling to abandon without support men already fighting. An honorable, decent, compassionate act of aiding those already in peril is not proof of consent to the actions that placed and continued them in that dangerous posture. We should not construe votes cast in pity and piety as though they were votes freely given to express consent.[22]

A major appropriations battle occurred in 1973. President Nixon's basis for military operations in Vietnam seemed to have disappeared with the signing of a cease-fire agreement in Paris on January 27, 1973, and the scheduled withdrawal of all American troops by the end of March. Congress had repealed the Gulf of Tonkin Resolution several years earlier. No longer could the president cite that as authority or offer as justification the need to protect American soldiers. Yet Nixon continued to maintain a massive bombing operation in Cambodia. When a supplemental appropriations bill reached the House floor in May, Cong. Clarence Long offered an amendment to prohibit the use of any funds authorized by the bill to support directly or indirectly U.S. combat activities in, over, or from off the shores of Cambodia or Laos (a restriction covering not only the supplemental funds but funds made available by previous appropriations). The bill presented to Nixon included the Senate version.[23]

Nixon vetoed the bill, claiming that the "Cambodian rider" would destroy the chances for a negotiated settlement in Cambodia. He also warned that nine agencies, dependent upon funds in the bill, would soon exhaust their authority to pay the salaries and expenses of their employees. According to his line of reasoning, the wheels of government would grind to a halt if Congress persisted in presenting objectionable statutory language to the president.

The issue of the appropriations power was now firmly joined. Congress could argue that the restrictions in the supplemental bill represented an appropriate effort to limit the president's ability to wage war and to commit the nation to vast expenditures. If Nixon refused to acknowledge congressional preeminence in matters of the purse, legislators could have held him responsible for the paralysis of agency operations. In this raw, high-noon confrontation, Congress backed off. It failed to override Nixon's veto. A revised bill delayed the cutoff of funds from June 30 to August 15, 1973, in effect giving the president freedom to bomb Cambodia for another forty-five days—which is what he did. But at least Congress, by agreeing to the compromise, succeeded in using its power of the purse to conclude military operations in Southeast Asia.

The "August 15 Compromise" aborted several cases that had been working their way through the federal courts. In a decision of July 25, 1973, a federal judge in New York held that Congress had not authorized the bombing in Cambodia. The fact that Congress could not muster a two-thirds majority to override the president's veto should not, he said, be interpreted as an affirmative grant of authority. This decision was later reversed, in part because an appellate court held that the August 15 date did indeed constitute congressional approval of the bombing.[24] In other decisions the courts accepted the compromise date as evidence that the two political branches were no longer in resolute conflict; therefore there was no need for the courts to act as referee.[25]

THE IRAN-CONTRA AFFAIR

Of all the revelations emanating from the Iran-Contra hearings in 1987, the most startling constitutional claim was the assertion that Congress cannot control foreign affairs by withholding appropriations. According to the argument advanced by some Reagan administration officials, if Congress prohibits the use of appropriations for foreign policy objectives—as it did with the Boland amendment—the president can nevertheless continue his goals by soliciting funds from the private sector and from foreign countries. If one well dries up, tap another. This theory, with roots dating back to Charles I, has profound implications for executive-legislative relations and constitutional government.

Beginning in 1982 Congress adopted a variety of statutory directives to restrict the Reagan administration's assistance to the Contras in Nicaragua. Language added to a continuing resolution in 1982 prohibited the Central Intelligence Agency or the Department of Defense from furnishing military equipment, military training or advice, or other support for military activities "to any group or individual, nor part of a country's armed forces, for the purpose of overthrowing the Government of Nicaragua or provoking a military exchange between Nicaragua and Honduras."[26] In a report issued on May 13, 1983, the House Permanent Select Committee on Intelligence described the statutory curb as ineffective. The Contras "openly acknowledged" their goal of overthrowing the Sandinistas and provoking a "military confrontation."[27] Congress discovered early in 1984 that the administration, operating through the CIA, had mined the harbors of Nicaragua. Congress responded with the following statutory language: "It is the sense of the Congress that no funds heretofore or hereafter appropriated in any Act of Congress shall be obligated or expended for the purpose of planning, directing, executing, or supporting the mining of the ports or territorial waters of Nicaragua."[28]

Finally, on October 12, 1984, Congress adopted strict language intended to prohibit all executive assistance of any kind to support the Contras. The language of the Boland amendment was intended to be all-embracing to prevent any further circumvention by executive officials:

> During fiscal year 1985, no funds available to the Central Intelligence
> Agency, the Department of Defense, or any other agency or entity of

the United States involved in intelligence activities may be obligated or expended for the purpose or which would have the effect of supporting, directly or indirectly, military or paramilitary operations in Nicaragua by any nation, group, organization, movement, or individual.[29]

Congress perfected this tortured language because the administration had demonstrated a disposition to exploit every possible loophole; it was the intention of Congress to close them all. Even with this explicit language, some legislators suspected that the Reagan administration might find ways to assist the Contras. During hearings on March 26, 1985, Sen. Christopher Dodd said that there

have been a number of rumors or news reports around this town about how the administration might go about its funding of the Contras in Nicaragua. There have been suggestions that it would be done through private parties or through funneling funds through friendly third nations, or possibly through a new category of assistance and asking the Congress to fund the program openly.[30]

Ambassador Langhorne A. Motely, appearing as the administration's spokesman, assured Senator Dodd that there would be no attempt to circumvent the Boland amendment by soliciting funds from private parties or from foreign governments. He offered his unqualified assurance that the Boland amendment would be complied with fully:

Nobody is trying to play games with you or any other Member of Congress. That resolution stands, and will continue to stand; and it says no direct or indirect. And that is pretty plain English; it does not have to be written by any bright, young lawyers. And we are going to continue to comply with that.[31]

Ambassador Motley provided similar assistance to the House Committee on Appropriations on April 18, 1985. He testified that the administration would not attempt to solicit funds from outside sources to assist the Contras.[32] When President Reagan signed the continuing resolution that contained the strict language of the Boland amendment, he did not issue a statement claiming that Congress had overstepped its powers and that the administration would continue its foreign policy course in Nicaragua. The attorney general did not challenge the constitutionality of the Boland amendment. The Office of Legal Counsel in the Justice Department did not conclude in any internal memorandum or report that the amendment was invalid or nonbinding.

Nevertheless, at the very moment Ambassador Motley testified before two congressional committees, executive branch officials were actively soliciting funds from private parties and from foreign governments to assist the Contras. Working closely with the White House and the National Security Council, private citizens raised money from private contributors to provide military weapons and supplies to the Contras.[33] Administration officials also made repeated efforts to obtain funds from foreign governments, succeeding with some countries (as with Saudi Arabia) and failing with others.[34] In a misguided moment, Congress even authorized the secretary of state in 1985 to solicit contributions from foreign governments for *humanitarian* assistance to the Contras.[35] On the basis of that authority, Assistant Secretary of State Elliott Abrams solicited $10 million from Brunei, and the money was promptly placed in the wrong account in Switzerland, never to reach the Contras.[36]

Only one document from the administration argued that the Boland amendment permitted some executive officials to assist the Contras. Bretton G. Sciaroni, counsel to the President's Intelligence Oversight Board, issued a memorandum on September 12, 1985, concluding that the National Security Council was not covered by the Boland amendment.[37] The memorandum was never made available to Congress or to the public; its existence was revealed only after the Iran-Contra affair became public in November 1986. If the legal analysis in the memorandum is correct, John Poindexter, Robert McFarlane, Oliver North, and other members of the NSC staff could do what the intelligence community, the Defense Department, and "any other agency or entity" had been prohibited from doing by the Boland amendment.

The Sciaroni memorandum is deficient in several respects. First, under the terms of the Boland amendment, the NSC is an "entity . . . involved in intelligence activities." The National Security Act provides that there "is established under the National Security Council a Central Intelligence Agency."[38] How can a subordinate body (the CIA) be involved in intelligence activities but not the controlling agency (the NSC)? Second, the NSC–CIA relationship is elaborated in Executive Order No. 12333, issued by President Reagan on December 4, 1981. The order states that the NSC "shall act as the highest Executive Branch entity that provides review of, guidance for and direction to the conduct of all national foreign intelligence, counterintelligence, and special activities [covert operations], and attendant policies and programs."[39] The order provides clear recognition that the NSC is "involved in intelligence activities" within the meaning of the Boland amendment. Moreover, as defined in the order, the director of Central Intelligence "shall be responsible directly to the President and the NSC."[40] The CIA shall "conduct services of common concern for the Intelligence Community as directed by the NSC."[41] The principal responsibility for implementing the order, entitled "United States Intelligence Activities," falls to the NSC.[42] Third, even if one rejects this line of argument, the plain fact is that the NSC under North and company was "involved in intelligence activities."

The idea that North and other members of the NSC could carry out a covert operation to assist the Contras is inconsistent with another section of Executive Order No. 12333. No agency except the CIA "may conduct any special activity [covert operation] unless the President determines that another agency is more likely to achieve a particular objective."[43] Reagan never determined that the NSC should conduct a covert action to replace the CIA. Such a determination would have deliberately undermined the Boland amendment, shifting the operating responsibility from an agency proscribed by law to one that attempts, by stealth and proxy, to achieve an end prohibited by Congress.

Had Reagan used the NSC as a substitute for the CIA, I think he would have committed an impeachable offense. Also impeachable would have been the attempt to conduct foreign policy by using private and foreign funds. Such funds may be used to finance governmental programs, but only when expressly authorized by Congress. Statutes have created trust funds to receive gifts from the private sector[44] and from foreign governments.[45] Gift funds must be placed in the Treasury Department and spent only for objects defined by Congress.[46] The purpose is to "ensure that the executive branch remains dependent upon the congressional appropriations process."[47]

Beginning with the Neutrality Act of 1794, Congress has specifically forbidden private citizens from organizing military expeditions against a foreign government.[48] U.S. foreign policy must be conducted through political institutions, not private parties. A Department of Justice analysis in 1979 concluded that the legislative history of the Neutrality Act "clearly shows that the evil it proscribes was precisely and exclusively one which threatens the ability of the Government to carry on a coherent foreign policy."[49]

Despite these precedents and principles, Colonel North asserted that the president "could authorize and conduct covert operations with nonappropriated funds."[50] He was asked at the hearings: "If Congress told the President he could not ask foreign countries or private individuals for financial or other official assistance for the Contras, there would be serious doubt whether Congress has exceeded its constitutional power, correct?" North replied, "If Congress passed such a measure, it would clearly, in my opinion, be unconstitutional."[51]

This argument suffers from weaknesses both political and constitutional. If Reagan had defied the Boland amendment by seeking financial or other assistance from foreign countries or private individuals, at a minimum this action would have subjected the United States to ridicule and humiliation. Having been rebuffed by Congress, the president would go, hat in hand, to foreign governments and private citizens for assistance in implementing the administration's foreign policy. Such conduct would risk a major collision with Congress, with the president acting in the face of a congressional policy enacted into law. In such circumstances, a president would invite, and deserve, impeachment proceedings. He would fail in his constitutional duty to see that the laws are faithfully executed, and he would precipitate a constitutional crisis by merging the power of the sword with the power of the purse.

Moreover, soliciting funds from foreign governments to promote U.S. foreign policy opens the doors to widespread compromise and corruption. Admiral Poindexter testified that the administration could withhold information from Congress because the Contras were being assisted with nonappropriated funds: "We weren't using appropriated funds. They were private, third-country funds."[52] Accepting funds from foreign governments to sustain U.S. policy creates an implicit quid pro quo, requiring the United States to reciprocate by giving contributing countries extra consideration in the form of foreign assistance, military assistance, arms sales, and trade concessions.[53]

Congress may pass legislation to stop quid pro quos. The Pell amendment in 1985 prohibited the use of any foreign assistance or military assistance to provide "assistance of any kind, either directly or indirectly, to any person or group engaging in an insurgency or other act of rebellion against the Government of Nicaragua." The purpose was to prevent recipients of U.S. funds and materials from giving assistance to the Contras as a condition, or quid pro quo, for obtaining aid.[54]

After the disclosure of the Iran-Contra affair, members of Congress proposed statutory language to prohibit all quid pro quos (also referred to as "leveraging"). Congress eventually reached an accommodation with the executive branch in 1989. The purpose was to prevent quid pro quos that attempt to circumvent statutory prohibitions. The statutory language states that appropriate funds for foreign assistance may not be provided to "any foreign government (including any instrumentality or agency thereof), foreign person, or United States person in exchange for that foreign government or person undertaking any action which is, if carried out by the United States Government, a United States official or employee, expressly prohibited by a provision of United States Law."[55] The statute also says it is not the intent of Congress to limit the ability of executive officials to make statements or express their views to foreign governments. In signing the bill, President Bush said it was his intent to construe the statutory language "narrowly" but agreed that the section prohibited quid pro quo transactions "in which U.S. funds are provided to a foreign nation on the express condition that the foreign nation provide specific assistance to a third country, which assistance U.S. officials are expressly prohibited from providing by U.S. law."[56]

CONCLUSIONS

For reasons that have both constitutional and practical dimensions, U.S. foreign policy must be conducted only with funds appropriated by Congress. Allowing the president to carry out foreign policy with private or foreign contributions would create what the Framers feared most: the union of the purse and the sword. The Framers deliberately separated those powers to protect individual liberties. Fusing the powers in today's world creates dangers far greater than in 1787. At the Iran-Contra hearings, Secretary of State George Shultz repudiated the idea of using nonappropriated funds for foreign policy: "You cannot spend funds that the Congress doesn't either authorize you to obtain or appropriate. That is what the Constitution says, and we have to stick with it."[57]

Beyond constitutional considerations is the practical necessity of cultivating congressional support for foreign policy. In a major address in 1984, Secretary of Defense Caspar W. Weinberger said that a prerequisite for using combat forces abroad is "some reasonable assurance we will have the support of the American people and their elected Representatives in Congress. . . . We cannot fight a battle with the Congress at home while asking our troops to win a war overseas."[58] After the damaging confrontations of the Vietnam years, Secretary of State Henry Kissinger expressed the need for executive-legislative cooperation:

> The decade-long struggle in this country over executive dominance in foreign affairs is over. The recognition that the Congress is a coequal branch of government is the dominant fact of national politics today. The executive accepts that the Congress must have both the sense and the reality of participation; foreign policy must be a shared enterprise.[59]

The president, his political appointees, and departmental careerists must construct a foreign policy that attracts the understanding and approval of Congress and the public. Only through such efforts can the United States create a foreign policy that has a chance of success and continuity.

NOTES

1. Paul Einzig, *The Control of the Purse* (London: Seckler and Warburg, 1959), pp. 57–62, 100–106.
2. William Blackstone, *Commentaries on the Laws of England* (1803), 2:237–80.
3. Max Farrand, ed., *The Records of the Federal Convention of 1787* (New Haven: Yale University Press, 1937), 1:65.
4. Ibid.
5. *The Writings of James Madison,* ed. Galliard Hunt, 9 vols. (New York: Putnam, 1900–1910), 6:148.
6. *The Writings of Thomas Jefferson,* ed. Paul Leicester Ford, 10 vols. (New York: Putnam, 1892–1899), 5:123.
7. Farrand, ed., *Records,* 1:139–40.
8. Bills of attainder: *United States v. Lovett,* 328 U.S. 383 (1946); *Blitz v. Donovan,* 538 F. Supp. 1119 (D.D.C. 1982); pardon power: *Hart v. United States,* 118 U.S. 62 (1886); *United States v. Klein,* 80 U.S. (13 Wall.) 128 (1871); religion: *Flast v. Cohen,* 392 U.S. 83, 104–5 (1968).
9. U.S. Const., Article II, section 1, and Article III, section 1; *United States v. Will,* 449 U.S. 200 (1980).
10. Kate Stith, "Congress' Power of the Purse," *Yale Law Journal* 97 (1988): 1343, 1351. However, the House of Representatives may deny appropriations to implement treaties (Louis Fisher, *Constitutional Conflicts Between Congress and the President* [Lawrence: University Press of Kansas, 1991], pp. 224–30).
11. Louis Henkin, *Foreign Affairs and the Constitution* (New York: W. W. Norton, 1972), p. 114.
12. *Fleming v. Page,* 50 U.S. (9 How.) 602, 615 (1850).
13. 87 Stat. 99, 129, sec. 307 (1973); 87 Stat. 130, 134, sec. 108 (1973).
14. 90 Stat. 729, 757, sec. 404 (1976).
15. 100 Stat. 3341–299, 3341–307, sec. 216 (1986), and 107 Stat. 1476, sec. 8151(b)(2)(B)(1993).
16. *INS v. Chadha,* 462 U.S. 919 (1983).
17. 54 *Department of State Bulletin* 487 (1966).
18. *Velvel v. Johnson,* 287 F. Supp. 846, 853 (D. Kans. 1968).
19. *Orlando v. Laird,* 317 F. Supp. 1013, 1018 (E.D. N.Y. 1970). See also *Davi v. Laird,* 318 F. Supp. 478, 481 (W.D. Va. 1970), and *Orlando v. Laird,* 443 F.2d 1039, 1042 (2d Cir. 1971).
20. *Berk v. Laird,* 317 F. Supp. 715, 724, 728 (E.D. N.Y. 1970). The position of expert witnesses for the plaintiffs appears at 718 and 721. See also *DaCosta v. Laird,* 448 F.2d 1368, 1369 (2d Cir. 1971).
21. *Atlee v. Laird,* 347 F. Supp. 689, 706 (E.D. Pa. 1972).
22. *Mitchell v. Laird,* 488 F.2d 611, 615 (D.C. Cir. 1973). Wyzanski's earlier position appears in *Massachusetts v. Laird,* 327 F. Supp. 378, 381 (D. Mass. 1971). For the ambivalent quality of defense appropriations, see *Campen v. Nixon,* 56 F.R.D. 404, 406 (N.D. Cal. 1972).
23. This paragraph, and the following two, are drawn from Louis Fisher, *Presidential Spending Power* (Princeton, N.J.: Princeton University Press, 1975), pp. 110–18.
24. *Holtzman v. Schlesinger,* 361 F. Supp. 553, 563–65 (E.D. N.Y. 1973), stayed by

the Supreme Court, 414 U.S. 1304, 1316, 1321, before being reversed, *Holtzman v. Schlesinger,* 484 F. 2d 1307, 1313–14 (2d Cir. 1973).

25. *Drinan v. Nixon,* 364 F. Supp. 854, 860–61, 864 (D. Mass. 1973).

26. 96 Stat. 1830, 1865, sec. 793 (1982).

27. H. Rept. no. 122 (Part 1), 98th Cong., 1st sess. (1983), p. 11.

28. 98 Stat. 494, 1210, sec. 2907 (1984).

29. 98 Stat. 1837, 1935, sec. 8066(a) (1984).

30. "Security and Development Assistance," Hearings Before the Senate Committee on Foreign Relations, 99th Cong., 1st sess. (1985), p. 908.

31. Ibid, p. 910. At the time he testified, Ambassador Motley was assistant secretary of state for Inter-American Affairs.

32. "Department of Defense Appropriations for 1986" (part 2), Hearings Before the House Committee on Appropriations, 99th Cong., 1st sess. (1985), p. 1092.

33. H. Rept. no. 433 and S. Rept. no. 216, 100th Cong., 1st sess. (1987), pp. 85–103 (hereafter Iran-Contra Report).

34. Ibid., pp. 38–39, 45, 63, 69–70.

35. 99 Stat. 1002, 1003, sec. 105(b)(2) (1985).

36. Iran-Contra Report, pp. 148–49, 352–53.

37. Memorandum from Bretton G. Sciaroni to Robert C. McFarlane, assistant to the president for National Security Affairs (September 12, 1985), "Iran-Contra Investigation" (vol. 100-5), Joint Hearings Before the Senate Select Committee on Secret Military Assistance to Iran and the Nicaraguan Opposition and the House Select Committee to Investigate Covert Arms Transactions with Iran, 100th Cong., 1st sess. (1988), p. 1988 (hereafter Iran-Contra Hearings).

38. 50 U.S.C. sec. 403(a) (1982).

39. 46 Fed. Reg. 59941, sec. 1.2 (1981).

40. Ibid., sec. 1.5.

41. Ibid., sec. 1.8(f).

42. Ibid., sec. 3.2.

43. Ibid., sec. 1.8(e).

44. 31 U.S.C. sec. 1321 (1988).

45. 5 U.S.C. sec. 7342 (1988).

46. 31 U.S.C. sec. 3302 (1988).

47. General Accounting Office, Principles of Federal Appropriation Law (1982), pp. 5-65; see also pp. 5-82 to 5-89.

48. 1 Stat. 369 (1794); 18 U.S.C. secs. 960–962 (1988).

49. Office of Legal Counsel, U.S. Department of Justice, Applicability of the Neutrality Act to Activities of the Central Intelligence Agency, memorandum from Larry L. Sims to Philip B. Heymann, assistant attorney general, Criminal Division (October 10, 1979), p. 5.

50. Iran-Contra Hearings, vol. 100-7, part 2, p. 37.

51. Ibid., part 1, p. 207.

52. Ibid., vol. 100-8, p. 158.

53. Ibid., vol. 100-1, pp. 25, 201, 279–80.

54. 99 Stat. 254, sec. 722 (d) (1985).

55. 103 Stat. 1251, sec. 582 (1989).

56. *The Public Papers of the Presidents: George Bush* (Washington, D.C.: Government Printing Office, 1990), 2:1573.

57. Iran-Contra Hearings, vol. 100-9, p. 75.

58. "The Uses of Military Power," remarks prepared for delivery by Secretary of Defense Caspar W. Weinberger, November 28, 1984, p. 6.

59. 72 *Department of State Bulletin* 562 (1975).

9

THE WAR POWERS RESOLUTION AND THE PERSIAN GULF WAR

EDWARD KEYNES

Since Congress adopted the War Powers Resolution in 1973 over Richard M. Nixon's veto, there has been a continuing debate over its efficacy and constitutionality as a means of reasserting legislative authority in military and foreign affairs.[1] The Persian Gulf War furnishes another occasion for examining the resolution's utility and constitutionality. As the history of the last twenty years suggests, the War Powers Resolution is ineffective in curbing presidential deployment of military forces abroad. It is probably unconstitutional because Congress cannot delegate authority that the Constitution vests in the legislature as a representative institution. Moreover, it is counterproductive because the resolution fails to focus attention, in a timely manner, on the military and foreign policy decisions underlying and preceding war and hostilities.

The Persian Gulf War promised to bring the War Powers Resolution center stage in the theater of constitutional law and foreign policy. Iraq's invasion of Kuwait on August 2, 1990, raised the specter of an assault on Saudi Arabia and the threat of an interruption of vital oil supplies to the United States. The War Powers Resolution, which was based on the premise of coordination and cooperation between the president and Congress, was ripe for a rigorous application. The Bush administration had time to consult with Congress. Indeed, it had time to seek authorization before responding militarily. But Bush ignored Congress altogether, and on August 7 he initiated a massive American troop buildup, dubbed Operation Desert Shield.

As a constraint, the resolution was unavailing. The White House did send a message to Congress, on August 9, "consistent with the War Powers Resolution," in which the president explained that he "did not believe involvement in hostilities" was imminent and that it was his "belief that this deployment will facilitate a peaceful resolution of the crisis," but he consistently maintained a posture of unilateralism, claiming that as commander-in-chief he possessed sufficient constitutional authority to initiate hostilities.[2] As a consequence, according to President Bush, congressional authorization was superfluous. In fact, the administration informed only one member of Congress, Sen. Sam Nunn (D.-Ga.), chairman of the Armed Services Committee, of its decision to deploy troops. Though Congress was not in session, the White House very easily could have reached members if it had been interested in consultation, or it could have convened a special session, as some members suggested. Within two weeks of the invasion, nearly 100,000 forces had been deployed in and around Saudi Arabia.[3] For its part, Congress was not aggressive in asserting either its role under the War Powers Resolution or its vast powers under the Constitution in the early period of the crisis. A few members complained, but as an institution Congress did not inject itself into the decisionmaking process. The portrait of a passive, quiescent Congress in the face of unilateral presidential military actions was painfully familiar.[4] However, the War Powers Resolution assumed congressional participation at take-off and not simply during landing. The decision to send several hundred thousand troops to the Gulf in August and early autumn and to have increased troop levels dramatically in November should have been debated in Congress and, indeed, across the nation. For all its promise, the War Powers Resolution failed to facilitate a congressional role in the planning and preparation for war in the Gulf, just as it had in other circumstances since its birth.

Despite congressional attempts to curb presidential warmaking, since 1974 every American president has deployed U.S. armed forces abroad in pursuit of the nation's security.[5] The War Powers Resolution of 1973 to the contrary notwithstanding, joint legislative-executive consultation and decisionmaking remain the exception rather than the rule in committing the nation's armed forces to foreign military operations and hostilities. Between 1973 and 1990, Congress did not employ the resolution effectively to promote executive accountability in military and foreign policymaking. Instead, presidents Ford, Carter, Reagan, and Bush found ways either to circumvent the resolution or to use its consulting and reporting requirements to legitimate their use of armed forces abroad.

In his brief interregnum, Gerald Ford dispatched military personnel to carry out approximately six rescue operations in Southeast Asia and the Middle East. And frustrated in his repeated diplomatic efforts to secure the release of American hostages being held in the U.S. embassy in Teheran, on April 24, 1980, Jimmy Carter ordered the military to rescue them.[6] The ill-fated clandestine mission renewed the debate, begun during the Vietnam War, about the scope of the president's military authority to order U.S. armed forces abroad and commit them to combat without prior congressional authorization or consultation.

Ronald Reagan's dispatch of 1,200 U.S. Marines to Beirut, Lebanon, in 1982 and the death of 269 marines at the Beirut airport in October 1983 rekindled the debate about the president's authority as commander-in-chief as well as the objectives of U.S. Middle East policy.[7] Reagan's invasion of Grenada in 1983, his bombing of Libya in 1986, the dispatch of fifty military advisers to El Salvador after his second inauguration, and the deployment of U.S. naval forces in the Persian Gulf in 1987 continued the struggle between Congress and the president over the conduct of American national-security policy and the use of force.[8] Following the failure of economic sanctions to topple Manuel Noriega, on December 20, 1989, George Bush dispatched 13,000 additional U.S. troops to Panama.[9] Finally, Bush's decision to send air, land, and naval forces to Saudi Arabia and the Persian Gulf in response to Iraq's invasion of Kuwait in August 1990 stimulated a brief, if melodramatic debate over the president's authority to commit American troops to combat.

The U.S.-led coalition's stunning military success in the Persian Gulf War, however, has since stifled both academic and congressional debate on the reassertion of presidential primacy in initiating military hostilities. Although Senate majority leader George Mitchell (D.-Maine) and House Speaker Thomas Foley (D.-Wash.) praised the congressional debates of January 10–12, 1991, as a historic exercise in joint legislative-executive responsibility under the War Powers Resolution, even a cursory examination of the "great debate" reveals that it was largely without substance. Indeed, the debates were little more than a call to support the president as commander-in-chief or, alternatively, an appeal to give economic sanctions more time to work.[10]

As the United Nations' deadline of midnight, January 15, 1991, approached, it was hardly surprising that the military imperative of supporting more than 430,000 U.S. armed forces facing imminent hostilities overshadowed such basic issues as the costs and benefits of employing military force in one of the world's most politically volatile regions. There was virtually no discussion of the postwar environment or balance of power that the United States and its coalition partner sought to achieve. As Sen. Bill Bradley (D.-N.J.) described the postwar uncertainties on January 10:

There could be a power vacuum and civil chaos in Iraq, because of the U.S. military action. We could be spilling American blood to make the region safe for Iranian and Syrian domination. Ambitious Baathist and Islamic powers in Syria and Iran would welcome the opportunity to fill a vacuum in Iraq.[11]

The great debate legitimated the president's conduct but did not illuminate the tortuous path to war or a safe passage in the war's aftermath.

Although Bush conferred with the congressional leadership concerning the dispatch of armed forces to the Persian Gulf, his decision raises, anew, questions about the allocation of constitutional authority for initiating military hostilities in the War Powers Resolution of 1973. Since its inception, American presidents have evaded the act's consulting and reporting requirements. Carter, for example, argued that his response to Iran's taking of diplomatic hostages was a defensive measure against a hostile act.[12] Since his intentions were defensive, Carter apparently believed he was not required to seek prior congressional approval.[13] Reagan circumvented the War Powers Resolution by calling his decision to position naval forces off Nicaragua a "maneuver" and conducting army "training exercises" in Honduras, in aid of El Salvador's armed struggle against Cuban- and Nicaraguan-backed rebels.[14]

Although Congress invoked the resolution in authorizing the stationing of marines in Lebanon, Reagan denied that the measure applied. Inasmuch as the marines were a "peacekeeping force," not in danger of becoming involved in hostilities, the president refused to concede his authority as commander-in-chief by invoking the War Powers Resolution.[15] Once again, in invading Grenada to protect American lives and to oust a radical Marxist regime, Reagan did not invoke the War Powers Resolution, but he did inform the congressional leadership about the military action.[16] When some members of Congress attempted to invoke the act, Reagan forestalled congressional action by declaring that he would withdraw U.S. armed forces prior to the sixty-day deadline, as the resolution mandates.[17]

Since 1973 U.S. presidents have employed armed forces abroad approximately thirty-one times, ranging from rescue attempts involving a few troops for a limited time to full-scale military deployments and hostilities in Panama and the Persian Gulf. In nineteen instances, various presidents reported their actions to Congress.[18] Yet in only two cases prior to the Bush administration did the president or Congress invoke the formal reporting requirements in section 4 (a) (1) of the War Powers Resolution, thereby triggering the requirement in section 5 (b) that the president terminate military hostilities and withdraw the armed forces in either sixty or ninety days unless Congress authorizes their continued deployment.[19]

Despite various presidents' avoidance of the resolution's formal reporting requirements, during the past eighteen years analysis and debate on the measure's efficacy and constitutionality have focused on the reporting and triggering mechanisms in section 4 (a) (1) and the legislative veto in section 5 (b), permitting Congress to order the president to withdraw armed forces from combat by concurrent resolution. This obsessive focus on the reporting-triggering mechanism and the constitutionality of the legislative veto has obscured the resolution's underlying rationales and has inhibited an evaluation of its overall effectiveness in promoting joint congressional-presidential participation in and responsibility for initiating, conducting, and terminating military hostilities. By enacting the War Powers Resolution, Congress hoped to redress the imbalance between itself and the president in any decision to transform the nation from a condition of peace to one of war or hostilities and to ensure that such decisions would evoke the public support necessary to wage war effectively. Given these objectives, the resolution attempts to create the conditions for consultation and decisionmaking prior to committing U.S. armed forces to combat or to regions where hostilities are imminent.[20]

Although U.S. presidents have submitted eighteen reports to Congress since 1973 (Ford submitted three, Carter one, and Reagan fourteen), these episodes do not reveal a pattern of prior consultation and joint decisionmaking that the resolution's authors hoped to achieve. In ten of twelve instances in which the president dispatched U.S. armed forces abroad without reporting to Congress, the number of troops and the duration of operations were too limited to test the resolution's efficacy. The dispatch of military advisers to El Salvador and the conduct of military training exercises in Honduras raised serious foreign policy questions, but Congress did not deal with these concerns within the framework of the War Powers Resolution. As a cursory analysis of the eighteen decisions that presidents Ford, Carter, Reagan, and Bush communicated to Congress indicates, presidential reporting has not achieved advance consultation and joint decisionmaking.

As the first four episodes (the Danang sealift, the evacuations from Saigon and Cambodia, and the *Mayaguez* rescue) reveal, Ford informed Congress shortly before the commencement of military operations.[21] Although the State Department's legal adviser, Monroe Leigh, claimed that the president's notification met the War Powers Resolution's reporting and consultation requirements, the timing and perfunctory nature of the reports do not represent either consultation or joint decisionmaking.[22] The president merely informed Congress that military operations were under way or were imminent. However, the limited scope and duration of the operations as well as their nonoffensive nature suggest that they were within the realm of the president's defensive authority as commander-in-chief.

Jimmy Carter failed to inform or consult Congress prior to the ill-fated attempt to rescue American hostages from the Teheran embassy. Arguing that prior consultation could jeopardize the security of the rescue operation, Carter simply ignored the requirement of reporting to Congress under section

3, "in every possible instance" in which the president introduces troops into hostilities or in which hostilities are imminent.[23] Furthermore, since the taking of hostages is an aggressive act under international law, one could describe the president's conduct as defensive and, therefore, within the zone of authority that the Constitution leaves to presidential discretion.

During Ronald Reagan's two administrations, the president's use of armed forces in Lebanon, the dispatch of naval forces to protect reflagged Kuwaiti tankers in the Persian Gulf, and aerial attacks against Libya indicate a pattern of presidential initiative and congressional deference, with the possible exception of Congress' decision to invoke section 4 (a) (1) of the resolution in September 1983. On July 6, 1982, Reagan announced his intention to send a contingent of marines to Beirut, Lebanon, as part of a multinational peacekeeping force. After withdrawing this first contingent on September 10, the president dispatched a second contingent on September 20, 1982. Clement Zablocki (D.-Wisc.), chairman of the House Foreign Affairs Committee, expressed his concerns in writing to the president, but Congress did not invoke the War Powers Resolution until September 1983. Then, as a response to a terrorist attack on the marines barracks on August 30, 1983, Congress enacted the Multinational Force in Lebanon Resolution (MFLR) on September 29.

Although Reagan did not report to Congress under section 4 (a) (1), after prolonged negotiations Congress agreed that the MFLR would indicate that section 4 of the War Powers Resolution had been operative since August 29. Congress also authorized the marines' continuing participation in Lebanon for eighteen months. Reagan never acknowledged that section 4 had become operative, but he did sign the MFLR into law. Nevertheless, he denied that his authority to dispatch armed forces for peacekeeping purposes could be "infringed by statute." Referring to the MFLR, Reagan rejected the interpretation that his signature acknowledged congressional power "to revise the President's constitutional authority to deploy United States armed forces."[24]

Since 1973 the War Powers Resolution's consulting, reporting, and triggering provisions have not appreciably altered the pattern of presidential initiative and congressional deference to various presidents' decisions to use military force as an instrument of U.S. foreign policy. Following the U.S. defeat in Vietnam, Gerald Ford's brief interregnum, and Jimmy Carter's failure in Iran, Ronald Reagan's decision to ignore or circumvent the War Powers Resolution's consulting and reporting requirements could be interpreted as a deliberate attempt to challenge congressional authority or, alternatively, as a successful strategy for restoring presidential power and U.S. military credibility. Were it not for the revelations of covert arms transfers to Iran and illicit aid for the Nicaraguan Contras, Reagan's reassertion of presidential power in military and foreign affairs might have gone completely unchallenged. Despite these misadventures, Reagan's successful restoration of the presidency enabled George Bush to take unparalleled initiatives in invading Panama and in dispatching armed forces to the Persian Gulf.

Notwithstanding the Bush administration's qualified success in Panama and its stunning military and political victories in Kuwait, the president's initiatives leave several unresolved questions in relation to the War Powers Resolution. Even if American presidents from Ford to Reagan had been faithful in meeting the resolution's various requirements, certain questions remain: Is the War Powers Resolution a politically desirable and constitutionally acceptable means of promoting joint congressional-executive responsibility for initiating war or military hostilities? Does the War Powers Resolution focus congressional and public attention on the conduct of American foreign policy in a timely way, i.e., well before the clock approaches midnight, when Congress must decide whether to support the commander-in-chief and the armies that are in harm's way? Does the resolution reduce the Constitution's broad provisions separating executive and legislative authority to a ritualistic formula that vitiates presidential-congressional responsibility and accountability to the American electorate for the foreign, military, and national security policies that lead the nation to the brink of war?

From its inception, the War Powers Resolution of 1973 has been constitutionally flawed. The Constitution (Article I, section 8) confers authority to declare war and initiate military hostilities exclusively on Congress. The only constitutional authority the president has is the power to respond to sudden attacks on U.S. territory, its armed forces, and its citizens at home and abroad.[25] By requiring the president to seek congressional authorization before initiating war or military hostilities, the Constitution's Framers hoped to make it more difficult to wage war than to conclude peace. In twentieth-century language, the Framers believed that the decision to spend American blood, lives, and treasure is so important that it should result from joint congressional-presidential action. They also recognized that, in a constitutional democracy, government cannot wage war effectively without an overwhelming consensus of the American people that war is necessary to preserve the nation's security. And they apparently believed that the separation of legislative policymaking from the executive's conduct of foreign and military policy would promote mutual restraint and accountability to the electorate.[26]

Unlike former British prime minister Margaret Thatcher, who went to war against Argentina over the Falkland Islands (1982), the U.S. president does not have constitutional authority to change the nation's condition from peace to war. Nor can Congress delegate this authority to the president. The constitutional authority to declare war and to initiate military hostilities inheres in Congress as a representative institution.[27] Under the British system, the House of Commons could have expressed its disapproval of Margaret Thatcher's decision by voting a lack of confidence in the prime minister's policy and bringing down the government. Although Commons rarely, if ever, topples a government, a vote of confidence is the ultimate constitutional check on the arbitrary exercise of executive power. In the U.S. constitutional system, the separation of the war powers from the office of the president theoretically serves a similar function in restraining executive power and promoting presidential accountability.[28]

Although the War Powers Resolution states that "it is the purpose of this resolution to fulfill the intent of the Framers of the Constitution," in the absence of a prior declaration of war the resolution delegates authority to the president to wage war for sixty or as many as ninety days, if he certifies that an additional thirty days are necessary to disengage the troops from combat and bring them home promptly.[29] Unless Congress authorizes continued military hostilities, the president is legally required to withdraw the armed forces from combat after this period has expired. In the absence of a declaration of war, the resolution provides that Congress can, by concurrent resolution, require the president to cease military hostilities at any time. Yet if the Constitution prohibits Congress from delegating authority to initiate war or military hostilities, then the time period—whether sixty or ninety days—is immaterial.

In providing that "any time U.S. armed forces are engaged in hostilities outside the territory of the United States . . . without a declaration of war or specific statutory authorization" Congress, by concurrent resolution, can require the president to withdraw those forces, the War Powers Resolution suffers from another fatal flaw.[30] Since concurrent resolutions are not subject to the president's veto, this feature of the resolution is constitutionally questionable, as the Supreme Court's decision in *Immigration and Naturalization Service v. Chadha* (1983) suggests.[31] In other words, Congress cannot legislate or make policy without presenting such legislation to the president for his signature. By circumventing the president's veto power (under Article I, section 7), the War Powers Resolution violates the constitutional separation of powers. Apparently, Congress recognized this flaw in 1983 when it adopted a measure providing for the use of joint resolutions requiring future presidents to withdraw troops from hostilities.[32] Inasmuch as joint resolutions are subject to the president's veto, this measure hardly reverses the erosion of congressional power. As amended, the War Powers Resolution indeed reinforces presidential power since the Constitution requires a two-thirds vote to override a veto.

In addition to these basic constitutional and pragmatic flaws, every American president from Richard Nixon through Ronald Reagan has found ways to circumvent triggering the resolution. By claiming that their actions were purely defensive, that the armed forces were on a peacekeeping mission, or that hostilities did not exist and were not imminent, American presidents have bypassed the resolution's requirement of reporting "within 48 hours to the Speaker of the House of Representatives and to the President pro tempore of the Senate a report, in writing, setting forth—(A) the circumstances necessitating the introduction of United States Armed Forces; (B) the constitutional and legislative authority under which such introduction took place; and (C) the estimated scope and duration of the hostilities or involvement."[33]

Until the president reports, the resolution's sixty- or ninety-day clock does not begin to tick. Under these circumstances, the only way that Congress can require the commander-in-chief to repatriate American troops is by passing a concurrent resolution, as the War Powers Resolution originally provided. Alternatively, Congress could enact a joint resolution, which would be subject to a presidential veto.[34] In either event, with American armed forces in the field, committed to combat, it would be virtually impossible to end military hostilities without provoking a political-constitutional crisis and causing a military and foreign policy disaster. Imagine, for example, Congress' ordering U.S. armed forces in the Kuwaiti theater of operations to cease operations if Iraqi armed forces had simply retreated, weapons intact, without surrendering to the U.S. and coalition military forces in hot pursuit.

Prior to the Persian Gulf War, President Bush dispatched approximately 430,000 troops to the region while Congress debated, reluctantly, authorizing military hostilities. In contrast to the Vietnam War, however, in this instance the international community supported economic sanctions, U.S. military deployments, and the use of force in the Gulf. Unlike with Vietnam, U.S. European allies, the Soviet Union, and most states in the region viewed Iraq's conduct as a threat to their security as well as to regional and international stability. As eleven UN Security Council resolutions indicate, both the United States and the international community exhausted various nonbelligerent means to restore peace and stability to the region.[35] In response, Iraq simply ignored these measures, arraying a 600,000-man army in Kuwait, along the Saudi Arabian border, and along Iraq's border with Turkey, a NATO ally.

Having failed to secure Iraq's peaceful withdrawal from Kuwait, on November 29, 1990, under considerable U.S. pressure, the UN Security Council adopted Resolution 678, which gave Iraq another opportunity to withdraw its forces, setting a deadline of midnight, January 15, 1991. Because the council recognized that Iraq probably would ignore this last appeal, the resolution authorized the member states "to use all necessary means to uphold and implement resolution 660 (1990) and all subsequent resolutions and to restore international peace and security in the area."[36] Although the president's supporters point to Resolution 678 as authority for U.S. military action, the measure lacks binding force. First, the resolution requests but does not require member states to provide appropriate military support. Second, Articles 42 through 44 of the UN Charter are not self-executing provisions. In each case, the Security Council must negotiate agreements with the member states to provide armed forces. Finally, Article 43 specifically provides that such agreements "shall be subject to ratification by the signatory states in accordance with their respective constitutional processes."[37]

Similar to the North Atlantic Treaty Organization's Charter, the UN Charter was never intended to displace the U.S. domestic constitutional process. Yet both Congress and the president delayed this constitutional process because of the potential international implications and because of adverse domestic responses. Bush sought to avoid a protracted debate that might divide Congress and the nation because he legitimately feared that Iraqi leader Saddam Hussein would misread U.S. intentions. Then, on January 8, the president sought a vote without a debate. On January 9, however, Bush reasserted his authority under UN Security Council Resolution 678 to take military action without further congressional approval or authorization.

Congress did not begin to consider the Gulf crisis seriously until late November, when Sen. Sam Nunn (D.-Ga.), chairman of the Senate Armed Services Committee, began hearings. Debating a Persian Gulf war in the long shadow of Vietnam, senators and representatives feared the domestic political consequences of casting a vote. Inasmuch as 25 percent of the men and women of operations Desert Shield and Desert Storm were African Americans, urban Democratic representatives, in particular, feared the political backlash that would result from potentially high casualty rates. Caught between constituency pressures and their sense of duty to support the president, both Democratic and Republican congressional leaders left their cohorts free to "vote their conscience."[38]

Following three days of "subdued, extended, often impassioned" debate, on January 12, 1991, Congress voted reluctantly to authorize Bush to use military force to carry out UN Security Council Resolution 678.[39] Before initiating military hostilities, however, the congressional resolution required the president to inform the Speaker of the House and the president pro tempore of the Senate that he had "(a) used all appropriate diplomatic and peaceful means to obtain compliance by Iraq with the United Nations Security Council resolutions; and (b) that those efforts have not been and would not be successful in obtaining such compliance."[40] Following the passage of the resolution by votes of 52 to 47 in the Senate and 250 to 183 in the House, Speaker Thomas Foley claimed that Congress had adopted " 'the practical equivalent' of a declaration of war."[41]

Yet neither UN Resolution 678 nor the congressional resolution is the functional equivalent of a declaration of war. If Congress cannot delegate the war-making authority to the president, certainly it can not delegate such plenary power, through the commander-in-chief, to the United Nations or any of its subsidiary organs. Furthermore, it would be imprudent to do so, given the equal voting status of the General Assembly's diverse membership, ranging from ministates to the Soviet Union and the United States, and the composition of the Security Council, the U.S. veto power to the contrary. Finally, the UN Charter does not contemplate such a broad delegation of power from its constituent members. Not unlike the government of the Articles of Confederation, the United Nations does not possess sovereign authority over its member states.

As for the congressional resolution "authorizing" the president to conduct military hostilities within the framework of UN Resolution 678, it is an open-ended grant of authority, which the Constitution does not contemplate. Similar to the Gulf of Tonkin Resolution, it gives the president power to name the time and the place; the enemy is clear.[42] With one possible exception, during the past two centuries Congress has enacted eleven declarations of war after, rather than before, the commencement of military hostilities. As these declarations demonstrate, the purpose for declaring war is to change the nation's legal status in domestic and international law. By declaring war, Congress and the president notify the nation's citizens, allies, enemies, and neutrals of their rights and responsibilities in relation to the belligerents.

Declarations of war do not furnish occasions for debating the wisdom of responding to immediate threats to the nation's armed forces or its international security. In the age of guided missiles and supersonic Stealth aircraft, focused congressional debate of the policy options should occur long before the president decides to deploy these weapons in politically unstable regions. Once an American president has decided to commit armed forces to a region in which hostilities are imminent, he is likely to ask Congress to support and legitimate his decisions to the American people. At this point, it is naive to believe that the president has come to Congress for a full debate of the issues, which would serve the enemy's interests more than it could fulfill the requirements of democratic accountability.

If the War Powers Resolution is both politically and constitutionally flawed, should Congress attempt to address these problems by revising the resolution or by scrapping it? Some critics argue that Congress should shorten the president's leash by revising the resolution. Among possible amendments are proposals to shorten the deadlines for withdrawing troops from combat operations, unless Congress authorizes their continued participation through legislation. Although this proposal is attractive to critics of presidential power, whether the president has thirty, sixty, or ninety days to withdraw armed forces is irrelevant since the Constitution simply does not permit Congress to delegate such authority, per se. Article I requires that Congress make such determinations itself. Pragmatically, the shorter the presidential leash, the greater is the pressure on Congress to support troops in the heat of combat.[43]

In addition to the shorter leash argument, other critics call for a clear definition of such terms as "hostilities," "imminent hostilities," "consultation," and "reporting."[44] Clarity may be desirable but often is elusive in drafting contingent legislation, since future contingencies are, by definition, unknown and often unforeseeable. In some circumstances, uncertainty may be more desirable than certainty. Indeed, the Framers believed that uncertainty is more likely to promote congressional control over presidential warmaking than predictability. Thus, they did not define the boundaries between presidential and congressional power regarding war and foreign affairs with great precision. They deliberately left twilight zones of constitutional power in order to restrain both the executive and legislative branches and to hold them mutually accountable to the American people. Finally, uncertainty may give international adversaries pause in deciding to launch military adventures.

Therefore, Congress should abandon the War Powers Resolution as a bad idea whose time has come and gone. The resolution is no substitute for the exercise of congressional responsibility for policymaking, i.e., for establishing wise and prudent policies that guide the executive's conduct of foreign and military policy and for overseeing the administration's execution of those policies. Congress can not substitute "precise language" for political will, party discipline, and responsible leadership. And it should not dissipate its responsibility for making policy in politically and constitutionally questionable attempts to run the State and Defense departments from Capitol Hill. Although Congress has authority to oversee the executive's conduct of foreign and military policy, it is neither constitutionally authorized nor politically equipped to administer cabinet agencies directly accountable to the president. By telescoping the policymaking process and focusing on the limited time frame in which the War Powers Resolution operates, Congress loses sight of its constitutional responsibilities, hampers the executive's effective performance of its functions, and fails to perform its legislative function as a representative institution. When actual events trigger the War Powers Resolution, usually it is too late to alter the course of war.

When the nation faces a war that may demand extraordinary sacrifices from its young men and women, the American people deserve more than a "vote of conscience," as House majority leader Richard A. Gephardt (D.-Mo.) described the decision to authorize military hostilities to eject Iraq from Kuwait.[45] Long before Congress voted to support the president, the American people were entitled to a debate of the foreign policy decisions leading to war. They deserved a debate of the postwar foreign policy consequences of stationing an occupation army in a region in which allies and adversaries are virtually indistinguishable, in which one person's terrorist is another's freedom fighter, and in which international political treachery is a norm rather than an aberration. They deserved a debate about the regional balance of power that the United States hopes to establish. And they deserved a debate about whether, in a constitutional democracy, the people are willing to sacrifice their blood and treasure to secure the national interest in distant lands and alien cultures.

NOTES

1. 87 Stat. 555, Public Law 93-148 (1973).
2. R. W. Apple, Jr., "U.S. Says Its Troops in the Gulf Could Reach 100,000 in Months," *New York Times,* August 11, 1990; Carroll J. Doherty, "Members Back Sending Troops to Gulf, but Worry About a Drawn-Out Crisis," *CQ Weekly Report,* August 11, 1990, pp. 2598–99; Susan F. Rasky, "Congress and the Gulf," *New York Times,* December 17, 1990. Bush's Message to Congress may be found in 26 *Weekly Comp. of Pres. Doc.* 1225 (1990).
3. Michael Wines, "Largest Force Since Vietnam Committed in 15-Day Flurry," *New York Times,* August 19, 1990. Various members of Congress also began to contend that any movement toward war would require close consultation with Congress, as well as formal authorization, but there were not enough members who shared that institutional concern. On November 20, fifty-three House members and one senator filed suit in U.S. District Court to obtain an injunction barring Bush from using force to remove Iraq from Kuwait without first seeking congressional authorization. In *Dellums et. al.* v. *George Bush,* 752 F. Supp. 1141 (D.D.C. 1990), Judge Harold H. Green ruled that the issue was not "ripe" since Congress had not yet acted on the issue. But Green did hold that only Congress may initiate war.
4. See, generally, Edward Keynes, *Undeclared War: Twilight Zone of Constitutional Power,* rev. paperback ed. (University Park: Penn State Press, 1991); Louis Fisher, *Presidential War Power* (Lawrence: University Press of Kansas, 1995); Adler, Chapter 7 of this volume.
5. See Ellen C. Collier, "The War Powers Resolution: Fifteen Years of Experience," in U.S. Congress, House of Representatives, Committee on Foreign Affairs, Subcommittee on Arms Control, International Security and Science, 100th Congress, 2d session, August 4 and September 27, 1988 (Washington, D.C.: Government Printing Office, 1989), pp. 255–64 (hereinafter cited as Collier, "War Powers Resolution").

6. *Public Papers of the Presidents of the United States: Jimmy Carter 1980–1981* (Washington, D.C.: Government Printing Office, 1981), pp. 771–72, White House Statement, April 25, 1980; p. 773, Address to the Nation, April 25, 1980; and pp. 793–94, President's News Conference of April 29, 1980.

7. *Congressional Quarterly Almanac 1982* (Washington, D.C.: Congressional Quarterly, 1983), pp. 167–71 (hereinafter cited as *CQ Almanac*).

8. Collier, "War Powers Resolution," pp. 255–57.

9. *CQ Almanac 1989*, pp. 595–96. A little more than five weeks later, on January 31, 1990, George Bush announced that he would withdraw the additional troops from Panama. Most members of Congress accepted National Security Adviser Brent Scowcroft's explanation of the president's decision as "precautionary as much as anything else." Congress did not attempt to invoke the War Powers Resolution (see *CQ Almanac 1989*, pp. 597–98).

10. *CQ Weekly Report*, January 12, 1991, pp. 65–71. On January 8, 1991, President Bush requested congressional authorization for military hostilities. But on January 9, in a press conference, he said, "I don't think I need [a congressional resolution]. . . . I feel I have the authority to fully implement the United Nations Resolution [678]" (p. 71). The resolution that Congress adopted on January 12 refers to UN Resolution 678 but does not invoke section 4 (a) (1) of the War Powers Resolution.

11. "Statement by Senator Bill Bradley on Use of Force in the Persian Gulf," issued January 10, 1991, U.S. Senate, Washington, D.C. (provided to the author by Senator Bradley).

12. *Public Papers: Jimmy Carter*, pp. 773 and 793–94.

13. Ibid.

14. *Public Papers of the Presidents of the United States: Ronald Reagan 1983* (Washington, D.C.: Government Printing Office, 1985), pp. 1066–67 and 1082–86, Remarks and a Question-and-Answer Session with Reporters on Domestic and Foreign Policy Issues, July 21, 1983, and the President's News Conference, July 26, 1983.

15. *CQ Almanac 1982*, pp. 168–69; *Public Papers: Reagan 1982*, pp. 1078–79 and 1238.

16. *Public Papers: Reagan 1983*, pp. 1505–8, Remarks of the President and Prime Minister Eugenia Charles of Dominica Announcing the Deployment of United States Forces in Grenada, October 25, 1983, and pp. 1520–22, Address to the Nation on Events in Lebanon and Grenada, October 27, 1983. Though Reagan informed Congress, he did not do so according to the reporting requirements in section 4 (a) (1), which would have triggered the sixty-to-ninety-day time limit on military operations.

17. Ibid., p. 1674, Letter to the Speaker of the House and the President Pro Tempore of the Senate, December 8, 1983; *CQ Almanac 1983*, pp. 134–36.

18. Collier, "War Powers Resolution," pp. 255–57.

19. Ibid., p. 240. In 1975 President Ford invoked section 4 (a) (1) of the War Powers Resolution in rescuing the crew of the *Mayaguez*, and in 1983 Congress invoked the provision during the deployment of marines to Beirut.

20. In fact, section 3 of the War Powers Resolution provides that

the President in every possible instance shall consult with Congress before introducing United States Armed Forces into hostilities or into situations where imminent involvement in hostilities is clearly indicated by the circumstances, and after every such introduction shall consult regularly with the Congress until United States Armed Forces are no longer engaged in hostilities or have been removed from such situations.

Quoted in W. Taylor Reveley, *War Powers of the President and Congress: Who Holds the Arrows and Olive Branch* (Charlottesville: University of Virginia Press, 1981), pp. 288.

21. *Public Papers of the Presidents of The United States: Gerald R. Ford 1975* (Washington, D.C.: Government Printing Office, 1977), p. 475, Statement on the Evacuation of the United States Mission in Phnom Penh, Cambodia, April 12, 1975; p. 476, Letter to the Speaker of the House of Representatives and the President of the Senate Reporting on the Evacuation of the United States Mission in Phnom Penh, April 14, 1975; p. 605, Statement Following the Evacuation of United States Personnel from the Republic of Vietnam, April 29, 1975; and pp. 669–70, Letter to the Speaker of the House of Representatives and the President Pro Tempore of the Senate Reporting on United States Actions in the Recovery of the SS *Mayaguez,* May 15, 1975.

22. Statement of Monroe Leigh, legal adviser, Department of State, U.S. Congress, House of Representatives, Committee on International Relations, Subcommittee on International Security and Scientific Affairs, "War Powers: A Test of Compliance Relative to the Danang Sealift, the Evacuation of Phnom Penh, the Evacuation of Saigon, and the *Mayaguez* Incident," 94th Cong., 1st sess., May 7 and June 4, 1975 (Washington, D.C.: Government Printing Office, 1975), pp. 76–79.

23. *Public Papers: Jimmy Carter,* pp. 773 and 793–94.

24. *Public Papers: Ronald Reagan 1983,* p. 1445, Statement on Signing the Multinational Force in Lebanon Resolution, October 12, 1983; *CQ Almanac 1983,* pp. 134–36.

25. See Keynes, *Undeclared War,* pp. 34–36 and 104–5.

26. Ibid. (see, generally, chapter 2, pp. 31–59).

27. Inasmuch as Article I specifically vests the war powers in Congress, it can not delegate this vast discretionary authority to the president without breaching the agency theory on which the Constitution rests.

28. Keynes, *Undeclared War,* pp. 22–30.

29. War Powers Act of 1973, Section 2 (a), quoted in Reveley, *War Powers of the President and Congress,* p. 287.

30. Ibid., section 5 (c), pp. 289–90.

31. 462 U.S. 919 (1983). Although *Chadha* applies to a one-house veto, the Court's opinion casts doubts on approximately 200 public laws that contain various forms of legislative vetoes.

32. Collier, "War Powers Resolution," p. 251.

33. War Powers Resolution of 1973, Section 4 (a) (3), quoted in Reveley, *War Powers of the President and Congress,* p. 288.

34. Ibid.

35. See UN Resolutions 660, 661, 662, 664, 665, 666, 667, 669, 670, 674, and 677 (1990).

36. UN Security Council Resolution 678, quoted in *CQ Weekly Report,* December 1, 1990, p. 4007.

37. UN Charter, Article 43, paragraph 3. For further discussion see, generally, Fisher, Chapter 14 of this volume.

38. *New York Times,* January 11, 1991, p. A9, col. 2.

39. R.W. Apple, Jr., *New York Times,* January 13, 1991, p. 1, col. 4, and p. 11, col. 3.

40. Ibid., p. 11, col. 3.

41. Ibid., p. 1, col. 4. As the vote revealed, Republicans in both houses generally supported the president, but Democrats were deeply divided on the issue. In the House, eighty-six Democrats joined the Republicans. Only three Republicans broke ranks to vote against the resolution. In the Senate, ten Democrats joined the Republicans to adopt the measure, but only two Republicans opposed using force. Southern Democrats tended to support the president. As the *New York Times* noted, not since the War of 1812 has Congress been so divided on launching war; at that time, the House voted 79 to 49 and the Senate 19 to 13 to authorize military hostilities (p. 11, col. 1).

42. See Keynes, *Undeclared War,* p. 150.

43. Collier, "War Powers Resolution," 282–87.

44. Ibid.

45. Noting that the whips would not line up votes, Cong. Richard A. Gephardt (D.-Mo.), the Democratic majority leader said, "We expect and want all of the members to vote their conscience, what in their mind is the right thing for this country to do" (*New York Times,* January 11, 1991, p. A9, col. 2).

PART FOUR

LAW AND FOREIGN POLICY: HISTORICAL PERSPECTIVES AND PRECEDENTS

10

THE WASHINGTON ADMINISTRATION, CONGRESS, AND ALGIERS

GERHARD CASPER

On the 25th of July, 1785, the schooner Maria, captain Stevens, belonging to a Mr. Foster, of Boston, was taken off Cape St. Vincents, by an Algerine corsair; and, five days afterwards, the ship Dauphin, captain O'Brien, belonging to Messieurs Irvins of Philadelphia, was taken by another Algerine, about fifty leagues westward of Lisbon. These vessels, with their cargoes and crews, twenty-one persons in number, were carried into Algiers.[1]

With those words, Secretary of State Thomas Jefferson described an event that posed one of the most intractable foreign policy problems the new country encountered, one which would occupy the Washington administration throughout its eight years. The Algiers episode illustrates vividly the foreign policy issues that arise under a system characterized by a three-way (executive, Senate, House) allocation of decisionmaking authority. In evaluating its significance, one must keep in mind that one of the Framers' central purposes in establishing the federal government was the effective and controlled conduct of foreign and defense policy.

Algiers, Tunis, and Tripoli were autonomous regencies of the Ottoman Empire, governed by a local and regularly replenished military establishment of Turks and financed by tributes from country tribes, agricultural trade, and piracy. For the purposes of piracy, fleets of cruisers were maintained under Turkish sea captains. The piracy policy was one of declaring "war" on countries big and small, taking ships and seamen captive, putting the "slaves" to work, and then selling "peace." A fourth participant in these activities was Morocco, an independent state under a sultan. These four powers, the Barbary Powers, exercised considerable control over Mediterranean and Atlantic shipping.[2] Because England withdrew her Mediterranean passes for American ships shortly after the outbreak of the War of Independence, the "American Revolution transferred from London to Philadelphia the problem of protecting American commerce."[3]

In 1784 the Continental Congress resolved to secure treaties with Morocco, Algiers, Tunis, and Tripoli. Indeed, a fifty-year treaty was concluded with Morocco in 1787.[4] Negotiations with the other Barbary Powers collapsed, however, and the capture of the *Maria* and *Dauphin* exacerbated the problem. The Continental Congress commissioned John Adams, Benjamin Franklin, and Thomas Jefferson to negotiate with the Barbary Powers. When these men sent an agent to Algiers, its ruler, the dey, demanded a $60,000 ransom. This sum amounted to more than $2,800 a head, considerably above the $200 that the commissioners had offered or the $550 that Jefferson was willing to pay in September 1788, when he employed the services of a French religious order to recover the hostages. In March 1790, Jefferson took up his new position of secretary of state, and the House of Representatives referred to him a petition for relief concerning the American captives in Algiers.[5] At this point it becomes interesting to explore the manner in which the executive branch and Congress interacted to find a solution.

On December 30, 1790, the president sent both houses of Congress a report on the prisoners of Algiers, which the House had requested, and which Jefferson had prepared for Washington. On the same date, Jefferson also sent the House a report on Mediterranean trade. The secretary of state had prepared the latter at the request of the House following the president's annual speech to his "Fellow Citizens of the Senate and House of Representatives" on December 8.[6] During that address, the president called the congressmen's attention to the "distressful" state of the Mediterranean trade.[7]

In the cover letter accompanying the first report, Washington said, "I lay before you a report of the Secretary of State on the subject of the citizens of the United States in captivity at Algiers, *that you may provide on their behalf, what to you shall seem most expedient.*"[8] Jefferson's report consisted of a detailed account of diplomatic activities since the days of the Continental Congress as well as of the "market" in Algerine captives—the per capita ransom paid by various European states.[9] Jefferson stated somewhat laconically that from "these facts and opinions, some conjecture may be formed of the terms on which the liberty of our citizens may be obtained."[10] He also pointed to the alternative of meeting force with force, suggesting the capture of Algerine mariners, or better still, of Turks, for purposes of exchange. Jefferson concluded by emphasizing the connection of the subject matter at hand with "the liberation of our commerce in the Mediterranean."[11] The report was accompanied by extracts from diplomatic and other correspondence,[12] which had received some "judicious editing" by Jefferson.[13]

In response to a House request, Jefferson sent the report on Mediterranean trade directly to the House after the president had approved it. In the report, Jefferson provided information about the importance of the Mediterranean ports for U.S. agricultural exports before the war. He stressed that navigation had not been resumed at all since the peace and discussed alternatives for coping with the situation, including the option "to obtain peace by purchasing it."[14] Jefferson relayed the opinion of a European source, "whose name is not free to be mentioned here,"[15] that the United States could not buy peace with Algiers for less than $1 million.[16]

Finally, Jefferson discussed "repel[ling] force by force" as an alternative.[17] He provided estimates of the strength of the Algerine naval force, suggested that the United States needed a naval force equal to it, and put forward the idea of an alliance with other countries. He pointed to the fact that Portugal, by keeping a naval watch before the Straits of Gibraltar, had contained the Algerines within the Mediterranean. "Should Portugal effect a peace with them, as has been apprehended for some time, the Atlantic will immediately become the principal scene of their piracies."[18] Jefferson concluded:

Upon the whole, it rests with Congress to decide between war, tribute, and ransom, as the means of re-establishing our Mediterranean commerce. If war, they will consider how far our own resources shall be called forth, and how far they will enable the Executive to engage, in the form of the constitution, the cooperation of other Powers. If tribute or ransom, it will rest with them to limit and provide the amount; and with the Executive, observing the same constitutional forms, to make arrangements for employing it to the best advantage.[19]

The report was so structured that Jefferson, while treating the alternatives fairly, made it clear where he stood (and, indeed had stood all along): giving in to ransom demands would only encourage further extortion. The report was again accompanied by a range of diplomatic and other correspondence.[20]

Jefferson submitted the report with a request to the Speaker of the House that it be treated as a secret document because it was not in the interest of the United States that countries at peace with Algiers learn about American plans for concerted action. The galleries were indeed cleared, and the House forwarded the report to the Senate on a confidential basis.[21]

When the Senate received Jefferson's report on January 3, William Maclay thought it breathed resentment and abounded "with martial estimates in a naval way."[22] Three days later, a Senate committee found that a naval force was necessary "and that it will be proper to resort to the same as soon as the state of the public finances will admit."[23] The committee was headed by Jefferson's friend John Langdon and included senators who were sympathetic to Hamiltonian trade policy.[24]

> On February 1, 1791, the Senate adopted a resolution that the Senate advise and consent that the President of the United States take such measures as he may think necessary for the redemption of the citizens of the United States now in captivity at Algiers, provided the expense shall not exceed forty thousand dollars; and, also, that measures be taken to confirm the treaty now existing between the United States and the Emperor of Morocco.[25]

The last item referred to the fact that the sultan had died and a customary payment was due his successor. The president responded to the Senate in a message dated February 22 in which he said he would act "in conformity with your resolution of advice" as soon as the necessary monies were appropriated and ready.[26] By a special appropriations act of March 3, 1791, Congress designated $20,000 for the Moroccan treaty.[27] No further steps were taken concerning a naval force or the Algiers prisoners, however.[28]

This first set of interactions between the executive branch and Congress was marked by a straightforward, detailed, and, on the whole, complete executive branch account to the Congress of the state of affairs.[29] It illustrated the president's inclination to wait for congressional judgment as well as Jefferson's inclination to make recommendations. No doubt was entertained about the ultimate authority of the Congress. Furthermore, both branches displayed a consensus that, at times, the interests of the country demanded secrecy. Perhaps the most important aspect is that, at the outset, the executive branch, because any solution depended on appropriations, recognized the need to deal with Congress as a whole. This last matter became controversial in spring 1792.

The previous December, Jefferson had forwarded new information to the Senate that suggested that accession of a new dey in Algiers provided a favorable moment for making a permanent arrangement with the regency. Also, Captain O'Brien urged, after six years of captivity, that something be done "to finally extricate your fourteen unfortunate subjects from their present state of bondage and adversity."[30] Of the twenty-one original captives, some had died and one had been privately ransomed. A Senate committee recommended a treaty.[31]

On March 11, 1792, in preparation for a meeting between the president and senators the next day, Washington and Jefferson discussed whether the former could proceed with treaty negotiations with only Senate authorization. Jefferson made notes on his consultation with the president:

> My opinions run on the following heads:
>
> We must go to Algiers with cash in our hands. Where shall we get it? By loan? By converting money now in the treasury?
>
> Probably a loan might be obtained on the President's authority; but as this could not be repaid without a subsequent act of legislature, the Representatives might refuse it. So if money in the treasury be converted, they may refuse to sanction it.
>
> The subsequent approbation of the Senate being necessary to validate a treaty, they expect to be consulted beforehand, if the case admits.
>
> So the subsequent act of the Representatives being necessary where money is given, why should not they expect to be consulted in like manner, when the case admits. A treaty is a law of the land. But prudence will point out this difference to be attended to in making them; viz. where a treaty contains such articles only as will go into execution of themselves, or be carried into execution by the judges, they may be safely made; but where there are articles which require a law to be passed afterwards by the legislature, great caution is requisite.
>
> For example; the consular convention with France required a very small legislative regulation. This convention was unanimously ratified by the Senate. Yet the same identical men threw by the law to enforce it at the last session, and the Representatives at this session have placed it among the laws which they may take up or not, at their own convenience, as if that was a higher motive than the public faith.
>
> Therefore, against hazarding this transaction without the sanction of both Houses.
>
> The President concurred. The Senate express the motive for this proposition, to be a fear that the Representatives would not keep the secret. He has no opinion of the secrecy of the Senate.[32]

Apparently Washington met with strong resistance from the senators, as is evidenced by Jefferson's notes from April 9:

> The President had wished to redeem our captives at Algiers, and to make peace with them on paying an annual tribute. The Senate were willing to approve this, but unwilling to have the lower House applied

to previously to furnish the money; they wished the President to take the money from the treasury, or open a loan for it. They thought that to consult the Representatives on one occasion, would give them a handle always to claim it, and would let them into a participation of the power of making treaties, which the constitution had given exclusively to the President and Senate. They said too, that if the particular sum was voted by the Representatives, it would not be a secret. The President had no confidence in the secresy [*sic*] of the Senate, and did not choose to take money from the treasury or to borrow. But he agreed he would enter into provisional treaties with the Algerines, not to be binding on us till ratified here. I prepared questions for consultation with the Senate, and added, that the Senate were to be apprized that on the return of the provisional treaty, and after they should advise the ratification, he would not have the seal put to it till the two Houses should vote the money. He asked me if the treaty stipulating a sum and ratified by him, with the advice of the Senate, would not be good under the constitution, and obligatory on the Representatives to furnish the money? I answered it certainly would, and that it would be the duty of the Representatives to raise the money; but that they might decline to do what was their duty, and I thought it might be incautious to commit himself by a ratification with a foreign nation, where he might be left in the lurch in the execution: it was possible too, to conceive a treaty, which it would not be their duty to provide for. He said that he did not like throwing too much into democratic hands, that if they would not do what the constitution called on them to do, the government would be at an end, and must *then assume another form*. He stopped here; and I kept silence to see whether he would say anything more in the same line, or add any qualifying expression to soften what he had said, but he did neither.[33]

Washington had obviously come to the conclusion that a negotiated redemption of the American prisoners was the only realistic option. Washington and Jefferson also believed that realism, if not constitutional necessity, made it highly desirable to have the House approve of the negotiations beforehand. Washington was not about to borrow the necessary money on his own authority. The Senate insisted on having a special role and brought the need for secrecy into play, although the president was not impressed by the Senate's allegedly superior capacity to keep secrets. After behind-the-scenes discussions, these considerations were brought into finely tuned balance; then on

May 8, 1792, the president formally asked the Senate whether it would approve both ransom and a treaty, and if so, at what price. The Senate advised the president that a peace treaty with Algiers not to exceed $40,000, plus subsequent annual tribute not to exceed $25,000, plus ransom not to exceed $40,000 would be approved.[34] Finally, the Congress made a special appropriation of $50,000 "to defray any expense which might be incurred in relation to the intercourse between the United States and foreign nations."[35] The purpose of this last appropriation was understood to be Algiers but this was not publicly stated to protect the negotiations.

Fearing interference from foreign countries, especially England, which was widely thought to be hostile to American interests and competition, the net steps were taken behind veils of extreme secrecy. George Washington, Thomas Jefferson, and Thomas Pinckney, the new American minister to London, were the only ones to know of the president's appointments of Adm. John Paul Jones, then in London, as commissioner for negotiations with Algiers, and of Thomas Barclay, the U.S. consul to Morocco, as his substitute should Jones not be available. Detailed instructions were issued for the negotiations.[36]

When Pinckney arrived in London, he learned of Jones's death. Barclay received the papers and prepared for his departure for Algiers but became ill and died in Lisbon in January 1793. At the end of March, Washington appointed the American minister to Portugal, David Humphreys, as commissioner. At this point the strategic situation deteriorated considerably. At the beginning of October 1793, in Gibraltar, Humphreys learned that the much-dreaded truce between Algiers and Portugal had been concluded and that Algerine corsairs were on their way to the Atlantic. The negotiations had been carried out by William Logie, the British consul in Algiers, on behalf of Portugal, although not necessarily with Portugal's informed consent. Edward Church, the U.S. consul in Lisbon, concluded that England was responsible:

The conduct of the British in this business leaves no room to doubt or mistake their object, which was evidently aimed at us. . . . As a further confirmation, it is worthy of remark, that the same British agent obtained a truce at the same time between the States of Holland and the Dey, for six months, whereby we and the Hanse Towns are now left the only prey to those barbarians.[37]

On December 16 the president presented to both houses of Congress a report from the secretary of state that contained much of the diplomatic correspondence. Washington requested secrecy:

While it is proper our citizens should know that subjects which so much concern their interests and their feelings, have duly engaged the attention of their Legislature and Executive, it would still be improper that some particulars of this communication should be made known. The confidential conversation stated in one of the last letters sent herewith is one of these. Both justice and policy require that the source of that information should remain secret. So a knowledge of the sums meant to have been given for peace and ransom might have a disadvantageous influence on future proceedings for the same objects.[38]

In connection with the House debates on the president's message, secrecy became controversial, and the House amended its standing order in favor of House discretion. The issue had acquired partisan overtones, with Republicans arguing for the amendment. This was also the time of heated controversy over the Neutrality Proclamation, the alliance with France, and relations with Great Britain. Nevertheless, after adoption of the amendment, the House defeated a motion to go into public session on Algiers by a one-vote margin.[39] Indeed, on January 2, 1794, the House adopted secret resolutions authorizing additional money for the negotiations and calling for a naval force "adequate to the protection of the commerce of the United States against the Algerine corsairs."[40] The House lifted the injunction of secrecy concerning these resolutions on January 7 and requested a committee to edit the president's communication in accord with his suggestions, a task accomplished by February 6.[41]

While Congress was considering possible responses to the changed circumstances, the administration received new information that made matters even worse. The president forwarded the information, on a confidential basis, on March 3, 1794.[42] During October and November, Algiers had taken eleven American vessels and 105 American seamen captive in the Atlantic, and the dey had firmly refused any negotiations with the United States.[43] Congress was bombarded with petitions not only from the hostages but also from merchants calling for adequate naval protection.[44] Insurance rates on American shipping increased from 10 to 30 percent.[45]

In a letter to Humphreys, Pierre Eric Skjoldebrand, brother of the Swedish consul in Algiers and an informal American agent, held out some hope that, if the dey could be talked to in a "favorable" moment, matters might be settled.[46] Apparently, on this basis, it was decided that Congress should make further efforts for a negotiated peace providing realistic amounts of ransom and naval armament.

Since 1790 Congress had made $40,000 available annually for "intercourse between the United States and foreign nations" and had given the president discretion not to account specifically for such expenditures that he thought it inadvisable to make public.[47] The latter procedure was regularized in 1793 by a formal system of certificates that were deemed to be a "sufficient voucher."[48] On March 20, 1794, Congress appropriated $1 million in addition to all previous appropriations "to defray any expenses which may be incurred in relation to the intercourse between the United States and foreign nations."[49] The legislation included authority to borrow the amount needed and called for an account of the expenditures "as soon as may be."[50] That it was almost half as much as regular 1794 appropriations for the support of the government and the military establishment gives a sense of the magnitude of this appropriation for a vaguely stated purpose.[51]

A naval bill called for additional monies. Almost three months after he had left the office of secretary of state, Jefferson, in a limited way, got what he had requested three years earlier and what he would use during his own presidency—a naval force to deal with the Barbary Powers. The proposal was, on the whole, not very popular in the House. Madison opposed it, arguing that it would be cheaper to purchase peace.[52] If the British were behind Algiers, as was widely assumed although not proven, then such a fleet would increase the danger of war with England.[53] Madison thus attempted to undercut the Federalists, who favored the naval bill, by linking the Algiers issue to the greater dispute over relations with England and France.[54] The House nevertheless approved the bill by an eleven-vote majority. The act of March 27, 1794, authorized six ships but also provided that the program should be dropped if "a peace shall take place between the United States and the Regency of Algiers."[55] Congress assigned priority to the negotiations.

The president took immediate steps to implement the legislation.[56] When a peace treaty with Algiers was eventually concluded, Congress reduced the shipbuilding program to three frigates that were launched in 1797.[57] The entire expense for building, arming, and keeping the ships in commission for the years 1794 to 1798 was about $2.5 million.[58] R. Irwin has argued that the great expense was dwarfed, however, by the savings in insurance premiums following the launching of the frigates.[59]

After considerable further difficulties, Humphreys's agent for these negotiations, Joseph Donaldson, agreed to a treaty at the end of 1795. Humphreys approved the treaty, "reserving the same, nevertheless, for the final ratification of the President of the United States of America, by and with the advice and consent of the Senate."[60] The terms had used up more money than Congress had appropriated and included maritime and military stores; in short, it was "cash and arms for hostages."[61]

The president submitted the treaty to the Senate on February 15, 1796, with much of the diplomatic correspondence.[62] It was promptly ratified. When the efforts to secure the necessary gold and silver in the war-torn European markets caused delays, the dey announced that he would declare war on the United States—the threat added a 36–gun frigate for "the Dey's daughter" to the previous expenses.[63] On May 30, 1796, Congress appropriated an additional $260,000 for treaties with the Barbary Powers.[64] The surviving American hostages were released in June 1796, some after eleven years of captivity.

The episode came to its end on February 22, 1797, when the House voted for still more appropriations, this time in the amount of approximately $350,000, for a total of Algiers expenditures in excess of $1.5 million.[65] In opening the session of Congress, Washington had said:

> After many delays and disappointments, arising out of the European war, the final arrangements for the fulfilling of the engagements made to the Dey and Regency of Algiers, will, in all present appearance, be crowned with success, but under great, though inevitable disadvantages in the pecuniary transactions, occasioned by that war, which will render a further provision necessary.[66]

The House resolved first to call for an accounting.[67] The president responded within a week, submitting to both Houses, "in confidence," detailed reports from the secretaries of state and treasury. On February 21, 1797, the House, after a secret debate on the appropriations, voted overwhelmingly that the injunction of secrecy imposed on the report be lifted and "that all future debates and proceedings thereon be had with open doors."[68] However, it exempted from publication an important letter detailing the matters of the additional frigate and payments made to various Algerine officials and an Algerine banker who had served as a go-between and financial broker.[69]

The United States' first encounter with hostage-taking had ended. The plight of the captives, merchant pressure, lack of a navy, geographical distance, and the European wars had forced the United States to behave in the same manner in which many, more important, European powers had behaved for a long time. When Jefferson, as president, faced the problem anew after the bashaw of Tripoli declared war in 1801, he sent the navy.[70] He justified his action as a training exercise, invoking an act of Congress passed during the last session of the Adams administration providing for a "Naval Peace Establishment."[71] Sending the navy helped to some extent. The bashaw, following the grounding of the frigate *Philadelphia,* captured more than 300 American seamen for whom the United States, as the result of a peace treaty in 1805, paid only $60,000 in ransom. That amount was much less than the $3 million originally demanded by the bashaw or the amount that was previously paid to Algiers.

Relations with Algiers began to sour once again in 1812. New hostages were taken. On February 23, 1815, Madison asked Congress for a declaration of war.[72] Congress responded on March 3, not with a formal declaration of war but with legislation authorizing the president to employ "such of the armed vessels of the United States as may be judged requisite."[73] This time it was the United States' turn to dictate a peace treaty to the dey on "unprecedented" terms.[74] When the dey reneged on that treaty, Madison, in his annual message on December 3, 1816, advised Congress that he would use naval force, if necessary.[75] The United States then compelled the dey, on December 23, to sign yet another treaty; however, given that the European powers had also become unwilling to put up with Barbary piracy, the treaty became more or less irrelevant.[76] In fact, it was forgotten in the State Department and not submitted by President Monroe for Senate ratification until December 1821.[77] In 1830 Algiers became part of the French colonial empire.

To say that the Algiers Episode is less well known than other foreign policy issues of the Washington administration would be an understatement. Because it did not generate the same partisan passions as the Neutrality Proclamation or the Jay Treaty, the episode has been largely ignored. The difficulties that it posed, however, were great and intractable. Precisely because it was relatively free of partisanship, it framed the questions concerning the distribution of powers in a more detached manner. In any event, Washington's actions surrounding his unilateral proclamation of neutrality (after France had declared war against England in 1793) and the Jay Treaty with England, concluded in 1795, displayed, by and large, the same constitutional circumspection that characterized his administration's conduct with respect to the Barbary Powers.[78]

The Constitution does not speak in such abstractions as *the* foreign affairs power or *the* war power. Nor, as the Washington administration addressed the Algiers problem, were these two powers thought of as meaningful. When Jefferson told Congress in 1790 that it had to decide "between war, tribute, and ransom,"[79] he said about the latter two that Congress had the duty to limit and provide the amount and that the executive had the duty "to make arrangements for employing it to the best advantage."[80] In context, he meant that negotiations and treaty drafts were the task of the executive department but that Congress shared responsibility and control through its power of the purse and the Senate through its treaty power.

As to Algiers, Washington sought advice,[81] and advice was rendered by the Senate, which set limits on the amount of ransom it would accept as the result of negotiations.[82] Although one may safely assume that informal discussions lay behind formal messages and resolutions, the administration did not proceed with negotiations without formal authority contained in Senate resolutions or congressional appropriations.[83] The instructions the administration unilaterally chose to give the commissioners were carefully framed in accordance with the stipulated monetary limitations.[84] To the extent that they were exceeded, it was because of the necessities faced by the negotiators. If Congress remained in the dark, so did the executive, due to the unsatisfactory communications system of the period. Yet the Senate's treaty functions were formally preserved by the appropriate treaty stipulations.[85]

The Washington administration did not always follow as strict a course of consultations as it did during the Algiers business.[86] It was quite conscious of the fact that occasionally the secrecy of diplomatic overtures was the condition of success. On the other hand, the extent to which the administration generally disclosed details of foreign negotiations to the Congress and to the public at large was remarkable and, indeed, it worried some political observers.[87] Frequently, Washington informed Congress literally by taking it into "his confidence," a mode of interaction that was subject to two limitations. On the one hand, the executive branch claimed the right to withhold information if even its limited publication would be against public interest.[88] On the other hand, the House eventually claimed the right to lift injunctions of secrecy.[89] Whether the practices of the government with respect to secrecy ran counter to the spirit of the Framers' plan and the demands of popular sovereignty is a difficult question.[90] Washington displayed awareness of these demands but was also troubled by "throwing too much into democratic hands."[91] On the whole, however, the administration seemed to be determined to achieve the highest possible degree of coordination for American policy toward Algiers and not only kept Congress informed but actually consulted it beforehand.

The shaping of governmental structures began in earnest in 1789 and, of course, has not concluded to this date. Precedents were set by the president and Congress in response to complex problems as they occurred and were influenced by earnest considerations of principles and practical considerations of statecraft but also, to be sure, by political considerations.[92] The process was helped initially by the relative absence of partisanship. It was also helped by the circumspection of Washington, who has found few matches among later presidents in the deliberateness with which he worried about what was right for the government as a whole rather than concentrating unduly on the powers of the presidency.

NOTES

This chapter has been excerpted from Gerhard Casper, "An Essay in Separation of Powers: Some Early Versions and Practices," *William and Mary Law Review* 30 (1989): 211–61.

1. *American State Papers: Foreign Relations,* ed. W. Lowrie and M. Clarke (Washington, D.C.: Gale and Seaton, 1832), 1:100.
2. For two detailed accounts of the Algiers episode, see R. W. Irwin, *The Diplomatic Relations of the United States with the Barbary Powers 1776–1816* (Chapel Hill: University of North Carolina Press, 1931), and H. G. Barnby, *The Prisoners of Algiers* (New York: Oxford University Press, 1966).
3. Irwin, *Diplomatic Relations,* p. 20 n. 153.
4. Ibid., pp. 28–33.
5. See *American State Papers: Foreign Relations,* 1:101.
6. *Annals of Cong. 1728* (1790), vol. 2.
7. Ibid., p. 1730.
8. *American State Papers: Foreign Relations,* 1:100 (emphasis added).
9. Prices ranged from $1,200 to $2,920 a man (see ibid., p. 101).
10. Ibid.
11. Ibid.
12. See list in *The Papers of Thomas Jefferson,* ed. J. Boyd, 25 vols. (Princeton: Princeton University Press, 1950–), 12:375 (editorial note).
13. Ibid., p. 404 (editorial note).
14. *American State Papers: Foreign Relations,* 1:104.
15. Ibid., p. 105.
16. In the end, the opinion turned out to be exceedingly accurate.
17. *American State Papers: Foreign Relations,* 1:105.
18. Ibid.
19. Ibid.
20. *The Papers of Thomas Jefferson,* 18:429–30 (editorial note).
21. Ibid., p. 410 (editorial note) and pp. 436–37.
22. E. Maclay, *The Journal of William Maclay,* 2d ed. (New York: Ungar Publishing, 1965), p. 353.
23. *American State Papers: Foreign Relations,* 1:108.
24. *The Papers of Thomas Jefferson,* 18:410 (editorial note).
25. *Annals of Cong.,* 2:1735.
26. *American State Papers: Foreign Relations,* 1:128.
27. An act making an appropriation for the purpose therein mentioned, 1 Stat. 214 (1791).
28. For a detailed account, see *The Papers of Thomas Jefferson,* 18:410–13 (editorial note).
29. Daniel Hoffman, *Governmental Secrecy and the Founding Fathers* (Westport, Conn.: Greenwood Press, 1981), pp. 68, 79. See also Chapter 12 of this volume.
30. *American State Papers: Foreign Relations,* 1:130.
31. Ibid., p. 133.
32. *The Complete Anas of Thomas Jefferson,* ed. F. Sawvel (New York: Round Table, 1903), pp. 63–64.

33. Ibid., pp. 72–73.

34. *American State Papers: Foreign Relations,* 1:136.

35. Ibid., p. 290; an act making certain appropriations therein mentioned, 1 Stat. 284–85 (1792).

36. See *American State Papers: Foreign Relations,* 1:288–300.

37. Ibid., p. 296.

38. Ibid., p. 288.

39. See the account in Hoffman, *Governmental Secrecy,* pp. 100–104.

40. *Annals of Cong.,* 4:154.

41. See Hoffman, *Governmental Secrecy,* p. 102.

42. See *American State Papers: Foreign Relations,* 1:413–23.

43. Irwin, *Diplomatic Relations,* p. 60.

44. See, e.g., *Annals of Cong.,* 4:481.

45. Irwin, *Diplomatic Relations,* p. 60.

46. *American State Papers: Foreign Relations,* 1:415.

47. An act providing the means of intercourse between the United States and foreign nations, 1 Stat. 128–29 (1790).

48. An act to continue in force for a limited time and to amend the act entitled "An Act providing the means of intercourse between the United States and foreign nations," 1 Stat. 299–300 (1793).

49. An act making further provision for the expenses attending the intercourse of the United States with foreign nations and further to continue in force the act entitled, "An act providing the means of intercourse between the United States and foreign nations," 1 Stat. 345 (1794).

50. Ibid.

51. See "An Act making Appropriations for the support of Government, for the year one thousand seven hundred and ninety four," 1 Stat. 342–45 (1794), and "An Act making appropriations for the support of the Military establishment of the United States, for the year one thousand seven hundred and ninety four," 1 Stat. 346–47 (1794).

52. *The Papers of James Madison,* ed. C. Hobson and R. Rutland (Charlottesville: University Press of Virginia, 1983–1991), 15:147 (editorial note).

53. Ibid., p. 249.

54. See ibid., p. 147 (editorial note).

55. An act to provide a naval armament, 1 Stat. 350–51 (1794).

56. Irwin, *Diplomatic Relations,* p. 66.

57. These frigates were the *United States,* the *Constitution,* and the *Constellation.*

58. Irwin, *Diplomatic Relations,* p. 79.

59. Ibid.

60. *American State Papers: Foreign Relations,* 1:532.

61. For the colorful details, see Barnby, *Prisoners of Algiers,* pp. 191–98.

62. *American State Papers: Foreign Relations,* 1:529–32.

63. Irwin, *Diplomatic Relations,* p. 74.

64. An act making further provision for the expenses attending the intercourse of the United States with foreign nations and to continue in force the act entitled "An act providing the means of intercourse between the United States and foreign nations," 1 Stat. 487–88 (1796).

65. *Annals of Cong.* (1797), 6:2245–46.

66. Ibid., p. 1764.

67. Ibid., pp. 1763–67.

68. Ibid., p. 2235.

69. Ibid., pp. 2235–45.

70. See Dumas Malone, *Jefferson and His Time,* 6 vols. (Boston: Little, Brown, 1948–1981), 5:37–49.

71. Abraham Sofaer, *War, Foreign Affairs, and Constitutional Power: The Origins* (Cambridge, Mass.: Ballinger, 1976), p. 210.

72. *Annals of Cong.* (1815), 28:269 (message of President Madison).

73. Ibid., p. 1943.

74. *American State Papers: Foreign Relations,* ed. W. Lowrie and W. Franklin (1834), vol. 4, and Irwin, *Diplomatic Relations,* pp. 176–86.

75. *Annals of Cong.* (1816), 30:13 (President Madison's annual message).

76. Irwin, *Diplomatic Relations,* p. 186.

77. *American State Papers: Foreign Relations,* ed. A. Dickens and J. Allen (1858), 5:133–34.

78. See Sofaer, *War, Foreign Affairs, and Constitutional Power,* pp. 103–16 (the Neutrality Proclamation), and pp. 85–93.

79. *American State Papers: Foreign Relations,* 1:105.

80. Ibid.

81. See text accompanying notes 8, 35.

82. See text accompanying notes 25–26, 35.

83. See text accompanying notes 27–28, 50.

84. See instruction to Jones, *American State Papers: Foreign Relations,* 1:290–92, and instructions to Humphreys, pp. 528–29.

85. See text following note 59.

86. See Sofaer, *War, Foreign Affairs, and Constitutional Power,* p. 96.

87. See Malone, *Jefferson,* 3:152, regarding Jefferson's disclosures as secretary of state.

88. See text accompanying note 13.

89. See text accompanying notes 39, 69.

90. Hoffman, *Governmental Secrecy,* p. 76.

91. See text accompanying notes 38 and 33 of this chapter and *Complete Anas of Thomas Jefferson,* p. 73.

92. For a similar assessment of relations between the judiciary and Congress, see Marcus and Van Tassel, "Judges and Legislators in the New Federal System, 1789–1800," in *Judges and Legislators: Toward Institutional Comity,* ed. R. Katzmann (Washington, D.C.: Brookings Institution, 1988), p. 31.

11

THE QUASI-WAR AND PRESIDENTIAL WARMAKING

DEAN ALFANGE, JR.

During the administration of John Adams, the United States engaged in an undeclared naval war with France—known commonly and, at least in the view of the navy, officially as the Quasi-War.[1] France, considering itself betrayed by American concessions to Great Britain in Jay's Treaty of 1795, undertook to prey upon and seize American merchant ships.[2] Following the humiliating treatment accorded to American envoys sent to France by President Adams in 1797 to negotiate a settlement to the disagreement, the United States, in 1798, determined to use force in response to the French spoliations.[3] The war that resulted involved numerous naval engagements and ship seizures on both sides,[4] and was finally ended by the Treaty of Mortefontaine in 1800.[5]

In addition to the fact that this was the first instance of military action against a foreign nation undertaken by the newly independent United States, there are at least two statements that may be made with certainty about this undeclared war. It was a war, and it was undeclared. If it were necessary to go beyond historical observation to confirm these assertions, it can be noted that the Supreme Court contemporaneously recognized the truth of the former and approved the constitutionality of the latter. In 1800 the Court unanimously acknowledged that by no other words could the relations between the two nations "be communicated, than by that of hostility or war."[6] Nor was the Court in any way perturbed by the absence of a formal declaration of war by Congress. None of the justices had the slightest doubt that "Congress is empowered to declare a general war, or Congress may wage a limited war."[7]

It is therefore perfectly proper to list this conflict among the instances in which the United States has engaged in military activity without a declaration of war, and its categorization as such in the various compilations of examples of presidential warmaking put together at the time of the Vietnam War in an effort to justify American involvement is unexceptionable.[8] But to characterize it as an undeclared war is not to impugn its constitutional validity. As was expressly recognized by the Supreme Court in 1800, and as was obviously taken for granted by Congress in providing authorization for the Persian Gulf War in 1991,[9] Congress may constitutionally authorize offensive military action by means other than a declaration of war.[10] However, in 1966, the Office of the Legal Adviser of the Department of State incautiously described the Quasi-War as the first among "at least 125 instances in which the President has ordered the armed forces to take action or maintain positions abroad without obtaining prior Congressional authorization."[11] There is a vast difference between an undeclared war and a war undertaken by the president "without obtaining prior Congressional authorization," and the failure of the legal adviser to heed that distinction left the assertion exposed to devastating criticism. Given such a golden opportunity, Francis Wormuth was able to produce copious evidence to disprove the claim,[12] and he concluded that the assertion was "altogether false. The fact is that President Adams took absolutely no independent action."[13]

Wormuth was able to cite no fewer than twenty-four acts of Congress passed between March 1798 and March 1799, which provided for arming ships, capturing armed French vessels, raising troops, acquiring ships of war, creating a Department of the Navy, establishing a Marine Corps, and suspending commercial intercourse and abrogating treaties of alliance with France.[14] The fact is that Congress and the public were outraged by the treatment accorded to the American envoys to France, Elbridge Gerry, John Marshall, and Charles Cotesworth Pinckney, in the XYZ affair of 1797, in which bribes and huge loans were demanded as a precondition to any negotiations over the French spoliations.[15] Once Adams turned over to Congress the dispatches from the envoys describing their treatment, American honor was seen to be at stake, and the opposition in Congress to a hostile response to the French depredations was quickly reduced to insignificance.[16] The public cry became "millions for defense, but not one cent for tribute," and Congress acted accordingly.[17] In addition to agreeing to a substantial enlargement of American armed forces, it gave authority for broad-ranging hostile actions against France, short of declaring war or approving offensive measures against unarmed French ships or private property.

For example, on May 28, 1798, Congress authorized the president to "direct the commanders of the armed vessels belonging to the United States" to capture any "armed vessel which shall have committed or which shall be found hovering on the coasts of the United States, for the purpose of committing depredations on the vessels belonging to the citizens thereof."[18] On June

25, it authorized American ships to use arms to "repel by force" any attack by a ship acting under French orders and to "subdue and capture the same," this authority to cease whenever the government of France should end "the lawless depredations and outrages hitherto encouraged and authorized by that government against the merchant vessel[s] of the United States."[19] On July 9, it authorized the president to allow the navy to "subdue, seize and take any armed French vessel," not only when it was "found hovering on the coasts of the United States" but also "elsewhere, on the high seas,"[20] whether or not it was engaged in depredations against American ships, and to take into custody "all French persons and others, who shall be found acting on board."[21] Prior to the passage of the first of these acts, the navy was restricted to defensive actions and the protection of the territorial waters of the United States,[22] but, as soon as the act of May 28 authorizing seizures became law, "express riders and dispatch boats rushed new instructions to American warships."[23] Any claim that John Adams undertook the Quasi-War "without obtaining prior Congressional authorization" thus cannot bear serious scrutiny. Over 100 years afterward, Adams's great-grandson was to write that "in regard to the policy of arming, the President and Congress were agreed."[24]

But in declaring that the State Department's statement was "altogether false" and that "President Adams took absolutely no independent action," Wormuth overstated his case. The Jeffersonian Republicans, who were keenly desirous of maintaining amity with France, understandably regarded one of the president's independent actions as constituting a unilateral act of belligerency.[25] The events leading up to that action may be briefly summarized. On April 8, 1797, shortly after Adams's inauguration, Secretary of the Treasury Oliver Wolcott had issued a circular of instructions to collectors of the Customs in the ports of the United States to outline the policy that was to be followed with regard to the arming of merchant vessels in light of the "depredations, to which the commerce of the United States is at present exposed."[26] The circular held the nation to the course of peace. It authorized continuation of the practice of arming vessels bound for the East Indies where pirates were likely to be encountered because "no doubt is entertained, that defence, by means of Military force, against mere Pirates and Sea Rovers, is lawful." Yet "as the arming of Vessels destined for European or West India commerce raises a presumption, that it is done with hostile intentions against some one of the belligerent Nations," the sailing of armed ships to these destinations was to "be restrained, until otherwise ordained by Congress."[27]

Congress chose not to ordain otherwise for over a year. In the meantime, the nation remained deeply divided over how to respond to the French provocations. James Monroe, American minister to France at the time of Jay's

Treaty and a Republican who sympathized with the French revolutionary cause and who was at odds with the Federalist administration over the wisdom of the treaty and over the administration's policy of coolness toward France, had been, to the consternation of the French, recalled by President Washington, who then dispatched Charles Cotesworth Pinckney as his replacement.[28] The Directory refused to receive Pinckney, threatened to arrest him, and ordered him from the country.[29] When news of this reached the new president, he was advised not to take any steps toward war without making a further attempt to reestablish amicable relations with France.[30] Heeding this advice, Adams determined to appoint a commission to seek a negotiated settlement,[31] ultimately choosing Gerry, Marshall, and Pinckney as its members.[32] He also called Congress into special session, however, and on May 16, 1797, only a month after the issuance of Secretary Wolcott's circular, asked for authority to arm merchant ships for self-defense, allow convoying of unarmed shipping, provide artillery and cavalry for the protection of sea ports, recruit a provisional army, and enhance the preparedness of the militia.[33] The Republicans were angered by what they regarded as the warlike implications of the requests, and the special session did little besides authorize completion of the construction of three warships already approved, improvement of coastal fortifications, and the provision of arms for the militia.[34]

When Congress reconvened in November, it continued to mark time pending word of the outcome of the negotiations undertaken by the commissioners, who had gathered in France in the preceding month. Adams repeated his call for adoption of "those precautionary measures" that he had recommended in May,[35] but Republican opposition in the House was still ample to preclude any action to implement the recommendations.[36] The first messages from the commissioners reporting the failure of their mission and the nature of the treatment they had received arrived in the United States on March 4, 1798, and were decoded over the next several days.[37] It was at this point that Adams took the action that can be described as tending to commit the nation to war "without obtaining prior Congressional authorization." On March 19, after the messages had been deciphered but before they had been disclosed to Congress (except for one that had not been sent in code),[38] the president sent a message to Congress stating that the dispatches had "been examined and maturely considered" and that they demonstrated that the mission had failed.[39] Then, in addition to urging Congress promptly to adopt the measures for military preparedness and self-defense that he had previously recommended, he announced that he was rescinding the instructions in Secretary Wolcott's circular of the year before that prohibited the arming of merchant ships sailing to European and West Indian destinations:

The present state of things is so essentially different from that in which instructions were given to collectors to restrain vessels of the United States from sailing in an armed condition that the principle on which those orders were issued, has ceased to exist. I therefore deem it proper to inform Congress, that I no longer conceive myself justifiable in continuing them.[40]

Those two sentences provide the sole basis for the claim that the Quasi-War provides a precedent for later presidential assertions of the authority to commit the United States to war "without the authority of Congress," and thus their import needs to be evaluated to determine what inferences may properly be drawn from them in this regard.[41] Initially, it is to be noted that Adams did no more than decline to continue in force an order issued by his administration, and, at first glance, it might seem difficult to argue that the president is without power to rescind instructions given under his authority. But, of course, if the earlier order had decreed the maintenance of a state of affairs that the president were without power to change, he could not validly effect the change by rescinding the order. Thus, in the absence of any congressional action to the contrary, the president may always proclaim that the United States is at peace with another nation and direct the armed forces to refrain from any acts of hostility toward that nation. Revocation of such instruction would merely be presidential discontinuance of a presidential order, but since the president is without power to order hostile action unilaterally, he cannot gain that power by the simple expedient of forbidding such action and then withdrawing the prohibition.

It would appear from the violence of the Republican reaction to the discontinuance of Secretary Wolcott's order against the arming of merchant ships that they believed that Adams could be initiating war by just such a process. Vice-President Jefferson urged in a letter to James Madison that, in view of the president's "insane message" declaring that "he has withdrawn the Executive prohibition to arm, the Congress should pass a legislative one."[42] Madison agreed but expressed doubt "that the Constitutional party in the H. of R. is strong eno' [to] do what ought to be done in the present instance."[43] It was clear to Madison that the president had exceeded his constitutional authority, and he wanted Adams to be called to account and required "to declare on what ground he undertook to grant an indirect licence to arm." In his view, the secretary had the power to issue the original order because that order was "in pursuance of the law of Nations, & consequently in execution of the law of the land," but its revocation was "a virtual change of the law, & consequently a Usurpation by the Ex. of a legislative power."[44]

This important constitutional issue was quickly mooted. After the House of Representatives called for the president to turn over to Congress the decoded dispatches from the commissioners in an overwhelming vote in which the Republicans, following Madison's advice to "insist on a full communication of the intelligence on which such measures are recommended,"[45] were joined by hard-line Federalists, who had a good idea of what those dispatches contained and of what the likely effect of their disclosure would be,[46] Adams promptly complied.[47] With their subsequent publication, the temper of both the public and the Congress shifted dramatically in favor of the president's policy of arming against the French.[48] Thereupon, Congress rapidly acted to augment the nation's capacity to fight a war and to authorize the use of force, both defensive and offensive, against armed French ships.[49]

But disregarding the mootness of the issue in the context of the Quasi-War, was Adams's March 19 announcement within the scope of his constitutional authority as president, or did it usurp Congress' responsibility to declare war? There is substantial justification for Madison's claim that Secretary Wolcott's 1797 order was consonant with international law while Adams's rescission was an "indirect licence" for its violation. France and England were at war. Under recognized rules of international law, ships of belligerent nations had the right to stop and search neutral ships on the high seas to ensure that they were not carrying contraband in aid of their enemy and to seize cargoes and ships as prizes of war where violations were discovered.[50] John Marshall has stated for the Supreme Court that "this is a belligerent right, which cannot be drawn into question."[51] As pointed out by Gen. Henry Halleck in his comprehensive nineteenth-century treatise on international law, "The *right* of search on the one side, implies the *duty* of submission on the other; and as the belligerent may lawfully apply his force to the neutral property, for the purpose of ascertaining its character and destination, it necessarily follows that the neutral may not lawfully resist the lawful exercise of the right of search."[52] The revocation of the prohibition against the arming of merchant ships could imply that this duty of submission to searches by belligerents was no longer to be respected, and, as Secretary Wolcott correctly stated in his initial instructions, could "[raise] a presumption, that it is done with hostile intentions."

Thus, by the revocation of this order, Adams could be seen as indirectly authorizing vessels sailing under the American flag to use force to resist the lawful actions of another nation. At least to the extent that it was inconsistent with international law, such resistance would be armed interference with the lawful military actions of a nation at war, and consequently an act of belligerency. But it is clear that Adams did not perceive himself as authorizing resistance to searches that were valid under international law. In his speech to the special session of Congress in the preceding May, he explained that he had prohibited the arming of merchant ships (except those whose voyages to the East Indies were endangered by pirates) to ensure the preservation of American neutrality and "not from any doubt entertained by me of the policy and propriety of permitting our vessels to employ means of defence, while engaged in a lawful foreign commerce."[53] Arming, therefore, was called for, not to prevent France from validly searching ships for contraband but for the defense of ships "engaged in a lawful foreign commerce," the searches and seizures of which were being carried out not to vindicate the proper rights of a belligerent under international law but solely for the purpose of demonstrating French discontent with American foreign policy. If Adams genuinely believed that the French depredations were hostile acts rather than the legitimate actions of a belligerent (and there is no evidence to indicate otherwise), his unilateral authorization for the arming of merchant vessels in March 1798 is entirely defensible as an appropriate measure for carrying out the president's constitutional responsibility to repel foreign attacks on the United States. It is well known that, at the Constitutional Convention, language that would have vested in Congress the power to "make war" was changed to "declare war" so that the president would be free to respond to sudden attacks without first having to obtain congressional approval.[54] Military force may thus be constitutionally employed by the president when the territory of the United States is attacked, and, if the possibility of an attack is perceived, there should be no constitutional obstacle to presidential action to ready the armed forces and to deploy them so that they will be in a position to meet it. Indeed, the Supreme Court has ruled that "the power to provide for repelling invasions includes the power to provide against the attempt and danger of invasion, as the necessary and proper means to effectuate the object. One of the best means to repel invasions is to provide the requisite force for action, before the invader himself has reached the soil."[55] An attack on an American ship is equivalent to an attack on American territory since "every merchant vessel on the high seas is regarded, in international law, as a part of the territory of the state to which it belongs," and, therefore, just as the president may ensure the readiness of troops who are facing a potential invasion, he may ensure that American vessels are prepared to defend themselves in the event of an unlawful attempt to seize them.[56] Thus, Adams's action, insofar as it was purely defensive in nature, was a constitutionally valid exercise of the president's power as commander-in-chief to repel actual attacks (whether sudden or anticipated should not matter) on the United States. It certainly provides no precedent for a claim of presidential prerogative to commit the United States to war without congressional authorization. Adams made absolutely no claim of a general presidential power to initiate hostilities. His authority to act was derived entirely from the need to provide American ships with the means to defend themselves against hostile attacks by a foreign power.

Nevertheless, although Adams's order fell within the range of actions that the president should constitutionally be able to take on his own initiative, the dismay of the Republicans at the issuance of the order is entirely understandable, not merely because even those military actions taken in self-defense necessarily exacerbate a conflict and make the restoration of peace more difficult, but because, once it is conceded that unilateral presidential defensive warmaking is constitutional, a risk of unilateral presidential offensive warmaking is created.[57] An assertion of the need for self-defense can be used as a pretext for the initiation of hostilities or for provocation of the very attack supposedly being guarded against.[58] Thus, if France had not been engaged in hostile harassment of American shipping but were merely seeking to ensure that contraband of war was not reaching its enemy, then the arming of merchant vessels to prevent French searches and seizures would not, in fact, have been a defensive measure but a hostile act quite likely to lead to American involvement in war—precisely the type of action that the president should have no power to order except on the specific authority of Congress. Moreover, even where self-defense is genuinely the basis for presidential action, there is a strong danger either that the urgency of the situation will make offensive action appear to be the proper course, on the theory—expressed in the maxim that "a good offense is the best defense"—that self-protection requires not merely repelling attacks that have actually occurred but also striking at the forces from which an attack is feared before any attack takes place, or that the preparation for effective self-defense will be misperceived as a threat of offensive action and thereby provoke an attack that otherwise might not have occurred.[59]

Prior to World War I, Woodrow Wilson faced a need for unilateral issuance of an order for the arming of merchant ships, analogous to Adams's, after Germany announced a policy of unrestricted submarine warfare against neutral as well as enemy commerce in certain specified zones, and some American ships had been sunk.[60] Wilson's experience demonstrates the danger that a recognized need for defense will generate a pressure to employ such offensive action as is necessary to make defensive measures effective. On February 26, 1917, Wilson, although of the opinion that he could, on his own authority, order the arming of merchant ships for self-defense "by the plain implication of my constitutional duties and powers," prudently asked Congress to institute a policy of "armed neutrality" by authorizing him "to supply our merchant ships with defensive arms, should that become necessary, and with the means of using them."[61] Although an overwhelming majority of Congress favored adoption of such a policy, eleven or twelve senators, anxious to avoid any action likely to lead to war—Wilson was to term them "a little group of willful men, representing no opinion but their own"[62]—undertook a successful filibuster to block Senate action prior to the adjournment of Congress.[63] Thereupon Wilson, like Adams, issued an order to arm without congressional authorization.[64] However, Wilson's order also authorized the armed ships to fire upon any approaching German submarine in a zone in which submarines had been directed to sink neutral vessels even before it launched an attack.[65] When, on April 2, 1917, Wilson asked Congress for a declaration of war, he explained that he had by then concluded that a policy of armed neutrality was "impracticable" as a means of maintaining defense but avoiding war. Although such a policy was feasible in an era when ships had only to "defend themselves against privateers or cruiser, visible craft giving chase upon the open sea," it is "worse than ineffectual" when the threat comes from submarines. Against submarines, attack—creating the likelihood of war, as Wilson fully recognized—is, he declared, the only possible defense since submarines "must be dealt with upon sight, if dealt with at all."[66]

But no matter how blurred the line between defense and offense may be, and no matter how great the pressure may be to employ offensive action in the name of self-defense, it is essential that, for the purpose of defining the constitutional limits on the president's power, the attempt to maintain that critical distinction not be abandoned. When the actions that are seen as needed for defensive purposes involve the offensive use of military force or the deployment of troops in a manner quite likely to provoke an attack upon them, the president's claim of constitutional authority to act on his own must be regarded as dubious at best. The importance of the distinction for determining the scope of presidential power has been recognized by the armed forces. In 1940, the judge advocate general of the U.S. Army, responding to a congressional query, properly stated that the president's authority as commander-in-chief to deploy and use the military extends only to the point beyond which "an intended use would constitute an initiation or declaration of war by the President, if carried through."[67]

Failure to respect the line between purely defensive actions and offensive actions that may be undertaken for defensive purposes can lead to remarkable conclusions regarding what the president may constitutionally do in the interest of self-defense. For example, Abraham Sofaer was able to infer from the president's undoubted power to repel sudden attacks a derivative power "to prevent attacks before they actually occur."[68] That is a disturbing proposition. Of course, the problem may simply lie in a poor choice of words. If by "prevent attacks," Sofaer merely meant "guard against" attacks, his inference is unexceptionable, and it describes the principal constitutional justification for John Adams's order authorizing the arming of merchant vessels. But the word "prevent" connotes more than that. The most direct way "to prevent attacks before they actually occur" is to disable the attacker, which means attacking first. Therefore, if Sofaer meant what he said, he managed the impressive logical feat of extrapolating a presidential power to initiate a preemptive strike against a foreign nation, without the need for congressional authorization, from the power to repel sudden attacks against the United States.

It is difficult to believe that one could seriously subscribe to the idea that, for purposes of determining the constitutional locus of the authority to commit the nation to war, the power to attack is to be equated with the power to defend. It would seem particularly difficult to make that argument in light of the devastating critique leveled at it in the oft-quoted letter of Abraham Lincoln to William Herndon in 1848. The letter was written specifically and solely to repudiate the position that one fears Sofaer may have been espousing, as Lincoln feared that Herndon was espousing it—viz., "that if it shall become necessary to repel invasion, the President may, without violation of the Constitution, cross the line and invade the territory of another country, and that whether such necessity exists in any given case the President is the sole judge."[69] Herndon had expressed disagreement with Lincoln's vote in the House of Representatives in January 1848 in favor of an amendment to insert in a resolution of thanks to Gen. Zachary Taylor for his achievements in the Mexican War a declaration that the war had been "unnecessarily and unconstitutionally begun by the President of the United States."[70] Following the annexation of Texas, the territory between the Nueces River and the Rio Grande remained in dispute between the United States and Mexico, and President Polk ordered troops into the disputed territory with authority to enter Mexico if their presence met with military resistance.[71] Lincoln saw this as a clear abuse of presidential authority. As he explained to Herndon:

Allow the President to invade a neighboring nation whenever he shall deem it necessary to repel an invasion, and you allow him to do so whenever he may choose to say he deems it necessary for such purpose, and you allow him to make war at pleasure. Study to see if you can fix any limit to his power in this respect, after you have given him so much as you propose. If to-day he should choose to say he thinks it necessary to invade Canada to prevent the British from invading us, how could you stop him? You may say to him, "I see no probability of the British invading us"; but he will say to you, "Be silent. I see it, if you don't."[72]

There have been numerous instances in American history of invasions uni-laterally ordered by the president, usually for the declared purpose of protect-ing American lives and property from the danger of violence, and, if these actions are short and successful, they are likely to be political as well as military triumphs.[73] But it is difficult to see how they can be defended as constitutional except on the theory that emergency must be allowed to determine constitu-tionality. As Lincoln saw so clearly, since the president acts in such circum-stances without the support of congressional authorization, it is left entirely to his discretion to determine when military action is warranted and also to determine the degree of force to be employed. If, therefore, presidential power to invade a foreign nation for reasons of self-defense or the protection of citizens is accepted as constitutional, there can be no practicable limits to presidential warmaking authority in such a context except those that are wholly self-imposed. When John Adams took the relatively mild and consti-tutionally defensible step of authorizing on his own the arming of merchant ships in the face of French depredations, James Madison responded with alarm. He saw serious constitutional objections to a process that promised to lead to the concession of warmaking authority to the president—objections that now seem prophetic in light of twentieth-century developments.[74] "The constitution supposes," Madison observed, "that the Ex[ecutive] is the branch of power most interested in war, & most prone to it. . . . But the Doc-trines lately advanced . . . will deposit the peace of the Country in that De-partment which the Constitution distrusts as most ready, without cause, to renounce it."[75]

Yet in contrast to the actions of James Polk and, arguably, of Woodrow Wilson, John Adams did not use the need for self-defense in the Quasi-War as a basis for authorizing offensive actions without congressional approval. His sole independent act providing for the use of force authorized no offensive ac-tivity and sanctioned only an armed defense against unlawful attacks. The power to ensure that American territory or American ships on the high seas can adequately be defended against invasion or attack is doubtlessly within the constitutional authority of the president, with or without prior congressional approval, provided only that it not be used as a pretext for the unauthorized initiation of hostilities. Because John Adams did not exceed his constitutional powers, the Quasi-War belongs on no list of instances in which the president unilaterally ordered American forces to commence military activity.

In fact, the Quasi-War, far from being a precedent to support the claim that the president's constitutional powers allow him to undertake hostile action whenever he deems it necessary, provides impressive evidence of the broad rec-ognition by the very persons who were participants in the drafting and ratifying of the Constitution that the president has no such power. This recognition was expressed not only by Jefferson and Madison and other Republican opponents of the war but also by leading Federalists, including Adams and Hamilton and the federal judiciary. Adams may have authorized arming for self-defense, but it is the responsibility of Congress "to prescribe such regulations as will enable our seafaring citizens to defend themselves against violations of the law of nations."[76] Even so strong an advocate of executive power as Alexander Hamilton, when asked by Secretary of War James McHenry, prior to the passage of the act of May 28, 1798, in which Congress authorized the navy to seize armed ships "hovering on the coasts,"[77] as to what instructions should be given to the captains of the newly acquired ships of the fleet who might encounter French privateers or French warships, in light of the need to "preserve the Executive from any future accusation, of having by its orders involved the country in war," advised that the administration should act with circumspection.[78] Because the president would be acting solely on the basis of his constitutional power and without the authority of an act of Congress, Hamilton replied that he was "not ready to say that [the President] has any other power than merely to employ the Ships as Convoys with authority to *repel* force by *force,* (but not to capture). . . . Any thing beyond this must fall under the idea of *reprisals* & requires the sanction of that Department which is to declare or make war."[79] McHenry's instructions to the captain of the first ship to put to sea constrained him to limit his ship's actions to those necessary for "the Prevention of Violations of our jurisdictional Rights and to Self-defence," because, as the secretary explained, "Congress possess exclusively the Power to declare War, grant Letters of Marque & Reprisal, and make Rules concerning Captures on Land and Water, and . . . neither has yet been done."[80]

Cases growing out of the Quasi-War that reached the Supreme Court provided an opportunity for the justices to make equally unambiguous pronouncements concerning the constitutional locus of warmaking authority. In the 1801 case *The Amelia,* John Marshall, one of the three envoys who had been spurned by France in the XYZ affair, declared for a unanimous Court that "the whole powers of war [were] by the constitution of the United States, vested in Congress."[81] And, in *The Flying Fish,* Marshall, again for a unanimous Court, held that whatever the president's inherent authority may be to determine military policy in the absence of express congressional directives, where such express directives exist, the president cannot order military activity that exceeds the authority that they grant.[82]

In short, for the purpose of determining the constitutional legitimacy of the executive department's exercise of the power to initiate war, the historical significance of the Quasi-War is not that it represents the first instance in which the president chose to disregard Congress and unilaterally to order the armed forces into combat, for it was not an instance of that at all. Rather, its significance is that it quite clearly demonstrates that, at a time essentially contemporaneous with the adoption of the Constitution, both Congress and the administration, Republicans and Federalists alike, fully recognized and understood the distinction articulated and affirmed by the Supreme Court between "that department which is entrusted with foreign intercourse, and . . . that which is invested with the powers of war."[83]

NOTES

1. See, e.g., Alexander DeConde, *The Quasi-War* (New York: Charles Scribner's Sons, 1966), and Navy Department, *Naval Documents Related to the Quasi-War Between the United States and France,* 7 vols. (Washington, D.C.: Government Printing Office, 1935–1938).

2. See Brooks Adams, "The Convention of 1800 with France," *Massachusetts Historical Society Proceedings* 44, (1911): 395. On Jay's Treaty, see, generally, Samuel Flagg Bemis, *Jay's Treaty* (New York: Macmillan, 1923).

3. See, generally, William C. Stinchcombe, *The XYZ Affair* (Westport, Conn.: Greenwood Press, 1980).

4. See, generally, *Naval Documents;* Gardner Allen, *Our Naval War with France* (Boston: Houghton Mifflin Company, 1909); Michael A. Palmer, *Stoddert's War* (Columbia: University of South Carolina Press, 1987); De Conde, *Quasi-War,* pp. 124–30.

5. See Allen, *Our Naval War,* pp. 245–51, and De Conde, *Quasi-War,* pp. 223–58.

6. *The Eliza* (alternate title *Bas v. Tingy*), 4 Dallas (4 U.S.) 37,38 (1800) (opinion of Moore, J.).

7. Ibid., p. 43 (opinion of Chase, J.).

8. See, e.g., J. Terry Emerson, "War Powers Legislation," *West Virginia Law Review* 74 (1971): 88, where the Quasi-War is listed at the top of a list of 192 instances of American foreign military engagements without a declaration of war. The list expanded to 197 by the following year—see J. Terry Emerson, "War Powers Legislation, an Addendum," *West Virginia Law Review* 75 (1972): 367—and to 199 by 1973 when a revised list was inserted into the Congressional Record by Sen. Barry Goldwater (119 *Cong. Rec.,* 93d Cong., 1st sess., 1973, pp. 25066–76). A 1967 study prepared by the State Department provided a similar list, identifying 137 instances, on which the Quasi-War was, chronologically, at the top (Department of State, *Armed Actions Taken by the United States Without a Declaration of War, 1789–1967* [1967]). An earlier State Department count put the number at "at least 125," starting with the Quasi-War (see text at note 11 of this chapter). As noted in a report prepared by the Foreign Affairs Division of the Legislative Reference Service (which provided its own summary): "The differences in numbers . . . reflect differences in individual interpretations" (U.S. House of Representatives, Committee on Foreign Affairs, *Background Information on*

the Use of *United States Armed Forces in Foreign Countries* [91st Cong., 2d sess., 1970], p. 15). The Quasi-War also appears first on the list prepared by the Legislative Reference Service.

9. Authorization for Use of Military Force Against Iraq, Pub. L. 102–1 (102d Cong., 1st sess., 1991); 105 Stat. 3. Section 2 (a) reads: "The President is authorized . . . to use United States Armed Forces pursuant to United Nations Security Council Resolution 678 (1990) in order to achieve implementation of Security Council Resolutions 660, 661, 662, 664, 665, 666, 667, 669, 670, 674, and 677.

10. In a 1967 report rejecting any claim of the president to independent warmaking authority, the Senate Committee on Foreign Relations, then chaired by Sen. J. William Fulbright, stated that it did "not believe that formal declarations of war are the only available means by which Congress can authorize the President to initiate limited or general hostilities. Joint resolutions . . . are a proper method of granting authority, provided that they are precise as to what is to be done and for what period of time, and provided that they do in fact *grant authority* and not merely express approval of undefined action to be taken by the President" (S. Rept. no. 797, 90th Cong., 1st sess., 1967, p. 25 [emphasis is in original]).

11. Department of State, Office of the Legal Adviser, *The Legality of United States Participation in the Defense of Viet Nam,* reprinted in *Yale Law Journal* 75 (1966): 1101.

12. Francis D. Wormuth, "The Vietnam War: The President Versus the Constitution," in *The Vietnam War and International Law,* ed. Richard A. Falk (Princeton, N.J.: Princeton University Press, 1969), 2:718–723.

13. Ibid., p. 718.

14. Ibid., pp. 718–19.

15. See DeConde, *Quasi-War,* pp. 8–80.

16. Ibid., pp. 89–92. Of the twenty-four statutes identified by Professor Wormuth (see "Vietnam War," 718–19), only one predated President Adams's disclosure to Congress of the contents of the XYZ dispatches on April 3, 1798. That was an act of March 27, 1798, providing an appropriation for completing the construction and the equipping of the frigates *United States, Constitution,* and *Constellation* and providing the funds for paying the crews and the expenses of maintenance and operation (1 Stat. 547). The remainder of the statutes on Professor Wormuth's list were enacted after disclosure of the documents.

17. The phrase was ascribed, apocryphally, to Charles Cotesworth Pinckney, one of the three American envoys. Pinckney later explained that what he had in fact said when they were asked to pay a bribe as a prerequisite for negotiations was "Not a sixpence!" But he saw no particular reason to disclaim utterance of a phrase that has become part of American legend. See Marvin R. Zahniser, *Charles Cotesworth Pinckney* (Chapel Hill: University of North Carolina Press, 1967), p. 170 n.10.

18. 1 Stat. 561.

19. 1 Stat. 572.

20. 1 Stat. 578.

21. 1 Stat. 578, 580.

22. See text at note 80 of this chapter.

23. Palmer, *Stoddert's War,* p. 16.

24. Adams, "Convention," p. 401.

25. See, e.g., Dumas Malone, *Jefferson and His Time* (Boston: Little, Brown, 1948–1981), 3:312–16.

26. *Naval Operations from February 1797 to October 1798, Naval Documents,* p. 4.

27. Ibid., p. 5.

28. See Harry Ammon, *James Monroe: The Quest for National Identity* (New York: McGraw-Hill Book Company, 1971), pp. 141–56.

29. Zahniser, *Pinckney,* pp. 142–47.

30. Page Smith, *John Adams* (Garden City, N.Y.: Doubleday and Company, 1962), 2:924.

31. DeConde, *Quasi-War,* pp. 16–23.

32. Ibid., pp. 28–30.

33. Charles Francis Adams, ed., *The Works of John Adams* (Boston: Little, Brown and Company, 1850–1856), 9:111–19.

34. DeConde, *Quasi-War,* pp. 30–31.

35. Adams, ed., *Works of John Adams,* 9:122.

36. See Manning J. Dauer, *The Adams Federalists* (Baltimore: Johns Hopkins University Press, 1953), pp. 137–38.

37. DeConde, *Quasi-War,* pp. 66–67.

38. Adams, ed., *Works of John Adams,* 9:156.

39. Ibid., pp. 156–57.

40. Ibid., p. 157.

41. See, e.g., J. Terry Emerson, "The War Powers Resolution Tested: The President's Independent Defense Power," *Notre Dame Lawyer* 51 (1975): 196–97: "On March 19, 1798, [Adams] issued an order, without the authority of Congress, allowing American merchant vessels to arm for defense against attacks by French warships. . . . His action was promptly questioned by Congress on the ground that if the President could take the measures which he had taken, 'he, and not Congress, had the power of making war.' "

42. Robert A. Rutland et al., eds., *The Papers of James Madison* (Charlottesville: University Press of Virginia, 1983–1991), 17:99.

43. Ibid., p. 105.

44. Ibid., p. 104. See also Abraham D. Sofaer, *War, Foreign Affairs, and Constitutional Power: The Origins* (Cambridge, Mass.: Ballinger Publishing Company, 1976), 1:143 n.

45. Rutland et al., eds., *Papers of James Madison,* 17:104.

46. See Dauer, *Adams Federalists,* pp. 141–42; for a breakdown of the voting on this request by individual members of the House, see pp. 306–9.

47. Adams, ed., *Works of John Adams,* 9:158.

48. DeConde, *Quasi-War,* pp. 72–76; Sofaer, *War,* 1:144; Malone, *Jefferson,* 3:371–74.

49. Wormuth, "Vietnam War," pp. 718–19. See note 16 and text at notes 14–24 of this chapter.

50. See Henry W. Halleck, *International Law* (San Francisco: H. H. Bancroft and Company, 1861), pp. 569–71, 606–10.

51. *The Anna Maria,* 2 Wheaton (15 U.S.) 327, 332 (1817).

52. Halleck, *International Law,* p. 609 (emphasis in original).

53. Adams, ed., *Works of John Adams,* 9:116.

54. See James Madison, *Notes of Debates in the Federal Convention of 1787* (Athens: Ohio University Press, 1966), p. 476. See also the discussion of the debate pertaining to this textual change in W. Taylor Reveley III, *War Powers of the President and Congress* (Charlottesville: University Press of Virginia, 1981), pp. 81–85; David Gray Adler, "The Constitution and Presidential Warmaking," *Political Science Quarterly*, 103 (1988): 4–5; and Wormuth, "Vietnam War," pp. 713–15.

55. *Martin v. Mott*, 12 Wheaton (25 U.S.) 19, 29 (1827). In this case, the Court unanimously upheld an act of Congress enacted February 28, 1795, which authorized the president, when there was an invasion or an imminent danger of invasion, to call up state militias in "such number . . . as he may judge necessary to repel such invasion" (1 Stat. 424).

56. Halleck, *International Law*, p. 592.

57. See text at note 75 of this chapter.

58. See Note, "Congress, the President, and the Power to Commit Forces to Combat," *Harvard Law Review* 81(1968): 1776–87.

59. Ibid., pp. 1785–87.

60. See Ray Stannard Baker, *Woodrow Wilson: Life and Letters* (New York: Doubleday, Doran and Company, 1927–1939), 6:444–60.

61. 54 *Cong. Rec.*, 64th Cong., 2d sess., 1917, p. 4273.

62. Ray Stannard Baker and William E. Dodd, eds., *The Public Papers of Woodrow Wilson* (New York: Harper and Brothers, 1925–1927), 4:435.

63. See Baker, *Wilson*, pp. 479–82.

64. The issuance of the order was announced on March 12, 1917, in a memorandum to all foreign embassies and legations. See Department of State, *Policy of the United States Toward Maritime Commerce in War* (1914–1918), 2:581 (1936).

65. Ibid., p. 582.

66. 55 *Cong. Rec.*, 65th Cong., 1st sess., 1917, p. 103.

67. Memorandum of the judge advocate general to the adjutant general, U.S. Army, June 17, 1940, quoted in U.S. House, *Background Information*, p. 23.

68. Testimony of Abraham D. Sofaer, in U.S. Senate, *War Powers Resolution, Hearings Before the Committee on Foreign Relations*, 95th Cong., 1st sess., 1977, p. 86.

69. Arthur B. Lapsley, ed., *The Writings of Abraham Lincoln* (New York: G. P. Putnam's Sons, 1905–1906), 2:51. There is an ambiguity in Lincoln's use of the word "repel," as there is in Sofaer's use of the word "prevent" (see text following note 68 of this chapter). The word could be understood as meaning that Lincoln was referring to an American invasion of a foreign nation undertaken as a defensive response to an invasion of American territory that had already taken place and needed to be "repelled." Fortunately, Lincoln dispelled any ambiguity by his hypothetical example of a possible British invasion from Canada (see text at note 72 of this chapter, in which it is clear that he is speaking of a preemptive response to a feared invasion that has not in fact occurred). Interestingly, in describing the hypothetical preemptive invasion, Lincoln uses Professor Sofaer's word, "prevent." The invasion of Canada would be "to prevent the British from invading us" (p. 51).

70. *Congressional Globe*, 30th Cong., 1st sess., 1848, p. 95. The amendment carried, 85 to 81. Lincoln's speech in defense of his vote appears in *Appendix to the Congressional Globe*, 30th Cong., 1st sess., 1847–48, pp. 93–95, and in Lapsley, ed., *Writings of Abraham Lincoln*, 2:27–44.

71. See Charles Sellers, *James K. Polk, Continentalist, 1843–1846* (Princeton, N.J.: Princeton University Press, 1966), pp. 261–62.

72. Lapsley, ed., *Writings of Abraham Lincoln*, 2:51–52.

73. See Department of State, memorandum of the solicitor, *Right to Protect Citizens In Foreign Countries by Landing Forces* (3d rev. ed., 1934), which lists the instances of such landings up to that date. The constitutionality of the practice of using military force to protect citizens' lives and property in foreign countries was defended by the solicitor of the State Department in this memorandum, written in 1912, on the ground that such interventions "do not constitute either a declaration of war or acts of war, though it is quite obvious that such acts may lead to a state of war if resistance is encountered" (p. 40). The solicitor even went so far as to argue that, in view of the president's duty to protect citizens, "it may be regarded as doubtful . . . that Congress has the constitutional power to pass" a law "prohibiting the President from using or directing him in his use of the forces of the United States for the protection of citizens abroad" (p. 41). For an analysis of these instances of foreign landings and a skeptical discussion of their constitutionality, see Wormuth, "Vietnam War," pp. 741–67. The recent invasions of Grenada and Panama suggest that the practice is becoming less popular neither with presidents nor the public.

74. See Harold Hongju Koh, *The National Security Constitution* (New Haven: Yale University Press, 1990), pp. 88–100. For an early demonstration that presidential assertions of a warmaking prerogative even in the first decades of the twentieth century were in marked contrast to the presidential attitudes that were generally characteristic of previous eras, see Albert H. Putney, "Executive Assumption of the War Making Power," *National University Law Review* 7 (1927): 1.

75. Rutland et al., eds., *Papers of James Madison*, 17:104.

76. Adams, ed., *Works of John Adams*, 9:116.

77. 1 Stat. 561. See text at note 18 of this chapter.

78. Harold C. Syrett, ed., *The Papers of Alexander Hamilton* (New York: Columbia University Press, 1961–1979), 21:459–60 (emphasis in original).

79. Ibid., pp. 461–62.

80. *Naval Operations from February 1797 to October 1798, Naval Documents*, p. 77.

81. *The Amelia* (alternate title *Talbot v. Seeman*), 1 Cranch (5 U.S.) 1, 28 (1801).

82. *The Flying Fish* (alternate title *Little v. Barreme*), 2 Cranch (6 U.S.) 170, 177–79 (1804).

83. *The Amelia*, p. 38.

12

SECRECY AND CONSTITUTIONAL CONTROLS IN THE FEDERALIST PERIOD

DANIEL N. HOFFMAN

Accountability is a central aspect of constitutionalism, and it is elementary that a government cannot be held accountable for actions that are not known to have occurred. If a constitution is to succeed in keeping government accountable, then, it must contrive somehow to limit the inevitable efforts of powerholders to conceal their acts and intentions. Yet total openness is neither possible nor perhaps, given the realistic concerns for efficient decisionmaking and national security, even desirable. The complexity of the practical and theoretical issues involved suggests that a sensitive control system, rather than a simple moral exhortation, is needed to deal at all successfully with the problem of secrecy. To what extent does the American constitutional system provide such a control?[1]

A look at the Constitution and the surrounding debates confirms that the Framers were well aware of the problem. The control system they established was indeed a complex one, consisting of three interwoven levels: explicit norms of official conduct, formal institutional checks, and procedures for public access and participation.

The Constitution in fact has little to say directly about secrecy. Article I, section 5 provides for publication of congressional journals, "excepting such parts as may in their judgement require secrecy." Article I, section 9 requires, without reservation, a periodic publication of governmental receipts and expenditures. Article II declares that, in connection with his legislative proposals, the president shall inform Congress from time to time of the state of the Union. Finally, the First Amendment guarantees that freedom of speech and of the press shall not be abridged.

Underlying these provisions was a theory of institutional specialization, according to which those military and diplomatic matters typically requiring secrecy were confided to the executive branch, which was to function discreetly—albeit under the policy guidance of a legislature whose proceedings would typically be public and which was empowered to engage in investigative oversight. The electorate, in turn, would play a more passive role, using such information as the government or the free press made available in performing its ultimate supervisory function. Typically, then, sensitive policy information would flow from the executive to Congress and from Congress to the public.

Communications from the executive to Congress were the key focus of secrecy conflict in the Federalist period. Such conflict seemed inherent in the constitutional plan; yet, save for the State of the Union clause, the Framers had not explicitly addressed the question of interbranch communications. The earliest problem that arose from the congressional perspective was not executive denial of information but executive efforts to guide the legislative process by submitting reports and proposals. Some elements in Congress sought to curtail communications from the executive in order to preserve the separation of powers, but these efforts were essentially unsuccessful. In 1790, the president introduced a practice of designating certain messages to Congress as confidential.[2] The ostensible purpose was to preserve secrecy for sensitive military and diplomatic information. Congress respected this policy and initially did not challenge the new procedures by which it was implemented. The timing and content of congressional briefings were left to the judgment of the president and his department heads.

Soon Jefferson and Hamilton began maneuvering to ensure an evenhanded flow of information to Congress, and inside the two houses emergent factions and nonaligned members struggled to establish publicity postures appropriate to their institutional or partisan concerns or both. A new kind of issue arose when Congress sought to call for papers on its own initiative. In the course of a long series of episodes the cabinet and the two houses began to develop more precise doctrines to regulate their respective roles in the policymaking process. Through a combination of formal and informal techniques, relying increasingly on legalistic and often public dialogue, the government as a whole made significant progress toward synthesizing these various doctrines into a relatively coherent, shared system of norms.

Certain routine reporting requirements had been imposed on the Treasury Department by law in 1789; Hamilton had welcomed and indeed lobbied for the opportunity of influencing legislation through this channel. But the first special investigation by Congress was less to his liking. In 1792 the House of Representatives, after adopting a new standing rule for the strict protection of confidential information, launched an inquiry into the failure of Gen. Arthur St. Clair's expedition against the Indians. Cabinet members decided upon a course of full cooperation with the House, although according to Jefferson's diary, they thought the president had a power in principle to withhold information if its release could harm the public interest.[3]

Late in 1793 the militant Third Congress began to challenge the executive branch's secrecy posture as well as its substantive policies. The House modified its standing rule, now proclaiming its right to disclose confidential communications on its own authority, and began to call for papers omitted from briefings submitted by the executive.[4] At first the president made no resistance. When the House sought to investigate charges that Hamilton had mishandled public funds, Washington cooperated fully. At one point Hamilton tried to claim that his confidential communications with the president were privileged from disclosure to the House; but the House overrode Hamilton's objection, and when it asked the president to comment on Hamilton's testimony, he found no impropriety in the request.[5]

Setting the stage for a decisive upheaval in interbranch communications was the outbreak of war in Europe. After Washington issued his Proclamation of Neutrality it was necessary to enlist congressional and public support in elaborating and enforcing that policy. More information was transmitted to Congress than ever before, some on a public and some on a confidential basis. The House, successfully at first, called for additional papers; and it exercised in a selective and temperate manner the previously asserted right to disclose information submitted to it in confidence. The Senate even prevailed upon the president to publicize his secret negotiations with Spain.[6] But Washington reacted sharply when, in spring 1794, the Senate moved to investigate the conduct of Gouverneur Morris, the president's hand-picked ambassador to France. Morris was suspected, and justly so, of contravening the official policy of recognition and friendship for the French Revolution. On this occasion the president departed from his previous policy of complete cooperation; he censored the papers supplied to the Senate, and the Senate made no protest. This episode, overlooked in most previous studies involving executive privilege, was accompanied by substantial bipartisan discussion involving executive officials, congressional leaders, and even a Supreme Court justice. All consulted were willing to admit that the president had some power to censor papers called for by Congress before submitting them if he deemed it necessary to protect personal safety, or perhaps, the national honor. The scope and limitations of this power, however, remained to be established.[7]

Early experiences indicated the likelihood that doctrine would continue to evolve by informal and relatively broad-based discussion. But the departure of

Jefferson from the Washington administration, the increasing partisan acrimony and anti-British sentiment in Congress, the Whisky Rebellion at home, and the revolutionary excesses abroad raised a specter of war and revolution that produced a strong conservative and pro-British reaction in the administration's outlook. In April 1794, John Jay was dispatched on a secret mission to London, and anti-British legislation pending in Congress was abandoned at Washington's request. When Jay returned with a commercial treaty in hand, the Senate's consent was obtained in total secrecy. A senator leaked what became known as the Jay Treaty to the public, but the president signed it despite a storm of protest. The opposition sought to block the funds for the treaty in the House of Representatives. An overwhelming bipartisan majority in the House won passage of a resolution that called for papers connected with the negotiations but only after a heated constitutional debate in which some Federalists questioned the propriety of the measure.[8] Washington, however, refused to comply. He did not rely on his established authority to censor the papers for public considerations but claimed instead that the House had no right to any information whatever since it has no constitutional role to play in treatymaking.[9] The House adopted strong resolutions of protest.[10] Though it ultimately granted the funds needed to implement the treaty, nothing could be further from the truth than the assertion, quoted with approval by Chief Justice Warren Burger, that Washington's act was "a refusal the wisdom of which was recognized by the House itself and had never since been doubted."[11] On the contrary, this episode threw the law of secrecy and indeed the whole constitutional system into turmoil and uncertainty.

An apparent return to orthodox practice came in the XYZ episode of 1798, when the House again demanded sensitive diplomatic papers in a context of impending war. President John Adams's compliance with that demand was consistent with his political interests, but it was more than that: it was a conscious repudiation of Washington's 1796 position, a return to the moderate ground that had been generally accepted in 1794 and that now seemed to command bipartisan and cross-institutional support once again.[12] This doctrine recognized the right of Congress to call for papers without restriction but recognized also a presidential power to censor the papers before supplying them—save perhaps where the Senate was acting in its executive capacity, or where a question of impeachment or of declaring war was before Congress. In those cases, the right to know might be absolute. Moreover, the only basis for presidential censorship that was unequivocally exercised and established as valid in the Federalist period was the protection of the safety of individuals. This is hardly the absolute privilege that recent executive spokesmen have purported to discover in the historical record, but neither is it the normless chaos that others have discerned.[13] Beyond this point of established consensus, of course, advocates remained free—memory and imagination permitting—to invoke and reinterpret a range of historic pronouncements and events whose exact legal status and significance were subject to continued dispute.

In point of fact, though, the aftermath of the XYZ affair was marked by disputes of a very different kind. Electoral vicissitudes had given the Federalist party control of every branch of the government, and elements of the Federalist leadership seized upon the chance to make their dominance permanent. The notions of "executive discretion" originally developed to serve the needs of nationbuilding and of interbranch conflict were now adapted, through enlargement of the "police power," to serve the pursuit of strict control over nongovernmental political activity through such measures as the sedition trials of 1798–1800. Whereas the constitutional issues of the earlier stages related to the separation of powers and the prerogatives of the several branches, now First Amendment issues came to the fore. When the courts proved unwilling to check the government's "law enforcement" program, the Republicans could only appeal to the people. In 1800, Jefferson's election as president ended the Federalist "reign of terror."

There are two central questions presented by this history: Why did the constitutional system of checks and balances and the norms of communication that evolved in the early years prove so relatively ephemeral in the crises of 1796 and 1798? Why did the system nevertheless emerge relatively intact, ideologically, institutionally, and politically, from these crises?

Several kinds of factors converged to make the situation inauspicious for the development of stable secrecy/publicity norms. Conceptually, I would distinguish three dimensions of the environment in which secrecy issues develop: the fluid context—the strategic and tactical constraints inherent in the fact that participants have various long-and-short-run objectives to consider, and the attitudes, beliefs, and skills that affect the techniques chosen to attain those ends; the rigid structure—the formal roles and channels through which contestants must largely operate; and finally, the law—established principles and precedents that, though mutable, cannot lightly be set aside, specifying what may and may not be done. These three dimensions are not strictly independent of each other; they interweave in a play of legal/political dynamics that defies reductionistic analysis. It is important, all the same, to draw attention to the special status of normative constraints among the operative factors. It is here that the fulcrum of coherent intentional regulation should reside. The "facts" can be fast-changing or seen in more than one light; sponsors may be shortsighted or corrupt and seek to manipulate issues for selfish ends; forums may be politically biased and their rules of procedure rigid and unrealistic or sketchy and inefficient. Amid this chaotic interplay, the logical discipline and universalizing tendencies of normative discourse, if carried on by competent advocates who take the effort at all seriously, supply a helpful buffering and rationalizing force. This effect makes constitutionalism more than a mere window-dressing; its possibility is what makes the process of legal development, and its failures, an important subject for study.

In the Federalist period, despite the respect accorded to the rule of law, precedential constraints were especially tenuous. A major reason was the simple immaturity of the norm system after a time of constitutional and ideological upheaval. The flexibility deliberately designed into the Constitution allowed a broad latitude for creative adaptation to an uncertain future and for the coexistence of diverse political creeds in political life. This flexibility was purchased, of course, at the expense of clarity in principle and stability in policy. In the period of nationbuilding, when precedents were intrinsically hard to come by, the temptation was powerful for government to rely on charismatic and traditional forms of authority. This reliance, however, delayed the institutionalization of political life under the new regime. In addition, because of primitive recordkeeping and, perhaps, inexperience, the available precedents were poorly exploited even in full-dress debates.

If the body of public law was immature and lacking in depth, the factual context was not conducive to its easy or rapid growth. For the constitutional system suffered a stressful infancy, with challenges ranging from intense class struggle to sectional jealousy to foreign menaces verging on overt warfare. It was, in short, a protracted state of emergency—a situation offering minimal support for constructions of the Constitution, or for rulemaking thereunder, that would place rigid limits on governmental power. Emergency, the Framers believed, requires discretion, vigor, secrecy, dispatch—in short, executive power.

On top of the difficult foreign and domestic policy questions confronting the government, the development of political parties distorted the structure of governmental interaction in ways with which the governing elites were poorly equipped to deal. Neither their organizational nor their conceptual system was designed with parties in mind. They saw issues as sponsored by individuals, responsible to constituencies and endowed with prerogatives and power resources that were largely defined in terms of official roles. The intricacies of federalism and separated powers were designed, in part, to diffuse and contain the clash of different social interests so that no single one could attain to a stable dominance of the governmental machinery. But this design did not anticipate the schism of the elite into two increasingly cohesive groupings that cooperated across institutional boundaries on a wide range of issues. Nor was the system designed to accommodate smoothly a rapidly growing democratic movement, pressing demands for information and access to policymaking that even in quieter and more trustful times it would have been difficult to absorb. In the context of the upheavals in France, this movement was terrifying to conservatives and made the party activities of the opposition seem doubly illegitimate. In taking the administration to task for excessive secrecy, therefore, opposition spokesmen ran the risk of identification as "disorganizers," "Jacobins," and demagogues of the "swinish multitude."

Though the Constitution was designed to maintain a flexible balance between separate institutions, between the values of energy and responsibility, the development of a party system did not facilitate smooth, moderate, or stable adjustments in the balance as the needs of the country changed. Instead, the workings of the electoral process tended to produce long periods of rigid interaction in which factions of stable size ritualistically confronted one another and reaffirmed their respective positions, punctuated by sudden and sharp alterations of the balance as election results were felt, often a year or more after citizens went to the polls. In these conditions even campaigning and voter behavior that met utopian standards of enlightenment and that focused squarely on secrecy issues could not have guaranteed rational, adaptive responses in governmental decisionmaking. And of course, it is by no means the case that secrecy issues were always a central concern and were explored with great insight and objectivity.

Madison had argued in *Federalist 51* that institutional self-interest would drive the separate branches to check each other so that ambition could be harnessed to the service of liberty.[14] But the emergence of parties greatly undercut the operation of this design. From the beginning, neither house of Congress was able to exert an effective check on the accelerating growth of "executive" power. The cabinet was seldom a force for executive self-restraint; and the courts, strongly Federalist in makeup, had no disposition to question the constitutionality of governmental action so long as their allies remained in power. The upshot was that the electoral system had to bear the brunt of conflict over secrecy, which became an issue of trust in the chief magistrate as much as one of regularity in decisionmaking procedures. Proposals for adjustments in interbranch relations by authoritative techniques such as constitutional amendment, legislation, or adjudication were seldom voiced and never acted upon in the Founding period.[15]

Some observers would view this record as supporting the propositions that secrecy is intrinsically insusceptible to constitutional restraint; that the Founders understood as much; that for theoretical and practical reasons they preferred to leave the matter to official discretion, loosely disciplined by the restraints of a competitive political process. Some might even wish to argue that, for a range of issues far broader than secrecy, constitutional restraints on governmental power are totally beside the point.[16]

To me the record shows not an inevitable but a highly contingent and partial failure of constitutional controls. After all, the Founding Fathers invested a substantial effort in constitutional analysis and debate. Many of their efforts were impressive in quality and were designed not for public effect but for decisionmakers' consumption. It was not just one group of "strict constructionists" who found constitutional argumentation meaningful; indeed, Hamilton's briefs on behalf of expansive readings of governmental power were among the most earnest and persuasive of the Founders' legal performances. Rules of procedure, like other kinds of policy, developed in fits and starts and sudden reversals rather than by a smooth, organic, and systematic path. Clearly no simple model of normative regulation can account for all the decisions made; yet it does not follow that what appeared to be a legal argument on a given day was really nothing but a naked power struggle.

Theorists of legal development sometimes speak as if legal systems grow inexorably, as if strife does not disrupt the process but feeds it. Thus Von Jhering wrote that "all the law in the world has been obtained by strife."[17] Yet on reflection it seems clear that not every instance of conflict results in the adoption or application of an identifiable rule, much less of a rule consistent with those applied in previous cases.[18] To the extent that legal rulemaking proves feasible, this may simply reflect a low level of concern or a high level of consensus about what ought to be done rather than a system well designed for the resolution of intense conflict. If in stages of high consensus participants may feel that any stable and reasonable procedure will do, in stages of rapid social change and heated partisan conflict the existing rules of procedure are likely to come under attack or evasion, and new rules will not easily be agreed upon. Rules adopted in such conflictual times are apt to reflect the ambiguities attendant on compromise; actual practice may, in contrast, reflect the extremism attendant on secret or preemptive unilateral action. In stages of repression the rules can be freely manipulated in accord with the wishes of the dominant group. The resulting system will have some of the attributes of "law" as manifested in other stages, but its real base of authority will rest on fundamentally different grounds. A pluralistic system uses competitive advocacy to maintain belief in the fairness of the rules of the game; a monolithic one may rely solely on coercive enforcement.

The prospects for lawful kinds of conflict resolution, then, appear to depend both on enduring traits of a political system, including cultural and structural features, and on situational factors that make the legal culture more or less vigorous, the institutional control system more or less balanced. The failures of legalization in the Federalist period involved the conjunction of serious destabilizing factors impinging on many different levels of the control system. Yet to an amazing extent the system held. Institutions stood; there were no political executions and relatively few and brief imprisonments, and the Constitution became widely revered. The contrast with, say, France, was obvious.

The Founders were obliged by the logic of their own Revolution, bolstered by earlier English traditions, to own the liberal-republican concepts of popular sovereignty and the rule of law as the fundamental legitimizing principles of their regime.[19] Whatever their private beliefs about the viability of these ideals, public discourse would submit their conduct to discussion and scrutiny in these terms. There was much room for official maneuver in deciding how, when, and by exactly whom this scrutiny should be performed; and that is what the secrecy issue ultimately was about. To call the secrecy issue a legal issue is to claim that the maneuvering was itself somehow disciplined by constitutional arrangements. This claim, I think, is amply substantiated by the record.

On the ideological plane, norms of constitutional stature dictated what could and what could not be said in debate. Secrecy could not be defended on the ground that it helped slow the process of democratization; it could be defended on national security grounds or on those of institutional integrity. The Founders accepted secrecy as essential to the performance of functions as diverse as diplomatic negotiations, executive and judicial deliberations, and even, for a time, the legislative work of the Senate. That institutionalized secrecy would bolster the elitist tendencies of the system escaped no one; and it is clear enough that for many this was a good thing. But they were also obliged to recognize that the government had to be sufficiently open and responsive to maintain the necessary degree of public acceptance and active support.[20] If the legitimate criteria for secrecy were abused, as they sometimes were, the guilty parties were subject to political attack and ultimate loss of public confidence. Neither officials nor the general public, obviously, typically engaged in a rational balancing of what the long-run public interest required before deciding whether to make particular information available or to keep it secret, whether to demand information or to acquiesce in secrecy for the time being. This does not mean that the process was utterly normless. A long-run trend toward greater publicity and broader participation was stimulated and supported by the rhetorical use made of the people's right to know.

The Constitution was also intermittently but powerfully operative through the mechanism of separated powers. Up to a point the several branches did tend to function as their formal structural attributes and official responsibilities would dictate.[21] The House of Representatives, directly elected, large in size, and excluded from the most sensitive executive functions, adopted a relatively open posture. The executive branch, tiny, hierarchically structured, and entrusted with the most sensitive duties, had no direct links with the public and few official ones even with Congress. The Senate was intermediate in size, hybrid in function, and showed some uncertainty as to the identity of its constituency and the appropriate communication posture to adopt. Each body went about its separate business, and each separately confronted the question of publicizing its proceedings or keeping them secret.

When the administration began to develop an agenda for the government as a whole, leaders were beset by crosscutting incentives for cooperation and competition, for sharing and for hoarding information. The resulting behavior was highly complex and not a straightforward product either of an individual's ideological temper or of his institutional affiliation.[22] Cabinet conservatives often found it prudent to advocate the release of sensitive information, sometimes officially, sometimes by informal leaks or even behind the president's back. Congressional liberals not only had secrets of their own but sometimes supported the executive in withholding information from the country and even from themselves.

The Framers had made the right of Congress to obtain information from the executive the key issue for lawful regulation of secrecy—not by express provision but in virtue of the separation of powers system. Secrecy debate was oriented toward this issue, and conflicts that could not be so formulated were hard to deal with in a legalistic or principled way. By the same token, the attempt to deal with an issue according to constitutional criteria did not necessarily facilitate a realistic description of the interests at stake. For example, defenders of Jay's Treaty were obliged to invoke presidential power, even though the mission was a senatorial inspiration.

In the long run Congress was unable to maintain a constant and unrelenting stand for publicity or to prevent the erosion of some of the powers the Framers had intended it to wield. Administration supporters usually were loath to assert congressional prerogative to the detriment of party interests, and even the opposition party often behaved as if it would rather capture the presidency than weaken it.[23]

In the Founding period neither party had a monolithic, ideologically determined posture on issues of secrecy and publicity. In fact, party cohesion in congressional votes on secrecy-related issues was often notably weak.[24] Still, if constitutional structures and principles provided the forums, mechanisms, and the language for meaningful debate and coherent regulation, it was party leaders who made the crucial strategic and tactical decisions on what information to demand or withhold and what grounds to rely upon in accusation or defense. Secrecy would not become an issue unless someone in a position to do so saw fit to make an issue of it. Like institutional considerations, party conflict provided incentives for publicity in some cases and for secrecy in others. Jefferson once suggested that party activity was justified by its role in informing the people, and it is true that party conflict obliged both sides to reach out for public support and to circulate information and propaganda for that end.[25] A united elite might have clung much longer to the old, closed form of politics. Yet it also seems clear that party opposition was the crucial factor in the drift of Washington's administration toward increasingly secretive and unilateral action vis-à-vis Congress from 1794 to 1796. The claims of presidential power were repeatedly expanded in order to preserve the Federalists' control over policymaking; when Madison and his allies finally determined to take a stand on the powers of Congress, it was too late. All that remained was to try to capture the presidency.

It may be valid from a broad historical perspective to say that the election of 1800 was a victory for constitutionalism and democratic ideology, though it cannot be proved that secrecy and repression were actually the decisive issues in the campaign. Jefferson's victory was certainly powerfully aided by other issues as well as by generous doses of wheeling, dealing, and sheer dirty tricks.[26] More important, his election gives no grounds for a claim that the electoral mechanism provides a reliable, speedy remedy for abuses of power. It is not only that the Federalists might have won but that Jefferson's election did not affect the structural weaknesses of the system. The electoral process is far less suitable than that of disciplined constitutional debate within specialized forums for isolating, refining, and resolving procedural questions in a timely and principled manner. The arguments useful for public opinion–molding are likely to be less complex and realistic than those officials, most of them lawyers, might find persuasive. Thus it is difficult to develop in campaign oratory an effective code of official conduct, even if that were a central aim of the leadership. In fact, of course, electoral controls operate in an analytically diffuse but rigidly timed manner, and the salience of any given issue is at the mercy of largely accidental forces.[27] By no means does the early history warrant us in saying that those who commit serious abuses are apt to be discovered and ousted before serious harm can be done to persons, to institutional integrities, and to the fabric of the law. Rather, the checks and balances built into the Constitution seem highly vulnerable to disruption in times of international crisis and especially in situations where Congress and the executive come under the control of the same party. At such times, opposition movements and media may become the crucial safeguard against tyranny. The historical record thus warrants an equivocal judgment on the effectiveness of constitutional controls. Although the Constitution seldom or never supplied strictly outcome-determining legal rules, it did supply a basis both for the elaboration of democratic ideology and for the increasing importance of public opinion. Appeals to norms of secrecy and publicity derived from the logic of the Constitution gained an important place in the broader scheme of political restraints on governmental decisionmaking.

The rhetorical function of secrecy issues was appropriate to the increasingly central role of the presidency and of presidential elections in American political life.[28] This development was not an explicit part of the Framers' program, though many of them may have hoped for something of the sort; but the leaders of the new government increasingly viewed the imperatives of nation-building and of an expansive foreign policy as demanding a strong, autonomous presidency. Not only Hamilton but Madison and Jefferson, too, were conscious of the fragility of the new regime and showed the greatest reluctance to challenge the character, the policies, or the emerging cult of George Washington. His personal popularity, his importance as a symbol of national unity, and the protracted crisis in which the country found itself made such challenges seem irresponsible and self-defeating.

It is hardly surprising that the leaders of a young, modernizing regime, tied economically and culturally to a world caught up in the throes of war and revolution, would look to presidential charisma for support and not always make strict constitutional orthodoxy their highest priority. No one before them had proved that a regime based on the rule of law could survive in such conditions, and surely they were agreed that "the Constitution is not a suicide pact."[29]

Yet the system the Federalists built and passed on to their successors was neither a monarchy nor a dictatorship. It was a pluralistic system based on diverse forms of authority, legitimacy, and participation—though, to be sure, at the same time a highly elitist one—and constitutional norms and structures were an integral functioning part of the system. The political process was disciplined by the law, within fluctuating limits. The constraints of checks and balances fluctuated with shifts in institutional power and authority; but the balance was not symmetrical, for claims asserted on behalf of the presidency were more consistently bold, assertive, ambitious. Those made on behalf of Congress tended to be, at best, weakened by compromises demanded by congressional supporters of the incumbent president.

And what about the courts? For complex reasons, they played little role in the great event of the Founding period. Their low prestige and strong partisan bias did not commend them as umpires; their conduct in the sedition trials and otherwise tended to show that, even if in the long run the courts might show some resistance to being used as a partisan weapon by the executive, they were most unlikely to lend themselves to use as an offensive weapon against it.[30]

We have come to think of the rule of law as virtually synonymous with the workings of the judicial process and to suppose that the law cannot be known or enforced by any other practice. Thus Charles Black, writing in praise of the Supreme Court's contribution, has said:

> A Government founded on the theory of limited powers faces and must solve the problem of legitimacy. . . . There are several hopeless ways to go about this. . . . First, the determinations of Congress and the President could simply have been made final on all questions affecting their own power. . . . It is not what happened, and I venture to say there is nothing in the history of this country to indicate it could ever have succeeded.[31]

Because the Supreme Court did not in the Federalist era play the role that, according to Black, only an independent, specialized legal tribunal can play, it must be his contention that the rule of law was not operative in America before the *Marbury v. Madison* decision in 1803. One way to test this claim is to focus on the special functional merits that Black and others have discerned in the judicial role and to inquire how far these qualities may not inhere in other aspects of the constitutional control system as well. These qualities include detachment (one must not judge his own case), respect for precedent, skill in following precedent and in discerning when it ought not to be followed, and attachment to the long-run interest of the whole people. Thus the strength of the rule of law can be assessed by the extent to which decisions are supported in principled terms, precedents are noted and reconciled or distinguished, and established rules and procedures are respected even when immediate interest might dictate otherwise.[32]

By these criteria there were distinct lacunae in the Founders' performance. This should not be surprising; even in a relatively open, modern, or modernizing system with a strong legal profession, informal techniques of conflict resolution will often be preferred. Where status hierarchy, voting, or other simple procedures can generate consensus there may be no incentive to undertake time-consuming and possibly divisive discussions of principle and precedent.[33] Of course a small, closed, and homogenous leadership group will be especially likely to eschew formalities.[34]

In the Founding period neither Congress nor the executive had an adequate system for collecting and analyzing relevant precedents. The president at least could require written opinions of the department heads and the attorney general; Congress had no mechanism for generating an institutional position save floor debate or referral to an ad hoc committee for report. Given the fairly rapid personnel turnover in both branches, it must be concluded that the government was poorly endowed in terms of memory. Inadequate recordkeeping made it difficult to collect precedents and to document the reasoning behind earlier decisions. Moreover, the legal opinions adopted by policymakers were often one-sided and self-serving. This was especially true of the legal advice that presidents received; and on crucial occasions opinions and precedents that ran counter to presidential inclination, or that of other powerful leaders, were simply ignored. Even the judiciary appears to have manifested these same weaknesses; in the Founding period, its work was distinctive more in subject matter than in intellectual method or political attitude.[35]

Much of this inadequacy could perhaps be explained away en masse by pointing to the intellectual and moral failures of specific persons or to the pervasive effects of class struggle and other corrupting forces; but explanations on those levels fail to do justice to a crucial postulate of constitutionalism: that the genius of a constitutional system is its capacity to perform in a rational and lawful manner even when powerful leaders and social forces are not oriented toward that goal. The Framers of the Constitution placed their faith neither in simple moral exhortation, nor in any elite censorial council empowered to enforce a code of public morality upon the officers of government, nor yet in a radical social reform but in a system of checks and balances ostensibly designed to prevent the worst abuses of power and to strike a long-run balance between competing, legitimate values and interests. The rule of law was not, in the Founding period at least, a professional shibboleth of the judiciary; it was claimed to be a virtue of the entire political order.[36]

Legalization was surely inhibited by the prevailing atmosphere of crisis, by the fact that secrecy issues were often bound up with the most intensely divisive issues of foreign policy and democratization, and by the fact that there was a valid argument for flexibility in dealing with some of these issues. Nevertheless the Founders never abandoned the search for viable constitutional standards of procedure; rather, they adhered to the constitutionalist premise that the virtue of the rulers need not and must not be the only safeguard of liberty. Thus it was that President Adams, presented with an opportunity to emulate Washington's handling of the Jay Treaty case, instead yielded up the XYZ papers to Congress and suffered the establishment of what had formerly been deemed an intolerably dangerous precedent. And thus it was that the Federalists, in the face of ample temptation and even provocation, suffered the survival of an opposition movement whose loyalty they sincerely doubted and peacefully surrendered power after the election of 1800.

Eventually First Amendment doctrine matured and the party system mellowed to the point where a repetition of the Federalist "reign of terror" against political critics seemed almost out of the question. The law of secrecy, however, remained inchoate and insensitive to the vicissitudes of shifting electoral returns and political crises. Hence, the institutional mechanisms for obliging a reluctant government to release the information necessary for effective criticism were periodically inactive; the specter of a renewed cycle of "irresponsible" opposition, secrecy, leaking, and repression lay dormant but unconquered.

Extrapolating a bit from the historical record, I would offer the following propositions, designed to illuminate these questions: When does secrecy become especially problematic for the system? How is the system likely to respond? What are the results?

1. Secrecy is most likely to become a bone of contention when (a) the pace of social change is rapid; (b) established status relations and limits on participation are under fire; and (c) foreign policy issues are salient and divisive.

2. Even under the above conditions effective challenges to secrecy will require inside sponsorship. The most likely sponsors are elites who (a) disagree with secret actions or plans, known or suspected; (b) possess the institutional leverage for demanding information; and (c) are not inhibited by party loyalty or the felt needs of national security from challenging the leadership.

3. The secrecy issue assumes a constitutional form when (a) Congress or a court seeks to extract information from a recalcitrant executive; (b) someone seeks to release information that has been designated secret by the executive; or (c) the government seeks to punish individuals who challenge official secrecy.

4. A principled resolution of these legal issues depends on (a) the climate of respect for law and the skills of legal advocates; (b) the structural mechanisms available for authoritative rulemaking; and (c) the situational factors that define the values at stake and constrain the strategies and tactics adopted.

5. The avoidance of legal solutions preserves a kind of flexibility that, for all its pragmatic advantages, may have serious costs. In particular, the possibility of unsuccessful legal regulation implicit in the above propositions is conducive to a particular scenario of abuses: (a) uni-

lateral and secret foreign policy initiatives by or in the name of the president that run directly counter to congressional and public expectation or desire; then (b) breakdown of information security due to loss of respect for official secrecy criteria and absence of alternative to leaking as a way of challenging established policy; then (c) harsh repressive measures against officials and private citizens classed as security risks, in part because they disclose official secrets or are deemed likely to do so.

Events of the 1960s, in fact, provided ideal conditions for a resurgence of the particular sort of crisis the Founders had experienced. By that decade great progress had ostensibly been made in building structural and cultural support for the rule of law. Both congressional oversight and judicial review were securely institutionalized; the executive branch had assumed ever more bureaucratic, and thus apparently rule-bound, organizational forms; and a much wider, more affluent public had gained the franchise, formal education, and presumably some sympathy for the values of a participant, libertarian political culture. Yet the crisis that appeared when the constitutional system was once more subject to the intense, simultaneous stresses of elite-sponsored radical protest at home and violent conflict abroad was remarkably like that of the Federalist period. In such cases presidents are prone to feel that their programs are essential to avert national disaster but find it imprudent or impossible to implement them openly and justify them by candid argument. The ensuing scenario followed parallel lines in the Founding and in recent eras: unilateral, secret initiatives, discovered by dissident elites, led in a seemingly inexorable sequence to credibility gaps, embarrassing leaks of inside information, and increasingly desperate efforts by the administration to silence opposition and restore consensus. The worst excesses of Vietnam and Watergate, like those of the Federalist "reign of terror," were exposed and ostensibly stopped; yet, in the absence of meaningful structural reform, what has happened at least twice could easily happen again. The Iran-Contra episode and the efforts of the Reagan and Bush administrations to bolster secrecy amply support this claim.

No doubt an intellectually respectable case, if not a politically realistic one, could be made for a major overhaul of the Constitution to redress the imbalance among the modern executive and the other branches. It seems more appropriate in the present context, however, to highlight some weaknesses in the system of checks and balances that might be redressed without constitutional amendment.

One kind of reform would consist of measures enhancing the institutional capabilities and incentives of Congress as a checking force. Insofar as the congressional tendency to acquiesce passively in presidential foreign policy initiatives arises from the sheer size and diversity of the legislature, it is not clear what remedies would be feasible or even desirable. Historically, the system of standing committees grew up in response to these and related problems; but the committee system has not consistently supported congressional powers vis-à-vis the executive, especially in the realm of foreign affairs. Congressional oversight was not highly effective in the Federalist period even though power was wielded by a mere handful of highly visible characters. The task of Congress is far more difficult today, when the activities of a vast, fragmented bureaucracy are in question. Even the president can oversee the whole to a very limited degree. A reliance on episodic investigations seems ill-suited to the chronic nature of this problem. The search for pertinent structural reform gains further impetus from seemingly permanent changes in the balance of power and allocation of functions between Congress and the president himself.

It was concerns like these, along with the shock value of events like the Pentagon Papers episode and Watergate, that led to the adoption of such reforms as the War Powers Resolution of 1973 and the strengthened Freedom of Information Act of 1974.[37] These efforts to address explicit legal prohibitions and requirements to the executive branch have not, unfortunately, always met with wholehearted acceptance; indeed, today even these mild measures are attacked as unconstitutional and unworkable. The presidency, at least in the international realm, seems to have largely recovered its imperial momentum; many of the audacious claims of executive power concocted by Richard Nixon's lawyers have already been echoed by his successors.

Insofar as these phenomena reflect widely shared and deeply ingrained American perceptions of the international situation, structural reforms are admittedly unlikely to have benevolent and far-reaching effect. Moreover, congressional leaders cannot be expected resolutely to support restraints on the presidency insofar as they themselves may entertain presidential ambitions. Still, it is worth noting that some of the imbalance in the control system reflects a simple want of institutional memory on the part of Congress; its inattention to questions of constitutional authority is in some measure attributable to a lack of alertness rather than to consciously fixed priorities.

From the outset presidents have been able to rely upon the legal as well as the political acumen of cabinet officers in defending and expanding the powers of their office. Attorneys general since Edmund Randolph have functioned less as neutral guardians of legality than as presidential advocates; indeed, to the extent that they have been prepared to adopt a more neutral stance, their advice has tended to be ignored. The cumulative effect has been substantial: today the collected opinions of the attorneys general provide a handy source of self-serving argument for virtually anything a president might wish to do. Congress, meanwhile, has no comparable officer or body of lore available to it. Lacking a single, specialized advocate endowed with an appropriate mandate, it is poorly equipped to confront the presidency with legal argument, either in the courts or at the bar of public opinion. This situation seems susceptible of an easy remedy: an office of legal counsel to the Congress, endowed with plenary subpoena powers and standing to sue in court, should be established by law.

Whatever the merits of such a proposal, we can be sure that Congress will not always stand up as a body to overreaching by presidents and their advisers. Historically, the second line of defense has been the competitive party system, appealing to the people through the media of mass communication. Such appeals, of course, depend for their efficacy on access to critical information and on the ability and the inclination to make that information public. Neither access, ability, nor inclination can be taken for granted; and it is doubtful whether any of the three can be directly and reliably legislated. It does not follow that legal reform is irrelevant. Perhaps the gravest legal deficiency of the constitutional control system today is the threat of criminal penalties and prior restraints against unauthorized disclosure of official information. It is commonly held that the Sedition Law of 1798 was a constitutional and political aberration, possible only because of the immaturity of the constitutional system and the unique crisis of the times. Yet in 1917 a broadly worded espionage law and in the 1950s a peacetime sedition law again appeared on the statute books. These laws today permit official intimidation of legitimate political speech and activity that in no way endanger the national security.[38] In the 1970s, Daniel Ellsberg was indicted for photocopying the Pentagon Papers, and several former CIA officials were enjoined from publishing any intelligence-related material without advance agency approval.[39] And recently there have been calls for a comprehensive Official Secrets Act, a measure spurned even by those men who passed the 1798 Sedition Law.

The laws and judicial doctrines abridging political speech and publication should not be toughened but repealed or overruled. In the present situation, as in the Founding era, their impact is not to protect the national interest but to maintain a rigid barrier between the rulers and the ruled, those with and those without a "need to know," those with and those without access to the private, elite channels of influence and information. Of course, no structural arrangement could guarantee that public debate would produce a wise consensus or any consensus at all. Even so, there are cogent grounds for insisting on timely public discussion of the fundamental moral, economic, and political commitments of a society dedicated to constitutional self-government.

NOTES

1. For a detailed study of this issue, see Daniel N. Hoffman, *Governmental Secrecy and the Founding Fathers: A Study in Constitutional Controls* (Westport, Conn.: Greenwood Press, 1981).

2. *Annals of Congress,* 1:936 (hereafter *Annals*).

3. *Annals,* 3:414; *The Writings of Thomas Jefferson,* Anas, ed. Lipscomb (New York: Round Table, 1903), 1:303–5.

4. *Annals,* 4:151.

5. *American State Papers, Finance* (Washington, D.C.: Gales and Seaton, 1832), 1:290–91.

6. *American State Papers, Foreign Affairs* (Washington, D.C.: Gales and Seaton, 1832), 1:454.

7. *Annals,* 4:34, 37–38, 56; George Washington manuscripts, series 4, reel 105, Library of Congress; *American State Papers, Foreign Affairs,* 1:329–412; President's Message to Senate, February 26, 1794, RG 46, National Archives, Washington, D.C.; Abraham D. Sofaer, "Executive Privilege," *Columbia Law Review* 75 (1975): 1318.

8. *Annals,* 5:400, 423–759.

9. *Annals,* 5:759.

10. *Annals,* 5:771, 782, 783.

11. *Nixon v. Administrator of General Services,* 433 U.S. 425, 510 (1977) (Burger, C.J., dissenting). The remark is quoted from a dictum of Justice Sutherland in 1936, in *United States v. Curtiss-Wright Export Corp.,* 299 U.S. 304, the inspiration for which is not known. Thus folly perpetuates itself.

12. *Annals,* 8:1358–74.

13. Compare Arthur M. Schlesinger, Jr., *The Imperial Presidency* (Boston: Houghton Mifflin, 1973); R. Swanstrom, *The Senate, 1787–1801,* S.Doc. No. 64 (Washington, D.C.: U.S. Government Printing Office, 1962); Louis Henkin, *Foreign Affairs and the Constitution* (Mineola, N.Y.: Foundation Press, 1972); David Frohnmayer, "An Essay on Executive Privilege," *Cong. Rec.,* April 30, 1974, p. S6603; J. R. Wiggins, *Freedom or Secrecy* (New York: Oxford University Press, 1964); Raoul Berger, *Executive Privilege: A Constitutional Myth* (Cambridge: Harvard University Press, 1974); J. W. Howard, "Constitutional Limitation and American Foreign Policy," in *Essays on the American Constitution,* ed. Gottfried Dietze (Englewood Cliffs, N.J.: Prentice-Hall, 1964).

14. *The Federalist,* ed. Edward Mead Earle (New York: Modern Library, 1937), *Federalist 51,* pp. 335–41.

15. I have found just two occasions when adjudication was mentioned as a possibility in the Federalist years. Several congressmen referred to it in the 1789 House debate on the president's power to remove department heads. There was no specific objection raised, but neither was the idea taken up. See Raoul Berger, *Congress v. the Supreme Court* (Cambridge: Harvard University Press, 1969), pp. 145–49. Hamilton suggested

to Washington that the constitutionality of Jay's Treaty might be adjudicated if Congress so desired; again, the suggestion was simply ignored. See *The Papers of Alexander Hamilton*, ed. Harold C. Syrett (New York: Columbia University Press, 1961–1979), 20:87–89.

16. Compare Schlesinger, *Imperial Presidency*, and Robert Dahl, *A Preface to Democratic Theory* (Chicago: University of Chicago Press, 1956); for radical views, see R. Lefcourt, ed., *Law Against the People* (New York: Random House, 1971), and Maureen Cain and Alan Hunt, *Marx and Engels on Law* (London and New York: Academic Press, 1979).

17. See Kocourek and Wigmore, eds., *Formative Influence of Legal Development*, Evolution of Law series, vol. 3 (New York: Little, Brown, 1918), chap. 17, p. 440.

18. The contrary proposition seems implicit in many treatments. See, for example, Coser, *The Functions of Social Conflict* (New York: Free Press, 1956), pp. 123f.; L. Coser, *Continuities in the Study of Social Conflict* (New York: Free Press, 1967); Kocourek and Wigmore, *Formative Influence;* G. Simmel, "The Secret and the Secret Society," in *The Sociology of George Simmel,* ed. K. Wolff (New York: Free Press, 1950), pt. 4, p. 365; Max Weber, *Wirtschaft and Gesellschaft,* pt. 3, chap. 6, in *From Max Weber,* ed. H. Gerth and C. W. Mills (Oxford: Oxford University Press, 1973), pp. 232–35; H. Wilensky, *Organizational Intelligence* (New York: Basic Books, 1967), p. 39; Nelson Polsby, "Legislatures," in *Governmental Institutions and Processes,* ed. Fred Greenstein and Nelson Polsby (Reading, Mass.: Addison Wesley, 1965); W. Chambers, *Political Parties in a New Nation* (Oxford: Oxford University Press, 1963), pp. 15, 36, 124; Denis Sullivan, Jeffrey Pressman, and F. Christopher Arterton, *Explorations in Convention Decision Making* (San Francisco: W. H. Freeman, 1976), pp. 38–39; Talcott Parsons, "An Outline of the Social System," in Parsons et al., *Theories of Society* (New York: Free Press, 1965), pp. 40, 41, 45, 55–59, 68–72, 75.

19. For an interesting treatment on perceptions of the rule of law in eighteenth-century England, see J. Brewer and J. Styles, eds., *An Ungovernable People* (New Brunswick, N.J.: Rutgers University Press, 1980), Introduction and chap. 4.

20. Compare the insights of modern writers such as Lon Fuller, "Governmental Secrecy and the Forms of Social Order," in *Community,* ed. Carl Friedrich (N.p.: Liberal Arts Press, 1959), Nomos 2, chap. 15; Carl Friedrich, *Constitutional Government and Democracy,* rev. ed. (1950); Robert Merton, *Social Theory and Social Structure* (New York: Free Press, 1957), pp. 199–202. See also note 18 above.

21. For structural perspectives see J. March, *Handbook of Organizations* (New York: Rand McNally, 1965), chap. 18, p. 785; Weber, *Wirtschaft;* Wilensky, *Organizational Intelligence;* F. Rourke, *Secrecy and Publicity* (Baltimore: Johns Hopkins University Press, 1961); L. Pye, *Politics, Personality, and Nationbuilding* (New Haven: Yale University Press, 1962), p. 27; Nelson Polsby, "The Institutionalization of the United States House of Representatives," *American Political Science Review* 62 (1968): 144.

22. For theoretical statements, compare Wilensky, *Organizational Intelligence,* pp. 128–29, 138–39; M. Goldschmidt, "Publicity, Privacy, and Secrecy," *Western Political Quarterly* 7 (1954): 401, 403; R. Dahl and C. Lindblom, *Politics, Economics, and Welfare* (New York: Harper, 1953), pp. 260–61; Simmel, "Secret," p. 336n.; Jurgen Habermas, *Legitimation Crisis* trans. Thomas McCarthy (Boston: Beacon, 1975), pp. 11–12; Greenstein and Polsby, eds., *Governmental Institutions,* chap. 3, p. 234.

23. Anthony King, "Executives," in Greenstein and Polsby, eds., *Governmental In-*

stitutions, remarks that "no one has explored to what extent congressmen and senators adopt . . . a posture . . . as defenders of Congress's prerogative per se against executive encroachments. This possibility has never been systematically investigated" (p. 234).

24. Reference should be made to a finding of Lowi that party cohesion tends to be strongest on "procedural" issues; see W. Chambers and W. D. Burnham, eds., *The American Party Systems: Stages of Political Development* (New York: Oxford University Press, 1967), p. 270. If secrecy issues such as resolutions calling for papers are "procedural," our data do not support this generalization. Some secrecy-related votes followed strict party lines, but more often than not at least one party would split on such issues.

25. See Chambers, *Political Parties,* p. 149. For perspectives on the role of party in the Federalist period, see R. M. Bell, *Party and Faction in American Politics: The House of Representatives, 1789–1801* (Westport, Conn.: Greenwood Press, 1973); N. E. Cunningham, *The Jeffersonian Republicans* (Westport, Conn.: Greenwood Press, 1973), p. 249; Chambers and Burnham, eds., *American Party Systems,* chaps. 1, 3, and 10; J. Charles, *Origins of the American Party System* (New York: Harper and Row, 1961).

26. For good general treatments, see Chambers, *Political Parties,* pp. 150f.; Cunningham, *Jeffersonian Republicans,* pp. 144f.; C. G. Bowers, *Jefferson and Hamilton* (New York: Houghton Mifflin, 1925), pp. 445f.

27. Some interesting remarks on the dysfunctionalities of the electoral cycle are offered by Wheeler, in "Constitutionalism," in Greenstein and Polsby, eds., *Governmental Institutions,* chap. 1, p. 6.

28. Young argues that the constitutional structure left the presidency at the mercy of congressional and cabinet factions until the party system gave presidents their own popular constituency; see J. S. Young, *The Washington Community* (New York: Harcourt Brace, 1966). But the rules of the game gave him plenary power to instruct, select, and remove department heads. The important restraints on the realization of this control came not from the formal legislative, impeachment, and appointing powers of Congress but from the practical needs of specific presidents to work amicably with specific other influentials, in or out of Congress. In the Federalist period, except for the closing years of Adams's term, these constraints were not a very important inhibition on presidential freedom of action.

29. Mr. Justice Goldberg, in *Kennedy v. Mendoza-Martinez,* 372 U.S. 144 (1962).

30. See generally, F. Wharton, *State Trials of the United States in the Administrations of Washington and John Adams* (Philadelphia: Carey and Hart, 1849); J. M. Smith, *Freedom's Fetters* (Ithaca, N.Y.: Cornell University Press, 1956); and J. C. Miller, *Crisis in Freedom: The Alien and Sedition Acts* (Boston: Little, Brown, 1951).

31. Charles Black, *The People and the Court* (New York: Macmillan, 1960), pp. 47–48.

32. Ibid., pp. 49–50; see also Lon Fuller, *The Morality of Law* (New Haven: Yale University Press, 1954), pp. 39f.

33. For a suggestive theoretical treatment of differential decisionmaking costs, see Thomas Sowell, *Knowledge and Decisions* (New York: Basic Books, 1980), chap. 2. The lines between purely ad hoc decisions, decisions involving informal rules or precedents, and those involving formal rules or precedents may not always be clear in practice. One key indicator of institutionalization of a rule or precedent, surely, is its reduction to written form, a practice thought by some theorists to be increasingly

common as systems "modernize" (Kocourek and Wigmore, *Formative Influence,* chaps. 23 and 25). As for the effect of institutionalization, the argument would seem to be that it makes the rule or precedent less ambiguous and more resistant to change, but the claim deserves careful empirical study.

34. The importance of class barriers and class conflict in understanding secrecy behavior has been noted by Habermas, *Legitimation Crisis,* pp. 116, 123, 132–34; J. Habermas, "A Theory of Communicative Competence," *Inquiry* 13 (1970): 360; B. Nelson, "Community," in Friedrich, ed., *Community;* Simmel, "Secret"; Coser, *Continuities;* H. Nieburg, *Culture Storm* (New York: St. Martin's, 1973); and S. M. Lipset, *The First New Nation* (New York: Doubleday, 1967). Lipset seems to imply that procedural regularity is an elitist value and that active public participation in politics is thus inimical to the rule of law (p. 308). Surely this is not invariably so, but it is likely to be true when public opinion is poorly socialized in liberal ideology, polarized on important substantive policy questions, and when governing institutions are "arenas" mirroring the lines of social cleavage rather than "transformative" agencies run by a cohesive and autonomous leadership group (for this last distinction see Polsby, *Institutionalization*).

35. See generally, J. Goebel, *History of the Supreme Court of the United States,* vol. 1 (New York: Macmillan, 1971).

36. According to Habermas, *Legitimation,* pp. 111–12, a separated powers system is conducive to compromise, not to discursive conflict resolution; this may imply a movement away from formal rulemaking.

37. War Powers Resolution, Public Law 93–148, 93d Cong., House Joint Res. 542, Nov. 7, 1973, 87 *Stat.* 55–60; Freedom of Information Act, 5 U.S.C. sec. 552, as amended by Public Law 93–502, 88 *Stat.* 1561–64. Additional legislative proposals designed to strengthen constitutional restraints are discussed in Morton Halperin and Daniel Hoffman, *Top Secret* (New York: New Republic Books, 1977).

38. See 18 U.S.C. secs. 792f., 238lf., 9371; 22 U.S.C. secs. 601f.; 42 U.S.C. secs. 2256f.; 50 U.S.C. secs. 781f. for the most important provisions.

39. See *United States v. Russo and Ellsberg,* no. 9373–WMB-CD (C.D. Cal. 1972); *United States v. Sneep,* 62 L. Ed. 2d 704 (1980); *United States v. Marchetti,* 466 F. 2d 1309 (4th Cir. 1972). The constitutional arguments against these sorts of proceedings are elaborated in Halperin and Hoffman, *Top Secret,* appendixes A and B, and M. Halperin and D. Hoffman, *Freedom vs. National Security* (New York: Chelsea House, 1977).

13
THE BARBARY WARS: LEGAL PRECEDENT FOR INVADING HAITI?

LOUIS FISHER

In 1994, during congressional debate on whether President Clinton could invade Haiti without first obtaining congressional authority, reference was often made to the Barbary Wars as an acceptable precedent. Senator John McCain described the wars as an example of Pres. Thomas Jefferson dispatching forces to the Mediterranean to engage in combat, with Congress never making "a declaration of war or even a declaration of approval."[1] Members of Congress may have received that impression from a memorandum opinion prepared for the attorney general in 1980 by John Harmon of the Office of Legal Counsel, U.S. Department of Justice.[2] The historical record, however, demonstrates that these military operations received advance authority from Congress in ten separate statutes. To the extent that Jefferson took initiatives before Congress acted, they were defensive in nature and not offensive (as was the action contemplated for Haiti).

During the presidencies of George Washington and John Adams, U.S. military action conformed to the Framers' expectation that the decision to go to war or to mount military operations was reserved to Congress and required advance authorization. For example, Washington's military actions against Indian tribes were initially authorized by Congress.[3] Consistent with these statutes, military operations were confined to defensive measures; offensive action required authority from Congress.[4] Similarly, when Washington used military force in the Whisky Rebellion of 1794, he acted on the basis of statutory authority.[5] John Adams engaged in the Quasi-War with France from 1798 to 1800, and although Congress did not declare war, military activities were fully authorized by more than two dozen statutes in 1798.[6]

Elected president in 1800, Thomas Jefferson inherited the pattern established during the Washington and Adams administrations: Congress had to authorize offensive military actions in advance. One of the first issues awaiting Jefferson was the practice of paying annual bribes ("tributes") to four states of North Africa: Morocco, Algiers, Tunis, and Tripoli. Regular payments were made so that these countries would not interfere with American merchantmen. A variety of local chieftains—with the titles of beys, deys, and pashas—grew wealthy from this custom as over a period of ten years, Washington and Adams had paid nearly $10 million in tributes.

In his capacity as secretary of state in 1790, Jefferson had identified for Congress a number of options for dealing with the demands of the Barbary powers. In each case it was up to Congress to establish national policy and the executive branch to implement it:

> Upon the whole, it rests with Congress to decide between war, tribute, and ransom, as the means of reestablishing our Mediterranean commerce. If war, they will consider how far our own resources shall be called forth, and how far they will enable the Executive to engage, in the forms of the constitution, the co-operation of other Powers. If tribute or ransom, it will rest with them to limit and provide the amount; and with the Executive, observing the same constitutional forms, to make arrangements for employing it to the best advantage.[7]

On March 3, 1801, one day before Jefferson took office as president, Congress passed legislation to provide for a "naval peace establishment."[8] On May 15, Jefferson's cabinet debated the president's authority to use force against the Barbary powers. The cabinet agreed that American vessels could repel an attack, but some departmental heads insisted on a larger definition of executive power. For example, Albert Gallatin, secretary of the treasury, remarked, "The Executive can not put us in a state of war, but if we be put into that state either by the decree of Congress or of the other nation, the command and direction of the public force then belongs to the Executive." Other departmental heads expressed different views.[9]

After hearing these opinions from his cabinet, Jefferson chose to rely on statutory authority rather than on theories of inherent presidential power. Citing the statute of March 3, the State Department issued a directive on May 20 to Capt. Richard Dale of the U.S. Navy, stating that under "this [statutory] authority" Jefferson had directed that a squadron be sent to the Mediterranean. In the event that Barbary powers declared war on the United States, American vessels were ordered to "protect our commerce & chastise their insolence—by sinking, burning or destroying their ships & Vessels wherever you shall find them."[10] Having issued that order based on congressional authority,

Jefferson also wrote that it was up to Congress to decide what policy to pursue in the Mediterranean: "The real alternative before us is whether to abandon the Mediterranean or to keep up a cruise in it, perhaps in rotation with other powers who would join us as soon as there is peace. But this Congress must decide."[11]

Insisting on a larger tribute, the pasha of Tripoli declared war on the United States. Jefferson did not interpret this action as authority for the president to engage in unlimited military activities. He informed Congress on December 8, 1801, about the demands of the pasha: unless the United States paid tribute, Tripoli threatened to seize American ships and citizens. Jefferson had sent a small squadron of frigates to the Mediterranean to protect against the attack and then asked Congress for further guidance, stating he was "unauthorized by the Constitution, without the sanction of Congress, to go beyond the line of defense." It was the responsibility of Congress to authorize "measures of offense also." Jefferson gave Congress the necessary documents and communications so that the legislative branch, "in the exercise of this important function confided by the Constitution to the Legislature exclusively," could examine the situation and act in the manner it considered most appropriate.[12]

Alexander Hamilton, writing under the pseudonym "Lucius Crassus," issued a strong critique of Jefferson's message to Congress. Hamilton believed that Jefferson had defined executive power too narrowly, deferring excessively to Congress. But even Hamilton, pushing the edge of executive power, never argued that the president had full power to make war on other nations. Hamilton merely argued that when a foreign nation declares war on the United States, the president may respond to that fact without waiting for congressional authority:

> The first thing in [the president's message], which excites our surprise, is the very extraordinary position, that though *Tripoli had declared war in form* against the United States, and had enforced it by actual hostility, yet that there was not power, for want of *the sanction of Congress,* to capture and detain her cruisers with their crews. . . . [The Constitution] has only provided affirmatively, that, "The Congress shall have power to declare War;" the plain meaning of which is, that it is the peculiar and exclusive province of Congress, *when the nation is at peace* to change that state into a state of war; whether from calculations of policy, or from provocations, or injuries received: in other words, it belongs to Congress only, *to go to War.* But when a foreign nation declares, or openly and avowedly makes war upon the United States, they are then

by the very fact *already at war,* and any declaration on the part of Congress is nugatory; it is at least unnecessary."[13]

Congress responded to Jefferson's message by authorizing him to equip armed vessels to protect commerce and seamen in the Atlantic, the Mediterranean, and adjoining seas. The statute also authorized American ships to seize vessels belonging to the bey of Tripoli, with the captured property distributed to those who brought the vessels into port.[14] Legislators had no doubt about their constitutional authority and duties. "The simple question now," said Cong. William Eustis, "is whether [the president] shall be empowered to take offensive steps." Congressman Samuel Smith added, "By the prescriptions of the law, the President deemed himself bound."[15]

Congress continued to pass measures authorizing military action against the Barbary powers. Legislation in 1803 provided additional armament for the protection of seamen and U.S. commerce.[16] The next year Congress gave explicit support for "warlike operations against the regency of Tripoli, or any other of the Barbary powers."[17] Duties on foreign goods were placed in a "Mediterranean Fund" to finance these operations.[18] Further legislation on the Barbary powers appeared in 1806, 1807, 1808, 1809, 1811, 1812, and 1813.[19]

Jefferson often distinguished between defensive and offensive military operations, permitting presidential initiatives for the former but not the latter. In 1805 he notified Congress about a conflict with the Spanish along the eastern boundary of the Louisiana Territory (West Florida). After detailing the problem, he noted: "Considering that Congress alone is constitutionally invested with the power of changing our condition from peace to war, I have thought it my duty to await their authority for using force in any degree which could be avoided."[20]

Military conflicts in the Mediterranean continued after Jefferson left office. The dey of Algiers made war against U.S. citizens trading in that region and kept some in captivity. With the conclusion of the War of 1812 with England, President Madison recommended to Congress in 1815 that it declare war on Algiers: "I recommend to Congress the expediency of an act declaring the existence of a state of war between the United States and the Dey and Regency of Algiers, and of such provisions as may be requisite for a vigorous prosecution of it to a successful issue."[21] Instead of a declaration of war, Congress passed legislation "for the protection of the commerce of the United States against the Algerine cruisers," the first line of the statute reading, "Whereas the Dey of Algiers, on the coast of Barbary, has commenced a predatory warfare against the United States." Congress gave Madison authority to use armed vessels for the purpose of protecting the commerce of U.S. seamen on the Atlantic, the Mediterranean, and adjoining seas. American vessels (both governmental and private) could "subdue, seize, and make prize of all vessels, goods and effects of or belonging to the Dey of Algiers."[22] An American flotilla set sail for Algiers, where it captured two of the dey's ships and forced him to stop the piracy, release all captives, and renounce the practice of annual tribute payments. Similar treaties were obtained from Tunis and Tripoli. By the end of 1815, Madison could report to Congress on the successful termination of the war with Algiers.[23]

The conduct of the Barbary Wars conformed to the Framers' expectations that Congress alone could authorize war or the initiation of lesser military hostilities abroad. It is clear that offensive actions that are contemplated by presidents, whether in the Mediterranean, Haiti, or elsewhere, require prior approval by Congress. It is equally clear that Congress may impose limits on its authorization of presidential actions.

Congress may not only authorize and declare war, it may also establish limits on prospective presidential actions. The statutes authorizing Washington to "protect the inhabitants" of the frontiers "from hostile incursions of the Indians" were interpreted by his administration as authority for defensive, not offensive, actions.[24] Secretary of War Henry Knox wrote to Gov. William Blount on October 9, 1792: "The Congress which possess the powers of declaring War will assemble on the 5th of next Month—Until their judgments shall be made known it seems essential to confine all your operations to defensive measures."[25] Washington consistently held to this policy. Writing in 1793, he said that any offensive operations against the Creek Nation must await congressional action: "The Constitution vests the power of declaring war with Congress; therefore no offensive expedition of importance can be undertaken until after they have deliberated upon the subject, and authorized such a measure."[26]

The 1792 statute upon which Washington relied for his actions in the Whisky Rebellion conditioned the use of military force by the president upon an unusual judicial check. The legislation provided that whenever the United States "shall be invaded, or be in imminent danger of invasion from any foreign nation or Indian tribe," the president may call forth the state militias to repel such invasions and to suppress insurrections.[27] However, whenever federal laws were opposed and their execution obstructed in any state "by combinations too powerful to be suppressed by the ordinary course of judicial proceedings, or by the powers vested in the marshals by this act," the president would have to be first notified of that fact by an associate justice of the Supreme Court or by a federal district judge. Only after that notice could the president call forth the militia of the state to suppress the insurrection.[28]

In the legislation authorizing the Quasi-War of 1798, Congress placed limits on what John Adams could and could not do. One statute authorized him to seize vessels sailing to French ports, but he acted beyond the terms of this statute by issuing an order directing American ships to capture vessels sailing *to or from* French ports. A naval captain followed his order by seizing a Danish ship sailing from a French port. He was sued for damages, and the case came to the Supreme Court, where Chief Justice John Marshall ruled for a unanimous Court that Adams had exceeded his statutory authority.[29]

The Neutrality Act of 1794 led to numerous cases before the federal courts. In one of the significant cases defining the power of Congress to restrict presidential war actions, a circuit court in 1806 reviewed the indictment of an individual who claimed that his military enterprise against Spain "was begun, prepared, and set on foot with the knowledge and approbation of the executive department of our government."[30] The court repudiated his claim that a president could authorize military adventures that violated congressional policy. Executive officials were not at liberty to waive statutory provisions: "If a private individual, even with the knowledge and approbation of this high preeminent officer of our government [the president], should set on foot such a military expedition, how can he expect to be exonerated from the obligation of the law?" The court said that the president "cannot control the statute, nor dispense with its execution, and still less can he authorize a person to do what the law forbids. If he could, it would render the execution of the laws dependent on his will and pleasure; which is a doctrine that has not been set up, and will not meet with any supporters in our government. In this particular, the law is paramount." The president could not direct a citizen to conduct a war "against a nation with whom the United States are at peace."[31] The court asked, "Does [the president] possess the power of making war? That power is exclusively vested in congress. . . . It is the exclusive province of congress to change a state of peace into a state of war."[32]

NOTES

1. 140 *Cong. Rec.* S10666 (daily ed., August 5, 1994).

2. 4A Opinions of Office of Legal Counsel 185, 187 (1980), reprinted in *Cong. Rec.* S14046 (daily ed., October 21, 1993), p. 139.

3. 1 Stat. 96, sec. 5 (1789); 1 Stat. 121, sec. 16 (1790); 1 Stat. 222 (1791).

4. *The Writings of George Washington,* ed. John C. Fitzpatrick (Washington, D.C.:

Government Printing Office, 1939), 33:73. For elaboration, see Louis Fisher, *Presidential War Power* (Lawrence: University Press of Kansas, 1995).

5. 1 Stat. 264, sec. 1 (1792).
6. 1 Stat. 547–611 (1798). For a fuller discussion, see Chapter 11 of this volume.
7. *American State Papers: Foreign Relations,* ed. Walter Lowrie and Matthew St. Clair Clarke (Washington, D.C.: Gales and Seaton, 1832), 1:105.
8. 2 Stat. 110, sec. 1 (1801).
9. Franklin B. Sawvel, ed., *The Complete Anas of Thomas Jefferson* (New York: Round Table Press, 1903), p. 213.
10. *Naval Documents Relating to the United States Wars with the Barbary Powers* (Washington, D.C.: Government Printing Office, 1939), p. 467.
11. *The Writings of Thomas Jefferson,* ed. P. L. Ford (Washington, D.C.: Thomas Jefferson Memorial Association, 1897), 8:63–64.
12. *Compilation of the Messages and Papers of the Presidents,* ed. James D. Richardson (Washington, D.C.: Washington Bureau of National Literature, 1909), 1:315.
13. *The Works of Alexander Hamilton,* ed. H. C. Lodge, 12 vols. (New York: Putnam, 1904), 8:249–50.
14. 2 Stat. 129 (1802).
15. *Annals of Cong.,* 7th Cong., 1st sess., 328–29 (1801).
16. 2 Stat. 106 (1803).
17. 2 Stat. 291 (1804).
18. Ibid., p. 292, sec. 2.
19. 2 Stat. 391 (1806); 2 Stat. 436 (1807); 2 Stat. 456 (1808); 2 Stat. 511 (1809); 2 Stat. 616 (1811); 2 Stat. 675 (1812); 2 Stat. 809 (1813).
20. Richardson, ed., *Compilation,* 1:377.
21. Ibid., 2:539.
22. 3 Stat. 230 (1815).
23. Richardson, ed., *Compilation,* 2:547.
24. 1 Stat. 96, sec. 5 (1789); 1 Stat. 121, sec. 16 (1790); 1 Stat. 222 (1791).
25. *The Territorial Papers of the United States,* ed. Clarence Edwin Carter (Washington, D.C.: Government Printing Office, 1936), 4:196.
26. *Writings of Washington,* 33:73.
27. 1 Stat. 264, sec. 1 (1792).
28. Ibid., sec. 2.
29. *Little v. Barreme,* 6 U.S. (2 Cr.) 169 (1804).
30. *United States v. Smith,* 27 Fed. Cas. 1192, 1229 (C.C.N.Y. 1806) (No. 16, 342).
31. Ibid., p. 1230.
32. Ibid.

14
TRUMAN IN KOREA

LOUIS FISHER

In June 1950 Pres. Harry Truman used military force against North Korea without seeking congressional authority. For legal basis he referred to resolutions passed by the United Nations Security Council, a source of authority that was in fact spurious. Because the Bush administration cited the Korean War as an acceptable precedent for taking offensive action against Iraq in 1991 without the need for congressional authority, we must understand Truman's actions and his reliance on UN resolutions.

THE UN CHARTER

In arguing that presidents need only authorization from the UN Security Council, not from Congress, the Truman administration violated the plain language and the clear legislative history of the UN Charter and the UN Participation Act. Nothing supports the notion that Congress, by endorsing the structure of the United Nations as an international peacekeeping body, amended the Constitution by reading itself out of the warmaking power. Congress did not—and could not—do so.

In response to any threat to the peace, breach of the peace, or act of aggression, the UN Security Council may decide under Article 41 of the UN Charter to recommend "measures not involving the use of armed force." If those measures prove to be inadequate, Article 43 provides that all members of the United Nations shall undertake to make available to the Security Council, "on its call and in accordance with a special agreement or agreements," armed forces and other assistance. The purpose of these agreements is to spell out the numbers and types of forces, their degree of readiness and general location, and the nature of the facilities and assistance to be provided. Could the president on his own enter into special agreements? Definitely not. Article 43 further provides that the measures shall be ratified by each nation "in accordance with their respective constitutional processes."

From July 9 to July 13, 1945, the Senate Foreign Relations Committee held hearings on the UN Charter. John Foster Dulles, an adviser to the U.S. delegation in San Francisco and an expert on the drafting of the charter, testified that the procedure for special agreements would need the approval of the Senate and could not be acted upon unilaterally by the president.[1] During floor debate, Sen. Scott Lucas (D.-Ill.) disagreed that special agreements could be disposed of solely by the Senate. Action by both Houses, he said, would be needed.[2] As the debate proceeded, Sen. Arthur Vandenberg (R.-Mich.) called Dulles to ask what he intended to say at the hearings. Dulles explained that he thought the issue was between unilateral presidential action (by executive agreement) or joint executive-legislative action. He definitely believed in the latter and assumed that joint action meant through the treaty process. The basic point he tried to make was that "the use of force cannot be made by exclusive Presidential authority through an executive agreement." On that point he was sure. Whether congressional action should be by treaty or by joint resolution he was less certain.[3]

Truman, aware of the Senate debate on which branch controlled the sending of armed forces to the UN, wired a note to Sen. Kenneth McKellar (D.-Tenn.) on July 27, 1945, from Potsdam, pledging, "When any such agreement or agreements are negotiated it will be my purpose to ask the Congress for appropriate legislation to approve them."[4] With Truman's reference to "the Congress," the senator understood him to mean that Congress "consists not alone of the Senate but of the two Houses."[5]

Having approved the charter, Congress then had to pass legislation to implement it and to determine the precise mechanisms for the use of force. The specific procedures, brought into conformity with "constitutional processes," are included in the UN Participation Act of 1945. The meaning of constitutional processes is defined by Section 6 of the act, which requires that the agreements "shall be subject to the approval of the Congress by appropriate Act or joint resolution." Statutory language could not be more clear. Two qualifications are included in Section 6:

> The President shall not be deemed to require the authorization of the Congress to make available to the Security Council on its call in order to take action under Article 42 of said Charter and pursuant to such special agreement or agreements the armed forces, facilities, or assistance provided therein: *Provided,* That nothing herein contained shall be construed as an authorization to the President by the Congress to make

available to the Security Council for such purpose armed forces, facilities, or assistance in addition to the forces, facilities, and assistance provided for in such special agreements or agreements.[6]

The first qualification states that once the president receives the approval of Congress for a special agreement, he does not need subsequent approval from Congress to provide military assistance under Article 42, by which the Security Council determines that peaceful means are inadequate and military action is necessary. Congressional approval is needed for the special agreement, not for subsequent implementations of the agreement. The second qualification states that nothing in the UN Participation Act of 1945 is to be construed as congressional approval of other agreements entered into by the president.

Thus, the qualifications do not eliminate the need for congressional approval. Presidents could commit armed forces to the UN only after Congress gave its explicit consent. That point is crucial. The League of Nations Covenant foundered precisely on the issue of the need for congressional approval before using armed force. The framers of the UN Charter knew of that history and consciously included protection for congressional prerogatives.[7] Senator Henry Cabot Lodge (R.-Mass.) presented fourteen "reservations" to the League Covenant in 1919; the second reservation expressly recognized the power of Congress to control military commitments:

> The United States assumes no obligation to preserve the territorial integrity or political independence of any other country or to interfere in controversies between nations—whether members of the league or not—under the provisions of article 10, or to employ the military or naval forces of the United States under any article of the treaty for any purpose, unless in any particular case the Congress, which, under the Constitution, has the sole power to declare war or authorize the employment of the military or naval forces of the United States, shall by act or joint resolution so provide.[8]

The legislative history of the UN Participation Act tracks this understanding perfectly and leaves no doubt about the need for advance congressional approval. In his appearance before the House Committee on Foreign Affairs, Undersecretary of State Dean Acheson explained that only after the president receives the approval of Congress is he "bound to furnish that contingent of troops to the Security Council; and the President is not authorized to furnish any more than you have approved of that agreement."[9] When Cong. Edith

Rogers (R.-Mass.) remarked that Congress "can easily control the [Security] Council," Acheson agreed unequivocally: "It is entirely within the wisdom of Congress to approve or disapprove whatever special agreement the President negotiates."[10] Congressman John Kee (D.-W.Va.) wondered whether the qualifications in Section 6 of the UN Participation Act permitted the president to provide military assistance to the Security Council without consulting or submitting the matter to Congress. Acheson firmly denied the possibility. No special agreement could have any "force or effect" until Congress approved:

> This is an important question of Judge Kee, and may I state his question and my answer so that it will be quite clear here: The judge asks whether the language beginning on line 19 of page 5, which says the President shall not be deemed to require the authorization of Congress to make available to the Security Council on its call in order to take action under article 42 of the Charter, means that the President may provide these forces prior to the time when any special agreement has been approved by Congress.
>
> The answer to that question is "No," that the President may not do that, that such special agreements refer to the special agreement which shall be subject to the approval of the Congress, so that until the special agreement has been negotiated and approved by the Congress, it has no force and effect.[11]

Other parts of the legislative history support this understanding. In reporting the UN Participation Act, the Senate Foreign Relations Committee anticipated a shared, coequal relationship between the president and Congress:

> Although the ratification of the Charter resulted in the vesting in the executive branch of the power and obligation to fulfill the commitments assumed by the United States thereunder, the Congress must be taken into close partnership and must be fully advised of all phases of our participation in this enterprise. The Congress will be asked annually to appropriate funds to support the United Nations budget and for the expenses of our representation. It will be called upon to approve arrangements for the supply of armed forces to the Security Council and thereafter to make appropriations for the maintenance of such forces.[12]

The House of Representatives also understood that the UN Participation Act protected congressional prerogatives over war and peace. In reporting the bill, the House Foreign Affairs Committee drew attention to the vote in the Senate rejecting the idea that special agreements could be handled solely by the Senate through the treaty process. The committee "believes that it is eminently appropriate that the Congress as a whole pass upon these agreements under the constitutional powers of the Congress."[13] During floor debate, Cong. Sol Bloom (D.-N.Y.), one of the delegates at the San Francisco conference, underscored that point:

> The position of the Congress is fully protected by the requirement that the military agreement to preserve the peace must be passed upon by Congress before it becomes effective. Also, the obligation of the United States to make forces available to the Security Council does not become effective until the special agreement has been passed upon by Congress.[14]

Some legislators thought that the UN Charter might allow the president to make military commitments through the treaty process, requiring only the Senate's approval, but that understanding was unfounded because the Participation Act requires approval of both houses. An amendment was offered in the Senate to authorize the president to negotiate a special agreement with the Security Council "and, by and with the advice and consent of the Senate, to enter into such agreement . . . provided two-thirds of the Senators present concur."[15] Senator Vandenberg made these points in opposing the amendment:

> If we go to war, a majority of the House and Senate put us into war. . . . The House has equal responsibility with the Senate in respect of raising armies and supporting and sustaining them. The House has primary jurisdiction over the taxation necessities involved in supporting and sustaining armies and navies, and in maintaining national defense. . . . [The Senate Foreign Relations Committee] chose to place the ratification of that contract in the hands of both Houses of Congress, inasmuch as the total Congress of the United States must deal with all the consequences which are involved either if we have war or if we succeeded in preventing one.[16]

Members of the Senate recognized that the decision to go to war must be made by both houses of Congress, and the amendment was defeated decisively, 57 to 14.[17]

The restrictions on the president's power under Section 6 to use armed force were clarified by amendments adopted in 1949, allowing the president on his own initiative to provide military forces to the United Nations for "cooperative action." However, presidential discretion to deploy these forces was subject to stringent conditions: they could serve only as observers and guards, could perform only in a noncombatant capacity, and could not exceed 1,000.[18] Moreover, in providing these troops to the UN the president shall ensure that they not involve "the employment of armed forces contemplated by Chapter VII of the United Nations Charter."[19] Clearly, there was no opportunity in the amendments to the UN Participation Act for unilateral military action by the president.

THE KOREAN WAR

With safeguards supposedly established to protect congressional prerogatives, on June 26, 1950, President Truman announced to the American public that he had conferred with the secretaries of State and Defense, their senior advisers, and the Joint Chiefs of Staff "about the situation in the Far East created by unprovoked aggression against the Republic of Korea."[20] He said that the UN Security Council had acted to order a withdrawal of the invading forces to positions north of the 38th parallel and that "in accordance with the resolution of the Security Council, the United States will vigorously support the effort of the Council to terminate this serious breach of the peace."[21] At that point, he made no commitment of U.S. military forces.

The next day, however, Truman announced that North Korea had failed to cease hostilities and to withdraw to the 38th parallel. He then summarized the UN action:

> The Security Council called upon all members of the United Nations to render every assistance to the United Nations in the execution of this resolution. In these circumstances I have ordered United States air and sea forces to give the [South] Korean Government troops cover and support.[22]

Moreover, Truman said that "the occupation of Formosa by Communist forces would be a direct threat to the security of the Pacific area and to United States forces performing their lawful and necessary functions in that area."[23] Finally, he advised that all members of the UN "will consider carefully" the consequences of Korea's aggression "in defiance of the Charter of the United Nations" and that a "return to the rule of force in international affairs" would have far-reaching effects. The United States, he said, "will continue to uphold the rule of law."[24]

In fact, Truman violated the unambiguous statutory language and legislative history of the UN Participation Act. How could he pretend to be under the UN umbrella in acting militarily in Korea without congressional approval? The short answer is that he ignored the special agreements that were the vehicle for ensuring congressional approval in advance of any military action by the president. With the Soviet Union absent, the Security Council voted 9 to 0 to call upon North Korea to cease hostilities and to withdraw their forces. Two days later the council requested military assistance from UN members to repel the attack, but by then Truman had already ordered U.S. air and sea forces to assist South Korea.

Truman's legal authority was nonexistent for two reasons. First, it cannot be argued that the president's constitutional powers vary with the presence or absence of Soviet delegates to the Security Council. As Robert Bork noted in 1971, "The approval of the United Nations was obtained only because the Soviet Union happened to be boycotting the Security Council at the time, and the President's Constitutional powers can hardly be said to ebb and flow with the veto of the Soviet Union in the Security Council."[25]

Second, the Truman administration did not act pursuant to UN authority, even though it strained to make that case. On June 29, 1950, Secretary of State Acheson claimed that all U.S. actions taken in Korea "have been under the aegis of the United Nations."[26] "Aegis" means shield or protection, and Acheson was expanding the definition to suggest that the United States was acting under the legal banner of the United Nations, which of course was not the case.

Acheson falsely claimed that Truman had done his "utmost to uphold the sanctity of the Charter of the United Nations and the rule of law" and that the administration was in "conformity with the resolutions of the Security Council of June 25 and 27, giving air and sea support to the troops of the Korean government."[27] Yet Truman had committed U.S. forces a day before the council called for military action. General Douglas MacArthur was immediately authorized to send supplies of ammunition to the South Korean defenders. On June 26, Truman ordered U.S. air and sea forces to give South Koreans cover and support.[28] After Acheson summarized the situation for some members of Congress at noon on June 27, Truman exclaimed, "But Dean, you didn't even mention the U.N.!"[29] Later that evening the Security Council passed the second resolution.

In his memoirs, Acheson admitted that "some American action, said to be in support of the resolution of June 27, was in fact ordered, and possibly taken, prior to the resolution."[30] After he left the presidency, Truman was asked whether he had been prepared to use military force in Korea without UN backing. He replied, with his usual bluntness, "No question about it."[31] Indeed, Truman did not seek the approval of members of Congress for his military actions in Korea. As Acheson suggested, Truman might only wish to "tell them what had been decided."[32] The president met with congressional leaders at 11:30 A.M. on June 27, after the administration's policy had been established and implementing orders issued.[33] He later met with congressional leaders to give them a briefing on developments in Korea but never asked for authority.[34] Some consideration was given to presenting a joint resolution to Congress to permit legislators to voice their approval, but the draft resolution never left the administration.[35]

On June 29, at a news conference, Truman was asked whether the country was at war. His response: "We are not at war."[36] Asked whether it would be more correct to call the conflict "a police action under the United Nations," he agreed: "That is exactly what it amounts to."[37] The United Nations exercised no real authority over the conduct of the war; other than token support from a few nations, it was an American war. The Security Council requested that the United States designate the commander of the forces and authorized the "unified command at its discretion to use the United Nations flag."[38] Truman designated General MacArthur to serve as commander of this so-called unified command.[39] Measured by troops, money, casualties, and deaths, it remained an American war.

Federal courts had no difficulty in defining the hostilities in Korea as war. A federal district court noted in 1953: "We doubt very much if there is any question in the minds of the majority of the people of this country that the conflict now raging in Korea can be anything but war."[40] During Senate hearings in June 1951, Secretary of State Acheson conceded the obvious by admitting "in the usual sense of the word there is a war."[41]

Truman's violation of constitutional and statutory requirements may have resulted from a mistaken reading of history. In deciding whether North Korean aggression could go unanswered, he looked, in his own lifetime, to Japan's invasion of Manchuria and Germany's reoccupation of the Rhineland. He did not consider other historical parallels where force had been used, such as the American Civil War or nineteenth-century efforts in Germany for unification. Apparently it did not occur to him that the situation in Korea resembled the attempts of the latter more than it did those in Manchuria or in the Rhineland.[42]

Even if a case could be made that the emergency facing Truman in June 1950 required him to act promptly without first seeking and obtaining legislative authority, nothing prevented him from returning to Congress and asking for a supporting statute or for retroactive authority. John Norton Moore has made this point: "As to the suddenness of Korea, and conflicts like Korea, I would argue that the President should have the authority to meet the attack as necessary but should immediately seek congressional authorization."[43] I would put it a little differently: in a genuine emergency, a president may act without congressional authority (and without express legal or constitutional authority), trusting that the circumstances are so urgent and compelling that Congress will endorse his actions and confer a legitimacy that only Congress, as the people's representatives, can provide.

The analysis of "constitutional processes" required for actions under Article 43 of the UN Charter applies also to mutual defense treaties entered into by the United States. Those treaties—NATO, SEATO, ANZUS, and so on—do not empower the president to use armed force abroad without congressional consent. The treaties merely authorize armed force. The principle that an attack on one nation is considered an attack on all does not require an immediate presidential response. There is no automatic commitment to war. Force is to be used only after following constitutional processes, which includes both houses of Congress.[44] Mutual defense treaties do not "transfer to the President the Congressional power to make war."[45] The Senate and the president cannot use the treaty process to take from the House of Representatives its constitutional role in the war power.[46]

POLITICAL RAMIFICATIONS

Congress was largely passive in its response to Truman's usurpation of the war power. Some members offered the weak justification that "history will show that on more than 100 occasions in the life of this Republic the President as Commander in Chief has ordered the fleet or the troops to do certain things which involved the risk of war [without seeking congressional consent]."[47] The list of alleged precedents for unilateral presidential action contains not a single military adventure that comes close to the dimensions of the Korean War. As Edward S. Corwin noted, the list consists largely of "fights with pirates, landings of small naval contingents on barbarous or semi-barbarous coasts, the dispatch of small bodies of troops to chase bandits or cattle rustlers across the Mexican border, and the like."[48]

A few legislators insisted that Truman should have gone to Congress for authority before he acted.[49] Congressman Vito Marcantonio (ALP-N.Y.) objected: "When we agreed to the United Nations Charter we never agreed to supplant our Constitution with the United Nations Charter. The power to declare and make war is vested in the representative of the people, in the Congress of the United States."[50]

Just as the Vietnam War spelled defeat for the Democrats in 1968, so did the Korean War help put an end to twenty years of Democratic control of the White House. "Korea, not crooks or Communists, was the major concern of the voters," writes Stephen Ambrose.[51] The high point of the 1952 campaign came on October 24, less than two weeks before the election, when Dwight D. Eisenhower announced that he would "go to Korea" to end the war.[52]

Once in office, Eisenhower concluded that Truman had made a serious mistake, politically and constitutionally, by going to war in Korea without congressional approval. Eisenhower thought that national commitments would be stronger if entered into jointly by both branches. Toward that end he asked Congress for specific authority to deal with crises in the Formosa Straits and in the Middle East, and Congress passed joint resolutions authorizing him to act in those regions.[53] He stressed the importance of collective action by Congress and the president: "I deem it necessary to seek the cooperation of the Congress. Only with that cooperation can we give the reassurance needed to deter aggression."[54]

Eisenhower's theory of government and international relations invited congressional support for area resolutions. On New Year's Day, 1957, he met with Secretary of State John Foster Dulles and congressional leaders of both parties. House majority leader John McCormack asked Eisenhower whether he, as commander-in-chief, already had sufficient constitutional authority to act in the Middle East without congressional approval. Eisenhower replied that he might have that power, in theory, but "greater effect could be had from a consensus of Executive and Legislative opinion. . . . I reminded the legislators that the Constitution assumes that our two branches of government should get along together."[55] Eisenhower knew that lawyers and policy advisers in the executive branch could always discover precedents for unilateral presidential action, but that did not satisfy him. It was his seasoned opinion that a commitment by the United States would impress allies and enemies more if it represented the collective judgment of the president and Congress.

Some leading academics, after rushing to Truman's support, later regretted their failure to give proper attention to constitutional principles. Henry Steele Commager, for example, had been quick to defend Truman. Writing for the *New York Times* on January 14, 1951, Commager remarked that the objections to Truman's unilateral actions "have no support in law or in history."[56] His own research into law and history, on this point, was superficial and misinformed; consider his reasoning:

It is an elementary fact that must never be lost sight of that treaties are laws and carry with them the same obligation as laws. When the Congress passed the United Nations Participation Act it made the obligation of the Charter of the United Nations law, binding on the President. When the Senate ratified the North Atlantic Treaty it made the obligations of that treaty law, binding on the President. Both of these famous documents require action by the United States which must, in the nature of the case, be left to a large extent to the discretion of the Executive.[57]

Commager not only overstated the president's power under mutual defense treaties but ignored, totally, the statutory text and the legislative history of the UN Participation Act.

Arthur S. Schlesinger, Jr., was also an early defender of Truman's action in Korea. In a letter to the *New York Times* on January 9, 1951, he disputed the statement by Sen. Robert Taft (R.-Ohio) that Truman "had no authority whatever to commit American troops to Korea without consulting Congress and without Congressional approval" and that by sending troops to Korea he "simply usurped authority, in violation of the laws and the Constitution." Schlesinger said that Taft's statements "are demonstrably irresponsible." Harkening back to Jefferson's use of ships to repel the Barbary pirates, Schlesinger claimed that American presidents "have repeatedly committed American armed forces abroad without prior Congressional consultation or approval."[58] Schlesinger neglected to point out that Jefferson told Congress he was "unauthorized by the Constitution, without the sanction of Congress, to go beyond the line of defense." It was the prerogative of Congress to authorize "measures of offense also."[59] Schlesinger did not cite, nor could he, a presidential initiative of the magnitude of the Korean War.

Edward S. Corwin took Commager and Schlesinger to task by labeling them the "high-flying prerogative men."[60] By the late 1960s, with the nation mired in a bitter war in Vietnam, Commager and Schlesinger publicly apologized for their earlier unreserved endorsements of presidential war power. By 1966 Schlesinger was counseling that "something must be done to assure the Congress a more authoritative and continuing voice in fundamental decisions in foreign policy."[61] In 1973 he stated that the "idea of prerogative was *not* part of presidential powers as defined by the Constitution," although it "remained in the back of [the Framers'] mind."[62] Commager told the Senate in 1967 that there should be a reconsideration of executive-legislative relations in the conduct of foreign relations.[63] Testifying before the Senate Foreign Relations Committee in 1971, he appealed for stronger legislative checks on presidential war powers.[64]

By the time of the Iraqi crisis in 1990–1991, this understanding of constitutional relations had faded in the collective memory, allowing the Bush administration to claim that it had sole authority to decide when to take the nation to war. Vague references were made to UN resolutions as an adequate source of legal authority. On January 8, 1991, Bush asked Congress to pass legislation authorizing his policy in the Gulf War. He was asked by reporters the next day whether he needed a resolution from Congress. He replied, "I don't think I need it. . . . I feel that I have the authority to fully implement the United Nations resolutions."[65] A week later Congress authorized the war, but the nation came perilously close to a constitutional crisis because we have yet to understand, and take to heart, the dangerous precedent established by Truman in Korea.

NOTES

1. "The Charter of the United Nations," Hearings Before the Senate Committee on Foreign Relations, 79th Cong., 1st sess. (1945), pp. 645–46.
2. 91 *Cong. Rec.* 8021 (1945).
3. Ibid., pp. 8027–28.
4. Ibid., p. 8145.
5. Ibid. (Senator Donnell).
6. 59 Stat. 621, sec. 6 (1945).
7. Michael J. Glennon, "The Constitution and Chapter VII of the United States Charter," *American Journal of International Law* 85 (1991): 74, 75–77.
8. 58 *Cong. Rec.* 8777 (1919).
9. "Participation by the United States in the United Nations Organization," Hearings Before the House Committee on Foreign Affairs, 79th Cong., 1st sess. 23 (1945).
10. Ibid.
11. Ibid., pp. 25–26.
12. S. Rept. no. 717, 79th Cong., 1st sess. (1945), p. 5.
13. H. Rept. no. 1383, 79th Cong., 1st sess. (1945), p. 7.
14. 91 *Cong. Rec.* 12267 (1945).
15. Ibid., p. 11296.
16. Ibid., p. 11301.
17. Ibid., p. 11303. See also H. Rept. no. 1383, 79th Cong., 1st sess. 7 (1945).
18. 63 Stat. 735–36, sec. 5 (1949).
19. Ibid.
20. *Public Papers of the Presidents: Harry Truman, 1950* (Washington, D.C.: Government Printing Office, 1950), p. 491.
21. Ibid.

22. Ibid., p. 492.

23. Ibid.

24. Ibid.

25. Robert Bork, "Comments on the Articles on the Legality of the United States Action in Cambodia," *American Journal of International Law* 65 (1971): 79, 81.

26. *Department of State Bulletin* 23 (1950): 43.

27. Ibid., p. 46.

28. *Public Papers of the Presidents: Harry Truman, 1950*, p. 529.

29. Glenn D. Paige, *The Korean Decision* (New York: Free Press, 1968), p. 188.

30. Dean Acheson, *Present at the Creation* (New York: W. W. Norton, 1969), p. 408. See also Edwin C. Hoyt, "The United States Reaction to the Korean Attack: A Study of the Principles of the United Nations Charter as a Factor in American Policy-Making," *American Journal of International Law* 55 (1961): 45, 53.

31. Merle Miller, *Plain Speaking: An Oral Biography of Harry S. Truman* (New York: Berkley, 1974), p. 297 n.

32. *Foreign Relations of the United States, 1950* (Washington, D.C.: Government Printing Office, 1976), 7:182.

33. Ibid., pp. 200–202.

34. Ibid., p. 257.

35. Ibid., pp. 282–83 nn. 1 and 2, and pp. 287–91.

36. *Public Papers of the Presidents: Harry Truman, 1951* (Washington, D.C.: Government Printing Office, 1951), p. 503.

37. Ibid., p. 504. On July 13, at a news conference, he again called the Korean War a "police action" (p. 522).

38. Ibid., p. 520.

39. Ibid.

40. *Weissman v. Metropolitan Life Ins. Co.*, 112 F.Supp. 420, 425 (S.D. Cal. 1953). See also *Gagliormella v. Metropolitan Life Ins. Co.*, 122 F.Supp. 246 (D. Mass. 1954); *Carius v. New York Life Insurance Co.*, 124 F.Supp. 388 (D. Ill. 1954); and A. Kenneth Pye, "The Legal Status of the Korean Hostilities," *Georgetown Law Journal* 45 (1956): 45.

41. "Military Situation in the Far East" (part 3), Hearings Before the Senate Committees on Armed Services and Foreign Relations, 82d Cong., 1st sess. (1951), p. 2014.

42. Richard S. Kirkendall, *Harry S. Truman and the Imperial Presidency* (St. Charles, Mo.: Forum Press, 1975), pp. 11, 16.

43. John Norton Moore, "The National Executive and the Use of Armed Forces Abroad," *Naval War College Review* 21 (1969): 28, 32.

44. Richard Heindel et al., "The North Atlantic Treaty in the United States," *American Journal of International Law* 43 (1949): 633, 649.

45. Ibid., p. 650.

46. Michael Glennon, "United States Mutual Security Treaties: The Commitment Myth," *Columbia Journal of Transnational Law* 24 (1986): 509.

47. 96 *Cong. Rec.* 9229 (1950). Statement of Sen. Scott Lucas (D.-Ill.).

48. Edward S. Corwin, "The President's Power," *New Republic,* January 29, 1951, p. 16.

49. 96 *Cong. Rec.* 9233 (1950). Statement of Sen. Arthur V. Watkins (R.-Utah).

See also Arthur V. Watkins, "War by Executive Order," *Western Political Quarterly* 4 (1951): 539.

50. 96 *Cong. Rec.* 9268 (1951).

51. Stephen E. Ambrose, *Eisenhower: Soldier, General of the Army, President-Elect* (New York: Simon and Schuster, 1983), 1:569.

52. Ibid.

53. 69 Stat. 7 (1955); 71 Stat. 4 (1957).

54. *Public Papers of the Presidents: Dwight D. Eisenhower, 1957* (Washington, D.C.: Government Printing Office, 1957), p. 11.

55. Dwight D. Eisenhower, *Waging Peace* (Garden City, N.Y.: Doubleday, 1965), p. 179.

56. Henry Steele Commager, "Presidential Power: The Issue Analyzed," *New York Times,* January 14, 1951, p. 11.

57. Ibid., p. 24.

58. Arthur Schlesinger, Jr., "Presidential Powers: Taft Statement on Troops Opposed, Actions of Past Presidents Cited," *New York Times,* January 9, 1951, p. 28.

59. James D. Richardson, ed., *A Compilation of the Messages and Papers of the Presidents* (New York: Bureau of National Literature, 1897–1925), 1:315.

60. Edward S. Corwin, "The President's Power," *New Republic,* January 29, 1951, p. 15.

61. Arthur M. Schlesinger, Jr., and Alfred de Grazia, *Congress and the Presidency* (Washington, D.C.: American Enterprise Institute, 1967), pp. 27–28.

62. Arthur Schlesinger, Jr., *The Imperial Presidency* (Boston: Houghton Mifflin, 1973), p. 9 (emphasis in original).

63. "Changing American Attitudes Towards Foreign Policy," Hearings Before the Senate Committee on Foreign Relations, 90th Cong., 1st sess. (1967), p. 21.

64. "War Powers Legislation," Hearings Before the Senate Committee on Foreign Relations, 92d Cong., 1st sess. (1971), pp. 7–74.

65. 27 *Weekly Comp. Pres. Doc.* 25 (1991).

APPENDIX A:
FEDERALIST PAPERS

FEDERALIST 64 (JAY): THE SENATE AND THE TREATY POWER

The second section [of Article II of the Constitution] gives power to the President, *"by and with the advice and consent of the Senate, to make treaties,* PROVIDED TWO THIRDS OF THE SENATORS PRESENT CONCUR.*"*

The power of making treaties is an important one, especially as it relates to war, peace, and commerce; and it should not be delegated but in such a mode, and with such precautions, as will afford the highest security that it will be exercised by men the best qualified for the purpose, and in the manner most conducive to the public good. The convention appears to have been attentive to both these points; they have directed the President to be chosen by select bodies of electors, to be deputed by the people for that express purpose; and they have committed the appointment of senators to the State legislatures. This mode has, in such cases, vastly the advantage of elections by the people in their collective capacity, where the activity of party zeal, taking advantage of the supineness, the ignorance, and the hopes and fears of the unwary and interested, often places men in office by the votes of a small proportion of the electors. . . .

Although the absolute necessity of system, in the conduct of any business, is universally known and acknowledged, yet the high importance of it in national affairs has not yet become sufficiently impressed on the public mind. They who wish to commit the power under consideration to a popular assembly, composed of members constantly coming and going in quick succession, seem not to recollect that such a body must necessarily be inadequate to the attainment of those great objects, which require to be steadily contemplated in all their relations and circumstances, and which can only be approached and achieved by measures which not only talents, but also exact information, and often much time, are necessary to concert and to execute. It was wise, therefore, in the convention to provide, not only that the power of making treaties should be committed to able and honest men, but also that they should continue in place a sufficient time to become perfectly acquainted with our national concerns, and to form and introduce a system for the management of them. The duration prescribed is such as will give them an opportunity of greatly extending their political information, and of rendering their accumulating experience more and more beneficial to their country. Nor has the convention discovered less prudence in providing for the frequent elections of senators in such a way as to obviate the inconvenience of periodically transferring those great affairs entirely to new men; for by leaving a considerable residue of the old ones in place, uniformity and order, as well as a constant succession of official information, will be preserved.

There are a few who will not admit that the affairs of trade and navigation should be regulated by a system cautiously formed and steadily pursued; and that both our treaties and our laws should correspond with and be made to promote it. It is of much consequence that this correspondence and conformity be carefully maintained; and they who assent to the truth of this position will see and confess that it is well provided for by making concurrence of the Senate necessary both to treaties and to laws.

It seldom happens in the negotiation of treaties, of whatever nature, but that perfect *secrecy* and immediate *despatch* are sometimes requisite. There are cases where the most useful intelligence may be obtained, if the persons possessing it can be relieved from apprehensions of discovery. Those apprehensions will operate on those persons whether they are actuated by mercenary or friendly motives; and there doubtless are many of both descriptions, who would rely on the secrecy of the President, but who would not confide in that of the Senate, and still less in that of a large popular Assembly. The convention have done well, therefore, in so disposing of the power of making treaties, that although the President must, in forming them, act by the advice and consent of the Senate, yet he will be able to manage the business of intelligence in such a manner as prudence may suggest.

They who have turned their attention to the affairs of men, must have perceived that there are tides in them; tides very irregular in their duration, strength, and direction, and seldom found to run twice exactly in the same manner or measure. To discern and to profit by these tides in national affairs is the business of those who preside over them; and they who have had much experience on this head inform us, that there frequently are occasions when days, nay, even when hours, are precious. The loss of a battle, the death of a prince, the removal of a minister, or other circumstances intervening to change the present posture and aspect of affairs, may turn the most favorable tide into a course opposite to our wishes. As in the field, so in the cabinet, there are moments to be seized as they pass, and they who preside in either should be left in capacity to improve them. So often and so essentially have we heretofore suffered from the want of secrecy and despatch, that the Constitution would have been inexcusably defective, if no attention had been paid to those objects. Those matters which in negotiations usually require the most secrecy and the most despatch, are those preparatory and auxiliary measures which are not otherwise important in a national view, than as they tend to facilitate the attainment of the objects of the negotiation. For these, the President will find no difficulty to provide; and should any circumstance occur which requires the advice and consent of the Senate, he may at any time convene them. Thus we see that the Constitution provides that our negotiations for treaties shall have every advantage which can be derived from talents, information, integrity, and deliberate investigations, on the one hand, and from secrecy and despatch on the other.

But to this plan, as to most others that have ever appeared, objections are contrived and urged.

Some are displeased with it, not on account of any errors or defects in it, but because, as the treaties, when made, are to have the force of laws, they should be made only by men invested with legislative authority. These gentlemen seem not to consider that the judgments of our courts, and the commissions constitutionally given by our governor, are as valid and as binding on all persons whom they concern, as the laws passed by our legislature. All constitutional acts of power, whether in the executive or in the judicial department, have as much legal validity and obligation as if they proceeded from the legislature; and therefore, whatever name be given to the power of making treaties, or however obligatory they may be when made, certain it is, that the people may, with much propriety, commit the power to a distinct body from the legislature, the executive, or the judicial. It surely does not follow, that because they have given the power of making laws to the legislature, that therefore they should likewise give them power to do every other act of sovereignty by which the citizens are to be bound and affected.

Others, though content that treaties should be made in the mode proposed are averse to their being the *supreme* laws of the land. They insist, and profess to believe, that treaties like acts of assembly, should be repealable at pleasure. This idea seems to be new and peculiar to this country, but new errors, as well as new truths, often appear. These gentlemen would do well to reflect that a treaty is only another name for a bargain, and that it would be impossible to find a nation who would make any bargain with us, which should be binding on them *absolutely,* but on us only so long and so far as we may think proper to be bound by it. They who make laws may, without doubt amend or repeal them; and it will not be disputed that they who make treaties may alter or cancel them; but still let us not forget that treaties are made, not by only one of the contracting parties, but by both; and consequently, that as the consent of both was essential to their formation at first, so must it ever afterwards be to alter or cancel them. The proposed Constitution, therefore, has not in the least extended the obligation of treaties. They are just as binding, and just as far beyond the lawful reach of legislative acts now, as they will be at any future period, or under any form of government.

However useful jealousy may be in republics, yet when like bile in the natural, it abounds too much in the body politic, the eyes of both become very liable to be deceived by the delusive appearances which that malady casts on surrounding objects. From this cause, probably, proceed the fears and apprehensions of some, that the President and Senate may make treaties without an equal eye to the interests of all the States. Others suspect that two thirds will oppress the remaining third, and ask whether those gentlemen are made sufficiently responsible for their conduct; whether, if they act corruptly, they can be punished; and if they make disadvantageous treaties, how are we to get rid of those treaties?

As all the States are equally represented in the Senate, and by men the most able and the most willing to promote the interests of their constituents, they will all have an equal degree of influence in that body, especially while they continue to be careful in appointing proper persons, and to insist on their punctual attendance. In proportion as the United States assume a national form and a national character, so will the good of the whole be more and more an object of attention, and the government must be a weak one indeed, if it should forget that the good of the whole can only be promoted by advancing the good of each of the parts or members which compose the whole. It will not be in the power of the President and Senate to make any treaties by which, they and their families and estates will not be equally bound and affected with the rest of the community; and, having no private interests distinct from that of the nation, they will be under no temptations to neglect the latter.

As to corruption, the case is not supposable. He must either have been very unfortunate in his intercourse with the world, or possess a heart very susceptible of such impressions, who can think it probable that the President and two thirds of the Senate will ever be capable of such unworthy conduct. The idea is too gross and too invidious to be entertained. But in such a case, if it should ever happen, the treaty so obtained from us would, like all other fraudulent contracts, be null and void by the law of nations.

With respect to their responsibility, it is difficult to conceive how it could be increased. Every consideration that can influence the human mind, such as honor, oaths, reputations, conscience, the love of country, and family affections and attachments, afford security for their fidelity. In short, as the Constitution has taken the utmost care that they shall be men of talents, and integrity, we have reason to be persuaded that the treaties they make will be as advantageous as, all circumstances considered, could be made; and so far as the fear of punishment and disgrace can operate, that motive to good behavior is amply afforded by the article on the subject of impeachments.

FEDERALIST 69 (HAMILTON): ANALYZING PRESIDENTIAL POWERS

The president is to be the "commander-in-chief of the army and navy of the United States, and of the militia of the several States, when called into the actual service of the United States. He is to have power to grant reprieves and pardons for offenses against the United States, *except in cases of impeachment;* to recommend to the consideration of Congress such measures as he shall judge necessary and expedient; to convene, on extraordinary occasions, both houses of the legislature, or either of them, and, in case of disagreement between them *with respect to the time of adjournment,* to adjourn them to such time as he shall think proper; to take care that the laws be faithfully executed; and to commission all officers of the United States." In most of these particulars, the power of the president will resemble equally that of the king of Great Britain and of the governor of New York. The most material points of difference are these:—*First.* The president will have only the occasional command of such part of the militia of the nation as by legislative provision may be called into the actual service of the Union. The king of Great Britain and the governor of New York have at all times the entire command of all the militia within their several jurisdictions. In this article, therefore, the power of the president would be inferior to that of either the monarch or the governor. *Secondly.* The president is to be commander-in-chief of the army and navy of the United States. In this respect his authority would be nominally the same with that of the king of Great Britain, but in substance much inferior to it. It would amount to nothing more than the supreme command and direction of the military and naval forces, as first general and admiral of the Confederacy; while that of the British king extends to the *declaring* of war and to the *raising* and *regulating* of fleets and armies,—all which, by the Constitution under consideration, would appertain to the legislature.

The governor of New York, on the other hand, is by the constitution of the state vested only with the command of its militia and navy. But the constitutions of several of the states expressly declare their governors to be commanders-in-chief, as well of the army as navy; and it may well be a question, whether those of New Hampshire and Massachusetts, in particular, do not, in this instance, confer larger powers upon their respective governors, than could be claimed by a president of the United States. . . .

The president is to have power, with the advice and consent of the Senate, to make treaties, provided two-thirds of the senators present concur. The king of Great Britain is the sole and absolute representative of the nation in all foreign transactions. He can of his own accord make treaties of peace, commerce, alliance, and of every other description. It has been insinuated, that his authority in this respect is not conclusive, and that his conventions with foreign powers are subject to the revision, and stand in need of the ratification, of Parliament. But I believe this doctrine was never heard of, until it was broached upon the present occasion. Every jurist of that kingdom, and every other man acquainted with its Constitution, knows as an established fact, that the prerogative of making treaties exists in the crown in its utmost plentitude; and that the compacts entered into by the royal authority have the most complete legal validity and perfection, independent of any other sanction. The Parliament, it is true, is sometimes seen employing itself in altering the existing laws to conform them to the stipulations in a new treaty; and this may have possibly given birth to the imagination, that its co-operation was necessary to the obligatory efficacy of the treaty. But this parliamentary interposition proceeds from a different cause: from the necessity of adjusting a most artificial and intricate system of revenue and commercial laws, to the changes made in them by the operation of the treaty; and of adapting new provisions and precautions to the new state of things, to keep the machine from running into disorder. In this respect, therefore, there is no comparison between the intended power of the president and the actual power of the British sovereign. The one can perform alone what the other can do only with the concurrence of a branch of the legislature. It must be admitted, that, in this instance, the power of the federal executive would exceed that of any state executive. But this arises naturally from the sovereign power which relates to treaties. If the Confederacy were to be dissolved, it would become a question, whether the executives of the several states were not solely invested with that delicate and important prerogative.

The president is also to be authorized to receive ambassadors and other public ministers. This, though it has been a rich theme of declamation, is more a matter of dignity than of authority. It is a circumstance which will be without consequence in the administration of the government; and it was far more convenient that it should be arranged in this manner, than that there should be a necessity of convening the legislature, or one of its branches, upon every arrival of a foreign minister, though it were merely to take the place of a departed predecessor.

The president is to nominate, and, *with the advice and consent of the Senate,* to appoint ambassadors and other public ministers, judges of the Supreme Court, and in general all officers of the United States established by law, and whose appointments are not otherwise provided for by the Constitution. The king of Great Britain is emphatically and truly styled the fountain of honor. He not only appoints to all offices, but can create an immense number of offices. He can confer titles of nobility at pleasure; and has the disposal of an immense number of church preferments. There is evidently a great inferiority in the power of the president, in this particular, to that of the British king; nor is it equal to that of the governor of New York, if we are to interpret the meaning of the constitution of the state by the practice which has obtained under it. The power of appointment is with us lodged in a council, composed of the governor and four members of the Senate, chosen by the Assembly. The governor *claims,* and has frequently *exercised,* the right of nomination, and is *entitled* to a casting vote in the appointment. If he really has the right of nominating, his authority is in this respect equal to that of the president, and exceeds it in the article of the casting vote. In the national government, if the Senate should be divided, no appointment could be made; in the government of New York, if the council should be divided, the governor can turn the scale, and confirm his own nomination. If we compare the publicity which must necessarily attend the mode of appointment by the president and an entire branch of the national legislature, with the privacy in the mode of appointment by the governor of New York, closeted in a secret apartment with at most four, and frequently with only two persons; and if we at the same time consider how much more easy it must be to influence the small number of which a council of appointment consists, than the considerable number of which the national Senate would consist, we cannot hesitate to pronounce that the power of the chief magistrate of this state, in the disposition of offices, must, in practice, be greatly superior to that of the chief magistrate of the Union.

Hence it appears that, except as to the concurrent authority of the president in the article of treaties, it would be difficult to determine whether that magistrate would, in the aggregate, possess more or less power than the governor of New York. And it appears yet more unequivocally, that there is no pretence for the parallel which has been attempted between him and the king of Great Britain. But to render the contrast in this respect still more striking, it may be of use to throw the principal circumstances of dissimilitude into a closer group.

The president of the United States would be an officer elected by the people for *four* years; the king of Great Britain is a perpetual and *hereditary* prince. The one would be amenable to personal punishment and disgrace; the person of the other is sacred and inviolable. The one would have a *qualified* negative upon the acts of the legislative body; the other has an *absolute* negative. The one would have a right to command the military and naval forces of the nation; the other, in addition to this right, possesses that of *declaring* war, and of *raising* and *regulating* fleets and armies by his own authority. The one would have a concurrent power with a branch of the legislature in the formation of treaties; the other is the *sole possessor* of the power of making treaties. The one would have a concurrent authority in appointing to offices; the other is the sole author of all appointments. The one can confer no privileges whatever: the other can make denizens of aliens, noblemen of commoners; can erect corporations with all the rights incident to corporate bodies. The one can prescribe no rules concerning the commerce or currency of the nation; the other is in several respects the arbiter of commerce, and in this capacity can establish markets and fairs, can regulate weights and measures, can lay embargoes for a limited time, can coin money, can authorize or prohibit the circulation of foreign coin. The one has no particle of spiritual jurisdiction; the other is the supreme head and governor of the national church! What answer shall we give to those who would persuade us that things so unlike resemble each other? The same that ought to be given to those who tell us that a government, the whole power of which would be in the hands of the elective and periodical servants of the people, is an aristocracy, a monarchy, and a despotism.

FEDERALIST 75 (HAMILTON): THE TREATY POWER

The President is to have power, "by and with the advice and consent of the Senate, to make treaties, provided two thirds of the senators present concur."

Though this provision has been assailed, on different grounds, with no small degree of vehemence, I scruple not to declare my firm persuasion, that it is one of the best digested and most unexceptionable parts of the plan. One ground of objection is the trite topic of the intermixture of powers: some contending that the President ought alone to possess the power of making treaties; others, that it ought to have been exclusively deposited in the Senate. Another source of objection is derived from the small number of persons by whom a treaty may be made. Of those who espouse this objection, a part are of the opinion that the House of Representatives ought to have been associated in the business, while another part seem to think that nothing more was necessary than to have substituted two thirds of *all* the members of the Senate, to two thirds of the members *present*. As I flatter myself the observations made in a preceding number upon this part of the plan must have sufficed to place it, to a discerning eye, in a very favorable light, I shall here content myself with offering only some supplementary remarks, principally with a view to the objections which have been just stated.

With regard to the intermixture of powers, I shall rely upon the explanations already given in other places, of the true sense of the rule upon which that objection is founded; and shall take it for granted, as an inference from them, that the union of the Executive with the Senate, in the article of treaties, is no infringement of that rule. I venture to add, that the particular nature of the power of making treaties indicates a peculiar propriety in that union. Though several writers on the subject of government place that power in the class of executive authorities, yet this is evidently an arbitrary disposition; for if we attend carefully to its operation, it will be found to partake more of the legislative than of the executive character, though it does not seem strictly to fall within the definition of either of them. The essence of the legislative authority is to enact laws, or, in other words, to prescribe rules for the regulation of the society; while the execution of the laws, and the employment of the common strength, either for this purpose or for the common defense, seem to comprise all the functions of the executive magistrate. The power of making treaties is, plainly, neither the one nor the other. It relates neither to the execution of the subsisting laws, nor to the enaction of new ones; and still less to an exertion of the common strength. Its objects are CONTRACTS with foreign nations, which have the force of law, but derive it from the obligations of good faith. They are not rules prescribed by the sovereign to the subject, but agreements between sovereign and sovereign. The power in question seems therefore to form a distinct department, and to belong, properly, neither to the legislative nor to the executive. The qualities elsewhere detailed as indispensable in the management of foreign negotiations, point out the Executive as the most fit agent in those transactions; while the vast importance of the trust, and the operation of treaties as laws, plead strongly for the participation of the whole or a portion of the legislative body in the office of making them.

However proper or safe it may be in governments where the executive magistrate is an hereditary monarch, to commit to him the entire power of making treaties, it would be utterly unsafe and improper to intrust that power to an elective magistrate of four years' duration. It has been remarked, upon another occasion, and the remark is unquestionably just, that an hereditary monarch, though often the oppressor of his people, has personally too much stake in the government to be in any material danger of being corrupted by foreign powers. But a man raised from the station of a private citizen to the rank of chief magistrate, possessed of a moderate or slender fortune, and looking forward to a period not very remote when he may probably be obliged to return to the station from which he was taken, might sometimes be under temptations to sacrifice his duty to his interest, which it would require superlative virtue to withstand. An avaricious man might be tempted to betray the interests of the state to the acquisition of wealth. An ambitious man might make his own aggrandizement, by the aid of a foreign power, the price of his treachery to his constituents. The history of human conduct does not warrant that exalted opinion of human virtue which would make it wise in a nation to commit interests of so delicate and momentous a kind, as those which concern its intercourse with the rest of the world, to the sole disposal of a magistrate created and circumstanced as would be a President of the United States.

To have intrusted the power of making treaties to the Senate alone, would have been to relinquish the benefits of the constitutional agency of the President in the conduct of foreign negotiations. It is true that the Senate would, in that case, have the option of employing him in this capacity, but they would also have the option of letting it alone, and pique or cabal might induce the latter rather than the former. Besides this, the ministerial servant of the Senate could not be expected to enjoy the confidence and respect of foreign powers in the same degree with the constitutional representatives of the nation, and, of course, would not be able to act with an equal degree of weight or efficacy. While the Union would, from this cause, lose a considerable advantage in the management of its external concerns, the people would lose the additional security which would result from the cooperation of the Executive. Though it would be imprudent to confide in him solely so important a trust, yet it cannot be doubted that his participation would materially add to the safety of the society. It must indeed be clear to a demonstration that the joint possession of the power in question, by the President and Senate, would afford a greater prospect of security, than the separate possession of it by either of them. And whoever has maturely weighed the circumstances which must concur in the appointment of a President, will be satisfied that the office will always bid fair to be filled by men of such characters as to render their concurrence in the formation of treaties peculiarly desirable, as well on the score of wisdom, as on that of integrity.

The remarks made in a former number, which have been alluded to in another part of this paper, will apply with conclusive force against the admission of the House of Representatives to a share in the formation of treaties. The fluctuating and, taking its future increase into the account, the multitudinous composition of that body, forbid us to expect in it those qualities which are essential to the proper execution of such a trust. Accurate and comprehensive knowledge of foreign politics; a steady and systematic adherence to the same views; a nice and uniform sensibility to national character; decision, *secrecy,* and despatch, are incompatible with the genius of a body so variable and so numerous. The very complication of the business, by introducing a necessity of the concurrence of so many different bodies, would of itself afford a solid objection. The greater frequency of the calls upon the House of Representatives, and the greater length of time which it would often be necessary to keep them together when convened, to obtain their sanction in the progressive stages of a treaty, would be a source of so great inconvenience and expense as alone ought to condemn the project.

APPENDIX B:
FOREIGN AFFAIRS CASES

BAS v. TINGY, 4 U.S. (4 DALL.) 37 (1800)

A limited war with France occurred between 1798 and 1801, although no formal declaration of war was ever made. As a result of French interference with American shipping, Congress passed two acts that became the focal point of this controversy. An act of June 28, 1798, provided that when an American vessel captured by the French was recaptured by another American ship, one-eighth of the value of the vessel and its cargo was to be awarded to the rescuers. The second act (March 2, 1799) declared that if ninety-six or more hours had elapsed before recapture of a vessel taken by the "enemy" then the rescuers were entitled to one-half the original value. In this case, the *Eliza,* a U.S. merchant vessel, was seized on the high seas by a French privateer. It was rescued by Captain Tingy about three weeks later, and he filed a claim based on the second act. The owners of the *Eliza* defended on the ground that the United States was not at war, France was not an enemy, and the act was not applicable. The Supreme Court unanimously held for Tingy.

Justice Washington. It may I believe, be safely laid down, that every contention by force between two nations, in external matters, under the authority of their respective governments, is not only war, but public war. If it be declared in form, it is called solemn, and is of the perfect kind; because one whole nation is at war with another whole nation; and *all* the members of the nation declaring war, are authorized to commit hostilities against all the members of the other, in every place, and under every circumstance. In such a war all the members act under a general authority, and all the rights and consequences of war attach to their condition.

But hostilities may subsist between two nations, more confined in its nature and extent; being limited as to places, persons, and things; and this is more properly termed *imperfect* war; because not solemn, and because those who are authorized to commit hostilities, act under special authority, and can go [no] further than to the extent of their commission. Still, however, it is *public war,* because it is an external contention by force, between some of the members of the two nations, authorized by the legitimate powers. It is a war between the two nations, though all the members are not authorized to commit hostilities such as in a solemn war, where the government restrain the general power.

Now, if this be the true definition of war, let us see what was the situation of the *United States* in relation to *France*. In *March* 1799, Congress had raised an army; stopped all intercourse with *France;* dissolved our treaty; built and equipped ships of war; and commissioned private armed ships; enjoining the former, and authorizing the latter, to defend themselves against the armed ships of *France,* to attack them on the high seas, to subdue and take them as prize, and to re-capture armed vessels found in their possession. Here, then, let me ask, what were the technical characters of an *American and French* armed vessel, combating on the high seas, with a view the one to subdue the other, and to make prize of his property? They certainly were not friends, because there was a contention by force; nor were they private enemies, because the contention was external, and authorized by the legitimate authority of the two governments. If they were not our enemies, I know not what constitutes an enemy.

But, secondly, it is said, that a war of the imperfect kind, is more properly called acts of hostility, or reprisal, and that Congress did not mean to consider the hostility subsisting between *France* and the *United States,* as constituting a state of war.

In support of this position, it has been observed, that in no law prior to *March* 1799, is *France* styled our enemy, nor are we said to be at war. This is true; but neither of these things were necessary to be done: because as to *France,* she was sufficiently described by the title of the *French* republic; and as to *America,* the degree of hostility meant to be carried on, was sufficiently described without declaring war, or declaring that we were at war. Such a declaration by Congress, might have constituted a perfect state of war, which was not intended by the government. . . .

What then is the evidence of legislative will? In fact and in law we are at war: An *American* vessel fighting with a *French* vessel, to subdue and make her prize, is fighting with an enemy accurately and technically speaking: and if this be not sufficient evidence of the legislative mind, it is explained in the same law.

The whole controversy turns on the single question, whether *France* was at that time *an enemy?* If *France* was an enemy, then the law obliges us to decree one half of the value of ship and cargo for salvage: but if *France* was not an enemy, then no more than one-eighth can be allowed. . . .

Congress is empowered to declare a general war, or Congress may wage a limited war; limited in place, in objects, and in time. If a general war is declared, its extent and operations are only restricted and regulated by the *jus belli,* forming a part of the law of nations; but if a partial war is waged, its extent and operation depend on our municipal laws.

What, then, is the nature of the contest subsisting between *America and France?* In my judgment, it is a limited, partial, war. Congress has not declared war in general terms; but Congress has authorized hostilities on the high seas by certain persons in certain cases. There is no authority given to commit hostilities on land; to capture unarmed *French* vessels, nor even to capture *French* armed vessels lying in a *French* port; and the authority is not given, indiscriminately, to every citizen of *America,* against every citizen of *France;* but only to citizens appointed by commissions, or exposed to immediate outrage and violence. So far it is, unquestionably, a partial war; but, nevertheless, it is a public war, on account of the public authority from which it emanates.

Justice Paterson. The *United States* and the *French* republic are in a qualified state of hostility. An imperfect war, or a war, as to certain objects, and to certain extent, exists between the two nations; and this modified warfare is authorized by the constitutional authority of our country. It is war *quoad hoc*. As far as Congress tolerated and authorized the war on our part, so far may we proceed in hostile operations. It is a maritime war; a war at sea as to certain purposes. The national armed vessels of *France* attack and capture the national armed vessels of the *United States;* and the national armed vessels of the *United States* are expressly authorized and directed to attack, subdue, and take, the national armed vessels of *France,* and also to re-capture *American* vessels. It is therefore a public war between the two nations, qualified, on our part, in the manner prescribed by the constitutional organ of our country.

LITTLE v. BARREME, 6 U.S. (2 CRANCH) 170 (1804)

On December 2, 1799, the Danish brigantine *Flying Fish* was captured, near the island of Hispaniola, by the U.S. frigates *Boston* and *General Greene,* upon suspicion of violating the act of Congress, usually termed the nonintercourse law, passed on February 9, 1799, vol. 4, p. 244, by the 1st section of which it is enacted, "That from and after the first day of March next no ship or vessel owned, hired or employed, wholly or in part, by any person resident within the United States, and which shall depart therefrom, shall be allowed to proceed directly, or from any intermediate port or place, to any port or place within the territory of the French Republic, or the dependencies thereof, or to any place in the West Indies, or elsewhere under the acknowledged government of France, or shall be employed in any traffic or commerce with or for any person, resident within the jurisdiction or under the authority of the French republic. And if any ship or vessel, in any voyage thereafter commencing, and before her return within the United States, shall be voluntarily carried or suffered to proceed to any French port or place as aforesaid, or shall be employed as aforesaid contrary to the intent hereof, every such ship or vessel, together with her cargo, shall be forfeited; and shall accrue, the one-half to the use of the United States, and the other half to the use of any person or persons, citizens of the United States, who will inform and prosecute for the same; and shall be liable to be seized, and may be prosecuted and condemned, in any circuit or district court of the United States, which shall be holden within or for the district where the seizure shall be made."

And by the 5th section it is enacted,

> That it shall be lawful for the President of the United States to give instructions to the commanders of the public armed ships of the United States, to stop and examine any ship or vessel of the United States on the high seas, which there may be reason to suspect to be engaged in any traffic or commerce contrary to the true tenor hereof; and if, upon examination, it shall appear that such ship or vessel is bound or sailing to any port or place within the territory of the French republic, or her dependencies, contrary to the intent of this act, it shall be the duty of the commander of such public armed vessel to seize every such ship or vessel engaged in such illicit commerce, and send the same to the nearest port in the United States; and every such ship or vessel, thus bound or sailing to

any such port or place, shall, upon due proof thereof, be liable to the like penalties and forfeitures as are provided in and by the first section of this act.

The instructions given in consequence of this section, bear date the 12th of March, 1799, and are as follows:

SIR—Herewith you will receive an act of Congress further to suspend the commercial intercourse between the United States and France, and the dependencies thereof, the whole of which requires your attention. But it is the command of the President that you consider particularly the fifth section as part of your instructions, and govern yourself accordingly.

A proper discharge of the important duties enjoined on you, arising out of this act, will require the exercise of a sound and impartial judgement. You are not only to do all that in you lies to prevent all intercourse, whether direct or circuitous, between the ports of the United States and those of France and her dependencies, in cases where the vessels or cargoes are apparently, as well as really, American, and protected by American papers only; but you are to be vigilant that vessels or cargoes really American, but covered by Danish or other foreign papers, and bound to or from French ports, do not escape you.

Whenever, on just suspicion, you send a vessel into port to be dealt with according to the aforementioned law, besides sending with her all her papers, send all the evidence you can obtain to support your suspicions, and effect her condemnation:

At the same time that you are thus attentive to fulfil the objects of the law, you are to be extremely careful not to harass or injure the trade of foreign nations with whom we are at peace, nor the fair trade of our own citizens.

February 27. MARSHALL, CH. J., now delivered the opinion of the Court.

The Flying Fish, a Danish vessel, having on board Danish and neutral property, was captured on the 2d of December, 1799, on a voyage from Jeremie to St. Thomas's, by the United States frigate Boston, commanded by Captain Little, and brought into the port of Boston, where she was libelled as an American vessel that had violated the non-intercourse law.

The judge before whom the cause was tried, directed a restoration of the vessel and cargo as neutral property, but refused to award damages for the capture and detention, because, in his opinion, there was probable cause to suspect the vessel to be American.

On an appeal to the circuit court this sentence was reversed, because the Flying Fish was on a voyage from, not to, a French port, and was, therefore, had she even been an American vessel, not liable to capture on the high seas.

During the hostilities between the United States and France, an act for the suspension of all intercourse between the two nations was annually passed. That under which the Flying Fish was condemned, declared every vessel owned, hired or employed, wholly or in part, by an American, which should be employed in any traffic or commerce with or for any person resident within the jurisdiction, or under the authority, of the French Republic, to be forfeited together with her cargo; the one half to accrue to the United States, and the other to any person or persons, citizens of the United States, who will inform and prosecute for the same.

The 5th section of this act authorizes the President of the United States to instruct the commanders of armed vessels "to stop and examine any ship or vessel of the United States on the high seas, which there may be reason to suspect to be engaged in any traffic or commerce contrary to the true tenor of the act, and if upon examination it should appear that such ship or vessel is bound, or sailing to, any port or place within the territory of the French republic or her dependencies, it is rendered lawful to seize such vessel, and send her into the United States for adjudication.

It is by no means clear that the President of the United States, whose high duty it is to "take care that the laws be faithfully executed," and who is commander in chief of the armies and navies of the United States, might not, without any special authority for that purpose, in the then existing state of things, have empowered the officers commanding the armed vessels of the United States, to seize and send into port for adjudication, American vessels which were forfeited by being engaged in this illicit commerce. But when it is observed that the general clause of the first section of the "act, which declares that such vessels may be seized, and may be prosecuted in any district or circuit court, which shall be holden within or for the district where the seizure shall be made," obviously contemplates a seizure within the United States; and that the 5th section gives a special authority to seize on the high seas, and limits that authority to the seizure of vessels bound, or sailing to, a French port, the legislature seems to have prescribed that the manner in which this law shall be carried into execution, was to exclude a seizure of any vessel not bound to a French port. Of consequence, however strong the circumstances might be, which induced Captain Little to suspect the Flying Fish to be an American vessel, they could not excuse the detention of her, since he would not have authorized to detain her had she been really American.

It was so obvious, that if only vessels sailing to a French port could be seized on the high seas, that the law would be very often evaded, that this act of Congress appears to have received a different construction from the executive of the United States; a construction much better calculated to give it effect.

A copy of this act was transmitted by the Secretary of the Navy, to the captains of the armed vessels, who were ordered to consider the 5th section as part of their instructions. The same letter contained the following clause: "A proper discharge of the important duties enjoined on you, arising out of this act, will require the exercise of a sound and an impartial judgment. You are not only to do all that in you lies to prevent all intercourse, whether direct or circuitous, between the ports of the United States and those of France or her dependencies, where the vessels are apparently as well as really American, and protected by American papers only, but you are to be vigilant that vessels or cargoes really American, but covered by Danish or other foreign papers, and bound to or from French ports, do not escape you."

These orders given by the executive under the construction of the act of Congress made by the department to which its execution was assigned, enjoin the seizure of American vessels sailing from a French Port. Is the officer who obeys them liable for damages sustained by this misconstruction of the act, or will his orders excuse him? If his instructions afforded him no protection, then the law must take its course, and he must pay such damages as are legally awarded against him; if they excuse an act not otherwise excusable, it would then be necessary to inquire whether this is a case in which the probable cause which existed to induce a suspicion that the vessel was

American, would excuse the captor from damages when the vessel appeared in fact to be neutral.

I confess the first bias of my mind was very strong in favor of the opinion that though the instructions of the executive could not give a right, they might yet excuse from damages. I was much inclined to think that a distinction ought to be taken between acts of civil and those of military officers; and between proceedings within the body of the country and those on the high seas. That implicit obedience which military men usually pay to the orders of their superiors, which indeed is indispensably necessary to every military system, appeared to me strongly to imply the principle that those orders, if not to perform a prohibited act, ought to justify the person whose general duty it is to obey them, and who is placed by the laws of his country in a situation which in general requires that he should obey them. I was strongly inclined to think that where, in consequence of orders from the legitimate authority, a vessel is seized with pure intention, the claim of the injured party for damages would be against that government from which the orders proceeded and would be a proper subject for negotiation. But I have been convinced that I was mistaken and I have receded from this first opinion. I acquiesce in that of my brethren, which is, that the instructions cannot change the nature of the transaction, or legalize an act which, without those instructions, would have been a plain trespass.

It becomes, therefore unnecessary to inquire whether the probable cause afforded by the conduct of the Flying Fish to suspect her of being an American would excuse Captain Little from damages for having seized and sent her into port, since, had she been an American, the seizure would have been unlawful?

Captain Little, then, must be answerable in damages to the owner of this neutral vessel, and as the account taken by order of the circuit court is not objectionable on its face, and has not been excepted to by counsel before the proper tribunal, this court can receive not objection to it.

There appears, then, to be no error in the judgment of the circuit court, and it must be affirmed with costs.

UNITED STATES v. SMITH, 27 F. Cas. 1192 (C.D.N.Y. 1806)

In this case, a Colonel William S. Smith was alleged to have assisted a General Miranda in outfitting a military expedition in New York against the Spanish province of Caracas and was indicted under a statute that forbade setting on foot a military expedition against a nation with which the United States was at peace. Smith subpoenaed the secretary of state, the secretary of the navy, and two other officers. They refused to appear, explaining that the president had specifically told them that he could not dispense with their services at that time. Smith sought a court order to compel them to attend, claiming in an affidavit that he hoped to prove by their testimony that the expedition "was begun, prepared, and set on foot with the knowledge and approbation of the president [Thomas Jefferson] of the United States, and with the knowledge and approbation of the Secretary of State [James Madison] of the United States." Associate Justice William Paterson of the Supreme Court, who had been a member of the Constitutional Convention, was riding circuit in New York and ruled that the trial should proceed without those witnesses because the testimony sought would be irrelevant.

Mr. Justice Paterson delivered the opinion of the Court.

Supposing then that every syllable of the affidavit is true, of what avail can it be on the present occasion? Of what use or benefit can it be to the defendant in a court of law? Does it speak by way of justification? The president of the United States cannot control the statute, nor dispense with its execution, and still less can he authorize a person to do what the law forbids. If he could, it would render the execution of the laws dependent on his will and pleasure; which is a doctrine that has not been set up, and will not meet with any supporters in our government. In this particular, the law is paramount. Who has dominion over it? None but the legislature; and even they are not without their limitation in our republic. Will it be pretended that the president could rightfully grant a dispensation and license to any of our citizens to carry on a war against a nation with whom the United States are at peace? Ingenious and learned counsel may imagine, and put a number of cases in the wide field of conjecture; but we are to take facts as we find them, and to argue from the existing state of things at the time. If we were at war with Spain, there is an end to the indictment; but, if at peace, what individual could lawfully make war or carry on a military expedition against the dominions of his Catholic majesty? The indictment is founded on a state of peace, and such state is presumed to continue until the contrary appears. A state of war is not set up in the affidavit. If, then, the president knew and approved of the military expedition set forth in the indictment against a prince with whom we are at peace, it would not justify the defendant in a court of law, nor discharge him from the binding force of the act of congress; because the president does not possess a dispensing power. Does he possess the power of making war? That power is exclusively vested in Congress; for, by the eighth section, of the 1st article of the constitution, it is ordained, that congress shall have power to declare war, grant letters of marque and maintain a navy, and to provide for calling forth the militia to execute the laws of the Union, suppress insurrections, and repel invasions. And we accordingly find, that Congress have been so circumspect and provident in regard to the last three particulars, that they have from time to time vested the president of the United States with ample powers.

Thus, by the act of the 28th of February, 1795 (3 Swift's Laws, 188 [1 Stat. 424]), it is made lawful for the president to call forth the militia to repel invasions, suppress insurrections, and execute the laws of the Union. Abstractedly from this constitutional and legal provision, the right to repel invasions arises from self-preservation and defense, which is a primary law of nature, and constitutes part of the law of nations. It therefore becomes the duty of a people, and particularly of the executive magistrate, who is at their head, and commander-in-chief of the forces by sea and land, to repel an invading foe. But to repel aggressions and invasions is one thing, and to commit them against a friendly power is another. It is obvious, that if the United States were at war with Spain at the time that the defendant is charged with the offense in the indictment, then he does not come within the purview of the statute, which makes the basis of the offense to consist in beginning or preparing the means to carry on a military expedition or enterprise against a nation with which the United States are at peace. If, indeed, a foreign nation should invade the territories of the United States, it would I apprehend, be not only lawful for the president to resist such invasion, but also to carry hostilities into the enemy's own country; and for this plain reason, that a state of complete and absolute war actually exists between the two nations. In the case of invasive hostilities, there cannot be war on the one side and peace on the other. There is a manifest distinction between our going to war with a nation at peace, and a war being made against us by an actual invasion, or a formal declaration. In the former case, it is the exclusive province of congress to change a state of peace into a state of war. A nation, however, may be in such a situation as to render it more prudent to submit to certain acts of a hostile nature, and to trust to negotiations for redress, than to make an immediate appeal to arms. Various considerations may induce to a measure of this kind; such as motives of policy, calculation of interest, the nature of the injury and provocation, the relative resources, means and strength of the two nations, &c. and, therefore, the organ intrusted with the power to declare war, should first decide whether it is expedient to go to war, or to continue in peace; and until such a decision be made, no individual ought to assume a hostile attitude; and to pronounce, contrary to the constitutional will, that the nation is at war, and that he will shape his conduct and act according to such a state of things. This conduct is clearly indefensible, and may involve the nation, of which he is a member, in all the calamities of a long and expensive war. It is a matter worthy of notice on the present occasion, that when the offense laid in the indictment is stated to have been committed, Congress were in session; and if, in their estimation, war measures were prudent or necessary to be adopted, they would no doubt, have expressed their sentiments on the subject, either by a public declaration of their will, or by authorizing the executive authority to proceed hostilely against the king of Spain. But nothing of this kind has been done, or at least appears to have been done. Congress does not choose to go to war; and where is the individual among us who could legally do so without their permission? . . .

THE PRIZE CASES, 2 BLACK (67 U.S.) 635 (1863)

Among other emergency actions in 1861, President Lincoln declared a blockade of ports controlled by persons in armed rebellion against the government. The owners of the captured ships and cargo (prize, or captured property) brought suit in federal court. To justify the blockade and seizure of neutral vessels, a state of war had to exist, but Congress had made no such declaration. Under what constitutional authority did Lincoln act? Does a state of war require a formal declaration? Three Lincoln appointees—Swayne, Miller, and Davis—joined Grier and Wayne to uphold presidential power.

Mr. Justice GRIER. There are certain propositions of law which must necessarily affect the ultimate decision of these cases, and many others, which it will be proper to discuss and decide before we notice the special facts peculiar to each.

They are, 1st. Had the President a right to institute a blockade of ports in possession of persons in armed rebellion against the Government, on the principles of international law, as known and acknowledged among civilized States?

2d. Was the property of persons domiciled or residing within those States a proper subject of capture on the sea as "enemies' property?"

I. Neutrals have a right to challenge the existence of a blockade *de facto,* and also the authority of the party exercising the right to institute it. They have a right to enter the ports of a friendly nation for the purposes of trade and commerce, but are bound to recognize the rights of a belligerent engaged in actual war, to use this mode of coercion, for the purpose of subduing the enemy.

That a blockade *de facto* actually existed, and was formally declared and notified by the President on the 27th and 30th of April, 1861, is an admitted fact in these cases.

That the President, as the Executive Chief of the Government and Commander-in-chief of the Army and Navy, was the proper person to make such notification, has not been, and cannot be disputed.

The right of prize and capture has its origin in the "*jus belli,*" and is governed and adjudged under the law of nations. To legitimate the capture of a neutral vessel or property on the high seas, a war must exist *de facto,* and the neutral must have a knowledge or notice of the intention of one of the parties belligerent to use this mode of coercion against a port, city, or territory, in possession of the other.

Let us enquire whether, at the time this blockade was instituted, a state of war existed which would justify a resort to these means of subduing the hostile force.

War has been well defined to be, "That state in which a nation prosecutes its right by force."

The parties belligerent in a public war are independent nations. But it is not necessary to constitute war, that both parties should be acknowledged as independent nations or sovereign States. A war may exist where one of the belligerents claims sovereign rights as against the other.

Insurrection against a government may or may not culminate in an organized rebellion, but a civil war always begins by insurrection against the lawful authority of the Government. A civil war is never solemnly declared; it becomes such by its accidents—the number, power, and organizations of the persons who originate and carry it on. When the party in rebellion occupy and hold in a hostile manner a certain portion of territory; have declared their independence; have cast off their allegiance; have organized armies; have commenced hostilities against their former sovereign, the world acknowledges them as belligerents, and the contest a war. . . .

As a civil war is never publicly proclaimed, *eo nomine,* against insurgents, its actual existence is a fact in our domestic history which the Court is bound to notice and to know.

The true test of its existence, as found in the writings of the sages of the common law, may be thus summarily stated: "When the regular course of justice is interrupted by revolt, rebellion, or insurrection, so that the Courts of Justice cannot be kept open, *civil war exists* and hostilities may be prosecuted on the same footing as if those opposing the Government were foreign enemies invading the land."

By the Constitution, Congress alone has the power to declare a national or foreign war. It cannot declare war against a State, or any number of States, by virtue of any clause in the Constitution. The Constitution confers on the President the whole Executive power. He is bound to take care that the laws be faithfully executed. He is Commander-in-chief of the Army and Navy of the United States, and of the militia of the several States when called into the actual service of the United States. He has no power to initiate or declare a war either against a foreign nation or a domestic State. But by the Acts of Congress of February 28th, 1795 and 3d of March, 1807, he is authorized to call out the militia and use the military and naval forces of the United States in case of invasion by foreign nations, and to suppress insurrection against the government of a State of the United States.

If a war be made by invasion of a foreign nation, the President is not only authorized but bound to resist force by force. He does not initiate the war, but is bound to accept the challenge without waiting for any special legislative authority. And whether the hostile party be a foreign invader, or States organized in rebellion, it is none the less a war, although the declaration of it be *"unilateral."* Lord Stowell (1 Dodson, 247) observes, "It is not the less a war on *that account,* for war may exist without a declaration on either side. It is so laid down by the best writers on the law of nations. A declaration of war by one country only, is not a mere challenge to be accepted or refused at pleasure by the other."

The battles of Palo Alto and Resaca de la Palma had been fought before the passage of the Act of Congress of May 13th, 1846, which recognized *"a state of war as existing by the act of the Republic of Mexico."* This act not only provided for the future prosecution of the war, but was itself a vindication and ratification of the Act of the President in accepting the challenge without a previous formal declaration of war by Congress.

This greatest of civil wars was not gradually developed by popular commotion, tumultuous assemblies, or local unorganized insurrections. However long may have been its previous conception, it nevertheless sprung forth suddenly from the parent brain, a Minerva in the full panoply of *war.* The President was bound to meet it in the shape it presented itself, without waiting for Congress to baptize it with a name; and no name given to it by him or them could change the fact.

Whether the President in fulfilling his duties, as Commander-in-chief, in suppressing an insurrection, has met with such armed hostile resistance, and a civil war of such alarming proportions as will compel him to accord to them the character of belligerents, is a question to be decided *by him,* and this Court must be governed by the decisions and acts of the political department of the Government to which this power was entrusted. "He must determine what degree of force the crisis demands." The proclamation of blockade is itself official and conclusive evidence to the Court that a state of war existed which demanded and authorized a recourse to such a measure, under the circumstances peculiar to the case.

The correspondence of Lord Lyons with the Secretary of State admits the fact and concludes the question.

If it were necessary to the technical existence of a war, that it should have a legislative sanction, we find it in almost every act passed at the extraordinary session of the Legislature of 1861, which was wholly employed in enacting laws to enable the Government to prosecute the war with vigor and efficiency. And finally, in 1861, we find Congress *"ex majore cautela"* and in anticipation of such astute objections, passing an act "approving, legalizing, and making valid all the acts, proclamations, and orders of the President, &c., as if they had been *issued and done under the previous express authority and direction of the Congress of the United States."*

The objection made to this act of ratification, that it is *expost facto,* and therefore unconstitutional and void, might possibly have some weight on the trial of an indictment in a criminal Court. But precedents from that source cannot be received as authoritative in a tribunal administering public and international law.

On this first question therefore we are of the opinion that the President had a right, *jure belli,* to institute a blockade of ports in possession of the States in rebellion, which neutrals are bound to regard.

[The Court then decides whether the property of all persons residing within the territory of the states in rebellion, captured on the high seas, is to be treated as "enemies' property" whether the owner be in arms against the government or not.]

Mr. Justice NELSON dissenting.

We are of opinion . . . that, according to the very terms of the proclamation, neutral ships were entitled to a warning by one of the blockading squadron and could be lawfully seized only on the second attempt to enter or leave the port.

It is remarkable, also, that both the President and the Secretary, in referring to the blockade, treat the measure, not as blockade under the law of nations, but as a restraint upon commerce at the interdicted ports under the municipal laws of the Government.

This power *[of announcing war]* in all civilized nations is regulated by the fundamental laws or municipal constitution of the country.

By our Constitution this power is lodged in Congress. Congress shall have power "to declare war, grant letters of marque and reprisal, and make rules concerning captures on land and water."

But we are asked, what would become of the peace and integrity of the Union in case of an insurrection at home or invasion from abroad if this power could not be exercised by the President in the recess of Congress, and until that body could be assembled?

The framers of the Constitution fully comprehended this question, and provided for the contingency. Indeed, it would have been surprising if they had not, as a rebellion had occurred in the State of Massachusetts while the Convention was in session, and which had become so general that it was quelled only by calling upon the military power of the State. The Constitution declares that Congress shall have power "to provide for calling forth the militia to execute the laws of the Union, suppress insurrections, and repel invasions." Another clause, "that the President shall be Commander-in-chief of the Army and Navy of the United States, and of the militia of the several States when called into the actual service of the United States;" and, again, "He shall take care that the laws shall be faithfully executed." Congress passed laws on this subject in 1792 and 1795. 1 United States Laws, pp. 264–424.

[In 1807 Congress passed additional legislation authorizing the President to call forth the militia to suppress insurrection.]

The Acts of 1795 and 1807 did not, and could not under the Constitution, confer on the President the power of declaring war against a State of this Union, or of deciding that war existed, and upon that ground authorize the capture and confiscation of the property of every citizen of the State whenever it was found on the waters. . . . This great power over the business and property of the citizen is reserved to the legislative department by the express words of the Constitution. It cannot be delegated or surrendered to the Executive. . . .

Congress on the 6th of August, 1862, passed an Act confirming all acts, proclamations, and orders of the President, after the 4th of March, 1861, respecting the army and navy, and legalizing them, so far as was competent for that body. . . .

Here the captures were without any Constitutional authority, and void; and, on principle, no subsequent ratification could make them valid.

Upon the whole, after the most careful consideration of this case which the pressure of other duties has admitted, I am compelled to the conclusion that no civil war existed between this Government and the States in insurrection till recognized by the Act of Congress 13th of July, 1861; that the President does not possess the power under the Constitution to declare war or recognize its existence within the meaning of the law of nations, which carries with it belligerent rights, and thus change the country and all its citizens from a state of peace to a state of war; that this power belongs exclusively to the Congress of the United States, and, consequently, that the President had no power to set on foot a blockade under the law of nations, and that the capture of the vessel and cargo in this case, and in all cases before us in which the capture occurred before the 13th of July, 1861, for breach of blockade, or as enemies' property, are illegal and void, and that the decrees of condemnation should be reversed and the vessel and cargo restored.

Mr. Chief Justice TANEY, Mr. Justice CATRON and Mr. Justice CLIFFORD, concurred in the dissenting opinion of Mr. Justice NELSON.

UNITED STATES v. CURTISS-WRIGHT EXPORT CORP., 299 U.S. 304 (1936)

The *Curtiss-Wright* case involves the delegation of legislative power to the president. In 1934, Congress authorized the president to place an embargo on the sale of arms and munitions to countries engaged in armed conflict in South America if the president determined that an embargo would contribute to the establishment of peace. The president did so and the defendants, indicted for violating the joint resolution, challenged its constitutionality on the theory that it unconstitutionally delegated legislative power to the executive.

JUSTICE SUTHERLAND delivered the opinion of the Court.

Whether, if the Joint Resolution had related solely to internal affairs, it would be open to the challenge that it constituted an unlawful delegation of legislative power to the Executive, we find it unnecessary to determine. The whole aim of the resolution is to affect a situation entirely external to the United States, and falling within the category of foreign affairs. The determination which we are called to make, therefore, is whether the Joint Resolution, as applied to that situation, is vulnerable to attack under the rule that forbids a delegation of the lawmaking power. In other words, assuming (but not deciding) that the challenged delegation, if it were confined to internal affairs, would be invalid, may it nevertheless be sustained on the ground that its exclusive aim is to afford a remedy for a hurtful condition within foreign territory?

It will contribute to the elucidation of the question if we first consider the differences between the powers of the federal government in respect of foreign or external affairs and those in respect of domestic or internal affairs. That there are differences between them and that these differences are fundamental, may not be doubted.

The two classes of powers are different, both in respect of their origin and their nature. The broad statement that the federal government can exercise no power except those specifically enumerated in the Constitution, and such implied powers as are necessary and proper to carry into effect the enumerated powers, is categorically true only in respect of internal affairs. In that field, the primary purpose of the Constitution was to carve from the general mass of legislative powers *then possessed by the states* such portions as it was thought desirable to vest in the federal government, leaving those not included in the enumeration still in the states. Carter v. Carter Coal Co. That this doctrine applies only to powers which the states had is self-evident. And since the states severally never possessed international powers, such powers could not have been carved from the mass of state powers but obviously were transmitted to the United States from some other source. During the Colonial period, those powers were possessed exclusively by and were entirely under the control of the Crown. By the Declaration of Independence, "the Representatives of the United States of America" declared the United (not the several) Colonies to be free and independent states, and as such to have "full Power to levy War, conclude Peace, contract Alliances, establish Commerce and to do all other Acts and Things which Independent States may of right do."

As a result of the separation from Great Britain by the colonies, acting as a unit, the powers of external sovereignty passed from the Crown not to the colonies severally, but to the colonies in their collective and corporate capacity as the United States of America. Even before the Declaration, the colonies were a unit in foreign affairs, acting through a common agency—namely, the Continental Congress, composed of delegates from the thirteen colonies. That agency exercised the powers of war and peace, raised an army, created a navy, and finally adopted the Declaration of Independence. Rulers come and go; governments end and forms of government change; but sovereignty survives. A political society cannot endure without a supreme will somewhere. Sovereignty is never held in suspense. When, therefore, the external sovereignty of Great Britain in respect of the colonies ceased, it immediately passed to the Union. See Penhallow v. Doane. The fact was given practical application almost at once. The treaty of peace, made on September 3, 1783, was concluded between his Brittanic Majesty and the "United States of America."

The Union existed before the Constitution, which was ordained and established among other things to form "a more perfect Union." Prior to that event, it is clear that the Union, declared by the articles of Confederation to be "perpetual," was the sole possessor of external sovereignty, and in the Union it remained without change save in so far as the Constitution in express terms qualified its exercise. The Framers' Convention was called and exerted its powers upon the irrefutable postulate that though the states were several their people in respect of foreign affairs were one. Compare The Chinese Exclusion Case. In that convention the entire absence of state power to deal with those affairs was thus forcefully stated by Rufus King:

> The states were not "sovereigns" in the sense contended for by some. They did not possess the peculiar features of sovereignty,—they could not make war, nor peace, nor alliances, nor treaties. Considering them as political beings, they were dumb, for they could not speak to any foreign sovereign whatever. They were deaf, for they could not hear any propositions from such sovereign. They had not even the organs or faculties of defense or offense, for they could not of themselves raise troops, or equip vessels, for war.

It results that the investment of the federal government with the powers of external sovereignty did not depend upon the affirmative grants of the Constitution. The powers to declare and wage war, to conclude peace, to make treaties, to maintain diplomatic relations with other sovereignties, if they had never been mentioned in the Constitution, would have vested in the federal government as necessary concomitants of nationality. Neither the Constitution nor the laws passed in pursuance of it have any force in foreign territory unless in respect of our own citizens and operations of the nation in such territory must be governed by treaties, international understandings and compacts, and the principles of international law. As a member of the family of nations, the right and power of the United States in that field are equal to the right and power of the other members of the international family. Otherwise, the United States is not completely sovereign. The power to acquire territory by discovery and occupation, the power to expel undesirable aliens, the power to make such international agreements as do not constitute treaties in the constitutional sense, none of which is expressly affirmed by the Constitution, nevertheless exist as inherently inseparable from the conception of nationality. This the court recognized, and in each of the cases cited found the warrant for its conclusions not in the provisions of the Constitution, but in the law of nations.

In Burnet v. Brooks, we said, ''As a nation with all the attributes of sovereignty, the United States is vested with all the powers of government necessary to maintain an effective control of international relations.'' Cf. Carter v. Carter Coal Co.

Not only, as we have shown, is the federal power over external affairs in origin and essential character different from that over internal affairs, but participation in the exercise of the power is significantly limited. In this vast external realm, with its important, complicated, delicate and manifold problems, the President alone has the power to speak or listen as a representative of the nation. He *makes* treaties with the advice and consent of the Senate; but he alone negotiates. Into the field of negotiation the Senate cannot intrude; and Congress itself is powerless to invade it. As Marshall said in his great argument of March 7, 1800, in the House of Representatives, ''The President is the sole organ of the nation in its external relations, and its sole representative with foreign nations.'' Annals, 6th Cong., col. 613. The Senate Committee on Foreign Relations at a very early day in our history (February 15, 1816), reported to the Senate, among other things, as follows:

> The President is the constitutional representative of the United States with regard to foreign nations. He manages our concerns with foreign nations and must necessarily be most competent to determine when, how, and upon what subjects negotiation may be urged with the greatest prospect of success. For his conduct he is responsible to the Constitution. The committee considers this responsibility the surest pledge for the faithful discharge of this duty. They think the interference of the Senate in the direction of foreign negotiations calculated to diminish that responsibility and thereby to impair the best security for the national safety. The nature of transactions with foreign nations, moreover, requires caution and unity of design, and their success frequently depends on secrecy and dispatch. 8 U.S. Sen. Reports Comm. on Foreign Relations, p. 24.

It is important to bear in mind that we are here dealing not alone with an authority vested in the President by an exertion of legislative power, but with such an authority plus the very delicate, plenary and exclusive power of the President as the sole organ of the federal government in the field of international relations—a power which does not require as a basis for its exercise an act of Congress, but which, of course, like every other governmental power, must be exercised in subordination to the applicable provisions of the Constitution. It is quite apparent that if, in the maintenance of our international relations, embarrassment—perhaps serious embarrassment—is to be avoided and success for our aims achieved, congressional legislation which is to be made effective through negotiation and inquiry within the international field must often accord to the President a degree of discretion and freedom from statutory restriction which would not be admissible were domestic affairs alone involved. Moreover, he, not Congress, has the better opportunity of knowing the conditions which prevail in foreign countries, and especially is this true in time of war. He has his confidential sources of information. He has his agents in the form of diplomatic, consular and other officials. Secrecy in respect of information gathered by them may be highly necessary, and the premature disclosure of it productive of harmful results. Indeed, so clearly is this true that the first President refused to accede to a request to lay before the House of Representatives the instructions, correspondence and documents relating to the negotiation of the Jay Treaty—a refusal the wisdom of which was recognized by the House itself and has never since been doubted. In his reply to the request, President Washington said:

> The nature of foreign negotiations requires caution, and their success must often depend on secrecy; and even when brought to a conclusion a full disclosure of all the measures, demands, or eventual concessions which may have been proposed or contemplated would be extremely impolitic; for this might have a pernicious influence on future negotiations, or produce immediate inconveniences, perhaps danger and mischief, in relation to other powers. The necessity of such caution and secrecy was one cogent reason for vesting the power of making treaties in the President, with the advice and consent of the Senate, the principle in which that body was formed confining it to a small number of members. To admit, then, a right in the House of Representatives to demand and to have as a matter of course all the papers respecting a negotiation with a foreign power would be to establish a dangerous precedent. Messages and Papers of the Presidents, p. 194.

We deem it unnecessary to consider, *seriatim,* the several clauses which are said to evidence the unconstitutionality of the Joint Resolution as involving an unlawful delegation of legislative power. It is enough to summarize by saying that, both upon principle and in accordance with precedent, we conclude there is sufficient warrant for the broad discretion vested in the President to determine whether the enforcement of the statute will have a beneficial effect upon the reestablishment of peace in the affected countries; whether he shall make proclamation to bring the resolution into operation; whether and when the resolution shall cease to operate and to make proclamation accordingly; and to prescribe limitations and exceptions to which the enforcement of the resolution shall be subject.

The judgement of the court below must be reversed and the cause remanded for further proceedings in accordance with the foregoing opinion.

It is so ordered.

MR. JUSTICE MCREYNOLDS does not agree. He is of opinion that the court below reached the right conclusion and its judgment ought to be affirmed.

MR. JUSTICE STONE took no part in the consideration or decision of this case.

UNITED STATES v. PINK, 315 U.S. 203 (1942)

Before the United States recognized the government of the Soviet Union in 1933, that government had expropriated various companies in the Soviet Union. Some of those companies maintained assets, including bank accounts, in the United States. These assets were claimed by the Soviet government. When Pres. Franklin Roosevelt recognized that government in 1933, he entered into an international agreement known as the "Litvinov Assignment." As part of the agreement, the Soviet government assigned to the United States its claims against those assets. When the federal government sought to recover those assets in the courts of the state of New York, however, the state courts dismissed the action as contrary to the public policy of the state.

MR. JUSTICE DOUGLAS delivered the opinion of the Court.

[The] power of New York to deny enforcement of a claim under the Litvinov Assignment because of an overriding policy of the State which denies validity in New York of the Russian decrees on which the assigned claims rest . . . was denied New York in United States v. Belmont. With one qualification . . . the Belmont case is determinative of the present controversy.

That case involved the right of the United States under the Litvinov Assignment to recover from a custodian or stakeholder in New York funds which had been nationalized and appropriated by the Russian decrees.

This Court, speaking through Mr. Justice Sutherland, held that the conduct of foreign relations is committed by the Constitution to the political departments of the Federal Government; that the propriety of the exercise of that power is not open to judicial inquiry; and that recognition of a foreign sovereign conclusively binds the courts and "is retroactive and validates all actions and conduct of the government so recognized from the commencement of its existence." It further held that recognition of the Soviet Government, the establishment of diplomatic relations with it, and the Litvinov Assignment were "all parts of one transaction, resulting in an international compact between the two governments." After stating that "in respect of what was done here, the Executive had authority to speak as the sole organ" of the national government, it added: "The assignment and the agreements in connection therewith did not, as in the case of treaties, as that term is used in the treaty making clause of the Constitution (Art. 2, § 2), require the advice and consent of the Senate." It held that the "external powers of the United States are to be exercised without regard to state laws or policies. The supremacy of a treaty in this respect has been recognized from the beginning." And it added that "all international compacts and agreements" are to be treated with similar dignity for the reason that "complete power over international affairs is in the national government and is not and cannot be subject to any curtailment or interference on the part of the several states." This Court did not stop to inquire whether in fact there was any policy of New York which enforcement of the Litvinov Assignment would infringe since "no state policy can prevail against the international compact here involved." United States v. Belmont, 301 U.S. 327.

The powers of the President in the conduct of foreign relations included the power, without consent of the Senate, to determine the public policy of the United States with respect to the Russian nationalization decrees. "What government is to be regarded here as representative of a foreign sovereign state is a political rather than a judicial question, and is to be determined by the political department of the government." Guaranty Trust Co. v. United States, 304 U.S. 137. That authority is not limited to a determination of the government to be recognized. It includes the power to determine the policy which is to govern the question of recognition. Objections to the underlying policy as well as objections to recognition are to be addressed to the political department and not to the courts. As we have noted, this Court in the Belmont case recognized that the Litvinov Assignment was an international compact which did not require the participation of the Senate. It stated: "There are many such compacts, of which a protocol, a modus vivendi, a postal convention, and agreements like that now under consideration are illustrations." Recognition is not always absolute; it is sometimes conditional. Power to remove such obstacles to full recognition as settlement of claims of our nationals certainly is a modest implied power of the President who is the "sole organ of the federal government in the field of international relations." United States v. Curtiss-Wright Corp., 299 U.S. 370. Effectiveness in handling the delicate problems of foreign relations requires no less. Unless such a power exists, the power of recognition might be thwarted or seriously diluted. No such obstacle can be placed in the way of rehabilitation of relations between its country and another nation, unless the historic conception of the powers and responsibilities of the President in the conduct of foreign affairs is to be drastically revised. It was the judgment of the political department that full recognition of the Soviet Government required the settlement of all outstanding problems including the claims of our nationals. Recognition and the Litvinov Assignment were interdependent. We would usurp the executive function if we held that that decision was not final and conclusive in the courts.

"All constitutional acts of power, whether in the executive or in the judicial department, have as much legal validity and obligation as if they proceeded from the legislature." The Federalist, No. 64. A treaty is a "Law of the Land" under the supremacy clause, Art. VI, Cl. 2, of the Constitution. Such international compacts and agreements as the Litvinov Assignment have a similar dignity. United States v. Belmont, 301 U.S. 331.

YOUNGSTOWN CO. v. SAWYER, 343 U.S. 579 (1952)

In April 1952, in an effort to avoid a nationwide strike of steelworkers that threatened American military interests in the Korean War, President Truman issued an executive order directing Secretary of Commerce Sawyer to seize and operate most of the steel mills. The order was not based on specific statutory authority. In fact, Truman decided not to use the statutory remedy available in the Taft-Hartley Act of 1947, which was enacted into law over his veto. In court, the administration justified the executive order on the basis of inherent presidential power. The district court issued a preliminary injunction against the seizure, rejecting the theory of inherent power, but the D.C. Circuit stayed this injunction pending review by the Supreme Court.

Mr. Justice BLACK delivered the opinion of the Court.

We are asked to decide whether the President was acting within his constitutional power when he issued an order directing the Secretary of Commerce to take possession of and operate most of the Nation's steel mills. The mill owners argue that the President's order amounts to lawmaking, a legislative function which the Constitution has expressly confided to the Congress and not to the President. The Government's position is that the order was made on finding of the President that his action was necessary to avert a national catastrophe which would inevitably result from a stoppage of steel production, and that in meeting this grave emergency the President was acting within the aggregate of his constitutional powers as the Nation's Chief Executive and the Commander in Chief of the Armed Forces of the United States. . . .

I.

[The Court rejects the administration's argument that the case should be resolved on nonconstitutional grounds. The constitutional question is "ripe for determination on the record presented."]

II.

The President's power, if any, to issue the order must stem either from an act of Congress or from the Constitution itself. There is no statute that expressly authorizes the President to take possession of property as he did here. Nor is there any act of Congress to which our attention has been directed from which such a power can fairly be implied. Indeed, we do not understand the Government to rely on statutory authorization for this seizure. . . .

Moreover, the use of the seizure technique to solve labor disputes in order to prevent work stoppages was not only authorized by any congressional enactment; prior to this controversy, Congress had refused to adopt that method of settling labor disputes. When the Taft-Hartley Act was under consideration in 1947, Congress rejected an amendment which would have authorized such governmental seizures in cases of emergency. Apparently it was thought that the technique of seizure, like that of compulsory arbitration, would interfere with the process of collective bargaining. Consequently, the plan Congress adopted in that Act did not provide for seizure under any circumstances. Instead, the plan sought to bring about settlements by use of the customary devices of mediation, conciliation, investigation by boards of inquiry, and public reports. In some instances temporary injunctions were authorized to provide cooling-off periods. All this failing, unions were left free to strike after a secret vote by employees as to whether they wished to accept their employers' final settlement offer.

It is clear that if the President had authority to issue the order he did, it must be found in some provision of the Constitution. And it is not claimed that express constitutional language grants this power to the President. The contention is that presidential power should be implied from the aggregate of his powers under the Constitution.

Particular reliance is placed on provisions in Article II which say that "The executive Power shall be vested in a President"; that "he shall take Care that the Laws be faithfully executed"; and that he "shall be Commander in Chief of the Army and Navy of the United States."

The order cannot properly be sustained as an exercise of the President's military power as Commander in Chief of the Armed Forces. The Government attempts to do so by citing a number of cases upholding broad powers in military commanders engaged in day-to-day fighting in a theater of war. Such cases need not concern us here. Even though "theater of war" be an expanding concept, we cannot with faithfulness to our constitutional system hold that the Commander in Chief of the Armed Forces has the ultimate power as such to take possession of private property in order to keep labor disputes from stopping production. This is a job for the Nation's lawmakers, not for its military authorities.

Nor can the seizure order be sustained because of the several constitutional provisions that grant executive power to the President. In the framework of our Constitution, the President's power to see that the laws are faithfully executed refutes the idea that he is to be a lawmaker. The Constitution limits his functions in the lawmaking process to the recommending of laws he thinks wise and the vetoing of laws he thinks bad. And the Constitution is neither silent nor equivocal about who shall make laws which the President is to execute. The first section of the first article says that "All legislative Powers herein granted shall be vested in a Congress of the United States." After granting many powers to the Congress, Article I goes on to provide that Congress may "make all Laws which shall be necessary and proper for carrying into Execution the foregoing Powers, and all other Powers vested by this Constitution in the Government of the United States, or in any Department or Officer thereof."

The President's order does not direct that a congressional policy be executed in a manner prescribed by Congress—it directs that a presidential policy be executed in a manner prescribed by the President. The preamble of the order itself, like that of many statutes, sets out reasons why the President believes certain policies should be adopted, proclaims these policies as rules of conduct to be followed, and again, like a statute, authorizes a government official to promulgate additional rules and regulations consistent with the policy proclaimed and needed to carry that policy into execution. The power of Congress to adopt such public policies as those proclaimed by the order is beyond question. It can authorize the taking of private property for public use. It can make laws regulating the relationships between employers and employees, prescribing rules designed to settle labor disputes, and fixing wages and working conditions in certain fields of our economy. The Constitution does not subject this lawmaking power of Congress to presidential or military supervision or control.

It is said that other Presidents without congressional authority have taken possession of private business enterprises in order to settle labor disputes. But even if this be true, Congress has not thereby lost its exclusive constitutional authority to make laws necessary and proper to carry out the powers vested by the Constitution "in the Government of the United States, or any Department or Officer thereof."

The Founders of this Nation entrusted the lawmaking power to the Congress alone in both good and bad times. It would do no good to recall the historical events, the fears of power and the hopes for freedom that lay behind their choice. Such a review would but confirm our holding that this seizure order cannot stand.

The judgment of the District Court is

Affirmed.

Mr. Justice FRANKFURTER.

Although the considerations relevant to the legal enforcement of the principle of separation of powers seem to me more complicated and flexible than may appear from what Mr. Justice Black has written, I join his opinion because I thoroughly agree with the application of the principle to the circumstances of this case. Even though such differences in attitude toward this principle may be merely differences in emphasis and nuance, they can hardly be reflected by a single opinion for the Court. Individual expression of views in reaching a common result is therefore important.

Mr. Justice Frankfurter, concurring.

Not so long ago it was fashionable to find our system of checks and balances obstructive to effective government. It was easy to ridicule that system as outmoded—too easy. The experience through which the world has passed in our own day has made vivid the realization that the Framers of our Constitution were not inexperienced doctrinaires. These long-headed statesmen had no illusion that our people enjoyed biological or psychological or sociological immunities from the hazards of concentrated power. It is absurd to see a dictator in a representative product of the sturdy democratic traditions of the Mississippi Valley. The accretion of dangerous power does not come in a day. It does come, however slowly, from the generative force of unchecked disregard of the restrictions that fence in even the most disinterested assertion of authority.

The issue before us can be met, and therefore should be, without attempting to define the President's powers comprehensively. I shall not attempt to delineate what belongs to him by virtue of his office beyond the power even of Congress to contract; what authority belongs to him until Congress acts; what kind of problems may be dealt with either by the Congress or by the President or by both, cf. *La Abra Silver Mng. Co. v. United States,* 175 U.S. 423; what power must be exercised by the Congress and cannot be delegated to the President.

To be sure, the content of the three authorities of government is not to be derived from an abstract analysis. The areas are partly interacting, not wholly disjointed. The Constitution is a framework for government. Therefore the way the framework has consistently operated fairly establishes that it has operated according to its true nature. Deeply embedded traditional ways of conducting government cannot supplant the Constitution or legislation, but they give meaning to the words of a text or supply them. It is an inadmissibly narrow conception of American constitutional law to confine it to the words of the Constitution and to disregard the gloss which life has written upon them. In short, a systematic, unbroken, executive practice, long pursued to the knowledge of the Congress and never before questioned, engaged in by Presidents who have also sworn to uphold the Constitution, making as it were such exercise of power part of the structure of our government, may be treated as a gloss on "executive Power" vested in the President by § 1 of Art. II.

Mr. Justice Douglas, concurring.

There can be no doubt that the emergency which caused the President to seize these steel plants was one that bore heavily on the country. But the emergency did not create power; it merely marked an occasion when power should be exercised. And the fact that it was necessary that measures be taken to keep steel in production does not mean that the President, rather than the Congress, had the constitutional authority to act. The Congress, as well as the President, is trustee of the national welfare.

The method by which industrial peace is achieved is of vital importance not only to the parties but to society as well. A determination that sanctions should be applied, that the hand of the law should be placed upon the parties, and that the force of the courts should be directed against them, is an exercise of legislative power. In some nations that power is entrusted to the executive branch as a matter of course or in case of emergencies. We chose another course. We chose to place the legislative power of the Federal Government in the Congress.

We pay a price for our system of checks and balances, for the distribution of power among the three branches of government. It is a price that today may seem exorbitant to many. Today a kindly President uses the seizure power to effect a wage increase and to keep the steel furnaces in production. Yet tomorrow another President might use the same power to prevent a wage increase, to curb trade-unionists, to regiment labor as oppressively as industry thinks it has been regimented by this seizure.

Mr. Justice Jackson, concurring in the judgement and opinion of the Court.

A judge, like an executive adviser, may be surprised at the poverty of really useful and unambiguous authority applicable to concrete problems of executive power as they actually present themselves. Just what our forefathers did envision, or would have envisioned had they foreseen modern conditions, must be divined from materials almost as enigmatic as the dreams Joseph was called upon to interpret for Pharaoh. A century and a half of partisan debate and scholarly speculation yields no net result but only supplies more or less apt quotations from respected sources on each side of any question. They largely cancel each other. And court decisions are indecisive because of the judicial practice of dealing with the largest questions in the most narrow way.

The actual art of governing under our Constitution does not and cannot conform to judicial definitions of the power of any of its branches based on isolated clauses or even single Articles torn from context. While the Constitution diffuses power the better to secure liberty, it also contemplates that practice will integrate the dispersed powers into a workable government. It enjoins upon its branches separateness but interdependence, autonomy but reciprocity. Presidential powers are not fixed but fluctuate, depending upon their disjunction or conjunction with those of Congress. We may well begin by a somewhat over-simplified grouping of practical situations in which a President may doubt, or others may challenge, his powers, and by distinguishing roughly the legal consequences of this factor of relativity.

1. When the President acts pursuant to an express or implied authorization of Con-

gress, his authority is at its maximum, for it includes all that he possesses in his own right plus all that Congress can delegate. In these circumstances, and in these only, may he be said (for what it may be worth) to personify the federal sovereignty. If his act is held unconstitutional under these circumstances, it usually means that the Federal Government as an undivided whole lacks power. A seizure executed by the President pursuant to an Act of Congress would be supported by the strongest of presumptions and the widest latitude of judicial interpretation, and the burden of persuasion would rest heavily upon any who might attack it.

2. When the President acts in absence of either a congressional grant or denial of authority, he can only rely upon his own independent powers, but there is a zone of twilight in which he and Congress may have concurrent authority, or in which its distribution is uncertain. Therefore, congressional inertia, indifference or quiescence may sometimes, at least as a practical matter, enable, if not invite, measures on independent presidential responsibility. In this area, any actual test of power is likely to depend on the imperatives of events and contemporary imponderables rather than on abstract theories of law.

3. When the President takes measures incompatible with the expressed or implied will of Congress, his power is at its lowest ebb, for then he can rely only upon his own constitutional powers minus any constitutional powers of Congress over the matter. Courts can sustain exclusive presidential control in such a case only by disabling the Congress from acting upon the subject. Presidential claim to a power at once so conclusive and preclusive must be scrutinized with caution, for what is at stake is the equilibrium established by our constitutional system.

We should not use this occasion to circumscribe, much less to contract, the lawful role of the President as Commander in Chief. I should indulge the widest latitude of interpretation to sustain his exclusive function to command the instruments of national force, at least when turned against the outside world for the security of our society. But, when it is turned inward, not because of rebellion but because of a lawful economic struggle between industry and labor, it should have no such indulgence. . . .

I have no illusion that any decision by this Court can keep power in the hands of Congress if it is not wise and timely in meeting its problems. A crisis that challenges the President equally, or perhaps primarily, challenges Congress. If not good law, there was worldly wisdom in the maxim attributed to Napoleon that "The tools belong to the man who can use them." We may say that power to legislate for emergencies belongs in the hands of Congress, but only Congress itself can prevent power from slipping through its fingers. . . . With all its defects, delays and inconveniences, men have discovered no technique for long preserving free government except that the Executive be under the law, and that the law be made by parliamentary deliberations.

Such institutions may be destined to pass away. But it is the duty of the Court to be last, not first, to give them up.

Mr. Justice Burton, concurring in both the opinion and judgment of the Court.

The present situation is not comparable to that of an imminent invasion or threatened attack. We do not face the issue of what might be the President's constitutional power to meet such catastrophic situations. Nor is it claimed that the current seizure is in the nature of a military command addressed by the President, as Commander-in-Chief, to a mobilized nation waging, or imminently threatened with, total war.

Mr. Justice Clark, concurring in the judgment of the Court.

In my view . . . the Constitution does grant to the President extensive authority in times of grave and imperative national emergency. In fact, to my thinking, such a grant may well be necessary to the very existence of the Constitution itself. As Lincoln aptly said, "[is] it possible to lose the nation and yet preserve the Constitution?" In describing this authority I care not whether one calls it "residual," "inherent," "moral," "implied," "aggregate," "emergency," or otherwise. I am of the conviction that those who have had the gratifying experience of being the President's lawyer have used one or more of these adjectives only with the utmost of sincerity and the highest of purpose.

I conclude that where Congress has laid down specific procedures to deal with the type of crisis confronting the President, he must follow those procedures in meeting the crisis; but that in the absence of such action by Congress, the President's independent power to act depends upon the gravity of the situation confronting the nation. I cannot sustain the seizure in question because here . . . Congress had prescribed methods to be followed by the President in meeting the emergency at hand.

Mr. Chief Justice Vinson, with whom Mr. Justice Reed and Mr. Justice Minton join, dissenting.

I.

In passing upon the question of Presidential powers in this case, we must first consider the context in which those powers were exercised.

Those who suggest that this is a case involving extraordinary power should be mindful that these are extraordinary times. A world not yet recovered from the devastation of World War II has been forced to face the threat of another and more terrifying global conflict.

Accepting in full measure its responsibility in the world community, the United States was instrumental in securing adoption of the United Nations Charter, approved by the Senate by a vote of 89 to 2. The first purpose of the United Nations is to "maintain international peace and security, and to that end: to take effective collective measures for the prevention and removal of the threats to the peace, and for the suppression of acts of aggression or other breaches of the peace." In 1950, when the United Nations called upon member nations "to render every assistance" to repel aggression in Korea, the United States furnished its vigorous support. For almost two full years, our armed forces have been fighting in Korea, suffering casualties of over 108,000 men. Hostilities have not abated. The "determination of the United Nations to continue its action in Korea to meet the aggression" has been reaffirmed. Congressional support of the action in Korea has been manifested by provisions for increased military manpower and equipment and for economic stabilization, as hereinafter described.

Congress recognized the impact of these defense programs upon the economy. Following the attack in Korea, the President asked for authority to requisition property and to allocate and fix priorities for scarce goods. In the Defense Production Act of 1950, Congress granted the powers requested and, *in addition,* granted power to stabilize prices and wages and to provide for settlement of labor disputes arising in the defense program. The Defense Production Act was extended in 1951, a Senate Committee noting that in the dislocation caused by the programs for purchase of military equipment "lies the seed of an economic disaster that might well destroy the military might we are straining to build." Significantly, the Committee examined the problem "in terms of just one commodity, steel," and found "a graphic picture of the over-all inflationary danger growing out of reduced civilian supplies and rising incomes." Even before Korea, steel production at levels above theoretical 100% capacity was not capable of supplying civilian needs alone. Since Korea, the tremendous military demand for steel has far exceeded the increases in productive capacity. This Committee emphasized that the shortage of steel, even with the mills operating at full capacity, coupled with increased civilian purchasing power, presented grave danger of disastrous inflation.

The President has the duty to execute the foregoing legislative programs. Their successful execution depends upon continued production of steel and stabilized prices for steel. . . .

III.

A review of executive action demonstrates that our Presidents have on many occasions exhibited the leadership contemplated by the Framers when they made the President Commander in Chief, and imposed upon him the trust to "take care that the Laws be faithfully executed." With or without explicit statutory authorization, Presidents have at such times dealt with national emergencies by acting promptly and resolutely to enforce legislative programs, at least to save those programs until Congress could act. Congress and the courts have responded to such executive initiative with consistent approval.

VI.

The diversity of views expressed in the six opinions of the majority, the lack of reference to authoritative precedent, the repeated reliance upon prior dissenting opinions, the complete disregard of the uncontroverted facts showing the gravity of the emergency and the temporary nature of the taking all serve to demonstrate how far afield one must go to affirm the order of the District Court.

The broad executive power granted by Article II to an officer on duty 365 days a year cannot, it is said, be invoked to avert disaster. Instead, the President must confine himself to sending a message to Congress recommending action. Under this messenger-boy concept of the Office, the President cannot even act to preserve legislative programs from destruction so that Congress will have something left to act upon. There is no judicial finding that the executive action was unwarranted because there was in fact no basis for the President's finding of the existence of an emergency for, under this view, the gravity of the emergency and the immediacy of the threatened disaster are considered irrelevant as a matter of law.

GOLDWATER v. CARTER, 444 U.S. 997 (1979)

On December 15, 1978, President Jimmy Carter terminated the 1954 Mutual Defense Treaty with Taiwan, an agreement that provided the cornerstone of U.S.–Taiwanese relations. Under the terms of the treaty, either "party" could end the pact after giving the other nation a year's notice. By the time the case reached the Court on appeal, President Carter's termination of the treaty was about to take effect. Without hearing oral argument, the Court dismissed the complaint by Sen. Barry Goldwater that Carter's unilateral action was unconstitutional. Goldwater argued that the termination of a treaty required legislative action.

Mr. Justice Powell, concurring in the judgment.

Although I agree with the result reached by the Court, I would dismiss the complaint as not ripe for judicial review.

I

This Court has recognized that an issue should not be decided if it is not ripe for judicial review. *Buckley v. Valeo,* 424 U.S. 1, 113–114 (1976) *(per curiam)*. Prudential considerations persuade me that a dispute between Congress and the President is not ready for judicial review unless and until each branch has taken action asserting its constitutional authority. Differences between the President and the Congress are commonplace under our system. The differences should, and almost invariably do, turn on political rather than legal considerations. The Judicial Branch should not decide issues affecting the allocation of power between the President and Congress until the political branches reach a constitutional impasse. Otherwise, we would encourage small groups or even individual Members of Congress to seek judicial resolution of issues before the normal political process has the opportunity to resolve the conflict.

In this case, a few Members of Congress claim that the President's action in terminating the treaty with Taiwan has deprived them of their constitutional role with respect to a change in the supreme law of the land. Congress has taken no official action. In the present posture of this case, we do not know whether there ever will be an actual confrontation between the Legislative and Executive Branches. Although the Senate has considered a resolution declaring that Senate approval is necessary for the termination of any mutual defense treaty, see 125 Cong. Rec. S7015, S7038–S7039 (June 6, 1979), no final vote has been taken on the resolution. See *id.,* at S16683–S16692 (Nov. 15, 1979). Moreover, it is unclear whether the resolution would have retroactive effect. See *id.,* at S7054–S7064 (June 6, 1979); *id.,* at S7862 (June 19, 1979). It cannot be said that either the Senate or the House has rejected the President's claim. If the Congress chooses not to confront the President, it is not our task to do so. I therefore concur in the dismissal of this case.

II

Mr. Justice Rehnquist suggests, however, that the issue presented by this case is a non-justiciable political question which can never be considered by this Court. I cannot agree. In my view, reliance upon the political-question doctrine is inconsistent with our precedents. As set forth in the seminal case of *Baker v. Carr,* 369 U.S. 186, 217 1962), the doctrine incorporates three inquiries: (i) Does the issue involve resolution of questions committed by the text of the Constitution to a coordinate branch of Government? (ii) Would resolution of the question demand that a court move beyond areas of judicial expertise? (iii) Do prudential considerations counsel against judicial intervention? In my opinion the answer to each of these inquiries would require us to decide this case if it were ready for review.

First, the existence of "a textually demonstrable constitutional commitment of the issue to a coordinate political department," *ibid.,* turns on an examination of the constitutional provisions governing the exercise of the power in question. *Powell v. McCormack,* 395 U.S. 486, 519 (1969). No constitutional provision explicitly confers upon the President the power to terminate treaties. Further, Art. II, § 2, of the Constitution authorizes the President to make treaties with the advice and consent of the Senate. Article VI provides that treaties shall be a part of the supreme law of the land. These provisions add support to the view that the text of the Constitution does not unquestionably commit the power to terminate treaties to the President alone. Cf. *Gilligan v. Morgan,* 413 U.S. 1, 6 (1973); *Luther v. Borden,* 7 How. 1, 42 (1849).

Second, there is no "lack of judicially discoverable and manageable standards for resolving" this case; nor is a decision impossible "without an initial policy determination of a kind clearly for nonjudicial discretion." *Baker v. Carr, supra,* 369 U.S., at 217. We are asked to decide whether the President may terminate a treaty under the Constitution without congressional approval. Resolution of the question may not be easy, but it only requires us to apply normal principles of interpretation to the constitutional provisions at issue. See *Powell v. McCormack, supra,* 395 U.S., at 548–549. The present case involves neither review of the President's activities as Commander in Chief nor impermissible interference in the field of foreign affairs. Such a case would arise if we were asked to decide, for example, whether a treaty required the President to order troops into a foreign country. But "it is error to suppose that every case or controversy which touches foreign relations lies beyond judicial cognizance." *Baker v. Carr, supra,* 369 U.S., at 211. This case "touches" foreign relations, but the question presented to us concerns only the constitutional division of power between Congress and the President.

A simple hypothetical demonstrates the confusion that I find inherent in *Mr. Justice Rehnquist's* opinion concurring in the judgment. Assume that the President signed a mutual defense treaty with a foreign country and announced that it would go into effect despite its rejection by the Senate. Under *Mr. Justice Rehnquist's* analysis that situation would present a political question even though Art. II, § 2, clearly would resolve the dispute. Although the answer to the hypothetical case seems self-evident because it demands textual rather than interstitial analysis, the nature of the legal issue presented is no different from the issue presented in the case before us. In both cases, the Court would interpret the Constitution to decide whether congressional approval is necessary to give a Presidential decision on the validity of a treaty the force of law. Such an inquiry demands no special competence or information beyond the reach of the Judiciary. Cf. *Chicago & Southern Air Lines v. Waterman S.S. Corp.*, 333 U.S. 103, 111 (1948).

Finally, the political-question doctrine rests in part on prudential concerns calling for mutual respect among the three branches of Government. Thus, the Judicial Branch should avoid "the potentiality of embarrassment [that would result] from multifarious pronouncements by various departments on one question." Similarly, the doctrine restrains judicial action where there is an "unusual need for unquestioning adherence to a political decision already made." *Baker v. Carr, supra,* 369 U.S., at 217.

If this case were ripe for judicial review, see Part I *supra,* none of these prudential considerations would be present. Interpretation of the Constitution does not imply lack of respect for a coordinate branch. *Powell v. McCormack, supra,* 395 U.S., at 548. If the President and the Congress had reached irreconcilable positions, final disposition of the question presented by this case would eliminate, rather than create, multiple constitutional interpretations. The specter of the Federal Government brought to a halt because of the mutual intransigence of the President and the Congress would require this Court to provide a resolution pursuant to our duty " 'to say what the law is.' " *United States v. Nixon,* 418 U.S. 683, 703 (1974), quoting *Marbury v. Madison,* 1 Cranch 137, 177 (1803).

III

In my view, the suggestion that this case presents a political question is incompatible with this Court's willingness on previous occasions to decide whether one branch of our Government has impinged upon the power of another. See *Buckley v. Valeo,* 424 U.S., at 138; *United States v. Nixon, supra,* 418 U.S., at 707; *The Pocket Veto Case,* 279 U.S. 655, 676–678, 49 S.Ct. 463, 73 L.Ed. 894 (1929); *Myers v. United States,* 272 U.S. 52, (1926). Under the criteria enunciated in *Baker v. Carr,* we have the responsibility to decide whether both the Executive and Legislative Branches have constitutional roles to play in termination of a treaty. If the Congress, by appropriate formal action, had challenged the President's authority to terminate the treaty with Taiwan, the resulting uncertainty could have serious consequences for our country. In that situation, it would be the duty of this Court to resolve the issue.

Mr. Justice Rehnquist, with whom *the Chief Justice, Mr. Justice Stewart, and Mr. Justice Stevens* join, concurring in the judgment.

I am of the view that the basic question presented by the petitioners in this case is "political" and therefore nonjusticiable because it involves the authority of the President in the conduct of our country's foreign relations and the extent to which the Senate or the Congress is authorized to negate the action of the President. . . .

I think that the justifications for concluding that the question here is political in nature are even more compelling than in *Coleman* because it involves foreign relations—specifically a treaty commitment to use military force in the defense of a foreign government if attacked. In *United States v. Curtiss-Wright Corp.,* 299 U.S. 304 (1936), this Court said:

Whether, if the Joint Resolution had related solely to internal affairs it would be open to the challenge that it constituted an unlawful delegation of legislative power to the Executive, we find it unnecessary to determine. The whole aim of the resolution is to affect a situation entirely external to the United States, and falling within the category of foreign affairs. *Id.*, at 315.

The present case differs in several important respects from *Youngstown Sheet & Tube Co. v. Sawyer,* 343 U.S. 579 (1952), cited by petitioners as authority both for reaching the merits of this dispute and for reversing the Court of Appeals. In *Youngstown,* private litigants brought a suit contesting the President's authority under his war powers to seize the Nation's steel industry, an action of profound and demonstrable domestic impact. Here, by contrast, we are asked to settle a dispute between coequal branches of our Government, each of which has resources available to protect and assert its interests, resources not available to private litigants outside the judicial forum. Moreover, as in *Curtiss-Wright,* the effect of this action, as far as we can tell, is "entirely external to the United States, and [falls] within the category of foreign affairs." Finally, as already noted, the situation presented here is closely akin to that presented in *Coleman,* where the Constitution spoke only to the procedure for ratification of an amendment, not to its rejection.

Having decided that the question presented in this action is nonjusticiable, I believe that the appropriate disposition is for this Court to vacate the decision of the Court of Appeals and remand with instructions for the District Court to dismiss the complaint. This procedure derives support from our practice in disposing of moot actions in federal courts. For more than 30 years, we have instructed lower courts to vacate any decision on the merits of an action that has become moot prior to a resolution of the case in this Court. *United States v. Munsingwear, Inc.,* 340 U.S. 36 (1950). The Court has required such decisions to be vacated in order to "prevent a judgment, unreviewable because of mootness, from spawning any legal consequences." *Id.,* at 41. It is even more imperative that this Court invoke this procedure to ensure that resolution of a "political question," which should not have been decided by a lower court, does not "spawn any legal consequences." An Art. III court's resolution of a question that is "political" in character can create far more disruption among the three co-equal branches of Government than the resolution of a question presented in a moot controversy. Since the political nature of the questions presented should have precluded the lower courts from considering or deciding the merits of the controversy, the prior proceedings in the federal courts must be vacated, and the complaint dismissed.

Mr. Justice Blackmun, with whom *Mr. Justice White* joins, dissenting in part.

In my view, the time factor and its importance are illusory; if the President does not have the power to terminate the treaty (a substantial issue that we should address only after briefing and oral argument), the notice of intention to terminate surely has no legal effect. It is also indefensible, without further study, to pass on the issue of justiciability or on the issues of standing or ripeness. While I therefore join in the grant of the petition for certiorari, I would set the case for oral argument and give it the plenary consideration it so obviously deserves.

Mr. Justice Brennan, dissenting.

I respectfully dissent from the order directing the District Court to dismiss this case, and would affirm the judgment of the Court of Appeals insofar as it rests upon the President's well-established authority to recognize, and withdraw recognition from, foreign governments.

In stating that this case presents a nonjusticiable "political question," Mr. Justice Rehnquist, in my view, profoundly misapprehends the political-question principle as it applies to matters of foreign relations. Properly understood, the political-question doctrine restrains courts from reviewing an exercise of foreign policy judgment by the coordinate political branch to which authority to make that judgment has been "constitutional[ly] commit[ted]." *Baker v. Carr*, 369 U.S. 186, 211–213, 217 (1962). But the doctrine does not pertain when a court is faced with the *antecedent* question whether a particular branch has been constitutionally designated as the repository of political decisionmaking power. Cf. *Powell v. McCormack*, 395 U.S. 486, 519–521 (1969). The issue of decisionmaking authority must be resolved as a matter of constitutional law, not political discretion; accordingly, it falls within the competence of the courts.

The constitutional question raised here is prudently answered in narrow terms. Abrogation of the defense treaty with Taiwan was a necessary incident to Executive recognition of the Peking Government, because the defense treaty was predicated upon the now-abandoned view that the Taiwan Government was the only legitimate political authority in China. Our cases firmly establish that the Constitution commits to the President alone the power to recognize, and withdraw recognition from, foreign regimes. See *Banco Nacional de Cuba v. Sabbatino*, 376 U.S. 398, 410 (1964); *Baker v. Carr, supra,* 369 U.S., at 212; *United States v. Pink*, 315 U.S. 203, 228–230 (1942). That mandate being clear, our judicial inquiry into the treaty rupture can go no further. See *Baker v. Carr, supra,* 369 U.S., at 212; *United States v. Pink, supra,* 315 U.S., at 229.

DAMES & MOORE v. REGAN, 453 U.S. 654 (1981)

After Iran seized American hostages in 1979, Pres. Jimmy Carter declared a national emergency and blocked the removal or transfer of all Iranian property subject to the jurisdiction of the United States. He also authorized certain judicial proceedings to handle consequent lawsuits brought by private parties seeking access to Iranian assets. When the American hostages were released on January 20, 1981, the United States and Iran entered into an agreement that required the termination of all legal proceedings in U.S. courts involving claims of U.S. nationals against Iran. Those claims would be submitted to binding arbitration before an Iran–United States Claims Tribunal. In this case, a private party seeks to prevent enforcement of various executive orders regulations issued to implement the agreement with Iran. The essential issue in this case is whether the administration exceeded its statutory and constitutional powers. Dames and Moore, a private company, sued Secretary of the Treasury Donald Regan.

JUSTICE REHNQUIST delivered the opinion of the Court.

We are confined to a resolution of the dispute presented to us. That dispute involves various Executive Orders and regulations by which the President nullified attachments and liens on Iranian assets in the United States, directed that these assets be transferred to Iran, and suspended claims against Iran that may be presented to an International Claims Tribunal. This action was taken in an effort to comply with an Executive Agreement between the United States and Iran. . . .

But before turning to the facts and law which we believe determine the result in this case, we stress that the expeditious treatment of the issues involved by all of the courts which have considered the President's actions makes us acutely aware of the necessity to rest decision on the narrowest possible ground capable of deciding the case. *Ashwander v. TVA,* 297 U.S. 288, 347 (1936) (Brandeis, J., concurring). . . .

I

On November 4, 1979, the American Embassy in Tehran was seized and our diplomatic personnel were captured and held hostage. In response to that crisis, President Carter, acting pursuant to the International Emergency Economic Powers Act, 91 Stat. 1626, 50 U.S.C. §§ 1701–1706 (1976 ed., Supp. III) (hereinafter IEEPA), declared a national emergency on November 14, 1979, and blocked the removal or transfer of "all property and interests in property of the Government of Iran, its instrumentalities and controlled entities and the Central Bank of Iran which are or become subject to the jurisdiction of the United States." On November 15, 1979, the Treasury Department's Office of Foreign Assets Control issued a regulation providing that "[u]nless licensed or authorized . . . any attachment, judgment, decree, lien, execution, garnishment, or other judicial process is null and void with respect to any property in which on or since [November 14, 1979,] there existed an interest of Iran." . . .

On November 26, 1979, the President granted a general license authorizing certain judicial proceedings against Iran but which did not allow the "entry of any judgment or of any decree or order of similar or analogous effect." § 535.504(a). On December 19, 1979, a clarifying regulation was issued stating that "the general authorization for judicial proceedings contained in § 535.504(a) includes pre-judgment attachment." § 535.418.

On January 20, 1981, the Americans held hostage were released by Iran pursuant to an Agreement entered into the day before. . . . The Agreement stated that "[i]t is the purpose of [the United States and Iran] . . . to terminate all litigation as between the Government of each party and the nationals of the other, and to bring about the settlement and termination of all such claims through binding arbitration." *Id.,* at 21–22. In furtherance of this goal, the Agreement called for the establishment of an Iran–United States Claims Tribunal which would arbitrate any claims not settled within six months. Awards of the Claims Tribunal are to be "final and binding" and "enforceable . . . in the courts of any nation in accordance with its laws." *Id.,* at 32. Under the Agreement, the United States is obligated

> to terminate all legal proceedings in United States courts involving claims of United States persons and institutions against Iran and its state enterprises, to nullify all attachments and judgments obtained therein, to prohibit all further litigation based on such claims, and to bring about the termination of such claims through binding arbitration. *Id.,* at 22.

In addition, the United States must "act to bring about the transfer" by July 19, 1981, of all Iranian assets held in this country by American banks. *Id.,* at 24–25. One billion dollars of these assets will be deposited in a security account in the Bank of England, to the account of the Algerian Central Bank, and used to satisfy awards rendered against Iran by the Claims Tribunal. *Ibid.*

On January 19, 1981, President Carter issued a series of Executive Orders implementing the terms of the agreement.

[On February 24, 1981, President Ronald Reagan issued an executive order in which he "ratified" the January 19 executive orders. In the meantime, a federal district court awarded Dames & Moore the amount claimed under the contract plus interest. Later, the company filed an action seeking to prevent enforcement of the executive orders and Treasury Department regulations implementing the agreement with Iran.]

II

[In this section, Justice Rehnquist finds Justice Jackson's concurring opinion in Youngstown Co. v. Sawyer (1952), classifying presidential actions into three general categories, to be analytically useful but somewhat too general to apply. Presidential action in any particular case does not fall "neatly in one of three pigeonholes, but rather at some point along a spectrum running from explicit congressional authorization to explicit congressional prohibition. This is particularly true as respects cases such as the one before us. . . ."]

III

In nullifying post–November 14, 1979, attachments and directing those persons holding blocked Iranian funds and securities to transfer them to the Federal Reserve Bank of New York for ultimate transfer to Iran, President Carter cited five sources of express or inherent power. The Government, however, has principally relied on § 203 of the IEEPA. . . .

[Dames and Moore argued that the Court should ignore the plain language of this statute and examine its legislative history and the history of the Trading With the Enemy Act (TWEA), which reveals that IEEPA "was not intended to give the President such extensive power over the assets of a foreign state during times of national emergency."

The Court disagreed, refusing to read out of IEEPA the meaning of certain words. To the Court, nothing in the history of that statute or of the TWEA requires such a result.]

To the contrary, we think both the legislative history and cases interpreting the TWEA fully sustain the broad authority of the Executive when acting under this congressional grant of power.

IV

Although we have concluded that the IEEPA constitutes specific congressional authorization to the President to nullify the attachments and order the transfer of Iranian assets, there remains the question of the President's authority to suspend claims pending in American courts. Such claims have, of course, an existence apart from the attachments which accompanied them. In terminating these claims through Executive Order No. 12294, the President purported to act under authority of both the IEEPA and 22 U.S.C. § 1732, the so-called "Hostage Act." 46 Fed. Reg. 14111 (1981).

We conclude that although the IEEPA authorized the nullification of the attachments, it cannot be read to authorize the suspension of the claims. The claims of American citizens against Iran are not in themselves transactions involving Iranian property or efforts to exercise any rights with respect to such property. . . . *[The Court also concludes that the Hostage Act does not provide specific authorization to the President to suspend claims in American courts.]*

Concluding that neither the IEEPA nor the Hostage Act constitutes specific authorization of the President's action suspending claims, however, is not to say that these statutory provisions are entirely irrelevant to the question of the validity of the President's action. We think both statutes highly relevant in the looser sense of indicating congressional acceptance of a broad scope for executive action in circumstances such as those presented in this case. As noted in Part III, *supra,* at 670–672, the IEEPA delegates broad authority to the President to act in times of national emergency with respect to property of a foreign country. The Hostage Act similarly indicates congressional willingness that the President have broad discretion when responding to the hostile acts of foreign sovereigns. . . .

Although we have declined to conclude that the IEEPA or the Hostage Act directly authorizes the President's suspension of claims for the reasons noted, we cannot ignore the general tenor of Congress' legislation in this area in trying to determine whether the President is acting alone or at least with the acceptance of Congress. As we have noted, Congress cannot anticipate and legislate with regard to every possible action the President may find it necessary to take or every possible situation in which he might act. Such failure of Congress specifically to delegate authority does not, "especially . . . in the areas of foreign policy and national security," imply "congressional disapproval" of action taken by the Executive. Haig v. Agee, 453 U.S. On the contrary, the enactment of legislation closely related to the question of the President's authority in a particular case which evinces legislative intent to accord the President broad discretion may be considered to "invite" "measures on independent presidential responsibility," Youngstown, 343 U.S., at 637 (Jackson, J., concurring). At least this is so where there is no contrary indication of legislative intent and when, as here, there is a history of congressional acquiescence in conduct of the sort engaged in by the President. It is to that history which we now turn.

Not infrequently in affairs between nations, outstanding claims by nationals of one country against the government of another country are "sources of friction" between the two sovereigns. *United States v. Pink,* 315 U.S. 203, 225 (1942). To resolve these difficulties, nations have often entered into agreements settling the claims of their respective nationals. As one treatise writer puts it, international agreements settling claims by nationals of one state against the government of another "are established international practice reflecting traditional international theory." L. Henkin, Foreign Affairs and the Constitution 262 (1972). Consistent with that principle, the United States has repeatedly exercised its sovereign authority to settle the claims of its nationals against foreign countries. Though those settlements have sometimes been made by treaty, there has also been a longstanding practice of settling such claims by executive agreement without the advice and consent of the Senate. . . .

Crucial to our decision today is the conclusion that Congress has implicitly approved the practice of claim settlement by executive agreement. . . .

The legislative history of the IEEPA further reveals that Congress has accepted the authority of the Executive to enter into settlement agreements. Though the IEEPA was enacted to provide for some limitation on the President's emergency powers, Congress stressed that "[n]othing in this act is intended . . . to interfere with the authority of the President to [block assets], or to impede the settlement of claims of U.S. citizens against foreign countries.'' S.Rep. No. 95–466, p. 6 (1977), U.S.Code Cong. & Admin. News, 1977, pp. 4540, 4544; 50 U.S.C. § 1706(a)(1) (1976 ed., Supp. III).

In addition to congressional acquiescence in the President's power to settle claims, prior cases of this Court have also recognized that the President does have some measure of power to enter into executive agreements without obtaining the advice and consent of the Senate. In *United States v. Pink,* 315 U.S. 203 (1942), for example the Court upheld the validity of the Litvinov Assignment, which was part of an Executive Agreement whereby the Soviet Union assigned to the United States amounts owed to it by American nationals so that outstanding claims of other American nationals could be paid. The Court explained that the resolution of such claims was integrally connected with normalizing United States' relations with a foreign state:

> Power to remove such obstacles to full recognition as settlement of claims of our nationals . . . certainly is a modest implied power of the President. . . . No such obstacle can be placed in the way of rehabilitation of relations between this country and another nation, unless the historic conception of the powers and responsibilities . . . is to be drastically revised. *Id.,* at 229–230.

In light of all of the foregoing—the inferences to be drawn from the character of the legislation Congress has enacted in the area, such as the IEEPA and the Hostage Act, and from the history of acquiescence in executive claims settlement—we conclude that the President was authorized to suspend pending claims pursuant to Executive Order No. 12294. . . . As Justice Frankfurter pointed out in *Youngstown,* 343 U.S., at 610–611, ''a systematic, unbroken, executive practice, long pursued to the knowledge of the Congress and never before questioned . . . may be treated as a gloss on 'Executive Power' vested in the President by § 1 of Art. II.'' Past practice does not, by itself, create power, but ''long-continued practice, known to and acquiesced in by Congress, would raise a presumption that the [action] had been [taken] in pursuance of its consent.'' *United States v. Midwest Oil Co.,* 236 U.S. 459, (1915). See *Haig v. Agee,* 453 U.S., at 291, 292. Such practice is present here and such a presumption is also appropriate. In light of the fact that Congress may be considered to have consented to the President's action in suspending claims, we cannot say that action exceeded the President's powers.

Just as importantly, Congress has not disapproved of the action taken here. Though Congress has held hearings on the Iranian Agreement itself, Congress has not enacted legislation, or even passed a resolution, indicating its displeasure with the Agreement. Quite the contrary, the relevant Senate Committee has stated that the establishment of the Tribunal is ''of vital importance to the United States.'' S.Rep. No. 97-71, p. 5 (1981). We are thus clearly not confronted with a situation in which Congress has in some way resisted the exercise of Presidential authority.

Finally, we re-emphasize the narrowness of our decision. We do not decide that the President possesses plenary power to settle claims, even as against foreign governmental entities. . . . But where, as here, the settlement of claims has been determined to be a necessary incident to the resolution of a major foreign policy dispute between our country and another, and where, as here, we can conclude that Congress acquiesced in the President's action, we are not prepared to say that the President lacks the power to settle such claims.

JUSTICE STEVENS, concurring in part.

JUSTICE POWELL, concurring and dissenting in part.

DELLUMS v. BUSH, 752 F. SUPP. 1141 (D.D.C. 1990)

After President Bush introduced U.S. troops into the Persian Gulf to create the potential for taking offensive action against Iraq, Cong. Ronald Dellums and fifty-three other members of Congress brought suit requesting an injunction to prevent Bush from going to war without first securing a declaration of war or other explicit congressional authorization. Although the district court declined to issue the injunction, the judge in this case, Harold H. Greene, issued a significant opinion rejecting many of the theories of presidential power advanced by the administration.

HAROLD H. GREENE, District Judge.

This is a lawsuit by a number of members of Congress who request an injunction directed to the President of the United States to prevent him from initiating an offensive attack against Iraq without first securing a declaration of war or other explicit congressional authorization for such action.

I

The factual background is, briefly, as follows. On August 2, 1990, Iraq invaded the neighboring country of Kuwait. President George Bush almost immediately sent United States military forces to the Persian Gulf area to deter Iraqi aggression and to preserve the integrity of Saudi Arabia. The United States, generally by presidential order and at times with congressional concurrence, also took other steps, including a blockade of Iraq, which were approved by the United Nations Security Council, and participated in by a great many other nations.

On November 8, 1990, President Bush announced a substantial increase in the Persian Gulf military deployment, raising the troop level significantly above the 230,000 then present in the area. At the same time, the President stated that the objective was to provide "an adequate *offensive* military option" should that be necessary to achieve such goals as the withdrawal of Iraqi forces from Kuwait. Secretary of Defense Richard Cheney likewise referred to the ability of the additional military forces "to conduct *offensive* military operations."

The House of Representatives and the Senate have in various ways expressed their support for the President's past and present actions in the Persian Gulf. However, the Congress was not asked for, and it did not take, action pursuant to Article I, Section, 8, Clause 11 of the Constitution "to declare war" on Iraq. On November 19, 1990, the congressional plaintiffs brought this action, which proceeds on the premise that the initiation of offensive United States military action is imminent, that such action would be unlawful in the absence of a declaration of war by the Congress, and that a war without concurrence by the Congress would deprive the congressional plaintiffs of the voice to which they are entitled under the Constitution. The Department of Justice, acting on behalf of the President, is opposing the motion for preliminary injunction, and it has also moved to dismiss. Plaintiffs thereafter moved for summary judgment.

The Department raises a number of defenses to the lawsuit—most particularly that the complaint presents a non-justiciable political question, that plaintiffs lack standing to maintain the action, that their claim violates established canon of equity jurisprudence, and that the issue of the proper allocation of the war making powers between the branches is not ripe for decision. These will now be considered seriatim.

II POLITICAL QUESTION

It is appropriate first to sketch out briefly the constitutional and legal framework in which the current controversy arises. Article, I, Section 8, Clause 11 of the Constitution grants to the Congress the power "To declare War." To the extent that this unambiguous direction requires construction or explanation, it is provided by the framers' comments that they felt it to be unwise to entrust the momentous power to involve the nation in a war to the President alone; Jefferson explained that he desired "an effectual check to the Dog of war"; James Wilson similarly expressed the expectation that this system would guard against hostilities being initiated by a single man. Even Abraham Lincoln, while a Congressman, said more than half a century later that *"no one man* should hold the power of bringing" war upon us.

The congressional power to declare war does not stand alone, however, but it is accompanied by powers granted to the President. Article II, Section 1, Clause 1 and Section 2 provide that "[t]he executive powers shall be vested in a President of the United States of America," and that "[t]he President shall be Commander in Chief of the Army and Navy. . . ."

It is the position of the Department of Justice on behalf of the President that the simultaneous existence of all these provisions renders it impossible to isolate the war-declaring power. The Department further argues that the design of the Constitution is to have the various war-and military-related provisions construed and acting together, and that their harmonization is a political rather than a legal question. In short, the Department relies on the political question doctrine.

That doctrine is premised both upon the separation of powers and the inherent limits of judicial abilities. *See generally, Baker v. Carr,* 369 U.S. 186 (1962); *Chicago & Southern Air Lines, Inc. v. Waterman Steamship Corp.,* 333 U.S. 103 (1948). In relation to the issues involved in this case, the Department of Justice expands on its basic theme, contending that by their very nature the determination whether certain types of military actions require a declaration of war is not justiciable, but depends instead upon delicate judgments by the political branches. On that view, the question whether an offensive action taken by American armed forces constitutes an act of war (to be initiated by a declaration of war) or an "offensive military attack" (presumably undertaken by the President in his capacity as commander-in-chief) is not one of objective fact but involves an exercise of judgment based upon all the vagaries of foreign affairs and national security. Motion to Dismiss at 1150. Indeed, the Department contends that there are no judicially discoverable and manageable standards to apply, claiming that only the political branches are able to determine whether or not this country is at war. Such a determination, it is said, is based upon "a political judgment" about the significance of those facts. Under that rationale, a court cannot make an independent determination on this issue because it cannot take adequate account of these political considerations.

This claim on behalf of the Executive is far too sweeping to be accepted by the courts. If the Executive had the sole power to determine that any particular offensive military operation, no matter how vast, does not constitute war-making but only an offensive military attack, the congressional power to declare war will be at the mercy of a semantic decision by the Executive. Such an "interpretation" would evade the plain language of the Constitution, and it cannot stand.

That is not to say that, assuming that the issue is factually close or ambiguous or fraught with intricate technical military and diplomatic baggage, the courts would not defer to the political branches to determine whether or not particular hostilities might qualify as a "war." However, here the forces involved are of such magnitude and significance as to present no serious claim that a war would not ensue if they became engaged in combat, and it is therefore clear that congressional approval is required if Congress desires to become involved.

[T]he Department goes on to suggest that the issue in this case is still political rather than legal, because in order to resolve the dispute the Court would have to inject itself into foreign affairs, a subject which the Constitution commits to the political branches. That argument, too, must fail.

While the Constitution grants to the political branches, and in particular to the Executive, responsibility for conducting the nation's foreign affairs, it does not follow that the judicial power is excluded from the resolution of cases merely because they may touch upon such affairs. The court must instead look at "the particular questions posed" in the case. *Baker v. Carr,* 369 U.S. at 211, 82 S. Ct. at 707. In fact, courts are routinely deciding cases that touch upon or even have a substantial impact on foreign and defense policy. . . .

[T]he Court has no hesitation in concluding that an offensive entry into Iraq by several hundred thousand United States servicemen under the conditions described above could be described as a "war" within the meaning of Article I, Section 8, Clause 11, of the Constitution. To put it another way: the Court is not prepared to read out of the Constitution the clause granting to the Congress, and to it alone, the authority "to declare war."

III STANDING

The Department of Justice argues next that the plaintiffs lack "standing" to pursue this action.

With close to 400,000 United States troops stationed in Saudi Arabia, with all troop rotation and leave provisions suspended, and with the President having acted vigorously on his own as well as through the Secretary of State to obtain from the United Nations Security Council a resolution authorizing the use of all available means to remove Iraqi forces from Kuwait, including the use of force, it is disingenuous for the Department to characterize plaintiffs' allegations as to the imminence of the threat of offensive military action for standing purposes as "remote and conjectural," Motion to Dismiss at 13, for standing purposes. *But see* Part V-B, *infra*. For these reasons, the Court concludes that the plaintiffs have adequately alleged a threat of injury in fact necessary to support standing.

IV REMEDIAL DISCRETION

Another issue raised by the Department which must be addressed briefly is the application to this case of the doctrine of "remedial" discretion developed by the Court of Appeals for this Circuit.
[Court will dismiss a case brought by a congressional plaintiff who could obtain substantial relief from fellow legislators through the enactment, repeal, or amendment of a statute.]

The plaintiffs in this case do not have a remedy available from their fellow legislators. While action remains open to them which would make the issues involved more concrete, and hence make the matter ripe for review by the Court, these actions would not remedy the threatened harm plaintiffs assert. A joint resolution counseling the President to refrain from attacking Iraq without a congressional declaration of war would not be likely to stop the President from initiating such military action if he is persuaded that the Constitution affirmatively gives him the power to act otherwise.

Plaintiffs in the instant case, therefore, cannot gain "substantial relief" by persuasion of their colleagues alone. The "remedies" of cutting off funding to the military or impeaching the President are not available to these plaintiffs either politically or practically. Additionally, these "remedies" would not afford the relief sought by the plaintiffs—which is the guarantee that they will have the opportunity to debate and vote on the wisdom of initiating a military attack against Iraq before the United States military becomes embroiled in belligerency with that nation.

V RIPENESS

Although, as discussed above, the Court rejects several of defendant's objections to the maintenance of this lawsuit, and concludes that, in principle, an injunction may issue at the request of Members of Congress to prevent the conduct of a war which is about to be carried on without congressional authorization, it does not follow that these plaintiffs are entitled to relief at this juncture. For the plaintiffs are met with a significant obstacle to such relief: the doctrine of ripeness.

In the context of this case, there are two aspects to ripeness, which the Court will now explore.

A. *Actions by the Congress*
No one knows the position of the Legislative Branch on the issue of war or peace with Iraq; certainly no one, including this Court, is able to ascertain the congressional position on that issue on the basis of this lawsuit brought by fifty-three members of the House of Representatives and one member of the U.S. Senate. It would be both

premature and presumptuous for the Court to render a decision on the issue of whether a declaration of war is required at this time or in the near future when the Congress itself has provided no indication whether it deems such a declaration either necessary, on the one hand, or imprudent, on the other.

In short, unless the Congress as a whole, or by a majority, is heard from, the controversy here cannot be deemed ripe; it is only if the majority of the Congress seeks relief from an infringement on its constitutional war-declaration power that it may be entitled to receive it.

B. *Action Taken by the Executive*

The second half of the ripeness issue involves the question whether the Executive Branch of government is so clearly committed to immediate military operations that may be equated with a "war" within the meaning of Article I, Section I, Clause 11, of the Constitution that a judicial decision may properly be rendered regarding the application of that constitutional provision to the current situation.

Plaintiffs assert that the matter is currently ripe for judicial action because the President himself has stated that the present troop build-up is to provide an adequate offensive military option in the area. His successful effort to secure passage of United Nations Resolution 678, which authorizes the use of "all available means" to oust Iraqi forces remaining in Kuwait after January 15, 1991, is said to be an additional fact pointing toward the Executive's intention to initiate military hostilities against Iraq in the near future.

The Department of Justice, on the other hand, points to statements of the President that the troops already in Saudi Arabia are a peacekeeping force to prove that the President might not initiate more offensive military actions. In addition, and more realistically, it is possible that the meetings set for later this month and next between President Bush and the Foreign Minister of Iraq, Tariq Aziz, in Washington, and Secretary of State James Baker and Saddam Hussein in Baghdad, may result in a diplomatic solution to the present situation, and in any event under the U.N. Security Council resolution there will not be resort to force before January 15, 1991.

[A]n injunction will be issued only if, on both of the aspect of the doctrine discussed above, the Court could find that the controversy is ripe for judicial decision. That situation does not, or at least not yet, prevail, and plaintiffs' request for a preliminary injunction will therefore not be granted.

For the reasons stated, it is this 13th day of December, 1990.

ORDERED that plaintiffs' motion for preliminary injunction be and it is hereby denied.

SELECTED BIBLIOGRAPHY

Adler, David Gray. *The Constitution and the Termination of Treaties*. New York: Garland, 1986.

Berger, Raoul. *Executive Privilege: A Constitutional Myth*. Cambridge: Harvard University Press, 1974.

Berman, Larry. *The New American Presidency*. New York: Little, Brown, 1987.

Bickford, Charlene Bangs, and Kenneth R. Bowling. *Birth of the Nation: The First Federal Congress, 1789–1791*. New York: First Federal Congress Project, 1989.

Bowling, Kenneth R., and Helen E. Veit, eds. *The Diary of William Maclay and Other Notes on Senate Debates*. Baltimore: Johns Hopkins University Press, 1988.

Caraley, Demetrios, ed. *The President's War Powers*. New York: Academy of Political Science, 1984.

Casper, Gerhard. "Constitutional Constraints on the Conduct of Foreign Policy: A Nonjudicial Model." *University of Chicago Law Review* 43 (1976): 463–98.

Christopher, Warren. "Ceasefire Between the Branches: A Compact in Foreign Affairs." *Foreign Affairs* 60 (Summer 1982): 989–1005.

Cooke, Jacob E., ed. *The Federalist*. Cleveland, Ohio: Meridian Books, 1961.

Corwin, Edward S. *The President: Office and Powers, 1787–1984: A History and Analysis of Practice and Opinion*. 5th rev. ed. New York: New York University Press, 1984.

Crabb, Cecil V., Jr., and Pat M. Holt. *Invitation to Struggle: Congress, the President, and Foreign Policy*. Washington, D.C.: CQ Press, 1989.

Cronin, Thomas E., ed. *Inventing the American Presidency*. Lawrence: University Press of Kansas, 1989.

——. *The State of the Presidency*. Boston: Little, Brown, 1980.

Crovitz, L. Gordon, and Jeremy Rabkin, eds. *The Fettered Presidency*. Washington, D.C.: American Enterprise, 1990.

Davidson, Roger N., ed. "Congress and the Presidency: Invitation to Struggle." *Annals of the American Academy of Political and Social Science* 499 (September 1988): 499–517.

Draper, Theodore. *A Very Thin Line: The Iran-Contra Affair*. New York: Hill and Wang, 1991.

Elliot, Jonathan, ed. *The Debates in the Several State Conventions on the Adoption of the*

Federal Constitution. Philadelphia: J. P. Lippincott, 1861. Reprint; 5 vols, New York: Burt Franklin, 1974.

Ely, John Hart. *War and Responsibility: Constitutional Lessons of Vietnam and Its Aftermath.* Princeton, N.J.: Princeton University Press, 1993.

———. "Suppose Congress Wanted a War Powers Act That Worked." *Columbia Law Review* 88 (1988): 1379–1431.

Farrand, Max. *The Records of the Federal Convention of 1787.* 4 vols. New Haven, Conn.: Yale University Press, 1966.

Fisher, Louis. *Constitutional Conflicts Between Congress and the President.* Lawrence: University Press of Kansas, 1991.

———. *Presidential War Power.* Lawrence: University Press of Kansas, 1995.

Glennon, Michael J. *Constitutional Diplomacy.* Princeton, N.J.: Princeton University Press, 1990.

———. "The Gulf War and the Constitution." *Foreign Affairs* 70 (1991): 84–101.

———. "The War Powers Resolution Ten Years Later: More Politics Than Law." *American Journal of International Law* 70 (1984): 571–81.

Henkin, Louis. *Constitutionalism, Democracy, and Foreign Affairs.* New York: Columbia University Press, 1990.

———. *Foreign Affairs and the Constitution.* New York: Free Press, 1972.

Hoffman, Daniel N. *Governmental Secrecy and the Founding Fathers: A Study in Constitutional Controls.* Westport, Conn.: Greenwood Press, 1981.

Johnson, Loch K. *America's Secret Power.* New York: Oxford University Press, 1989.

———. *The Making of International Agreements.* New York: New York University Press, 1984.

Keynes, Edward. *Undeclared War: Twilight Zone of Constitutional Power.* University Park: Pennsylvania State University Press, 1982.

Koh, Harold Hongju. *The National Security Constitution: Sharing Power After the Iran-Contra Affair.* New Haven, Conn.: Yale University Press, 1990.

Kurland, Philip B. *Watergate and the Constitution.* Chicago: University of Chicago Press, 1978.

———. "The Impotence of Reticence." *Duke University Law Journal* (1968): 619–36.

Levy, Leonard W. *Original Intent and the Framers' Constitution.* New York: Macmillan, 1988.

Lobel, Jules. "Covert War and Congressional Authority: Hidden War and Forgotten Power." *University of Pennsylvania Law Review* 1340 (1986): 1035–1110.

Lofgren, Charles A. "War-Making Under the Constitution: The Original Understanding." *Yale Law Journal* 81 (1972): 672–702.

Lowi, Theodore J. *The Personal President.* Ithaca, N.Y.: Cornell University Press, 1985.

Mann, Thomas E., ed. *A Question of Balance: The President, Congress, and Foreign Policy.* Washington, D.C.: Brookings Institution, 1990.

Moffett, George D., III. *The Limits of Victory: The Ratification of the Panama Canal Treaties.* Ithaca, N.Y.: Cornell University Press, 1985.

Page, Benjamin I., and Mark P. Petracca. *The American Presidency.* New York: Mc-Graw-Hill, 1983.

Pious, Richard M. *The American Presidency.* New York: Basic Books, 1979.

Reveley, W. Taylor, III. *War Powers of the President and Congress.* Charlottesville: University of Virginia Press, 1981.

Robinson, Donald L., ed. *Government for the Third American Century.* Boulder, Colo.: Westview, 1989.

————. *To the Best of My Ability.* New York: Norton, 1987.

Robinson, James A. *Congress and Foreign Policy-Making.* Homewood, Ill.: Dorsey, 1967.

Rossiter, Clinton. *The American Presidency.* New York: New American Library, 1960.

————. *Constitutional Dictatorship.* New York: Harcourt, Brace and World, 1948.

Schlesinger, Arthur M., Jr. *The Imperial Presidency.* Boston: Houghton Mifflin, 1973.

Schwartz, Bernard. *A Commentary on the Constitution of the United States.* 2 vols. New York: Macmillan, 1963.

Scigliano, Robert. *The Supreme Court and the Presidency.* New York: Free Press, 1971.

Sofaer, Abraham D. *War, Foreign Affairs, and Constitutional Power: The Origins.* Cambridge, Mass.: Ballinger, 1976.

Spitzer, Robert J. *President and Congress: Executive Hegemony at the Crossroads of American Government.* New York: McGraw-Hill, 1993.

————. "Presidential Prerogative Power: The Case of the Bush Administration and Legislative Powers." *Political Science and Politics* 24 (March 1991): 38–41.

————. *Presidential Veto: Touchstone of the American Presidency.* Albany: State University of New York Press, 1988.

Story, Joseph. *Commentaries on the Constitution of the United States.* Durham, N.C.: Carolina Academic Press, 1987.

Sutherland, George S. *Constitutional Power and World Affairs.* New York: Columbia University Press, 1919.

Whicker, Marcia, Raymond A. Moore, and James Pfiffner, eds. *The Presidency and the Persian Gulf War.* Lexington: University Press of Kentucky, 1992.

Wormuth, Francis D. "The Nixon Theory of the War Power: A Critique." *University of California Law Review* 60 (1972): 623–703.

————. "The Vietnam War: The President Versus the Constitution." In *The Vietnam War and International Law.* Edited by Richard Falk. Vol. 2. Princeton, N.J.: Princeton University Press, 1969.

Wormuth, Francis D., and Edwin B. Firmage. *To Chain the Dog of War: The War Powers of Congress in History and Law.* Dallas: Southern Methodist University Press, 1986.

ABOUT THE CONTRIBUTORS

DAVID GRAY ADLER is a professor of political science at Idaho State University and is the author of *The Constitution and the Termination of Treaties.* He has contributed articles and essays on the Constitution and foreign policy to various books and journals, including *Political Science Quarterly, Presidential Studies Quarterly,* and *Encyclopedia of the American Presidency.*

DEAN ALFANGE, JR., is a professor of political science at the University of Massachusetts, Amherst. He has written numerous articles on American constitutional law and the Supreme Court in *Supreme Court Review* and such journals as *Yale Law Journal, George Washington Law Review, Pennsylvania Law Review, Cornell Law Review,* and *Hastings Constitutional Law Quarterly.*

GERHARD CASPER is president of Stanford University. A former dean of the University of Chicago Law School and editor of *Supreme Court Review,* Casper has authored numerous articles and essays in various law journals, including *University of Chicago Law Review, Stanford Law Review, University of California Law Review,* and *Supreme Court Review.*

LOUIS FISHER is senior specialist in Separation of Powers at the Congressional Research Service, Library of Congress. He has published extensively in the areas of constitutional law, administrative law, and the Supreme Court. His books include *Constitutional Conflicts Between Congress and the President, Presidential Spending Power, The Politics of Shared Power, Constitutional Dialogues,* and, most recently, *Presidential War Power.* He has twice received the Louis Brownlow Book Award from the National Academy of Public Administration and was a coeditor of *Encyclopedia of the American Presidency.*

LARRY N. GEORGE is an associate professor of political science at California State University, Long Beach. He has twice earned a Fulbright Fellowship and has contributed articles and essays in the field of American foreign policy and politics to various books and journals, including *Polity.*

DANIEL N. HOFFMAN, a professor of political science at Johnson C. Smith University, has published numerous works in the areas of constitutional law, judicial politics, and national security. He is the author of *Governmental Secrecy and the Founding Fathers* and coauthor of *Top Secret: National Security and the Right to Know*.

EDWARD KEYNES is a professor of political science at Penn State University. He has contributed articles to various books and journals and to *Encyclopedia of the American Presidency*. His books include *Undeclared War: Twilight Zone of Constitutional Power* and *Court v. Congress: Prayer, Busing and Abortion*.

HAROLD HONGJU KOH is Gerard C. and Bernice Latrobe Smith Professor of Law and director of the Orville H. Schell, Jr., Center for International Human Rights, Yale Law School. A former clerk to U.S. Supreme Court Justice Harry Blackmun, Koh is the author of *The National Security Constitution: Sharing Power After the Iran-Contra Affair*, which received the 1991 Richard Neustadt Book Award.

DONALD L. ROBINSON is a professor of government at Smith College. He served as a principal adviser on the five-part series, "The Presidency and the Constitution," which was produced by CBS News on the occasion of the bicentennial celebration of the Constitution. He is the author of *Slavery in the Structure of American Politics*, *"To the Best of My Ability": The Presidency and the Constitution*, and editor of *Reforming American Government*. He has contributed articles and essays to various publications, including *Yale Review*, *Presidential Studies Quarterly*, and *Nation*.

ARTHUR SCHLESINGER, JR., recently retired from the Albert Schweitzer Chair in the Humanities at the City University of New York. Schlesinger won the Pulitzer Prize for History in 1946 for *The Age of Jackson* and the Pulitzer Prize for Biography in 1966 for *A Thousand Days: John F. Kennedy in the White House*. He has authored scores of articles, essays, and chapters and has written several other books, including *The Age of Roosevelt* (3 vols.), *The Cycles of American History*, and the widely praised work, *The Imperial Presidency*.

ROBERT J. SPITZER is a professor of political science at the State University of New York College at Cortland. He has contributed articles and essays on American politics to various journals and books and is the author of *The Presidency and Public Policy*, *The Right to Life Movement and Third Party Politics*, *The Presidential Veto*, and, most recently, *The Politics of Gun Control*.

INDEX